The International Commission of Jurists

University of Pennsylvania Press
Pennsylvania Studies in Human Rights
Edited by Bert B. Lockwood, Jr.

A complete listing of the books in this series appears at the back of this volume.

The International Commission of Jurists

Global Advocates for Human Rights

Howard B. Tolley, Jr.

University of Pennsylvania Press
Philadelphia

Printed in the United States of America

Library of Congress Cataloging-in-Publication Data
Tolley, Howard.
The International Commission of Jurists: global advocates for human rights / Howard B. Tolley, Jr.
p. cm.—(Pennsylvania studies in human rights)
Includes bibliographical references and index.
ISBN 0-8122-3254-2
1. International Commission of Jurists (1952–) 2. Rule of law. 3. Human rights. I. Title. II. Series.
K110.I46T65 1994
341.4′81—dc20 94-4457
CIP

This work is dedicated to the spirit of my son, Naren Justin Tolley, who died ten days after his seventeenth birthday on January 29, 1991. A poem Naren wrote appears below as a father's

TRIBUTE

This poem is for you
In this feeling of excitement which never dies
This is for the power you have to bring people alive
With your strong reassuring hands
Lifting us to the summit of emotions
Your powerful voice willing us to endeavor past our dreams
A search for inner fulfillment your powerful form
Rising from the churches, synagogues, temples and forest
Leaping like a panther
Strong and able to race into any soul in the farthest recess of
the mind
Always helping
Always strong
Never a dim spirit dispelling doubt
This poem is for you—will of man.

Contents

List of Illustrations ix
Acknowledgments xi
Preface xiii

Introduction: Human Rights NGOs, World Politics, and International Law 1

Part I. 1952–1955: Cold Warriors against Socialist Legality

1. Recruiting Free World Jurists 25

Part II. 1956–1963: Liberal Idealists for the Rule of Law

2. Organizing a Global Network 49
3. Defining the Rule of Law 68
4. Protecting Victims 79

Part III. 1963–1970: NGO Pioneers for International Human Rights

5. Building Coalitions for Global Change 97
6. Responding to Crisis 114

Part IV. 1970–1990: Elite Advocates for Economic and Social Justice

7. Mobilizing Advocates for Development 137
8. Setting Standards and Procedures 165
9. Enforcing Civil Liberties 187
10. Representing the Bench and Bar 218

Part V. 1990–1993: Third World Leadership for a New Order

11. Turning Forty 243

Conclusion: Politics, Law, and Human Rights NGOs 271

Appendices
1. ICJ/CIJL National Sections and Affiliates, 1993 283
2. ICJ/CIJL Periodicals, Yearbooks, and Activity Reports 287
Notes 289
Bibliography 333
Index 345

Illustrations

Tables

1.1. ICJ Officers, Members, and Meetings, 1952–1955 37
2.1. ICJ Officers, Members, and Meetings, 1956–1963 56
2.2. ICJ Regional Contacts as of 1963 59
3.1. ICJ Reports Defining the Rule of Law 75
5.1. ICJ Officers, Members, and Meetings, 1963–1970 103
7.1. Revenue Sources for ICJ Expenses, 1990 143
7.2. ICJ Officers, Members, and Meetings, 1970–1990 158
7.3. ICJ Regional Contacts as of 1970 and 1990 160
9.1. ICJ Protection Activities, 1970–1990 194
10.1. CIJL Directors and Advisory Board, 1978–1992 220
10.2. CIJL Protection Activities, 1978–1992 222
11.1. ICJ Officers, Members, and Meetings, 1990–1993 251
11.2. ICJ Regional Contacts as of 1990–1993 253

Photographs

1. Secretary A. J. M. "Bart" van Dal of the Netherlands and former U.S. High Commissioner in Berlin John J. McCloy at an April 10, 1956 New York City Bar Association meeting. 32
2. Dudley Bonsal, the first Executive Committee chairman, addressing the 1956 New York City Bar Association meeting. 35
3. Norman S. Marsh, ICJ Secretary-General from 1956 to 1958, and Administrative Secretary Edward Kozera. 53
4. Seán MacBride, ICJ Secretary-General from 1963 to 1970. 101

5. Niall MacDermot, Q.C., ICJ Secretary-General from 1970 to 1990. 140
6. William Butler, Kéba Mbaye, and T. O. Elias at the 1986 ICJ meeting in Nairobi. 147
7. ICJ Secretary-General Niall MacDermot and CIJL Director Reed Brody attending a 1988 meeting of the U.N. Commission on Human Rights. 212
8. Adama Dieng of Senegal, ICJ Secretary-General (1990). 245
9. ICJ legal officers in 1992. 249
10. Michael Kirby, ICJ Executive Committee chairman (1991), meeting with the Dalai Lama. 265

Acknowledgments

Bert Lockwood, director of the Urban Morgan Institute for Human Rights at the University of Cincinnati College of Law, initiated this study in 1983. He sent two fellows from the Institute, Fred Woodbridge and Richard Rosswurm, to gather materials and conduct interviews at the ICJ headquarters in Geneva. ICJ Secretary-General Niall MacDermot and Executive Committee chairman Bill Butler extended full cooperation to the law students. While conducting my own research in Geneva on the U.N. Human Rights Commission, I became interested in the ICJ's lobbying and human rights casework. Following the students' graduation and my completion of the U.N. Commission study, I prepared an ICJ book prospectus and was provided the files and materials gathered at the Institute. Nancy Ent, the Institute's administrative assistant, capably helped navigate often troubled waters. During my five years of research and writing, Bert Lockwood continued to support the project by providing travel grants for my 1987 and 1992 research trips to Geneva and New York, as well as extraordinary personal encouragement. These words can not adequately acknowledge how much the study owes to his creative inspiration and unflagging generosity.

The University of Cincinnati's Taft Fund has also provided vital support at several key points in the project. A summer research grant in 1988 supported the preparation of two conference papers on the ICJ's rule of law confrontation with socialist legality and its lobbying strategies at international organizations. One conference paper revised for Chapter 8 originally appeared as "Popular Sovereignty and International Law: ICJ Strategies for Human Rights Standard Setting," *Human Rights Quarterly* 11, no. 4 (November 1989): 561–85. My University of Cincinnati sabbatical leave in 1991–92, extended with a second Taft Fund summer research grant, enabled me to complete the ICJ project. Following acceptance of the book manuscript, the Taft Fund provided a small travel grant for a brief detour from London to Geneva, where I conducted final interviews, updated developments through the June 1993 World Conference on Human Rights, and planned for a French translation of this work.

Numerous colleagues and friends offered critical encouragement that sustained me on a difficult path that on several occasions appeared to have reached a dead end. At the outset, a generous colleague and department head, Norman Thomas, shared his valuable experience with the case study method and reviewed my preliminary efforts. David Forsythe at the University of Nebraska also responded promptly with wise counsel to a request for guidance in the early stages of my research. David Weissbrodt at the University of Minnesota and Laurie Wiseberg of Human Rights Internet intervened at a critical moment to revive my work. I am also indebted to several scholars for their thoughtful, encouraging comments on draft chapters: Larry LeBlanc at Marquette University and Paul Lauren at the University of Montana. Richard Claude of the University of Maryland provided guidance of extraordinary value to my revisions of the final manuscript.

ICJ staff, leaders, and members have been unusually forthcoming, even when aware that my analysis criticized aspects of their work. Their dedication to the rule of law and their personal integrity are matched by an incredible workload. Friends in Geneva, George and Mary Haour, offered unparalleled family hospitality that enriched each research trip and was deeply appreciated.

My wife Nina and son Mark helped me through the incalculable loss of a cherished son/brother with the love so essential to our transformed lives. This work is dedicated to my son Naren's enduring spirit, which will forever challenge my own effort to realize our common humanity.

Preface

Critics around the world condemn privileged lawyers as arrogant, greedy, manipulative, and self-serving. The stereotype does not fit the International Commission of Jurists (ICJ), an organization of human rights lawyers based in Geneva, Switzerland. While its members and staff would never be faulted for excessive humility, their pride arises from a lofty commitment to the rule of law rather than from winning immense monetary judgments. Like ambitious Davids confronting Goliath, the self-selected ICJ judges, law professors, and practicing attorneys have challenged a state system whose sovereign governments choose to be a law unto themselves. Their goal is to create a new, international political and legal order that prevents historically sovereign governments from kidnapping, torture, murder, and arbitrary detention. An exclusive professional elite motivated by noble ideals has campaigned for universal democratic principles.

This book presents a five-part history of the ICJ from 1952 to mid-1993 as a case study of political science and legal theories about interest groups in a changing world. Part I describes how the ICJ began in response to Stalinist totalitarianism.[1] The United States Central Intelligence Agency (CIA) covertly arranged an inaugural conference in Berlin to counter the Soviet-controlled International Association of Democratic Lawyers (IADL). The CIA supported more than two hundred organizations through foundations that most recipients believed were privately funded. Unaware of any CIA connection, lawyers recruited "free world" jurists for an ICJ that proclaimed the rule of law and denounced "socialist legality." A small governing Commission of elite judges, scholars, and practicing lawyers hired a Secretary-General to direct a permanent staff.

Part II details how a new Secretary-General in 1956 and superpower rivalry in the third world led the ICJ to attack fascism and apartheid as well as the dictatorship of the proletariat. Highly publicized and well-attended congresses on the rule of law in New Delhi,

Lagos, and Rio de Janeiro created a global network of members in thirty-four national sections. The ICJ defined universal rule of law principles obligating all states to honor both procedural and substantive rights. ICJ activists then initiated enforcement tactics involving trial observers, country reports, negative publicity, and inquiry committees. Balanced criticism directed at noncommunist dictators in Spain and South Africa improved the ICJ's reputation for impartiality. Partisan anticommunism compromised major inquiries on China and Cuba.

Part III examines how Secretary-General Seán MacBride reoriented the ICJ after 1963. A confirmed internationalist, MacBride fashioned a coalition of nongovernmental organizations (NGOs) that linked the East and the West, the IADL and the ICJ. In a worldwide campaign, the NGOs called for a U.N. High Commissioner for Human Rights and Geneva Convention protocols to improve humanitarian law. The ICJ also attempted to protect individual victims through quiet diplomacy, trial observers, fact-finding missions and publications, and interventions with international organizations and national foreign policy makers. MacBride's pioneering campaign for global citizenship rights produced successes and failures that guided other NGOs.

Public disclosure brought an end to covert CIA funding in 1967. Soviet bloc and third world tyrants embarrassed by ICJ publicity sought to revoke U.N. consultative status for the U.S.-funded group. Other third world governments appreciated that MacBride had applied a nonpartisan approach that also shamed pro-Western dictators. Suspicions always lingered about the early years, but until this study there has been no full accounting of CIA involvement. The ICJ retained its good reputation and U.N. consultative status but lost most of its income. The Ford Foundation provided an interim grant and then recommended that the ICJ wind up operations in 1970. Drastic retrenchment and MacBride's departure left the ICJ leaderless and without funds. MacBride shifted his energies to Amnesty International, which grew rapidly through mass membership organizing efforts and a world campaign against torture.

Part IV covers the twenty-year tenure of Secretary-General Niall MacDermot. European government grants saved the ICJ from bankruptcy, and a scaled-down program achieved remarkable impact. Observers typically rank the ICJ as among the most influential and respected human rights NGOs. The ICJ won the first European Human Rights Prize in 1980, the Wateler Peace Prize in 1988, and the Erasmus Prize in 1989. MacDermot directed a three-part campaign of promotion, standard setting, and protection activities. Chapter 7 describes how the ICJ adapted classical liberal ideology to promote human rights in one-party and developing states. As the Association of Soviet Lawyers came to recognize the virtues of Western due process models, the ICJ progressively expanded its rule of law principles to include the right to development.

Chapter 8 examines how ICJ elite advocacy contributed significantly to new international law on torture, principles for an independent judiciary, and an African Commission on Human Rights.[2] Coalition building with other NGOs, standard setting by expert consultants, and "tree top" lobbying with heads of state and cabinet ministers maximized the ICJ's impact. The ICJ lobbied effectively for international human rights standards adopted by the United Nations, the Council of Europe, the Organization of African Unity, and the Japanese Diet. Chapter 9 details the protection activities, fact-finding missions, and reports that helped win release of detainees. Its leaders, staff, and admirers have credited the ICJ with effectively pressuring regimes such as Argentina and Chile to curtail abuses.

Chapter 10 describes how the ICJ Centre for the Independence of Judges and Lawyers combined promotion, standard setting, and protection. Legal expertise and persistent lobbying produced U.N. Principles on the Independence of the Judiciary and the Role of Lawyers. The ICJ promoted those principles in third world seminars and sought to protect human rights defenders under government attack. When governments harass independent judges and lawyers defending political dissidents, professional colleagues often ignore national loyalties and pursue solidarity in a global bar that invokes universal standards.

Part V introduces the changes and growth initiated in 1990 by an African Secretary-General, Adama Dieng of Senegal. Western European governments substantially increased funding for ICJ technical assistance programs in the third world to further legal reforms that were seen as prerequisites of economic development. The ICJ's expanded legal education program promoted Legal Services in Rural Areas. Welcomed as a nonthreatening form of aid, seminars to recruit and train paralegals for India's untouchables or Latin America's landless peasants could also be seen as undermining national sovereignty.

In the struggle for power between states and within countries, NGOs increasingly influence who governs and by what rules. For forty years the ICJ has accepted government money while attempting to make states comply with universal human rights. Has the ICJ independently used that funding to limit state sovereignty, or has the organization been manipulated by its government sponsors? Has the ICJ progressively challenged Western economic injustice or mainly promoted Western political institutions in the third world? As a transnational professional movement, the ICJ contributes to interdependence by socializing lawyers to global norms enforced by international procedures. Whether or not the ICJ's forty-year quest for the rule of law has contributed to a new world order, its work makes clear that public interest idealists differ from traditional lawyer mercenaries.

The ICJ story adds a unique piece to the incomplete puzzle of world politics and international law. Some international relations and legal scholars theorize that transnational organizations such as the ICJ are part of an emerging new world order based on universal norms. This case study tests those legal and political science theories about interest groups, world politics, and international law.

The Introduction reviews the academic literature on interest groups, international relations theory, and natural law to identify research questions and propositions for the study. Each of the five stages in the ICJ's organizational development provides new material for testing theories about realism and idealism, pluralism and corporatism, natural law monism and positivist dualism. A concluding section in each chapter links the developments reported to selected theories from the larger case study.

Chapters 1, 2, 5, 7, and 11 apply interest group theory to the ICJ's founding, its subsequent changes in membership and finances, and the policy initiatives of its new leaders. How do the ICJ's internal governance, strategies of influence, and government contacts compare with what is known about domestic interest groups? What ethical considerations should guide organizations that receive government funds? U.S. pluralism insists that private citizens create and finance groups entirely free of government influence; European corporatism embraces state sponsorship and funding of quasi-nongovernmental organizations. The ICJ received both covert and public government support that illustrates problems of funding and accountability.

Chapters 4, 6, and 9 test claims of a new world order by evaluating the ICJ's success in enforcing the rule of law against repressive governments. Chapter 7 examines ICJ socialization of third world elites to universal norms that promote world citizenship over national loyalty. Most international relations research adopts the realist premise that relations between sovereign states fundamentally differ from domestic politics. World order theorists envision a transformation of the state system with growing restraints on sovereignty.

Chapters 3, 8, and 10 evaluate the ICJ campaign to make rule of law procedural and substantive norms into legal duties that bind even nonconsenting governments. Natural law monists regard fundamental human rights standards as legally binding on all governments. Positivist dualism treats such unenforceable norms as *morality*; *laws* are officially adopted rules that states can be compelled to obey. The ICJ's natural law jurisprudence and human rights standard setting put the competing theories to the test. The book's Conclusion draws final lessons about the application of legal and political theory to the ICJ and offers suggestions for further research.

Academic specialists and general readers, theorists and practitioners often speak different languages. The portions of this book that are written for social scientists, historians, and legal scholars may contain too much academic terminology and theoretical abstraction for practicing lawyers, NGO activists, and nonspecialist readers. The most idealistic human rights advocates resent analysis that compares their selfless pursuit of universal justice to political lobbying by special interest groups. Practitioners and general readers interested in the human drama may not care about the academic theories.

The book has been organized to make a scholarly work on a citizen's movement accessible to the widest possible audience. Readers interested primarily in a narrative history should skip the Introduction and Conclusion as well as the concluding sections in each chapter. The substantive sections in Chapters 1 through 11 present a complete history of the ICJ's fascinating evolution and its role in the international human rights movement. That history sheds new light on U.S. Cold War strategy at a time when new Eastern bloc leaders begin to reveal communist secrets. The ICJ's Western founders were early pioneers in a worldwide human rights movement; in 1993 the organization remained on the cutting edge as a genuinely transnational organization under third world leadership. This case study of ICJ global advocates tests academic claims of the new world order, describes one NGO model for human rights practitioners, and offers an interesting history for general readers.

Introduction:
Human Rights NGOs, World Politics, and International Law

> The great violators of human rights are sovereign governments, . . . when they choose to be a law unto themselves, there is no effective power to stop them. . . . The task before us is to find the way to diffuse that power. It needs to be dispersed in two directions. Firstly, downwards to the provinces, to the communities and ultimately to the individuals who constitute our nations, . . . And secondly, upwards to the continents or regions, and ultimately to Tennyson's dream of "the Parliament of Man, the Federation of the World."
>
> —ICJ Secretary-General Niall MacDermot[1]

Is the International Commission of Jurists part of a "new world order?" Theorists make conflicting claims about the influence of nongovernmental organizations (NGOs). The first section of this Introduction explores the debate between realists and idealists and proposes a functional analysis of human rights institutions. The second section presents research questions about ICJ functions to test rival claims. The third section compares pluralism and corporatism to raise questions about the ICJ's origins, funding, and governance. A final section explains the methodology used to conduct this case study. Activists and practitioners who read an early draft of this Introduction disagreed with its academic reviewers on how much theory was appropriate for this book. The revised text attempts to make the study accessible to the widest possible audience. Readers who regard academic terminology as impossible jargon should begin with Part I rather than this Introduction. A complete ICJ history begins in Chapter 1. Readers with a broader interest in political and legal theory can trace the analytical framework of this Introduction through selected findings in the concluding section of each chapter and a comprehensive analysis in the Conclusion. Following an appendix of ICJ publications, a four-part research bibliography lists works on (1) world politics and international law; (2) international nongovernmental organizations; (3) human rights NGOs; and (4) interest groups, pluralism, and corporatism.

Catalyst for a New World Order? Realists versus Idealists

Realists, Positivism, and State Sovereignty

Realists would consider an ICJ study no more promising than would readers who never met a lawyer they could trust. Most international relations scholars continue to view states as the unchallenged masters of world politics; they dismiss NGOs as being mostly "trivial" with "minimal" capabilities.[2] NGOs can only influence the "low" politics of economic and social concerns. States alone are significant players in the "high" politics of security and diplomacy. Realists treat past as prologue: the current state system will continue indefinitely into a future governed by superior political and economic power rather than by international law and organization.[3] According to that pessimistic appraisal, war and gross human rights violations not only will persist but are unavoidable features of any conceivable inter-state system.[4] In a Machiavellian world where might continues to make right, history proves that the rule of law is unattainable. State power configurations may have changed over the past three centuries, but the different bipolar, multipolar, and unipolar patterns have not been influenced by international organizations. Highly touted new global forces may occasionally influence government decisions, but they demonstrate no real power to control.

In Zbigniew Brzezinski's view, global turmoil remains out of control. He tallies the unprecedented body count of the twentieth century and forecasts undiminished carnage in the twenty-first.[5] Samuel Huntington anticipates a renewed clash of civilizations more profound than nation-state rivalry as fundamentalist Islamic, Hindu, Confucian, and other non-Western cultures challenge European world dominance.[6]

Legal positivism parallels political science realism. Dualism treats international and municipal law as distinct, so that local courts give national law priority over any conflicting international duty. Positivists also regard states as beyond regulation unless a government consents to accept a particular international law.

> Since the late eighteenth century, "positivism" in international law has been identified above all with two propositions: (1) that "law," properly so called, is a set of rules distinct from "natural law or morality," and (2) that the source of all law, so understood, that is binding on the citizens and officials of a state is the will of the sovereign as expressed internally through legislation and externally through explicit agreement (treaties) or tacit agreement (custom) with other states.[7]

Deriding "monistic idealists," a positivist critic asserted that international human rights laws and enforcement procedures are "so ineffective as to be completely worthless."[8] Coercive enforcement distinguishes positive law from morality. States alone are the subjects of international law; individuals derive rights solely from municipal law. Soviet and Chinese communist doctrine has also demanded nonintervention, limiting the enforcement of international law to those provisions adopted in national legislation. "Unlike the bourgeois normative theory of law, the Marx-Lenin theory . . . regards legal norms as instruments of the class struggle in the hands of the dominant class. . . . [L]aw is not above the State, but emanates from it . . . and cannot become an impediment to [the Socialist State's] realization of its historical tasks."[9] Louis Henkin "characterizes the . . . statist worldview in a form that shows its mockery of its Jeffersonian antithesis":

> All states are [created] equal. They are endowed [by their Creator] with certain [unalienable] inherent rights. Among these are [life] *existence*, [liberty] *independence/autonomy*, and the pursuit of [happiness] *national interest*. To secure these rights [governments] law is instituted among *states*, deriving *its* [just powers] legitimate authority from the consent of the [governed] states. (Brackets and italics provided by Henkin.)[10]

The ever-growing number of international NGOs and their political campaigns have not impressed skeptics. Governments at the United Nations retain conrol over which international groups receive consultative status; national groups are accepted only after their governments have been consulted.[11] At the 1993 World Conference on Human Rights in Vienna, states severely limited NGO access to the drafting committee and totally excluded several unacceptable groups from the U.N. Centre. States reaffirm their own supremacy by characterizing citizen's groups as "nongovernmental" rather than "transnational" organizations. The ICJ is one of many organizations heavily dependent on government funds. NGOs still do not have legal personality under public international law. Except for the International Committee of the Red Cross (ICRC), NGO personnel do not enjoy the formal legal status and protection conferred on diplomats.[12] Private international law merely grants corporate status under municipal law. No matter how transnational the membership, each organization is subject to the laws of the incorporating state. Postwar negotiations never produced a statute to recognize nationally registered NGOs. Outside the European Community no international treaties confer legal status and rights on transnational NGOs. From the realist perspective, sovereign states retain legal autonomy beyond the influence of either the United Nations or interest groups. Neither the United Nations nor large NGOs such as the Red Cross and Amnesty International have significantly breached the citadel of national sovereignty. In the absence of coercive power to control, mere influence is unworthy of a realist's attention.

Idealists, Natural Law, and International Regimes

Idealists envision a different world order where international organizations finally chain the dogs of war and find global alternatives to the unjust features of an outmoded state system.[13] James Rosenau forecasts a growing role for transnational groups in a "post-international" world political/legal order.[14] In his view, multinational corporations, revolutionary terrorist groups, environmentalists, pacifists, and human rights activists have gained significant political clout that governments can no longer monopolize. Stanley Hoffman sees a "collision between man as a citizen of his national community and what could be called an incipient cosmopolitanism, or man as a world citizen."[15] Internationalists confidently predict further inexorable erosion of state sovereignty, which nationalist patriots have become powerless to resist. Effective international regulation of mail, telecommunications, and commercial aviation and shipping illustrates the functional encroachment on national jurisdiction.

The optimists are not so utopian as to expect completion in their lifetimes. The process of international transformation has been underway for many years, and it is still not clear what form the governing institutions of an increasingly interdependent world will take. After each major war since 1800, states established stronger intergovernmental organizations and their citizens forged new transnational private groups. In each instance government leaders chastened by wartime devastation recognized that the national interest would be served by multilateral planning that progressively limited independent action. The international organizations' founders in each case struck a pragmatic balance between realism and idealism. The Cold War's end reinforced progressive aspirations for new initiatives of transnational cooperation.

Natural law monists promote a single legal system in which international law is superior to municipal law and both are governed by fundamental general principles.[16] They challenge dualism by insisting that governments are legally bound by universally recognized principles whether or not they willingly consent. Hersch Lauterpacht argued that international law grants to individuals fundamental rights enforceable against sovereign states.[17] He regarded the Geneva Conventions as approaching "international legislation," that declares "universally binding international custom" based on "compelling considerations of humanity."[18] Peremptory norms of international law against genocide, torture, slavery, and apartheid criminalize atrocities by all tyrants whether or not their governments have ratified any human rights treaties.[19] Natural law monists consider many other fundamental rights as legal norms, even though few governments have endorsed those higher standards.

The Nazi holocaust rekindled efforts to strengthen international law and institutions. Leo Gross advocated slowly emerging standards for a world legal community. In a time of rapid social change, Quincy Wright favored new law as a stabilizing influence.[20] He theorized that "law and society reciprocally influence each other. . . . [A]s man progresses . . . law exerts a positive influence, adapting society to the values which it sanctions."[21] By ratifying the U.N. Charter, states consented to new limits on the use of force and pledged to respect human rights. NGOs successfully lobbied for Charter provisions that granted them consultative status and established a U.N. Commission on Human Rights.

Idealists advocate popular sovereignty, citizen participation in creating and enforcing international law. NGOs should be free of state control in order to participate in the rudimentary legislative and judicial procedures of the primitive international order.[22] NGOs helped draft a Universal Declaration of Human Rights exhorting "every individual and every organ of society . . . to promote respect for these rights and freedoms, and by progressive measures, national and international, to secure their universal and effective recognition and observance." The Statute of the International Court of Justice creates nonconsensual sources for law. Article 38(1) empowers the court if necessary to look beyond (a) treaties and (b) custom to consider (c) "general principles of law" and (d) "judicial decisions and the teaching of the most highly qualified publicists of the various nations, as subsidiary means for the determination of rules of law."[23] Positivists view ratified treaties as states' primary legal code. Monists impose additional obligations based on state custom, common national principles, court opinions, and legal scholarship. They contend that NGOs contribute to international legislation by articulating customary norms and by lobbying governments for new treaties. The governments of Sweden, France, and Norway have recognized the importance of NGOs by appointing ambassadors to manage relations with them.[24] Human rights activists view the people as superior to both national and intergovernmental bodies. They claim that emerging custom has legitimized NGOs' semiofficial trial observer missions, fact-finding investigations, and quasi-diplomatic interventions.

The earliest transnational federations, such as the 1855 World Alliance of YMCAs, admittedly had minimal impact. Yet by 1900 the International Parliamentary Union and the Institut de Droit greatly influenced the Hague Peace Conferences of 1899 and 1907. More than one thousand NGOs functioned during the League of Nations.[25] The International Chamber of Commerce had three million firms, and the International Federation of Trade Unions twenty million members. Lawyers from the American Institute of International Law helped write eleven conventions adopted by the 1928–1933 Pan-American Conference.[26] The united front tactics of the Comintern compromised other groups in which communist agents manipulated politically innocent or disinterested individuals.[27]

Since 1945 the number of international NGOs has grown to more than five thousand and has stimulated hopes for greater citizen influence in world politics.[28] Advocates of "people power" celebrate nongovernmental organizations as tools for democratization. Citizens make common cause with like-minded souls in other countries, forging loyalties to transnational interests that undercut loyalty to their own nations. The United Nations has granted consultative status to more than nine hundred groups. Pacifists have organized across national boundaries to challenge nuclear weapons, and the "greens" have placed environmental concerns on the global agenda.[29]

Idealists argue that the steady development of international law and organization has brought non-state actors into a global political system that transcends and shapes intergovernmental relations.[30] Within that system, theorists have identified distinct "regimes" that govern environmental, economic, military, and other practices.[31] The expert policy makers of those transnational norms and institutions have been characterized as an "epistemic" community. Selected elites now circulate among leadership posts with the U.N. Secretariat, specialized agencies, regional organizations, national ministries, and NGOs.

The emerging international policy community resembles issue networks identified in the United States. Scholars in the 1960s identified U.S. "subgovernments" or "iron triangles" composed of interest group representatives, executive department administrators, and legislators.[32] Key lobbyists, Congressional staff members, and health department bureaucrats, for example, decided national health policy. Critics charge that medical interest groups capture regulatory agencies and control enforcement. Others have complained that some environmental reform groups have been co-opted by the establishment. The most recent research suggests that the Reagan administration successfully weakened interest group–dominated subgovernments. Washington in the 1980s was characterized not by iron triangles, but by more open issue networks with fluid memberships.[33] In practice there remains as much collaboration as confrontation between public officials and private groups. Legislators, bureaucrats, and lobbyists regularly shift between the legislature and executive, and move in and out of government. A similar revolving door circulates human rights activists within international policy-making institutions.

Public Interest NGOs and Human Rights

At the time of this study in early 1993, international human rights institutions appeared to comprise at best a weak regime. Jack Donnelly identified it as a promotional regime that had not developed enforcement powers.[34] Forsythe described the internationalization of human rights, but he questioned whether a "regime" decisively constrains state power.[35] My prior study, *The U.N. Commission on Human Rights*,[36] found that intergovernmental procedures provide minimal checks on governments that unjustly kill, torture, kidnap, and imprison their own citizens. Other scholars have traced the dramatic growth of NGOs in a policy community that created human rights standards and implementation procedures.

The movement began with nineteenth-century abolitionist societies that lobbied for treaties against slavery. French activists founded the International Federation of Human Rights in the early twentieth century. After World War I, lawyers first proposed a universal declaration of rights.[37] The ICJ organized in 1952, well before the movement took off in the 1970s. By the 1980s reference directories identified eight hundred human rights NGOs in Europe, five hundred in the United States and Canada, and four hundred in Latin America, Africa, and Asia.[38] More than 140 sent representatives to the 1992 session of the U.N. Commission on Human Rights in Geneva. More than two thousand NGO delegates attended the 1993 World Conference on Human Rights in Vienna.[39] In size and limited resources the ICJ currently resembles other midsized NGOs; Amnesty International is now in a league by itself with more than a million members in six thousand local groups, forty-eight national sections, and an International Secretariat staff of 290.[40]

Is the movement shadow without substance or part of an emerging world order? Human rights activists and their academic supporters claim that NGOs now function as influential actors in world politics. In their view, groups communicating universal values can spark mass political movements that challenge local officials. Transnational citizen networks weaken national loyalty, stimulate new demands on local officials, socialize individuals to global citizenship, and hold states accountable to law.[41] Political scientists Richard Claude and Laurie Wiseberg have identified critical NGO functions, such as information processing and dissemination, advocacy, developing norms, influencing policy, building solidarity, offering condemnation and praise, and providing legal assistance.[42] International law scholars David Weissbrodt and Virginia Leary hailed NGOs' contributions to rule making and enforcement.[43]

This case study offers a slightly different analytical framework for evaluating human rights institutions. Gabriel Almond's functional analysis of different political systems offers a useful framework for examining the human rights policy community.[44] Almond's work on comparative government identified eight basic functions performed by different structures in national political systems—legislatures, bureaucracy, courts, political parties, interest groups, and so forth. The human rights community performs quite similar functions through comparable institutions: the U.N. Commission on Human Rights, the U.N. Secretariat, regional human rights courts, state voting blocs, and NGOs as well as states. Prior research has described U.N. activities in terms of promotion, standard setting, and protection. That three-part framework encompasses all eight of the functions identified by Almond. Promotion involves socialization, communication, and recruitment; standard setting includes articulation, aggregation, and policy making; and protection entails policy implementation and adjudication.

Research documenting significant global influence by one NGO would support but not validate theories of a new world order. The highly regarded ICJ, with a forty-year record of purported success, appeared likely to offer more supporting evidence than any other human rights group except Amnesty International. Prior case studies of Amnesty International, the Red Cross, and the International Rescue Committee concentrated on activity programs or employed a different analytical framework.[45] Most research generalizing about the entire NGO network has concentrated on only one function, such as rule making or enforcement. Regime theorists give little or no attention to socialization and recruitment. The human rights network now has so many institutions performing varied functions that comprehensive systems analysis requires far more extensive empirical work. This case study should indicate whether functional analysis provides an appropriate framework for future research.

Research Questions on ICJ Functions

The functions of interest groups vary in different political systems. In democracies independent groups participate actively in policy making. In totalitarian societies government-controlled groups socialize victims not to articulate demands. As international human rights institutions slowly developed, the ICJ attempted to perform all possible functions, including adjudication of state crimes. Activists and scholars have not agreed on a single list of functions and have given different labels to similar NGO activities, roles, and methods. Terminology has proliferated:[46]

Promotion:
- socialization/promotion/education
- communication/information gathering, evaluation, and dissemination
- recruitment/mobilization/building solidarity

Standard Setting:
- articulation/lobbying/agenda building
- aggregation/solidarity/representation/coalition building/lobbying
- policy making/rule making/standard setting

Protection:
- policy implementation/rule supervision/monitoring/service delivery
- adjudication/rule enforcement/protection/advocacy/litigation

This study identifies eight functions under the three program headings used by the ICJ in its own literature: (1) promotion, (2) standard setting, and (3) protection. These correspond to a similar division of domestic interest group activity on (1) public education, (2) lobbying, and (3) litigation. This study does not identify any new functions or attach new labels. It creates a framework for analysis of human rights institutions with a unique combination of functions and terms extensively employed in other studies.[47]

Promotion

Socialization. Has the ICJ effectively socialized world citizens and leaders to a global consciousness and liberal democratic values?

Self-interested rulers and passive citizens are the unacceptable norm. Idealists envision self-reliant citizens holding responsive leaders accountable to the rule of law. The ICJ attempted to empower victims for political action and to educate elites for democratic governance. Educational conferences presented rule of law materials to public officials, judges, law professors, and practicing lawyers. Training seminars for paralegals disseminated information among third world community groups on several continents.

Was the rule of law message heard? Did elites in newly independent states resist universal norms enforced by supranational institutions? Were activists emboldened to protest local violations? Did members welcome or protest ICJ criticism of their governments? Chapter 7 evaluates charges that two ICJ "fallen angels" betrayed human rights ideals in return for high office and legal fees from a multinational corporation. Are legal elites more likely to promote a new order or be co-opted by the old?

Recruitment. Did the ICJ mobilize new human rights activists, leaders, and organizations from Western and third world countries for both national and international service?

Western missionaries for human rights have proselytized widely, with mixed results. Developing countries have few private voluntary associations, and their citizens have little influence in European-based transnational NGOs. Many groups have made third world organizational development a high priority.[48] The ICJ defined itself as a global jurists' organization. Was it, like other human rights NGOs, built from the top down by Western elites? How successfully did the ICJ recruit staff, members, leaders, and local affiliates from developing countries? Did the appointment of a Senegalese attorney as Secretary-General in 1990 signify a shift from Western control?

Case studies of Amnesty International and the International League for Human Rights describe federated organizations like the ICJ with numerous national sections.[49] How do NGOs overcome the language barriers and state-imposed legal obstacles to building a transnational organization? Did autonomy for national affiliates minimize fears of neo-imperialist penetration? How did ICJ elites promote solidarity with other professional, religious, labor, and grassroots organizations? Did the ICJ recruit eminent jurists for new posts as human rights experts? Did younger recruits make careers in the international network?

Communication. Did the ICJ provide public officials and citizens with reliable information needed for promotion, standard setting, and protection?

Information exchange lubricates human rights mechanisms. Lawmakers track violations, advocates require new case law, and scholars hunger for detail. ICJ publications and press relations link activists across national boundaries and the public-private divide. How did the ICJ obtain reliable, timely information? Who were the consumers and how were they identified? Which language groups were included, and which left out? Did state censors limit distribution? Has the ICJ kept up with new communication technology and information media?

Standard Setting

Articulation. How effectively has the ICJ articulated the rule of law as a universal value?

A 1960s realist concluded that transnational groups worked "through their own governments rather than articulating independently in international relations."[50] Independent demands by NGOs may indicate a decline in state power; U.S. domestic interest groups have increased their representation functions as political parties have weakened. Idealists regard human rights as new global values that promote world unity. R. J. Vincent suggests that "realists . . . may be missing a transformation from international relations to world politics as significant as that which established the society of states, and for which the idea of human rights is a kind of midwife."[51] Seyom Brown wrote: "The capacity of national governments to maintain sovereign authority over what happens within their jurisdiction is also being weakened by the worldwide popular embrace of the idea that a government is legitimate only to the extent that it rests on the noncoerced consent of the governed and secures their basic "human rights."[52]

Scholars and activists continue to debate whether the human rights most often promoted are Western values elevated to universal norms. Von Laue characterizes the new global consciousness as a *World Revolution of Westernization*.[53] Under predominantly Western leadership, most human rights NGOs have attacked gross civil liberties violations occurring in third world countries. They have treated liberal democratic principles as nonpolitical legal mandates binding all governments. Many third world activists treat gross violations as symptoms of economic injustice caused by landholding, military, and financial structures. Legal remedies alone cannot provide human dignity without major political reforms. Western activists have resisted utopian goals and strategies that would make human rights NGOs no different from other political interests competing for power.[54]

The ICJ's forty-year search for universal values progressively expanded rule of law ideals. A U.S.-inspired and funded anticommunist crusade dominated the early years. A new Secretary-General in 1956 adopted broad liberal democratic goals. In the 1980s the ICJ alone among major NGOs advocated economic rights as well as civil liberties. Was the change a result of increased support from European democratic socialists, a leadership search for doctrine appealing to elites from developing countries, or a sign of growing third world influence within the ICJ? Did the jurists independently synthesize universal human rights that incorporate third world concerns, or were they agents of socialization for Western values? Does the ICJ provide democratic representation for world citizens in the international political system?

Aggregation. Did the ICJ enhance broad-based demands through NGO coalitions and collaboration with government policy makers?

Regional voting blocs at the United Nations reconcile governments' conflicting demands and produce common proposals. Human rights activists occasionally use NGO coalitions to get their proposals on the legislative agenda. Collaboration can assure consideration if not approval. Does ICJ seniority and expertise make it a leader in aggregating NGO demands? How does the elite ICJ relate to grassroots organizations, other lawyers' groups, churches, and powerful newcomers like Amnesty International? When have coalition strategies worked and when has NGO rivalry prevented collaboration? Has the ICJ collaborated with government sponsors and U.N. experts to advance demands? How do participants compromise their positions, divide responsibility, and share the credit?

Domestic interest group lobbyists interact regularly with elected legislators and bureaucrats; they effectively mobilize information, expertise, and grassroots support to shape legislative proposals by bargaining, accommodation, and compromise. Is there an international human rights network comparable to policy communities in the United States? Does the ICJ aggregate demands from different racial, ethnic, religious, and social groups?

Lawmaking. Has ICJ expertise and lobbying significantly influenced customary international law as well as human rights conventions?

Some of the ICJ's eminent judges, legal scholars, and practitioners might qualify as "highly qualified publicists." They proclaimed a rule of law based on general principles that should govern all states. Are their declarations evidence of international custom or general principles of law? Chapter 3 evaluates the ICJ conference procedure used to recommend universal norms for adoption as municipal law. Was the rule of law a synthesis of civil and common law that ignored non-Western, Islamic, and socialist legal doctrines? If the rule of law includes more than procedural guarantees, which substantive rights should be universally guaranteed and on what authority?

In a legal order dictated by states, ICJ interpretation of international law had less authority than intergovernmental agreements. For thirty years, the ICJ has contributed expertise to governments drafting international legislation—conventions, treaties, declarations, and principles adopted by the United Nations and regional human rights bodies. Prior research has detailed the NGO lobbying tactics and insider contacts that supported negotiation, adoption, and ratification of human rights standards.[55] Diplomats negotiating treaties may be less susceptible to constituent pressure than elected national legislators.[56] Feld concludes that lobbying at the United Nations might occur too late to change policy decisions made earlier in national capitals.[57] How did the ICJ use personal diplomatic contacts and local affiliates to influence appointed government representatives? How do ICJ elites maximize insider contacts without being tainted by association with government officials? Chapters 8 and 10 examine how ICJ lobbyists capitalized on legal expertise to influence international as well as national legislation.

Protection

Implementation. How have ICJ advocates moved national, intergovernmental, and expert monitors to demand compliance by state offenders?

Post–World War II human rights treaties empowered both national and intergovernmental institutions to investigate, denounce, and remedy violations. The ICJ lobbied diplomats and friendly legislatures to insist that treaty partners and aid recipients respect human rights. For victims organizing in self-defense, the ICJ provided legal assistance and solidarity with support groups abroad. Trusted NGOs increasingly administer bilateral and multilateral humanitarian relief and services.

The ICJ frequently challenged state offenders by presenting evidence to intergovernmental bodies, treaty-based expert committees, rapporteurs, and Secretariat staff that monitor human rights violations. NGO complaints activated procedures neglected by officials reluctant to investigate and condemn offenders. Have ICJ elites "captured" some monitors who sympathetically respond to NGOs? How has the ICJ overcome target governments' objections that NGOs lack standing to bring complaints? The Human Rights Committee has rejected petitions from NGOs unable to demonstrate that a victim requested such representation.[58] Chapter 9 describes an important victory for all NGOs when in 1982 the U.N. Commission on Human Rights allowed an ICJ representative from Argentina to give testimony despite his government's objection.

Enforcement. Have ICJ interventions and public judgments of state crimes induced government compliance?

When the state kills, NGOs do much more than promote global values. Immediate intervention to protect victims from oppression takes many forms. ICJ fact-finding missions have investigated, exposed, and embarrassed state offenders. This study asks whether a major NGO has had discernible impact on government misconduct. ICJ denunciation of miscreants violates a cardinal norm of the state system when private organizations judge sovereign governments. How has the ICJ identified situations requiring action and decided which tactics to employ? Do tyrants care? Has ICJ intervention freed political prisoners, saved any condemned from execution, or protected local human rights defenders?

In the 1950s the ICJ initiated NGO enforcement measures inspired by the intergovernmental tribunal at Nuremberg. Did findings of law by ICJ inquiry commissions have legal or moral authority, or both? Did ICJ trial observers contribute to a customary norm that states must allow international visitors to attend open criminal proceedings? As more and more NGO trial observers and fact-finding missions passed judgment on state crimes, scholars recommended investigation guidelines to insure reliability.[59] Chapters 4 and 9 evaluate whether ICJ investigations observed the due process and rule of law principles urged on governments. Did the ICJ select targets for investigation based on purely legal rather than political criteria? Were ICJ missions conducted by impartial experts? Should powerful government defendants placed in the NGO dock have the right to confront their victim accusers? How can self-selected NGO prosecutors and judges be held accountable without compromising their independence?

Human Rights NGOs: Global Pluralism or Corporatism?

Is the ICJ a sibling or distant cousin of domestic public interest groups? The literature describing human rights NGOs has made little use of extensive research on the origins, leadership, funding, and membership of national organizations.[60] Research in Europe and the United States has distinguished public from sectional or economic interest groups. "Public" interest groups seek a "collective good . . . which will not selectively and materially benefit the membership or activists of the organization."[61] The weak international system has proportionately fewer economic groups and more public interest NGOs.[62] Several case studies examine U.S. public interest groups, and Jeffrey Berry has prepared a general overview.[63] His call for further research applies with equal force to human rights NGOs:

> An interest group's ability to accomplish its goals is affected by its organizational strengths and weaknesses. Its allocation of resources, setting of priorities, leadership, and adaptation to change in the environment are all critical in determining how well it gets its political job done. . . . Few political scientists have tried to systematically study interest groups to find the kinds of structures that are most productive. Little research has been done on the decision-making process of lobbying organizations. The organizer of a new interest group who wants to go by the book in setting up the organization can't—there is no book.[64]

Research on interest groups in Western democracies has compared pluralism in the United States with corporatist systems in Europe. Phillipe Schmitter defined pluralism as a system with an "unspecified number of multiple, voluntary, competitive, nonhierarchically ordered and self-determined categories that are not specifically licensed, recognized, subsidized, created or otherwise controlled . . . by the state." In a corporatist system Schmitter finds groups "organized into a limited number of singular, compulsory, noncompetitive, hierarchically ordered and functionally differentiated categories, recognized or licensed (if not created) by the state and granted a deliberate representational monopoly."[65]

European corporatist models differ markedly from the U.S. pluralist ideal of independent citizens organizing to challenge the state.[66] Many American pluralists associate corporatism with its fascist perversion, a totalitarian regime dominating nominally private groups to control the population. Europe's democratic socialist governments practice a more benign variant. They promote and fund privately directed organizations that enjoy considerable autonomy.[67] Government-supported farmers, merchants, religious and other societies share in policy making and program administration. State-approved bar associations have sole responsibility for representing and disciplining lawyers.

Without recognizing the practice as corporatism, U.S. policy makers have also encouraged and supported new citizen groups to represent the disadvantaged. The Economic Opportunity Act of 1964 sought "maximum feasible participation" by the poor in publicly funded community action programs. "Liberals hoped that government-sponsored pluralism would nourish a failing system."[68] Government-funded legal aid groups illustrate public-private collaboration that provides services as well as policy input for an unrepresented sector of the population. This study asks whether the ICJ's origins, funding, membership, and leadership fit a pluralist or corporatist model of the international political system.[69]

Origins. Did the ICJ's founding contribute to interest group pluralism in world politics?

Pluralists and their critics in the United States have disagreed over how and why new interest groups begin. David Truman theorized that U.S. groups organized in response to a "disturbance" created by a political crisis, rival group, or new government policy.[70] Farmers organized in response to declining prices, workers unionized to compete with management groups, and so on. In terms of "disturbance" theory, outraged citizens founded the public interest lobby Common Cause after the Watergate scandal in order to demand campaign finance reform. The ACLU organized to assist aliens deported after World War I. The French League for the Rights of Man and the Citizen was a 1902 response to French anti-Semitism and the Dreyfus case.

Robert Salisbury's "exchange" theory treats entrepreneurial founders rather than political upheaval as the major catalysts for new organizations.[71] Without patrons John Gardner and Roger Baldwin, Common Cause and the ACLU would never have organized. The entrepreneur Baldwin also founded the International League for Human Rights in New York.[72] European governments may create and license groups. Berry concludes that no single theory satisfactorily explains the origins of interest groups: "Interest groups have prospered because of broad political changes that have made people aware of the advantages of interest group advocacy, and because individual entrepreneurs have grown skilled in organizing and maintaining interest groups."[73] Chapter 1 asks whether the ICJ was a creation of U.S. patrons or a response to the "disturbance" of Soviet atrocities and the International Association of Democratic Lawyers (IADL).

Funding. When is it ethical and politic for governments to grant, and NGOs to accept, public funding?

Pluralists question the propriety and wisdom of government subsidies for interest groups. U.S. economic interest groups receive 76.8 percent of their funds from dues, but citizen groups and nonprofit organizations receive only one-third to one-half of their funding from their members.[74] Foundation grants sustain many nonprofit groups; fees and publications generate limited revenue. Like European democracies, the United States uses private voluntary organizations extensively for humanitarian relief and foreign aid development projects.[75] Many private charities distributing government assistance have become quasi-nongovernmental organizations (QUANGOs). Critics charged that China and other Asian states funded and directed government NGOs (GONGOs) to defend their interests at the 1993 World Conference on Human Rights in Vienna.[76]

Human rights NGOs enjoy the greatest independence with private funding for uninhibited challenges to government abuse of political dissidents. Amnesty International refuses government support, but many other NGOs accept public subsidies. In a form of global corporatism, Western democratic governments have funded NGOs that challenged non-Western tyrants. Both liberals and conservatives have objected. Idealists worry that NGOs that accept government grants may be co-opted or may lack credibility. They insist on private funding as a matter of principle; public support for human rights NGOs is improper, not merely unwise. Conservatives oppose public grants to unaccountable NGOs that capture government agencies for liberal programs opposed by the majority.

Both political groups and governments are using nonprofits, aided by taxpayers' money, to pursue goals not necessarily supported by a majority of citizens in either developed or developing countries. For these reasons, clear accountability and full disclosure to the public at large, as well as to governments, are not always forthcoming.[77]

The ICJ offers an ideal case to apply the conflicting views on public funding for human rights NGOs. Did covert CIA grants from 1952 through 1967 co-opt the organization and compromise its independence? Since 1967 has the ICJ used its political connections with European governments to finance programs opposed by democratic majorities? Has public funding enhanced or diminished the ICJ's influence and credibility? How does the ICJ account for its use of public funds and private contributions? In conclusion the case study recommends guidelines for human rights NGOs derived from the ICJ's experience with government grants.

Membership. Did the ICJ effectively recruit an exclusive membership supported by a broad base of lawyers from many different countries?

Government and foundation grants to the ICJ meant that a large membership was not needed for raising financial support. Groups with few dues-paying members may enhance their credibility by claiming to represent a mass base. The ICJ claimed legitimacy from no more than forty eminent Commissioners, staff experts, and thousands of local supporters in highly autonomous affiliates. Were selfless members and supporters serving a cause or were they recruited with personal benefits? Mancur Olson's rational interest model argues that personal gain even more than common purpose leads individuals to join interest groups.[78] Founding patrons offer a mix of purposive, material, and solidary incentives that attract members.[79] Public interest groups provide ideology, information, and camaraderie. The ICJ's American founders promoted the new organization as a movement of "free world" lawyers to combat communist and other totalitarian regimes. Presumably, human rights NGOs do not attract powerful elites seeking to maintain their privilege, and the ICJ recruited members purely with solidarity appeals to promote the rule of law. Chapter 2 identifies the incentives offered through 1963 when the organization enlisted twenty-five Commissioners, thirty-one ICJ national groups, and claimed forty thousand supporters worldwide. Chapter 7 examines membership development from 1970 through 1990.

Leadership. Did the elite membership of jurists practice the democracy they preached?

Whether pursuing the public good or private advantage, domestic interest groups rarely govern themselves as participatory democracies. "Just as it is true that interest groups almost always appear on the outside to be democratic, it also seems that they are almost always oligarchic on the inside. . . . A small cadre of workers invariably seem to dominate such organizations."[80] Elite leadership and staff make key decisions, even in mass membership organizations.[81] Despite by-law provisions for democratic governance, many interest groups become identified with one dominant leader. Nonprofit groups' governing boards meet infrequently and routinely endorse staff recommendations. Terms in office continue indefinitely. Public interest groups with mass constituencies are no more democratically governed than are corporate special interests.

Nor do members represent a broad cross section of the community; upper-income, well-educated individuals are typically the most active supporters, creating notable class bias.[82] Like U.S. groups with state affiliates, groups such as the International League for Human Rights organized as coalitions of national sections; very few are mass membership organizations whose supporters vote on policy.[83] Third world activists complain that dominant Western-based NGOs are unrepresentative and paternalistic.[84] At the 1993 World Conference on Human Rights in Vienna, new southern NGOs rebelled against leadership by well established European-funded groups, insiders with U.N. consultative status. Whether national or international, most groups function as staff-dominated oligarchies rather than participatory democracies.

Chapters 2, 5, 7, and 11 test whether those findings hold true for the ICJ at each transition to new leadership. Has a dominant Secretary-General, an exclusive inner circle, or the membership controlled the organization? Did the selection of an African as Secretary-General in 1990 herald a genuine shift to third world leadership and control that helps bridge North-South differences in the human rights movement?

Methodology

Three individuals conducted field research for this study in Geneva, London, and New York between 1983 and 1993. Two law students from the University of Cincinnati's Morgan Institute[85] began collecting materials for the ICJ project while I was completing a study on the U.N. Human Rights Commission that revealed significant ICJ influence. My subsequent visits to the Geneva Secretariat and to affiliate offices in New York and London provided access to budget data, committee minutes, and correspondence files. Interviews were conducted with five of the seven individuals who served as Secretary-General; three of the five chairmen of the Executive Committee; twelve current and former legal officers; and the leaders of three national affiliates. Additional interviews with leaders of NGOs, government officials, U.N. staff, and other observers provided independent evaluation. The ICJ's numerous publications were reviewed along with press accounts of ICJ activities and published commentary on its work.

Forsythe notes the difficulty in isolating and measuring the precise influence of human rights lobbyists.[86] This study presents some data to test claims of interest group impact. ICJ subscription lists, correspondence, membership, and national affiliates indicate the extent of transnational links. The number of U.S. libraries with ICJ publications was determined through OCLC, an on-line computer system. No objective standard can determine whether the ICJ has passed the new world order test. Successful interest groups function at varying levels of effectiveness in different activity areas; some concentrate on lobbying, with no attention whatever to public education. Coercion of governments is the critical variable for realists, but it would be impossible to prove decisive control. In order to test claims that NGOs enhance supranational authority, this study asks instead whether the ICJ has significantly influenced governments, either directly or indirectly. Even if growing interdependence has not diminished state sovereignty, international NGOs may have enhanced citizen influence in national politics.[87]

ICJ leaders, staff, and other practitioners were invited to review the accuracy of draft chapters that reported their work and views. Eleven chapters cover the period from 1952 to 1993 in Parts I through V. Within each part, the chapters offer a functional analysis of the ICJ's changing approach to promotion, standard setting, and protection. The forty-year chronology reveals how an NGO adapts under different leaders to a changing political environment and to its own shifting needs. As the human rights network changed, the ICJ altered its program priorities, funding base, and membership criteria. Chapters on promotion track the ICJ's development through affiliate organizing and recruitment. Conclusions at the end of each chapter offer political and legal analysis related to selected research questions from this Introduction.

The Conclusion of this book compares the ICJ with the nineteenth-century Anti-Slavery Society to assess whether a contemporary NGO has greater influence than an eminent predecessor. The findings provide an interdisciplinary perspective for students of human rights, public law, and international politics. What difference will it make to realists and idealists, proponents of natural law monism and positivist dualism, pluralists and corporatists, academics and activists? For realists and positivists a tiny lawyers' organization, whatever its lofty intentions, would contribute nothing significant to either real world politics or binding international law. A smaller cadre of idealists and monists would expect the ICJ to support their claims that a new world order is emerging. The ICJ history could also clarify whether interest group activity in world politics corresponds to a pluralist or corporatist model. In terms of normative theory, the study proposes standards for funding and accountability of human rights NGOs. Activists put off by theories of world politics, international law, and citizen loyalty should find value in learning what worked and what did not for a highly regarded NGO.

Part I
1952–1955: Cold Warriors against Socialist Legality

Chapter 1
Recruiting Free World Jurists

> Investigators digging at the site of a Soviet-run prison camp in the former East Germany have uncovered mass graves containing the bodies of 12,500 people. . . . The camp was at Sachsenhausen, north of Berlin, and was open from 1945 to 1950. . . . In the years after the end of World War II, occupying Soviet forces imprisoned thousands of Germans. . . . Some were simply picked off the street, victims of Stalinist crackdowns.
>
> —*The New York Times*, September 24, 1992, p. 7

Cold War Containment

The war that ended Hitler's genocidal crimes against humanity left a rival mass murderer in control of Eastern Europe. Stalinism appeared on the march in Czechoslovakia, Greece, China, and Korea. The United States feared that communist totalitarianism was spreading throughout Europe and beyond. The International Commission of Jurists (ICJ) was a small offshoot of a comprehensive U.S. policy to contain Soviet expansion. Containment brought aid to the Greek government, the Marshall Plan, the North Atlantic Treaty Organization, and the U.N.-endorsed defense of South Korea.

The United States also created a Central Intelligence Agency (CIA) with covert action capability.[1] A top secret National Security Council Directive (10/2) in June 1948 authorized clandestine

> propaganda, economic warfare, preventative direct action including sabotage, anti-sabotage, demolition and evacuation measures . . . subversion against hostile states, including assistance to underground resistance move-

ments, guerrillas and refugee liberation groups, and support of indigenous anti-Communist elements in threatened countries of the free world.

Radio Free Europe and Radio Liberty began broadcasting with agency support and a private fund-raising cover.

Divided Berlin in East Germany became a Cold War flash point and the ICJ's birthplace. Over Western objections in 1949, the USSR created a new German Democratic Republic in Soviet-occupied Eastern Germany. Stalinists arrested and summarily executed thousands of former Nazis and pro-democracy dissidents. The Soviets blockaded Berlin, and the United States mounted a massive airlift to retain control of the Western-occupied zone. In 1952 the U.S. Information Service Daily Wireless reported: "The swelling mass of refugees fleeing from East Germany into anti-Communist West Berlin during the last several days is now estimated by Western officials at about 200,000 men, women and children."[2]

The U.S. High Commissioner for Germany, John J. McCloy, supervised both civilian and paramilitary intelligence operations. His two chief deputies, Bethuel Webster and Eli Whitney Debevoise, were also leaders of the New York bar. An associate in McCloy's law firm, Benjamin Shute, was director of intelligence for the Allied High Commission for Occupied Germany (HICOG). All three belonged to the presitigious Council on Foreign Relations, which helped initiate the containment policy. Since 1921 the Council's elite, exclusive membership of bankers, lawyers, and government advisers had encouraged U.S. policy makers to assume global leadership responsibilities.[3]

Shute helped recruit, equip, train, and finance German groups to undermine communist authority in the Soviet zone.[4] The United States conducted a "sophisticated . . . campaign designed to persuade left-of-center European intellectuals to oppose communist political influence. Thousands of Germans . . . were drawn into this intelligence network as informants, agents of influence, and propagandists."[5] Nazis eagerly joined the anticommunist campaign: The U.S. Army Counter Intelligence Corps used war criminal Klaus Barbie. Shute recommended that McCloy appoint another Hitler intelligence expert as a security adviser to the new German government.[6] U.S. sponsors did not always care about or carefully check records. A founding member of the ICJ, Dr. Theo Friedenau, had created a false identity to conceal his Nazi past. A self-proclaimed Jewish lawyer and survivor of Gestapo imprisonment, Friedenau directed a publicly funded Investigating Committee of Free Jurists in West Berlin.[7] In fact, Friedenau was Horst Erdmann, born of German parentage and a Stammführer in Hitler Youth responsible for a battalion-size force. He had attended university for only one term and was a lawyer in name only.[8]

Friedenau applied the Nuremberg principles to warn individual communist officials that they would be held criminally liable for abuse of power. His government-funded staff of thirty used a network of informers and agents in the Soviet zone.[9] Their evidence documented how the communists had destroyed the independence of bench and bar and used nonlawyer judges responsible to the party.

> Between April 21st and July 1st, thirty-five hundred people were sentenced to prison terms ranging from six to twenty-five years, on the usual manufactured charges. A few were even executed. The shortest trial lasted fourteen minutes, the longest forty-five. The arraignments were written up, at the rate of more than a hundred a day, by seventeen-year-old students in the Criminal Police School in Arnsdorf.[10]

The committee lawyers submitted their "indictments" to the West German Ministry of Justice for possible prosecution, distributed the charges throughout the Soviet zone, and broadcast individual warnings over the Radio in the American Sector.[11] The communists offered a reward for Friedenau's capture, and the committee's Berlin headquarters was heavily guarded. East German courts convicted several captured committee agents on espionage and sabotage charges. Friedenau's family had been sent to safety in Western Germany. Unaware of his alleged Nazi background, *The New Yorker*, *Time*, and *The American Mercury* carried highly favorable accounts praising Friedenau's invaluable work for human rights.

Nongovernmental Rivals

Postwar human rights activists challenged not only Stalinist repression in Eastern Europe, but also fascist rule in Spain, European colonialism in Asia and Africa, and South Africa's emerging apartheid system. With some reluctance, the major powers accepted demands for a Commission on Human Rights in the postwar United Nations. The United States and its Western allies won the 1948 U.N. debate over the contents of a Universal Declaration of Human Rights. The USSR and its satellites abstained in that vote—strange bedfellows with members of the American and Canadian Bar Associations. Conservative American lawyers had regarded the U.N. declaration as a socialist document because it endorsed limited economic as well as familiar civil and political rights. Under pressure from conservative isolationists, the United States after 1950 refused to support binding human rights treaties. The Soviet Union hypocritically endorsed unenforceable human rights covenants in order to embarrass the United States.

The USSR also controlled major NGOs with U.N. consultative status that disseminated anti-American propaganda. Since the 1930s, Comintern agents had been used to infiltrate, influence, and control noncommunist leftist groups.

> Their purpose was to reach beyond the limited number of committed communists to large, functional groups within society which could be appealed to by offering them memberships in organizations that appeared to serve their social and economic needs, and to offer a hope of redress for their grievances. The fact of Communist control was hidden behind the facade of generous social purpose. As these "front" groups proliferated, they opened up new avenues for propaganda and political action that would have been closed to communists identified for what they were.[12]

Major communist front groups included the International Union of Students, the World Peace Council, the International Organization of Journalists, and the World Federation of Trade Unions. The Soviets spent an estimated $250 million annually on the ostensibly private groups.[13]

Propaganda from the Soviet-funded International Association of Democratic Lawyers (IADL) particularly aggravated U.S. officials during the Korean War. The IADL offered "'documented proof' that U.S. forces in Korea were dropping canisters of poisoned mosquitoes on North Korean cities and were following a 'systematic procedure of torturing civilians, individually and en masse.'"[14] A French lawyers' resistance organization had begun the IADL at an October 1946 congress in Paris attended by practitioners and judges from twenty-four nations. The congress established the IADL ostensibly to support the United Nations in restoring, defending, and developing democratic liberties as well as in removing all vestiges of fascism from the field of law. In practice the IADL's global activities stridently attacked the United States. In Calcutta the All-India Association of Democratic Lawyers attacked U.S. practices in occupied Okinawa. An IADL Vienna Conference for the Defense of Democratic Liberties denounced U.S. Senator McCarthy's persecution of communists and the Rosenbergs' prosecution as Soviet spies.

The IADL's increasingly communist orientation prompted France's René Cassin to resign its presidency; the U.S. National Lawyers Guild ended its affiliation in 1951. The CIA widely publicized the USSR's sponsorship of the communist front groups and persuaded the French government to expel those based in Paris. The IADL moved to Brussels in 1950; other communist fronts relocated in Eastern Europe. Following U.S. complaints about politically inspired propaganda, the U.N. Economic and Social Council (ECOSOC) rescinded consultative status for the IADL and the Women's International Democratic Federation in 1951.

CIA planners reasoned that private Western groups needed covert government support to compete against Soviet-controlled groups. Private foundations not only lacked the necessary resources but had been intimidated by Senator Joseph McCarthy from supporting the noncommunist left. A Georgia representative who chaired the committee to investigate tax-exempt foundations in 1952 felt that "un-American or subversive" Ford Foundation actvities tended to "weaken or discredit the capitalistic system as it exists in the United States and to favor Marxist socialism."[15] There was no prospect of winning Congressional approval for U.S. grants to socialists in Europe that McCarthyites regarded as communist sympathizers. The CIA's liberal anticommunist lawyers concealed their NGO support from both the Soviet adversary and the right-wing conservatives in the U.S. Congress. Presidents Truman and Eisenhower, their top national security advisers, and selected Congressional representatives responsible for overseeing the CIA all approved the clandestine effort.[16]

Allen Dulles, President of the Council on Foreign Relations, became the CIA's deputy director of plans for clandestine services in 1950. Dulles recruited Tom Braden to head up a new CIA International Organization Division.[17] Braden was a liberal Dartmouth College English professor, former executive secretary of New York's Museum of Modern Art, and director of the American Committee for a Free Europe. His deputy and successor, Cord Meyer, had led the World Federalists and battled communist sympathizers in the American veterans movement.[18] Braden, Meyer, and their CIA superiors, Frank Wisner and Richard Bissell, were all nonresident members of the council.[19]

The CIA covertly supported existing groups and established new organizations in fields where powerful communist fronts operated unopposed. Braden lamented that pro-Soviet groups like the IADL had stolen the great words—"Peace, Freedom, Justice." A salaried CIA officer arranged the 1950 inaugural convention of the Congress for Cultural Freedom in Berlin. More than one hundred prominent artists resolved to create a permanent Congress. "In the early years, it sponsored any number of arts and writers' 'festivals' as part of a sophisticated campaign of psychological warfare against communists and fellow travelers. A half-dozen magazines were sponsored to spread the message, the most prominent and long-lasting of them being *Encounter* in London."[20]

The International Organizations Division grew rapidly with unvouchered funds from a CIA budget that had tripled by 1955. Braden was responsible for a network of labor, student, and professional groups that rivaled the massively supported Soviet propaganda offensive. "By 1953 we were operating or influencing international organizations in every field where Communist fronts had previously seized ground."[21] Recipients included the International Confederation of Free Trade Unions, the World Assembly of Youth, the Coordinating Organization of National Unions of Students, and its American affiliate, the National Student Association. Braden explained the operating guidelines: "Limit the money to amounts private organizations can credibly spend. . . . Use legitimate, existing organizations; disguise the extent of American interest; protect the integrity of the organization by not requiring it to support every aspect of official American policy."[22]

Only selected recipients knew of CIA sponsorship and performed assigned tasks. The CIA used the Asia Foundation "through penetrations among the officers and members to find anticommunist academicians . . . to disseminate throughout Asia a negative vision of mainland China, North Vietnam and North Korea, and to recruit foreign agents and new case officers."[23] Other paid agents aided the CIA in the "spotting, assessing and recruiting of student and youth leaders as long term agents."[24]

In many organizations, genuinely independent leaders and staff had no knowledge of CIA support. Each CIA dollar spent passed through several conduit foundations in order to conceal its origin. Socialist Norman Thomas operated labor programs in Latin America apparently unaware that the foundation grants received were a CIA investment in the noncommunist left. Highly independent writers for *Encounter* criticized the United States, even though one of the editors was a CIA agent. While undertaking this research, I learned for the first time of CIA funding for Operation Crossroads Africa, which sponsored my 1963 summer work camp in Sierra Leone. Press revelations in 1967 exposed CIA connections to about sixty different foundations that had funded more than one hundred organizations.[25] The disclosures ended the covert program but left unanswered questions. Most of the organizations that survived, including the ICJ, never fully accounted for their original funding and minimized the CIA's contribution. When interviewed for this study, Tom Braden confirmed my finding that his CIA office helped set up the ICJ.[26]

The 1952 International Congress of Jurists in Berlin

To counter the communist-dominated IADL, the CIA decided to create a new organization rather than to build up one of the very few existing international human rights NGOs. During World War II, ACLU founder Roger Baldwin provided a New York base for exiled French leaders of the Paris-based International Federation of Human Rights. After the war he continued the International League for the Rights of Man in New York. The small League was not a lawyers' organization; it refused government support and pursued a broad agenda that included decolonization in Africa and Asia.

Other New York lawyers who belonged to the Council on Foreign Relations decided to promote a new organization exclusively for jurists. CIA planning director Allen Dulles had been president of the council and had worked extensively with McCloy and their New York bar associates in Germany. A salaried CIA lawyer, Robert Bass, had primary responsibility for operational details.[27] The ICJ inaugural convention resembled the Berlin Congress of Cultural Freedom covertly arranged by the CIA in 1950.[28] Friedenau's investigating committee was the designated host for a meeting of eminent jurists in 1952; unnamed Americans of German origin interested in German reunification were identified as the funding sponsors.[29] The all-expenses-paid meeting cost $142,000.

The 106 voting delegates included thirty-one ministers and statesmen, thirty-two professors, and thirty-five judges, counsel, and presidents of high courts. Representatives of thirty-two free world countries participated, along with eleven refugee delegations representing the Baltic Republics, Russia, Georgia, and the Eastern European satellites. McCloy and his associates invited several of their colleagues from the New York bar and the Council on Foreign Relations. Whitney North Seymour, president of the New York Bar Association, invited Dudley Bonsal, a council member working in London on the German-Dutch debt settlement.[30] The past and current presidents of the American Bar Association also joined the American delegation.[31] McCloy advised Debevoise not to attend, in order to avoid the appearance of U.S. sponsorship. Friedenau asked foreign representatives in Bonn to identify prospective participants and toured seven European capitals to promote the congress.

The East German press characterized congress participants as "gangsters in the guise of jurists." Immediately before the congress convened, a staff lawyer on Friedenau's Investigating Committee was kidnapped and taken to East Germany. The abduction outraged

Secretary A. J. M. "Bart" van Dal of the Netherlands (left) and former U.S. High Commissioner in Berlin John J. McCloy at an April 10, 1956 meeting of the New York City Bar Association to promote American support for the ICJ.

the jurists, who denounced the disappearance.[32] East German officials sought to discredit Friedenau and his associates during the congress by conducting a well-publicized trial of seven committee investigators on espionage and economic sabotage charges. The president of the German section of the IADL urged one participant to leave the congress and condemned Friedenau's "U.S. paid espionage organization."[33]

Undeterred, the assembled jurists heard witnesses and reviewed documents presented by Friedenau's committee under the rubric "Injustice and the System." The International Congress of Jurists functioned as a tribunal to review Friedenau's complaints of injustice in the Soviet zone. Separate committees examined penal law, public law, civil and economic law, and labor law. Committee reports found that the East Germans had violated provisions of their own constitution taken from the Universal Declaration of Human Rights. By applause acclamation and without a recorded vote, the congress accepted the "authentic nature of the material" presented and resolved that "generally accepted principles of law have been violated by the administration of the Soviet zone." The congress resolved to send its findings and the supporting documents to the German government, the Occupation Authorities of the Soviet Zone, and the United Nations for appropriate action.

British and Dutch jurists resisted an Indian delegate's efforts to discuss other human rights issues, including racial discrimination in South Africa and colonized peoples' quests for independence.[34] Without regard for impartial fact finding, the congress allowed government officials exiled from Soviet-ruled territories to participate. In a public report, the ICJ vouched for the truth of its findings based on the eminence of the jurists attending the congress.[35] Stefan Osusky, a former minister of Czechoslovakia exiled in Washington, organized other refugees in attendance to create a standing council of exile jurists from countries behind the Iron Curtain. They planned a new investigating committee to publicize injustices in the satellite countries.

At Friedenau's request, the participants elected a standing committee of five to continue their work in support of his investigating committee. The congress elected as committee chairman Joseph T. Thorson, President of Canada's Exchequer Court and Minister of National War Services.[36] A. J. M. "Bart" van Dal of the Netherlands was named Secretary. Van Dal, a staunch cold warrior, had been a journalist before studying law. His office at The Hague became the committee's secretariat.[37] The resolution granted the members the "power to replace and co-opt," and authorized "such further action as the Standing Committee may deem desirable to implement the objectives of the Congress."[38]

The American Fund for Free Jurists

By late 1953 American support had transformed the International Congress of Jurists Standing Committee into the International Commission of Jurists. Members of the liberal New York Bar Association, rather than the more conservative ABA, took the lead. The U.S. founders were deeply committed to civil liberties both at home and abroad.[39] They shared a commitment to individual liberty under the rule of law and an antipathy for "socialist legality." They promoted the new international organization as public servants summoning like-minded colleagues to contain communism's spread.

After leaving his post as counsel to the U.S. High Commissioner in

Germany, Bethuel Webster became president of the New York Bar Association. He appointed Dudley Bonsal to chair a special New York City Bar committee to cooperate with "The International Commission of Free Jurists." Born of an early American family, Bonsal held "that personal security and rights of the individual are important aspects of national security." He also advocated efforts to extend freedom "back into areas which have fallen victims to totalitarian oppression."[40] Another committee member, Whitney North Seymour, was "a liberal champion of unpopular causes and a recognized authority in the field of civil liberties."[41] In the 1930s, while representing a black communist, he persuaded the U.S. Supreme Court to hold as unconstitutional Georgia's anti-insurrection statute. Seymour's commitment to effective counsel for the poor led him from Yale Law School to the presidency of New York's Legal Aid Society. He belonged to a conservative anticommunist majority on the ACLU board, but protested a loyalty oath for ABA members.

The New York bar committee sponsored a special meeting in May 1953 that featured van Dal as keynote speaker.[42] Van Dal stressed the Commission's Cold War mission to "mobilize the forces—in particular the juridical forces—of the free world for the defense of our fundamental legal principles, and in doing so to organize the fight against all forms of systematic injustice in the Communist countries."[43] Bonsal and Debevoise also arranged for an ABA committee to cooperate with the new international organization. Council member and national ACLU chairman Ernest Angell became chairperson of that ABA group, which included members from twelve cities. Angell was an American Legion member and chaired a regional Federal Loyalty Board.[44]

Bonsal then incorporated a nonprofit Delaware corporation the American Fund for Free Jurists (AFFJ). Bonsal became the fund's president, Seymour its vice-president, and J. Grafton Rogers its chairman.[45] The board of directors included Webster, Debevoise, and Shute from McCloy's staff in Germany. All but one of the directors belonged to the Council on Foreign Relations.[46] Bonsal advised the New York bar committee that the AFFJ would take responsibility for soliciting contributions to the ICJ.[47] A fund-raising letter sent to prospective donors raised $53,000.[48] To conceal its contributions, the CIA passed funds designated for the ICJ first through dummy foundations and then through several legitimate foundations. The M. D. Anderson Foundation's IRS reports from 1958 to 1964 show $655,000 received from the conduit foundations and the same amount disbursed to the AFFJ.[49] The CIA officer responsible for the ICJ, Robert Bass, served as the first AFFJ executive secretary. When interviewed

Dudley Bonsal, the first Executive Committee chairman, addressing the 1956 New York City Bar Association meeting to promote the ICJ. ICJ President Joseph Thorson of Canada (left) and A. J. M. van Dal of the Netherlands are seated.

for this study, Debevoise acknowledged that he knew about the CIA funding.

Organizing the International Commission of Jurists

With AFFJ funding in place, the U.S. sponsors established the ICJ as a separate international nongovernmental organization. Bonsal became the unelected leader of a five-member Executive Committee that included only two individuals from the Standing Committee chosen in Berlin.[50] The new group included Friedenau but not Thorson, the titular Standing Committee chairman.

The Executive Committee renamed the organization "The International Commission of Jurists," with Thorson designated President and van Dal Secretary-General. The committee initially identified eleven Commissioners: the five Executive Committee members, four other Standing Committee members elected in Berlin, and two new Commissioners.[51] The Committee selected only men with high standing and considerable experience in public life—cabinet ministers, parliamentary deputies, appeals court judges. Elite status would give access to national officials as well as to international organizations where the ICJ obtained consultative status, including the Council of Europe and the United Nations.[52] The entire Executive Committee and all but two of the first eleven Commissioners were from continental Europe and North America. To provide greater balance, the Committee soon added to the Commission four new members who had not attended the Berlin Congress: the former U.K. Attorney General, a senior advocate from India, Lebanon's former Minister of Justice and President of the Court of Appeal, and a law professor from Uruguay.[53] Table 1.1 lists the first members.

Bonsal rarely attended Committee meetings, but he dominated the critical organizing sessions with correspondence and a designated alternate. A letter from Bonsal to the first Executive Committee meeting called attention to the upcoming session of the IADL, "a camouflaged communist organization." He recommended countermeasures to inform the press and delegates about the IADL. Bonsal's alternate was James L. McDonnell, a New York attorney based in London. McDonnell did not belong to the ICJ, the AFFJ, or the New York Committee; he effectively overruled Friedenau's attempts to direct independent national sections and branch offices. When a Polish seaman sought political asylum in Britain, McDonnell presided over an ICJ group that investigated.[54]

The ICJ opened branch offices in Munich and Istanbul similar to Friedenau's Berlin operation in order to receive refugees from Czechoslovakia, Romania, and Bulgaria. U.S. sponsors soon insisted on centralizing ICJ operations in The Hague, and the branch activities lasted only two years. Friedenau wanted ICJ agents to challenge regimes behind the Iron Curtain; Bonsal opposed direct ICJ involvement that could lead to criminal prosecution by communist authorities. Broadcasts prepared for Radio Free Europe, Voice of America, and the BBC offered a safe alternative.

TABLE 1.1. ICJ Officers, Members, and Meetings, 1952–1955.

Secretariat (47 Buitenhof, The Hague, Netherlands)
Secretary-General, A. J. M. van Dal, July 1952–April 1, 1956
Administrative Secretary, Edward Kozera, April 1954–November 1964
AFFJ Executive Secretary, New York, Robert Bass

Executive Committee, 1953–1956
Dudley Bonsal, U.S., *de facto* Chairman; alternate James McDonnell
Theo Friedenau, Germany (a.k.a. Horst Erdmann)
Axel Henrik Munktell, Sweden
A. J. M. van Dal, Netherlands
Edouard Zellweger, Switzerland

American Fund for Free Jurists Board of Directors
Dudley Bonsal, President
Whitney North Seymour, Vice President
J. Grafton Rogers, Chairman
Whitney Debevoise
Earnest Medina
Benjamin Shute
Bethuel Webster

Original Members of the ICJ

Year elected		*Final year*
1952	Joseph T. Thorson, Canada, President, 1952–1959	1971[a]
	A. J. M. van Dal, Netherlands, Executive Secretary	1973[a]
	Per T. Federspiel, Denmark	1978[a]
	José T. Nabuco, Brazil	1973[a]
	Hatim Badrudin Tyabji, Pakistan	1971[a]
	Edouard Zellweger, Switzerland	1960
1953	Dudley Bonsal, U.S., Executive Committee Chair	1974[a]
	Theo Friedenau, (a.k.a. Horst Erdmann), Germany	1958
	Axel Henrik Munktell, Sweden	1963
	Stefan Osusky, Czechoslovakia/U.S.	1973
	Giuseppe Bettiol, Italy	1973[a]
1954	Philippe N. Boulos, Lebanon	1971[a]
	Sir Hartley Shawcross, U.K.	1971[a]
	Purshottam Trikamdas, India	1969
	Juan José Cabajal Victorica, Uruguay	1962

Meetings

International Congress of Jurists, West Berlin, 1952
International Congress of Jurists, Athens, 1955

[a] Year elected as honorary member.

In addition to American Bar Association supporters, lawyers in Greece, Turkey, and Sweden formed national ICJ sections. The CIA was particularly concerned about the communist threat in Greece and provided a subsidy to army colonel George Papadopoulos after 1952.[55] The CIA may have used paid agents to establish the Greek National Section.[56] Axel Henrik Munktell, a professor at Uppsala University and a member of Parliament, became Vice President of the Swedish Association. He complained about the ICJ's identification with Friedenau's anticommunist committee in Berlin and urged attention to injustices in South Africa, Spain, Argentina, and Yugoslavia.

On Bonsal's recommendation, the committee hired Edward Kozera as ICJ administrative secretary at The Hague. Kozera, a U.S. citizen of Polish descent, had been a Ph.D. candidate and lecturer in government at Columbia University. He appears to have collaborated actively with the CIA. Before coming to the ICJ in April 1954, Kozera had worked for the CIA's covertly funded Radio Free Europe. Kozera's $9,000-employment contract was with the AFFJ rather than the ICJ; he, rather than van Dal, managed the organization's finances.[57] The Executive Committee approved only an expenditure budget without considering income; Kozera then consulted the U.S. office to determine what resources would be available. Kozera removed all ICJ financial documents from Executive Committee files,[58] and his assistant complained about the excessive secrecy. When forced to resign in 1964, Kozera took ICJ mailing lists of more than forty thousand names without authorization.[59]

McDonnell told ICJ Executive Committee members that the New York City Bar Association and ABA were funding the AFFJ; he strongly urged them to obtain similar financial support from the European bar.[60] The European jurists felt that Americans could be more generous because of their greater wealth and the U.S. tax laws that allowed deductions for charitable gifts. The ICJ Executive Committee approved a general policy that funds were to be received exclusively from lawyers and lawyers' associations, although legacies, bequests, and foundation grants would also be accepted. The first ICJ publications stated: "Financial support for the work of the Commission comes entirely from private voluntary contributions of individual jurists or from the national organizations."[61]

Whose False Colors?

Administrative Secretary Kozera managed an extensive publication program that included monographs, documents, a newsletter, and radio broadcasts. The first publications described the ICJ as "a world-wide organization of lawyers and jurists dedicated to the preservation and, if necessary, restoration of the rule of law in every country." In practice ICJ reports only faulted regimes behind the Iron Curtain. Key Commission members and Secretariat staff forced into exile by Soviet occupation had a personal stake in removing communist dictators.

Kozera hired for an ICJ investigation and information division two militantly anticommunist Czech refugees, Vladimir E. Kabes and Karel Vasak. Kabes was an organizer, speaker, and writer in the anti-communist movement. As an ICJ consultant he had published a three-hundred-page attack on the IADL, *Blueprint of Deception*, that did not identify a publisher. In November 1954 the ICJ published eleven thousand copies of its first *Bulletin* in English, French, and German. The issue attacked Communist Party control of judges and was distributed without charge on request.[62] In the second *Bulletin*, a Kabes article condemned "Socialist Legality." Other ICJ pamphlets criticized Soviet-ruled Estonia and communist China.[63]

An ironically titled 1955 publication set out to expose the ICJ's Cold War rival—*Under False Colours: A Report on the Character of the International Association of Democratic Lawyers*. In an introduction to the thirty-two-page pamphlet, van Dal explained the ICJ's "deviation from its main tasks." The pamphlet was an "incidental" publication to overcome confusion about the stated goals of the two organizations. "The commission does . . . object to the fact that the IADL pursues aims which it does not honestly and openly manifest." A quote from Klara Zetkin on Cominform strategy exposed the duplicity of front groups:

> These organizations must not carry placards with the words "communist organization" visible from afar by their red letters. On the contrary they should appear from outside as neutral organizations. It is indispensable that their committees should include representatives of all types of opinion. What is essential is that the Communist Party should, surreptitiously, give to each organization its aims and its program.[64]

The IADL countered with a pamphlet that attacked the ICJ and exposed Friedenau's Nazi past: "*The Law above the Rule of Law: A criticism of an enterprise of the cold war.*"[65]

In a published report on the 1952 Berlin Congress, the ICJ Secretariat assured that resolutions were "unprejudiced by political questions of the day . . . not for propaganda purposes, but with the object of spreading the truth in order to maintain and defend Law against an imminent danger not yet sufficiently understood by the Free World." In its first *Bulletin* the ICJ proclaimed: "Honesty and fairness in the presentation of our evidence will be one of our leading motives. The world of today does not need more doctrinaire material; what it does need is honest reflection, and men who have the courage to form and voice a conviction."[66]

Deliberate misrepresentation of the ICJ's funding belies those claims and raises questions about the documentary evidence presented by Friedenau and Kozera. The CIA produced both "grey propaganda"—valid information disseminated without disclosing the true source—as well as disinformation or "black propaganda."[67] By accepting covert government funds and relying extensively on victims seeking personal redress, the new organization compromised its professed principles. Nongovernmental public interest groups for the rule of law invariably confront political power. A state-funded organization targeted exclusively at a rival government is something quite different.

The 1955 Athens Congress

Within two years, the ICJ began its transformation into a more principled human rights NGO. The ICJ's formal debut came at a 1955 meeting in Athens arranged by McDonnell. Friedenau had sought $150,000 to $200,000 for an international congress in a country bordering the Soviet Union. Bonsal directed that expenditures not exceed $100,000 and wanted delegates to pay some of their own expenses. The ICJ invited jurists from throughout the noncommunist world. Friedenau, Kozera, and Vasak prepared a 499-page briefing book of materials on Eastern Europe published in English and German entitled *Justice Enslaved: A Collection of Documents on the Abuse of Justice for Political Ends.*

"The First International Congress of Jurists sponsored by the International Commission of Jurists" attracted to Athens 150 leading experts from thirty-nine noncommunist countries and political exiles from nine Soviet satellites. Future ICJ members included Supreme Court judges from Burma, India, and Israel as well as the chief justice of Pakistan. Eminent U.S. delegates included Angell, Bonsal, Debevoise, McDonnell, Charles Raphael, Rogers, and Webster.

The documents in *Justice Enslaved* clarified the conflict between the ICJ's Rule of Law doctrine and Eastern European "socialist legality." The Rule of Law meant individual liberties guaranteed by an independent judiciary in a democratic political system. Communist doctrine subjected individuals, lawyers, and judges to arbitrary action by the state or party. Under Stalin, law became an instrument of the state to secure the dictatorship of the proletariat. In a 1941 book on criminal evidence, chief prosecutor Audrey Vyshinsky wrote that "neither court nor criminal procedure is or could be outside politics. This means that the contents and form of judicial activities cannot avoid being subordinated to political class aims and strivings."[68]

Stalin's notorious show trials perverted the judicial system and fatally compromised the independence of both bench and bar. The Soviets elected judges to fixed terms but could recall jurists at any time. Professional judges shared the power to decide cases with lay assessors elected by the party.[69] The Ministry of Justice and the Procuracy closely supervised judges.[70] Lawyers engaged in private practice paid higher taxes than those serving an attorney's collective.[71] The government determined which individuals could obtain professional training for the bar and thereby controlled admission to colleges of advocates. Most authorities insisted that defense counsel disclose a client's confidences about counterrevolutionary crimes.[72]

The independent delegates attending the First International Congress of Jurists recognized that communist governments were not the only regimes breaching the Rule of Law. To the consternation of South Africa's anticommunist participants, non-Western jurists also strongly condemned apartheid. Scandinavian delegates objected to Spanish fascism, and Greeks challenged British colonialism in Cyprus. Bonsal objected to making Spain a target, but the ICJ initiated a study. In a concluding resolution the participants directed the ICJ to investigate systematic injustice wherever found.[73] In the "Act of Athens," the ICJ's founders drafted and the congress unanimously approved their basic formulation for the Rule of Law.

> We free jurists . . . devoted to the Rule of Law which springs from the rights of the individual . . . for freedom of speech, press, worship, assembly and association and the right to free elections to the end that laws are enacted by the duly elected representatives of the people and afford equal protection to all, Being concerned by the disregard of the Rule of Law in various parts of the world, . . . Do solemnly declare that:
>
> 1. The State is subject to the law.
> 2. Governments should respect the rights of the individual under the Rule of Law and provide effective means for their enforcement.
> 3. Judges should be guided by Rule of Law, protect and enforce it without fear or favor and resist any encroachments by governments or political parties on their independence as judges.
> 4. Lawyers of the world should preserve the independence of their pro-

fession, assert the rights of the individual under the Rule of Law and insist that every accused is accorded a fair trial.[74]

Conclusions

Origins

Corporatism and exchange theory rather than pluralism and disturbance theory best explain the ICJ's creation. Government patrons and private entrepreneurs responding to Stalinist totalitarianism and Soviet expansionism collaborated to organize new NGOs. State patronage made a critical difference. Independent lawyers' organizations that challenged human rights atrocities by Stalin and Hitler in the 1930s were quickly forgotten.[75]

The postwar superpowers practiced a perverted corporatism behind a pluralist facade. Both manipulated citizen groups to advance their strategic interests. The United States approved U.N. consultative status for NGOs that challenged communists' sovereignty and excluded Soviet fronts that criticized American policy. Soviet-manipulated front groups and their CIA-sponsored adversaries peddled a pluralist myth of a genuine citizens' movement.

The ICJ did not begin as a citizen-initiated transnational movement that challenged state sovereignty. The United States created the lawyers' organization to counter subversion of Western European democracies and to help destabilize communist states behind the Iron Curtain. Stalin committed gross human rights violations, but the CIA was more concerned about the Soviet threat to U.S. allies and strategic interests. New York lawyers from the Council on Foreign Relations supplied CIA funds received through conduit foundations to aid refugee jurists from Eastern Europe and anticommunist advocates in Western democracies. Human rights advocates genuinely committed to an independent bench and bar became unwitting associates of covert CIA operatives and a former Nazi who concealed their true identities.

Funding

Tom Braden publicly acknowledged that the covert CIA program was "immoral."[76] He argued that good results justified the shady means. President Truman had articulated a moral goal: "to help free peoples to maintain their free institutions and their national integrity against aggressive movements that seek to impose upon them totalitarian regimes."[77] The CIA fought fire with fire, using undemocratic tactics against totalitarian rivals. The Executive subverted the U.S. Constitution by concealing from Congress covert CIA operations. Lies to Congress and pardons for well-motivated Iran-Contra patriots continued through the Bush administration in 1992. The ICJ's founders recruited staff and members using false pretenses and jeopardized the reputations of independent jurists who would be embarrassed by public disclosure of a CIA connection.

Neither the elected legislators who appropriated U.S. tax dollars nor the ICJ recipients of those funds understood the public-private partnership engineered by the CIA. Secrecy prevented accountability.[78] Unelected CIA patriots fixed the terms for commingling public and private functions. U.S. democracy was founded on Madisonian ideals of competing power centers to check arbitrary state power. Ironically, the United States fought Soviet totalitarianism by manipulating private organizations in violation of its own pluralist principles. The United States also frustrated NGO pluralism at the United Nations by stripping organizations that made unacceptable political statements of their consultative status. Open U.N. or state funding of competing groups might have promoted pluralist ends with corporatist means. Covert funding and restrictions on consultative status left states the primary but inadequate representatives of public opinion at the United Nations.

Policy Making

The ICJ appears like the handiwork of a foreign policy subgovernment composed of individuals from the CIA and Council on Foreign Relations: Allen Dulles, Frank Wisner, Richard Bissell, Tom Braden, Cord Meyer. That sub-government also embraced the U.S. High Commissioner's staff in Germany and prominent members of the private New York City Bar Association, including John McCloy, Bethuel Webster, Eli Whitney Debevoise, and Benjamin Shute. Liberal CIA decision makers excluded Congressional participation in the "iron triangle" because of conservative legislators' well-known hostility toward communist sympathizers. Without fully accounting to Congress for unvouchered funds, the public-private collaboration organized several new anticommunist groups and financed many others.

Enforcement

The eminent jurists attending the ICJ's first conferences did not create a satisfactory model for NGO enforcement of universal human rights. Using questionable procedures, they hastily condemned Stalin's notorious atrocities. Eastern European exiles striving to regain power in the Soviet satellites sat in judgment on their communist enemies. Jurists from other countries vouched for the exiles' testimony and validated documentary evidence with only cursory review. Participants did not know that the CIA had paid their expenses as part of a Cold War containment policy. The jurists selectively attacked Stalin's egregious violations, and very few applied the rule of law to other human rights offenders. Friedenau and Kozera had no legal training and pursued a political agenda.

The ICJ had a limited effect on Eastern European governments. Communist officials sought to discredit the jurists and to intimidate prospective members. The number of refugees fleeing the Soviet zone was estimated at two hundred thousand in the week after the Berlin Congress.[79] The major goals to reunify Germany, roll back the Iron Curtain, and change Eastern Europe's legal systems took thirty-five years and involved factors far beyond the ICJ's influence. The Athens Congress improved on the inaugural meeting in Berlin by endorsing general rule of law principles. Following the Athens Congress, a new Secretary-General administered a considerably broader ICJ program that redirected the Commission's development through 1963.

ICJ Publications, 1952–1955

International Congress of Jurists, Complete Report: Discourses, Protocols. West Berlin: ICJ, 1952.
Injustice as a System. Documentary Supplement. West Berlin, 1952.
Right vs. Injustice: The 1952 Berlin Congress. The Hague: ICJ, 1952.
Poom, Paul. *Sovietization of Estonia's Law Courts*. The Hague: ICJ, 1953.
Bulletin of the International Commission of Jurists. Numbers 1 (1954)–2 (1955).
Report of the 1955 International Congress of Jurists. Athens, Greece.
Justice Enslaved: A Collection of Documents on the Abuse of Justice for Political Ends. The Hague: ICJ, 1955.
Bonnichon, Father André. *Law in Communist China*. The Hague: ICJ, 1955.
Gsovski, Vladimir. *The Essence of a Totalitarian State*. The Hague: ICJ, 1955.
Under False Colors: A Report on the Character of the International Association of Democratic Lawyers. The Hague: ICJ, 1955.

Articles by ICJ Founders

Angell, Ernest. "Communism or Freedom: The Legal Profession and the Rule of Law." *ABA Journal* 43 (1957): 924–27.
Bonsal, Dudley B. "Gangsters in the Guise of Jurists." *The Record of the Association of the Bar of the City of New York* 7 (1952): 445–46.
———. "Lawyers and the Cold War in Cooperation with the ICJ." *Minutes of the Association of the Bar of the City of New York* (May 4, 1953): 4, 8–9.

———. "Free Lawyers in Athens." *The Record of the Association of the Bar of the City of New York* 10, no. 7 (October 1955): 352.
———. "The Judiciary and the Bar—Socialist Legality vs. the Rule of Law." *Texas Law Review* 40 (1961): 1–17.
———. "The Lawyer's Role in the Search for Peace." *The Record of the Association of the Bar of the City of New York* 16 (June 1961).
Thorson, Joseph T. "The International Commission of Jurists." *Canadian Bar Review* 33 (1957): 898–901.

Part II
1956–1963: Liberal Idealists for the Rule of Law

Chapter 2
Organizing a Global Network

> The COMMISSION WILL . . . by mobilizing the jurists of the world in support of the Rule of Law . . . advance and fortify the independence of the judiciary and the legal profession and promote fair trial for all persons accused of crime. The COMMISSION will foster understanding of and respect for the Rule of Law and give aid and encouragement to those peoples to whom the Rule of Law is denied.
>
> —ICJ Statute, Article 4, "Aims and Objectives"

Part II Overview, 1956–1963

After 1955 the ICJ deliberately turned away from strident anticommunism directed exclusively at Eastern Europe. As the British and French empires crumbled, the Cold War sparked intense competition for control of newly independent governments in Africa and Asia. Legal idealists confronted third world political rivalry over who would govern and under what rules.[1] Under new leadership, the ICJ campaigned worldwide for the rule of law.

Colonialism, nationalism, communism, totalitarianism, and the Cold War all threatened democratic ideals. Colonized Africans and Asians fighting for independence denounced European common law and constitutional democracy as alien impositions. Totalitarian regimes in Spain, Portugal, and South Africa systematically violated fundamental rights. France's colonial wars in Vietnam and Algeria, the Anglo-French attack on Suez, and racial segregation in the United States further alienated new third world leaders; they launched a nonaligned movement at Bandung. Communists charged that Western capitalism unjustly subordinated vital economic rights to ersatz political and civil liberties. Chinese leaders touted an economic development model that sacrificed representative institutions and individual liberties. Fidel Castro exported revolutionary nationalism from Cuba; the Berlin Wall imprisoned East Germans. The CIA countered KGB subversion with covert actions in Tibet, Cuba, and the Congo, as well as with plots to assassinate Castro, Trujillo, and Lumumba.

State representatives to the U.N. Commission on Human Rights refused to address even the most flagrant government disregard for the Universal Declaration. Instead, that Commission drafted two international covenants on economic and political rights that languished for twelve years in the General Assembly. At the insistence of the United States, the U.N. Commission contented itself with nonthreatening studies, international seminars, and advisory services to promote rather than protect human rights. Delegates to the General Assembly passionately disputed major power invasions of Hungary, Egypt, Tibet, and Cuba; they demonstrated no principled commitment to human rights standard setting or enforcement.

Three chapters in Part II trace ICJ initiatives to define, promote, and enforce the rule of law. This chapter examines the ICJ's rapid growth into a global jurists' network of thirty-one affiliates on five continents with a professional Secretariat in Geneva. The group adopted a statute and was legally incorporated. A new Secretary-General, unaware of CIA funding, recruited an independent, professional Secretariat staff. Distinguished jurists from Asia and Africa were elected as Commissioners and national sections were organized. The Secretary-General made world tours to meet post-colonial rulers and to recruit local jurists for national sections. The Secretariat organized conferences to popularize democratic principles, conducted multinational surveys on the rule of law, and published a scholarly journal (*Journal of the International Commission of Jurists*). Literature in three languages was mailed free of cost to more than forty thousand recipients, a number surpassing the audience for U.N. promotional materials. Since the ICJ was promoting pro-Western, anticommunist movements, the CIA increased its indirect, covert support.

Chapter 3 examines how the jurists defined a universal rule of law based on common principles from different Western legal systems. Three ICJ congresses formulated standards for both substantive rights and procedural means. Rather than lobbying for international treaties at the United Nations, ICJ experts recommended principles for governments to adopt as municipal law. CIA strategists combatting Marxism welcomed the alternative due process synthesis.

Chapter 4 shows how principled ICJ human rights advocates denounced—with neither political bias nor the U.N.'s timidity—violations by China and Spain, the USSR and South Africa. Several governments allowed ICJ observers to attend politically sensitive criminal trials. Brief reports in the ICJ *Bulletin* exposed misconduct by governments on both sides of the Iron Curtain. For selected miscreants, the ICJ carried out in-depth investigations and published detailed special reports. The United States selectively used ICJ inquiries on Hungary and Tibet to embarrass rivals at the United Nations, but ignored ICJ accounts of fascism and apartheid by anticommunist allies.

The International Commission

The ICJ's founders confronted major political obstacles to mobilizing a global constituency. The organization needed both staff and volunteers to influence national governments, the United Nations, its specialized agencies, and the Council of Europe. Staff from different countries needed government-approved visas and permits to work for an international secretariat. At the national level, dictatorships and one-party regimes denied the free association needed to foster volunteer groups. Domestic NGOs linked to foreign agents are immediately suspect, even in democratic states, and in many countries all lawyers were obligated to belong to a government-controlled national law society.

Several national and international NGOs provided organizing models. The AFFJ directors favored the Council on Foreign Relations approach—the organization of a highly exclusive elite, selected and governed by a small inner circle. AFFJ directors Angell and Seymour were also directors of the American Civil Liberties Union. The ACLU had both individual members and state affiliates with shared power to elect a national board and make policy. The International Bar Association and International League for the Rights of Man were coalitions of highly autonomous national sections. The committee member from Switzerland, Edouard Zellweger, was most familiar with the International Committee of the Red Cross (ICRC), which admitted independent national societies to a loose global confederation.[2] The ICJ founders settled on a two-tier organization: an International Commission with a permanent secretariat in Europe and highly autonomous, loosely affiliated national sections.

Statute

Bonsal proposed a draft statute for approval at the organization's first official meeting in Athens. Ten Commissioners formally approved the

ICJ Statute on July 16, 1955, and the organization officially incorporated in the Netherlands.[3] The Statute made no reference to the AFFJ, but the parent corporation effectively directed the new ICJ Executive Committee. A "Webster Commission" of three AFFJ directors made nine specific recommendations.[4] The Executive Committee dutifully elected Bonsal as its chairman, shifted van Dal from Secretary to Vice President, and approved a new Secretary-General recruited by the U.S. sponsors.

Secretariat

The Statute allowed, and the Secretary-General enjoyed, freedom to act within a broad policy established by the Executive Committee. The prestigious Commission required a well-connected Secretary-General to recruit and direct a professional staff, manage publications and press relations, organize national sections, identify candidates for election to the Commission, target situations for investigation, and intervene with governments. Between 1956 and 1963 three individuals held the post for terms ranging from nine months to three years.

From 1956 to 1958 Secretary-General Norman S. Marsh set the ICJ on a quest for universal rule of law principles.[5] A Fellow of University College, Oxford with an interest in comparative law, Marsh was a barrister-at-law, M.A., B.C.L. of the Middle Temple. The ICJ had such a highly negative, anticommunist reputation that Marsh had little interest in the post. James McDonnell convinced him that the ICJ wanted someone to change its image and to get the ICJ known in England. The American Master of University College, William Goodhart, advised him that the New York lawyers were "first-rate" people; Marsh was granted a two-year academic leave. The Executive Committee agreed that Marsh could end the negative Cold War propaganda and begin to develop common principles for the rule of law. Marsh left the finances to Kozera and was unaware of CIA funding.[6] His primary goal was to define the rule of law as understood in differing legal traditions.

When Marsh returned to Oxford, the AFFJ alternate recruited Jean-Flavien Lalive as the new ICJ Secretary-General.[7] A Swiss national, Lalive had been Secretary-General of the Joint Relief Commission of the International Red Cross, General Counsel of the U.N. Relief and Works Agency in Beirut, and First Secretary of the International Court of Justice at The Hague.[8] Lalive's U.N. background generated greater ICJ support for international standards and enforcement procedures. With Executive Committee approval, Lalive immediately transferred the ICJ offices from The Hague to Geneva,

Norman S. Marsh, ICJ Secretary-General from 1956 to 1958, working with Administrative Secretary Edward Kozera (standing).

site of the U.N.'s European headquarters.[9] In seeking a successor to Lalive in 1961, the AFFJ leaders favored another U.N. insider, Sir Leslie Munro. As New Zealand's U.N. Ambassador, Munro had served as President of the General Assembly. Like van Dal, he became both a Commission member and its Secretary-General. Munro had a drinking problem and was forced to resign after a 1962 Commission meeting in Rio de Janeiro.[10] ICJ President Vivian Bose of India served as acting Secretary-General in 1963.

Administrative Secretary Edward Kozera remained the power behind six different Secretaries-General from 1954 to 1964. Marsh recruited new legal officers for the staff and complained about nonlawyer Kozera's unprofessional, political approach. Kozera traveled extensively on recruiting missions and assiduously developed media contacts. The AFFJ administered Kozera's employment contract and assigned him exclusive responsibility for the budget provided by CIA sponsors. Charles Raphael became the AFFJ's Executive Director in New York, capably managing the ICJ's new consultative status with the U.N. Economic and Social Council. Raphael, a Greek American, earned a law degree at Harvard and held several government posts before joining the American Fund. Vladimir Kabes, a Czech refugee, served as Raphael's alternate at the United Nations.

By 1963 the fifteen-member staff included legal officers from Argentina, Britain, Cuba, Czechoslovakia, India, and Thailand. The ICJ attracted young activists dedicated to promoting the rule of law. The legal officers earned considerably less than lawyers in private practice: the Secretary-General received a modest $10,000 annual salary with $2,000 for expenses. The job offered considerable independence and responsibility for legal officers who exposed offending governments in their respective regions to public rebuke. Staff experience and expertise led several to important posts. Karel Vasak left the ICJ Secretariat to work for the European Community; other legal officers became consultants to new governments in Libya and the Congo. The Secretariat acquired an impressive law library replete with the statutes and case law required for comparative analyses and country inquiries. A South African opposition party requested the ICJ to retain apartheid documents and treason trial materials.

Executive Committee

Although the Statute vested "directive authority" in the full Commission, other provisions made the ICJ at best a guided democracy. Commission meetings were only required once every three years. Five Executive Committee members elected to three-year terms were to meet three times yearly. They had "full power and authority" to act "in any and all matters." The committee could elect new members, amend the statute, dissolve the Commission, or decide other urgent matters. The committee appointed the Secretary-General and approved his choice of Administrative Secretary; both officers attended committee meetings. Committee members unable to attend meetings could designate an alternate who would exercise all "rights power, duties and privileges" of a member of the Executive Committee. Most alternates were not ICJ members.[11] ICJ governance illustrated the iron law of oligarchy. At its first two meetings in 1955 and 1958, the Commission did not hold elections for either its Executive Committee or President. The founding Executive Committee and President Thorson simply continued in office until the first elections in 1959.

Even when elected, the President did not preside over or belong to the Executive Committee; in theory, that group selected its own chairman from year to year. By unwritten rule, an AFFJ director or alternate always chaired Executive Committee meetings. The AFFJ's New

York office instructed Bonsal's two alternates, McDonnell and John Ferguson. Bonsal resigned and gave his post to Benjamin Shute in 1959, but then returned as chairman in 1961.[12] Shute, former intelligence director for the Allied High Commission in occupied Germany, was a New York attorney and Council on Foreign Relations member; he only stayed on the Commission during his brief tenure on the Executive Committee. Bonsal's 1961 return to the committee was even more short-lived. Eli Whitney Debevoise took over as chairman of both the AFFJ board and the ICJ Executive Committee. During his fifteen-year term he attended ICJ committee meetings himself and rarely used a designated alternate.[13] Debevoise had served as Deputy High Commissioner for Germany and was well aware of CIA grants to the AFFJ. He had chaired the executive committee of Radio Free Europe, was legal adviser to the Ford Motor Company, and served as defense counsel for Alger Hiss in two perjury trials.

Membership

In contrast to mass membership organizations like the ACLU, the ICJ in its original Statute provided for no more than twenty-five members selected for life.[14] Commissioners were to provide wide geographic representation of the free world. As was the case for the Council on Foreign Relations, an exclusive inner circle controlled election to the Commission. New members required sponsorship by two Commissioners and recommendation by the Executive Committee before approval by the full Commission. Other individuals and organizations could join as nonvoting associates, paying whatever dues might be proscribed. The ICRC reassured governments of its principled neutrality by limiting membership to Swiss citizens. The multinational ICJ would inspire trust by the eminence of its members. Presitigous jurists with establishment connections would have the greatest access to those in power and the greatest freedom to organize professional volunteer groups.

The ICJ successfully recruited as members five current or former chief justices,[15] prestigious former ministers, legislators, judges, bar association leaders, successful practitioners, law school deans, and published scholars. Among the notable early members were the Rt. Hon. Lord Hartley Shawcross, former Attorney General and Britain's Chief Prosecutor at the Nuremberg trials; Vivian Bose, Judge of India's Supreme Court; Philippe Boulos, Lebanon's former Minister of Justice; Per Federspiel, Minister of Special Affairs and member of Denmark's Parliament and the Council of Europe's Consultative Assembly; A. Henrik Munktell, a Swedish Parliamentarian; Arturo

TABLE 2.1. ICJ Officers, Members, and Meetings, 1956–1963.

Secretariat (6 Rue de Mont de Sion, Geneva [beginning 1958])
Secretary-General: Norman Marsh, April 1, 1956–Sept. 1958[a]
Jean Flavien Lalive, Sept. 1958–July 1, 1961[a]
Sir Leslie Munro, July 1, 1961–March 3, 1963
Vivian Bose, (acting), March–Oct. 10, 1963
Administrative Secretary, Edward Kozera
AFFJ Executive Secretary, New York, Charles Raphael

Executive Committee
Chairman: Dudley Bonsal, U.S., 1956–1959, 1961–1962
Benjamin R. Shute, U.S., 1959–1961
Eli Whitney Debevoise, U.S. (beginning 1962)
Jean Kréher, France (beginning 1959)
Axel Henrik Munktell, Sweden
Sir Hartley Shawcross, U.K. (beginning 1960)
A. J. M. van Dal, Netherlands
Edouard Zellweger, Switzerland

President
Vivian Bose, India, 1959–1966

New Members

Year elected		*Final year*
1957	Jean Kréher, France	1971
	Vivian Bose, India, President, 1959–1966	1970[a]
1958	Arturo Alafriz, Philippines	1975[a]
	Osvaldo Illanes Benitez, Chile	1974[b]
	Sir Owen Dixon, P.C., G.C.M.G., Australia	1976[b]
	Paul-Maurice Orban, Belgium	1975[a]
	Kotaro Tanaka, Japan	1961[b]
1959	U Chan Htoon, Burma	1975
	Benjamin R. Shute, U.S., Chairman, Executive Committee, 1959–1961	1962[b]
1960	Sir Adetoklunbo A. Ademola, Nigeria	1975[b]
	Rudolf Katz, Germany	1974
1961	Isaac Forster, Senegal	1972[a]
1962	Eli Whitney Debevoise, U.S., Executive Committee Chairman, 1962	1980[a]
	Manuel G. Escobedo, Mexico	1975
	Thusew S. Fernando, Ceylon/Sri Lanka, President, 1966–1977	1980[a]
	Fernando Fournier, Costa Rica, Vice President	1980[a]
	Sir Leslie Munro, New Zealand, Secretary-General	1974
	Sebastian Soler, Argentina	1972[b]
1963	Hans-Heinrich Jescheck, Germany	1980[a]

TABLE 2.1. (*continued*)

Commission Meetings	
	The Hague, Netherlands, July 7–8, 1958
	New Delhi, India, Jan. 10, 1959
	Rio de Janeiro, Brazil, Dec. 11–15, 1962

[a] Year elected as honorary member. Masatoshi Yokota was also named an honorary member in 1981.
[b] Year the member resigned.

Alafriz, President of the Philippines Bar Association; Professor Giuseppe Bettiol, member of the Italian Parliament; and Osvaldo Illanes Benitez, Judge of Chile's Supreme Court. Table 2.1 identifies the Commissioners elected through 1963.

Founding member Theo Friedenau of Germany became a potential embarrassment when the East German IADL exposed his false identity and Nazi background in 1956. The Statute authorized resignation with notice or Commission action for termination of membership. Friedenau simply disappeared from the organization and its Executive Committee without any explanation made to the members.

Limited membership sparked disputes over representation. In theory, all agreed on universal principles embodied in the rule of law; in practice, conservatives and liberals in multiparty democracies often disagreed. The Council on Foreign Relations deliberately maintained a membership balance between top Republicans and Democrats. With only one member per country,[16] the ICJ had to choose between a jurist associated with the opposition or the party in power. However prestigious the choice, there could be suspicions of preference for or hostility toward the current government. The limit of one jurist per country also severely disadvantaged minority, women, and Jewish candidates. The Commission was enlarged to forty members but still could not provide representation for every U.N. member state. French and British members were elected to create greater European diversity, but non-Western countries fell far short of proportionate representation.

Finances

With ample funding assured from the AFFJ, the Executive Committee did not need to organize private fund raising. The ICRC had become a respected NGO with recognized government financial contributions. Open public funding for the avowedly nonpolitical ICJ might compromise its independent ability to challenge injustice in all countries. At an early meeting, Executive Committee members objected to taking government funds. The ICJ Statute neither expressly prohibits state grants nor identifies governments as a source of income: resources were to "derive from subscription fees, from voluntary contributions by way of gift, devise or bequest from Members, affiliates or other legal associations, private trusts and individuals."[17] The Statute also required an annual audit and Executive Committee financial reports at Commission meetings. There was no treasurer, and the committee never arranged for audits or presented financial reports.

Even if the original Statute had authorized membership dues, the annual fee for twenty-five Commissioners would have provided little revenue. AFFJ members encouraged their European associates to seek contributions similar to the donations received from wealthy U.S. donors. The Executive Committee did not solicit contributions from members, nor did the committee arrange for annual audits. The Secretariat distributed ICJ publications cost-free, even to subscribers unwilling to pay the nominal two-dollar *Journal* fee initiated in 1960. Affluent lawyers did not underwrite the ICJ program. The CIA successfully concealed the main revenue source, even from appropriations committees of the U.S. Congress.

The AFFJ paid most of the bills with CIA funds that had passed through conduit foundations. By 1962 the ICJ annual general budget had grown to $350,000; the M. D. Anderson Foundation provided $190,000[18] of the covert CIA funds through the AFFJ in that year. For a 1959 New Delhi Congress, the AFFJ authorized $140,000, and the covertly funded Asia Foundation agreed to pay travel expenses for jurists from the region.[19] AFFJ President Ernest Angell obtained a $54,000 Ford Foundation grant to cover travel and meeting expenses for a 1961 Lagos conference. The Nigerian government contributed an additional 12,000 pounds toward conference expenses. A few national sections made annual grants of up to $3,000 annually.

Publications

By 1962 the Commission had distributed more than two million individual units of publications in four languages to lawyers, government officials, law school libraries, and institutions in ninety territorial areas.[20] In 1957 Marsh launched the *Journal of the International Commission of Jurists*, which published scholarly articles on national legal systems, comparative jurisprudence, and book reviews. Prominent scholars and practitioners wrote for an elite audience of opinion leaders and prominent officials, following the model of the journal *Foreign*

TABLE 2.2. ICJ Regional Contacts as of 1963.

Region	*ICJ members*	*National sections*	*Mailing list (1966)*	*Countries visited*	*Executive Committee*
W. Europe	9	12	16,698	8	4
Asia	8	10	10,536	14	(President)
Africa	2	2	3,186	16	
S. America	3	8	10,953	17	(Vice President)
N. America	4	2	4,439	2	1
Total	26	34	45,812	57	5

Affairs, published by the Council on Foreign Relations. An ICJ information *Bulletin* carried brief reports on selected country situations and theme articles; the ICJ *Newsletter* summarized organizational developments. Congress proceedings and major country studies were also widely circulated in several languages.

Missions

The jurists' social and professional status gave the ICJ remarkable access to government leaders and lawyers' organizations. Top staff members and officers conducted world tours and organizing missions to fifty-seven countries. They spoke at bar association functions, recruited leaders for national sections, and identified possible Commission members. In courtesy visits, the Secretary-General and Executive Committee members met with ministers of justice, legislators, Supreme Court judges, and nine heads of state.[21] Local contacts identified more than forty thousand professionals interested in receiving ICJ publications.

Well-attended congresses in New Delhi, Lagos, and Rio de Janeiro further enhanced the organization's reputation. Between 1955 and 1958 the press carried more than seventeen hundred articles, reports, or references to the ICJ.[22] The Academy of Moral and Political Sciences of the Institut de France awarded the Henri Texier Prize of 300,000 francs to the ICJ for "action in the defence of individual freedom."[23] By 1961 the ICJ had members from twenty-three countries and listed thirty-four national sections. Table 2.2 displays the global network in a tally of regional contacts.

National Sections

The ICJ created a loose network of independent local groups rather than a unified global movement. The International Federation of Human Rights and the ICRC had organized similar transnational coalitions. Once recognized by the Swiss ICRC, local Red Cross and Red Crescent societies freely adapted the humanitarian program to local political and religious institutions. Unlike the League of Red Cross societies, the ICJ did not bring national sections together for policymaking conferences.

By 1963 the ICJ had founded thirty-one national sections and affiliated with three existing organizations. The Secretariat provided a model statute for prospective groups, and the Executive Committee granted formal recognition. Most ICJ-created national sections of lawyers did not name their groups a "Commission of Jurists"; affiliated organizations could have nonlawyer members. New sections all became fully independent entities not readily distinguishable from other organizations that affiliated with the ICJ. Whether national section or affiliate, group or individual, legal or nonprofessional, those recruited were not designated as "members"; they were not required to provide financial support, and were not enfranchised to decide policy. After receiving ICJ funds to organize and incorporate, national sections became autonomous; they rarely solicited contributions for the ICJ and had no formal role in its governance. Active sections assisted the Secretariat in conducting surveys, issuing press releases, and organizing Human Rights Day activities. Eight ICJ Commissioners participated actively in their national sections, but ten did not.

Local autonomy for ICJ sections avoided divisive conflicts. Early rivalry between sections in Greece and Turkey, India and Pakistan required reciprocal concessions. The French section claimed Executive Committee membership for its leader, but it was impossible to accommodate all the groups seeking representation. ICJ control of national sections might give governments an excuse to shut down vigorous local groups as subversive international agents. Irresponsible section leaders might conduct unauthorized political activities, damaging the ICJ's carefully nurtured reputation for professional expertise. National sections investigating violations in other countries might duplicate or contradict the international Secretariat's fact-finding missions. ICJ leaders preferred a loose association with local groups that avoided both the risks and potential benefits of closer transnational integration.

North America

As a funding agent, the AFFJ was not an ICJ national section. Authorizing legislation prohibited CIA programs within the United States.

While chairman of the AFFJ, Angell organized and led an ABA Committee to cooperate with the ICJ.[24] Accompanied by Angell and Raphael, Marsh visited lawyers in several U.S. cities in 1957; on a return visit in 1958, Marsh spoke at the Council on Foreign Relations. By 1961 the ICJ had more than twenty-five hundred names on its U.S. mailing list and an additional thirteen hundred in Canada. The large Canadian section held business sessions at meetings of the Canadian Bar Association but had no regular activities. AFFJ directors Angell and Seymour also held leadership posts in the ACLU, which could have affiliated with the ICJ; however, founder Roger Baldwin had never been able to persuade the ACLU Board to include international human rights on its agenda.

Western Europe

The twelve national sections in Europe became the most active. More than 40 percent of the ICJ mailings went to the twenty-four Western countries. Nine Europeans comprised one-third of the Commission's membership; four joined a U.S. chairman to constitute its Executive Committee. The Committee made small grants to help start European sections after closing the ICJ's Berlin and Munich refugee offices. The most active sections employed staff, published newsletters, and sponsored programs. Others simply functioned as discussion groups for an aging elite; young lawyers in Sweden formed a junior section. A few inactive sections produced little more than a letterhead.

"Justice" began in 1956, when London attorney Peter Benenson convened lawyers from the three main British political parties. During a celebrated treason trial in South Africa, the founders created an all-party Commonwealth organization devoted to justice in the British colonies. At the same time, Marsh and McDonnell were inviting jurists to form an ICJ national section.[25] The organizers combined to create an ICJ section in 1957, retained the name "Justice," and invited Lord Shawcross to serve as chairman.[26] The ICJ granted a startup loan and circulated a membership appeal to British lawyers. By 1964 the section had more than one thousand members and was regarded as an organization of great prominence, reputation, and importance. "Justice" sent trial observers and fact-finding missions to Commonwealth territories and then became a watchdog group monitoring prison conditions in the United Kingdom. A large delegation attended the ICJ New Delhi conference, and the section made small annual contributions to the international Secretariat.

In 1961 Benenson made a public international appeal for a year-long amnesty campaign. He described how Portugal imprisoned two students for making a public toast calling for liberty, and he urged citizens to demand that governments release political prisoners.[27] The response led to the formation of a new mass membership organization, Amnesty International, separate from the ICJ and "Justice." The ICJ Executive Committee decided to cooperate with the new group, and a Secretariat observer served as liaison.[28]

The large French national section, "Libre Justice," held a joint meeting with its British counterpart on human rights in the colonies. Jean Kréher, the section President, replaced Friedenau on the Executive Committee. (A socialist active in the resistance during World War II, Kréher had been sent to Buchenwald and slated for the gas chambers.) The three-hundred-member German section published a survey report on the rule of law and contributed toward the cost of translating the *Journal*. At the invitation of sections in Greece, Turkey, Italy, and Norway, the Executive Committee held business meetings in those countries. Following Munktell's death, the Swedish section conducted few activities.

The European sections convened a joint 1957 meeting in Vienna to examine "Legal Limits to Freedom of Opinion" and procedures applicable for political crimes.[29] The conference drew 158 participants from eighteen countries. Jurists from Poland and Yugoslavia were invited but did not attend. Support for the European Commission and Court of Human Rights grew steadily, and the ICJ obtained consultative status with the Council of Europe. A representative of the European Community's Human Rights Department attended the Vienna meeting.

Asia

The Executive Committee selected New Delhi for a 1959 Congress, despite concerns that third world participants might attack apartheid and colonialism rather than communism. Prior to the meeting, Marsh and Administrative Secretary Kozera conducted a world tour that took them to eleven Asian and three European countries. The ICJ spokesmen gave press conferences and interviews and had sixty-five meetings with justices of the high courts, executive branch officials, and law school faculty. Representatives of the Asia Foundation and U.S. embassies assisted in establishing local contacts. Lawyers in Ceylon questioned the ICJ's motives and characterized its publications as American propaganda. In the Philippines the ICJ officers were the only NGO observers at a U.N. seminar on "Protection of Human Rights in Criminal Law and Procedure." Commission member Alafriz organized an active section in the Philippines. Lalive and Kozera made a goodwill mission to eleven Asian countries immediately after the 1959 Congress.

The five-day New Delhi Congress hosted 185 eminent scholars, judges, and practicing lawyers from fifty-three countries. Jurists from the United Kingdom, fifteen Commonwealth partners, and former Asian and African colonies comprised the majority.[30] Among the fifteen American delegates were former U.S. Attorney General Herbert Brownell and former Assistant Secretary of State for Policy Planning Robert Bowie. Seán MacBride, President of the European Council of Foreign Ministers, represented Ireland, and Legal Director Oscar Schachter represented the United Nations, despite Secretary-General Dag Hammarskjold's concern that the ICJ was a partisan, Cold War organization.[31] In contrast to the Berlin and Athens meetings, the Congress planners did not invite exiles to represent the USSR and its satellites. In a provocative opening address, Prime Minister Nehru complained that the Cold War undermined the rule of law; he urged the jurists to adapt outmoded laws to modern realities and advocated freedom for subject peoples. Indian Supreme Court Justice Vivian Bose chaired the Congress.

Asians comprised the second largest regional bloc of members and national sections in the ICJ. India had the most effective nonwestern section as well as two Commission members, Bose and the socialist Purshottam Trikamdas. Following election as ICJ President in 1959, the Cambridge-educated Bose offered a third world perspective as a nonvoting observer at Executive Committee meetings. Bose toured African colonies and European countries on behalf of the ICJ and was received by the king of Norway.[32] He filled an awkward leadership void as acting Secretary-General after Munro resigned in 1963.

Following Marsh's 1958 visit, U Chan Htoon, a Judge of Burma's Supreme Court and former Attorney General, attended the New Delhi Congress. He was elected to the Commission and organized a Burmese national section. The Burmese government censored incoming letters, removed him from the court, placed him under house arrest, and denied him a visa to attend Commission meetings. In Australia, democratic traditions offered fertile soil for the region's model section. Ceylon's active section distributed ICJ publications and reissued press releases. The other sections founded after the New Delhi Congress conducted few activities. ICJ members from Japan, Lebanon, and Pakistan did not organize sections in their countries. In the Middle East, Israelis organized the only ICJ section in the region. The

IADL had greater support than the ICJ in Islamic countries; Algeria's war for independence from France set back organizational activities in North Africa.

Africa

Despite ICJ members' visits to fifteen countries and a regional conference, the Commission established only two sections in Africa. Lalive and ICJ members Eduard Hambro of Norway, Edouard Zellweger of Switzerland, and President Bose made separate speaking trips to prepare for a 1961 Lagos regional conference. Administrative Secretary Kozera and African legal officer Kabes also undertook organizing efforts. Ethiopia's Emperor Haile Selassie granted Kozera an audience. Nigeria's Chief Justice, Sir Adetokunbo A. Ademola, and former Chief Justice Isaac Forster of Senegal were elected to the Commission, providing representation for both Anglophone and Francophone Africa.

The ICJ brought together nearly two hundred experts from twenty-three African nations and nine other countries for the 1961 Lagos conference. Many jurists from East and West Africa, former French and English colonies, met for the first time.[33] Noting the impressive participation of many ministers and vice ministers of justice, heads of university law faculties, and judges of the highest rank, the Ford Foundation provided partial funding: "it is essential . . . that the new countries embrace the system of the rule of law designed to protect the rights of individuals."[34] Nigeria's Chief Justice presided at the conference sessions, and Governor-General Nnamdi Azikiwe addressed the final dinner. Nigerian lawyers established "Liberty," an ICJ national section.

Government opposition intimidated activists and frustrated organizing efforts in two other countries. Ghana's Minister of Information promoted an organization of nonaligned jurists at the conference and also appeared to be instructing the country's Chief Justice.[35] The Nkrumah regime detained ICJ section chairman J. B. Danquah with other opposition leaders. Ghana denied ICJ observer Judge Mookerjee permission to visit and refused to grant Danquah a visa to attend the ICJ's Rio Congress.[36] Liberia's Supreme Court disbarred Christian A. Cassell for life because he wrote a "contemptuous" paper for the Lagos Conference. The Liberian Chief Justice who attended strongly disapproved of Cassell's moderately balanced comments on national laws limiting free speech. An outraged Liberian court punished Cassell for presenting his criticisms to an international conference in a sister state.[37] Slightly more than three thousand subscribers received ICJ publications in Africa.

South America

Van Dal conducted the first goodwill mission, an eight-country tour of Central and South America, from April to June 1956. Commission member Osvaldo Illanes Benitez directed extensive section activities in Chile. Lalive and Kozera toured seventeen countries and met five heads of state from February to May 1961. Disaffected CIA agent Philip Agee revealed many years later how the deputy chief of station in Ecuador arranged for them to meet Juan Yepez del Pozo. Yepez was working as a propaganda agent for the CIA to support an anti-communist government. He became Secretary-General of the ICJ affiliate in Ecuador and attended the 1962 Rio Congress.[38] With Leslie Munro presiding, the ICJ brought nearly three hundred eminent jurists from seventy-five countries to Brazil in December 1962 for its largest International Congress.[39] Publications in Spanish reached nearly eleven thousand in the region. Most of the South American sections were mainly paper organizations, even in Brazil, after the Rio Congress.

Conclusions on Organizational Structure and Promotion

Leadership

The ICJ's internal governance resembled the undemocratic features of other interest groups. Like the ICRC and the Council on Foreign Relations, the Commission began as a selective elite directed by an exclusive inner circle. A self-selected Executive Committee led by AFFJ sponsors made key decisions without democratic accountability to the members. Unlike the case in many nonprofit groups, staff did not dominate the governing oligarchy. The Secretary-General was fully accountable to the Executive Committee, and the early ICJ leadership replaced both van Dal and Munro.

Membership

Jurists who joined the Commission and its national groups, like recruits of other interest groups, appeared to be inspired by mixed motives of public service and personal benefit. Pluralist theory suggests that like-minded individuals join organizations that support their political values.[40] ICJ supporters shared a belief in the rule of law and backed its campaign for an independent judiciary. The rational interest model argues that material as well as purposive incentives persuade individuals to join.[41] The opinion leaders recruited by the ICJ received free publications, invitations to international congresses, and inexpensive opportunities to meet eminent colleagues from other countries. There were no membership dues. The "big names" recruited brought stature to the Commission and its national sections, conferring status on others who joined. Inspired by common ideals and a sense of noblesse oblige, many jurists volunteered their time for the cause. Others merely lent their names and prestige to an organization that provided valuable information and contacts.

Recruitment

A global constituency of concerned jurists did not create and sustain the ICJ. Instead, the ICJ became an agent for mobilizing legal professionals for a nascent human rights network. Two officials with U.N. experience, Lalive and Munro, were recruited for human rights service as ICJ Secretaries-General. An Indian Supreme Court justice, Bose, became active in the international movement as ICJ President. The Secretariat recruited legal officers from six countries, and one early recruit moved on to the European human rights system. As the international political culture became more favorable, lawyers and other Western activists began organizing human rights NGOs with similar agendas. The ICJ had considerably more financial resources and a much larger staff than did other groups. The International League for Human Rights had no staff, and Amnesty International was just beginning.

By 1963 the ICJ had fashioned the first weak links in a network of noncommunist lawyers and national groups. ICJ groups had great national autonomy. Successful local groups depended on both citizen initiative and government policy. In at least one country, a section provided cover for a local CIA recruit. But covert funding alone did not assure viability. Most local groups, including one in Ecuador with CIA links, had little or no professional support.

European countries and Commonwealth democracies offered the most fertile soil for public interest groups. Democratic countries allowed lawyers to organize, and their political culture favored private groups. In many third world countries, political repression and local tradition frustrated organizing efforts. Regimes in Burma and Ghana imprisoned prestigious jurists who created ICJ national sections; Liberia disbarred a lawyer for writing a conference paper. Two ICJ visits and repeated prodding failed to energize Argentina's bar. Recruiting efforts in five Muslim countries brought three members to the Commission but no national sections. The ICJ did not publish in Arabic.

The following chapters examine how the ICJ used its network assets to articulate rule of law principles and to challenge state offenders.

Chapter 3
Defining the Rule of Law

> The State is subject to the law.
> —ICJ, *Act of Athens*

> The Rule of Law is a dynamic concept for the expansion and fulfillment of which jurists are primarily resposible and which should be employed not only to safeguard and advance the civil and political rights of the individual in a free society, but also to establish social, economic, educational and cultural conditions under which his legitimate aspirations and dignity may be realized.
> —ICJ, *Declaration of Delhi*

In the late 1980s liberal democratic values enjoyed spectacular triumphs. Eastern Europe and the USSR repudiated Marxism and socialist legality; multiparty democratic reforms swept Latin America and Africa. Academic theorists hotly debated the significance. Was there now universal acceptance of liberal democracy? Had Westernization created a global culture?[1] In the 1950s the United Nations brought together representatives of different legal systems to identify universal human rights. The Universal Declaration affirms: "Human rights should be protected by the rule of law." Two UNESCO-sponsored colloquia at Chicago and Warsaw examined the rule of law and socialist legality. The U.N. Commission on Human Rights drafted treaty language to make rights from the Universal Declaration legally binding and enforceable under international law. The United States insisted on separate covenants, one for nonbinding economic rights and a second with enforceable guarantees of political liberty.

The ICJ created an independent NGO procedure for defining rule of law principles and did not seek to influence the U.N. treaties. The jurists became liberal agents of socialization; Western idealists defined the rule of law and influenced elite opinion at the national level. The ICJ convened four international consultations for eminent jurists in Athens, New Delhi, Lagos, and Rio de Janeiro. In preparation for a Delhi Congress working paper, Norman Marsh conducted a survey of seventy-five thousand lawyers from twenty-four countries. Cooperating groups in the United States, Germany, and Italy published survey results describing how the rule of law worked in national practice.[2] Based on questionnaire responses from ABA committee members in seventeen cities, Ernest Angell prepared a one hundred-page publication setting forth the principles of U.S. constitutional democracy.[3]

At each congress, American, British, and European jurists led debates on natural law ideals from the Anglo-American common law and continental civil law traditions. The congresses did not include advocates of Marxist, Islamic, or precolonial systems. Communist jurists were regarded as party loyalists incapable of independent judgment. The Koran and Shari'a as enforced in traditional Muslim Qadi courts had been superseded in many European colonies. No lawyers' meeting would be possible without philosophical differences, and the ICJ congresses worked to reconcile conflicting views on economic rights, self-determination, and international enforcement.

Natural Law versus Positivism

Liberal idealists differed with conservative positivists on both substance and procedure. In its most conservative sense, the rule of law assures only procedural fairness. A law-based state respects published rules enforced by independent courts. Such procedural due process leaves the state unlimited power to grant or withdraw substantive rights such as welfare entitlements or religious liberty. If a state requires monogamy for example, the rule of law would not guarantee Muslims or Mormons religious liberty to practice polygamy; it would only guarantee the procedural right to a fair trial. In positivist theory, sovereign states decide which substantive rights to confer; there is no higher natural law that governs how states treat their own citizens.

Natural law advocates insist that the rule of law also requires governments to grant fundamental substantive rights. For Thomas Jefferson in the U.S. Declaration of Independence, equality and liberty were "self-evident." Civil libertarians treat individual political rights as inalienable, free market advocates give personal property highest priority, and socialists insist on economic justice. American and European jurists agreed that the rule of law includes basic civil and political liberties—speech, press, religion, assembly, free elections, privacy. There were minor differences on the scope of those negative rights that limit government power. The U.S. Constitution expresses fundamental liberties in absolute terms; European laws confer emergency powers on governments to limit incendiary speech and to use preventive detention. Unlike most American civil libertarians, European and non-Western jurists also favored positive economic rights to health care, education, and social security. Some advocated not only citizen rights but also civic responsibilities, especially for lawyers.

When debating procedures to enforce substantive rights, the ICJ congresses examined different national and international, common and civil law approaches. The Europeans favored considerably more supranational enforcement than did the Americans, proud of the U.S. constitutional order.[4] Conservative dualists opposed liberal monist efforts to create a global bill of rights superior to national law. Positivists insisted that sovereign governments could reject human rights treaties and international courts.

All favored an independent national judiciary, but some questioned judges' power to make law. U.S. and British judges have considerably more lawmaking power than do continental civil law courts. Judicial review enables U.S. judges to negate Congressional acts as unconstitutional. Legal realists demonstrated how judges who claimed that they merely interpreted law in fact created new rules. British judges cannot overrule Parliament but do make common law to resolve disputes not covered by existing statutes. In theory, the continent's civil law system restricts judges to statutory interpretation. In practice, French courts have made administrative law by reading the code broadly. Common law systems that acknowledge judicial lawmaking assure democratic control through popular election of judges or executive/legislative appointment. Civil law systems often use merit selection by professional jurists. Anglo-American criminal courts presume innocence in an accusatory system that historically employed juries to determine guilt or innocence. The French inquisitorial system places greater evidentiary burdens on defendants, whose guilt is determined by the court rather than a jury.

At each ICJ congress, committees revised and approved staff-prepared recommendations on topics such as the role of the executive, the legislature, the judiciary, criminal procedure, and the legal profession. After Athens, no other congress reviewed evidence of violations to support resolutions that named offending governments.

Marsh insisted that governments could not be held accountable until there were clearly defined universal standards. Each congress added new elements to a rule of law synthesis that included both substantive and procedural rights. After accepting committee recommendations, each congress, in a final plenary session, adopted a one-page summary resolution: the Act of Athens, Declaration of Delhi, Law of Lagos, and Resolution of Rio. As initially defined in the American-inspired 1955 Act of Athens, the Rule of Law included fundamental political and civil rights—of speech, press, worship, assembly, association, free elections, and equal protection—to be enforced by independent judges and lawyers in domestic courts.

The Declaration of Delhi and Economic Justice

As ICJ Secretary-General, Norman Marsh wanted to take the rule of law beyond the individualism espoused in the ICJ Act of Athens and in nineteenth-century British works.[5] Twentieth-century welfare state proponents and socialists also wanted positive legal guarantees of economic rights to insure human dignity. Those "second-generation" positive human rights had particular appeal in underdeveloped countries such as India. Marsh described the rule of law doctrine as a dynamic "politico-legal" ideology not tied to a laissez-faire theory limiting the state's role in economic affairs.[6] "Far from being opposed to the welfare state, [the Rule of Law] is an essential instrument of its purposes."[7] American and Canadian Bar Association members, however, had objected to the economic and social provisions in the Universal Declaration of Human Rights. After insisting on separate U.N. covenants for political and economic rights, the United States withdrew from the effort to draft binding international norms.[8]

Marsh prepared a working paper for the Delhi Congress that defined the rule of law in terms the ICJ repeatedly used as a basic text:

> By the Rule of Law the Commission means adherence to those institutions and procedures, not always identical, but broadly similar, which experience and tradition in the different countries of the world, often having themselves varying political structures and economic backgrounds, have shown to be essential to protect the individual from arbitrary government and to enable him to enjoy the dignity of man.[9]

At the congress Seán MacBride and third world participants firmly insisted that the rule of law incorporate an element of economic justice not traditionally associated with American capitalism. Committee I called on legislatures to recognize not only civil and political rights but also to establish "the social, economic, educational and cultural conditions which are essential to the full development of individual dignity." Rather than repudiate socialism, the congress affirmed that different political and economic systems could honor the rule of law. Lalive stressed that the rule of law was "not a weapon to protect vested rights and to stifle social progress."[10]

Four committees at the congress endorsed a variety of procedural safeguards, primarily for civil rights in a constitutional, representative democracy guaranteed by an independent judiciary and bar. Committee IV recommended secure tenure for judges and disapproved elections that compromised judicial independence. Committee III recommended that criminal defendants be protected by procedures employed in adversarial systems: the right to bail, counsel, presumption of innocence, public trial, the exclusionary rule, production of witnesses, cross examination of accusers, and appeal. Committee I called on legislatures to implement the Universal Declaration of Human Rights and called for international agreements patterned on the European Human Rights Convention with a right of individual appeal to a regional court. In plenary session the delegates accepted the committee recommendations and adopted the Declaration of Delhi.

The Law of Lagos and Representative Democracy

African jurists at the 1961 Lagos Conference wanted the rule of law to affirm rights of self-governance. Nigeria's Attorney-General and Minister of Justice T. O. Elias prepared the conference working paper. Disputes over Pan-Africanism had divided the continent's thirty new governments into rival political blocs whose representatives clashed at the meeting. Ghana's Minister of Information appeared to be giving directions to that country's Chief Justice. With some difficulty, ICJ President Vivian Bose rejected proposals to recognize colonized peoples' right to independence and to investigate racial discrimination in Britain's three Southern Africa territories. Noting that he too felt the humiliation of racial discrimination and colonial rule, Bose praised the restraint of those whose defeated proposals would have alienated friends and embarrassed the ICJ.[11]

The African jurists declared the Delhi principles applicable to "all countries, whether dependent or independent." In another departure, the Law of Lagos proclaimed that the standards "should apply to any society, whether free or otherwise" and insisted that "the Rule of Law cannot be fully realized unless legislative bodies have been estabished in accordance with the will of the people who have adopted their Constitution freely." Without expressly referring to apartheid, the African jurists repeatedly called for democratic representation in legislatures.[12]

The Law of Lagos also significantly increased ICJ support for U.N. and regional protection measures. In order to give full effect to the Universal Declaration, the conference invited study of an African Convention of Human Rights and the creation of a regional court. One Lagos committee recommendation conflicted with an Athens committee standard that opposed preventive detention. The African jurists familiar with European colonial practice condoned emergency detention within limits set by the legislature and subject to judicial review.

The Resolution of Rio: Administrative Law and Professional Ethics

The first ICJ rule of law declarations sought economic justice and the right to education but had not proposed substantive guarantees for health care or social security. Western industrialized democracies increasingly administered a broad range of entitlements and regulated destructive business practices. The 1962 Rio Congress examined "Executive Action," or due process by administrators. The jurists recommended administrative procedures to assure that legislatively delegated economic authority would be fairly exercised. Legislatures granted the executive considerable discretionary power for welfare benefits and business regulation. What legal restraints checked arbitrary administrative action? Sweden pioneered the Ombudsman complaint system and required public disclosure of government documents; the U.S. Congress mandated judicially reviewable administrative procedures to insure fairness. One Rio committee endorsed quasi-autonomous administrative law judges in the executive. Such procedural safeguards would assure nondiscriminatory administration of public entitlements, but could not guarantee minimum conditions of human dignity.

The Rio Congress went far beyond prior ICJ statements in defining lawyers' responsibility. They should "concern themselves with the prevalence of poverty, ignorance and inequality . . . and inspire and promote economic development and social justice." How incredible that recommendation must seem to those who jokingly compare lawyers to leeches.[13] The lawyers' skill and knowledge are "not to be employed solely for the benefit of clients, but should be regarded as held in trust for society." A committee on legal education concluded that lawyers properly trained in the rule of law would recognize a professional responsibility to work not merely for procedural fairness but for economic development and social justice as well:

> It is not enough that faculties of law and other institutions specially engaged in the teaching of law endeavour to attain the highest levels of technical preparation of students. They must also make a special effort to shape their characters, to develop their sense of social responsibility and to strengthen their moral discipline.[14]

That approach sounds remarkably like endorsing socialist conscience and using law to achieve political change, concepts of which the ICJ's anticommunist founders heartily disapproved. The visionary goal was to achieve independent judicial protection for individual liberty rather than to foster adversarial procedures in expensive courts that enriched combative counsel. European socialists and third world jurists clearly influenced the ICJ's natural law principles. By 1962 the jurists at Rio also disregarded conservative reservations about international enforcement and forthrightly encouraged regional human rights courts.

Promotion

The Secretariat published in four languages and disseminated materials promoting the rule of law to an audience of more than forty thousand. Marsh edited the scholarly *Journal of the ICJ*, which appeared twice a year. Articles described how different judicial systems functioned and compared the uses and abuses of preventive detention. A global survey enlisted twenty-four thousand lawyers in the Rule of Law project. Reports on the rule of law in the United States, Germany, and Italy were published for international consumption. *The Rule of Law in a Free Society* reproduced Marsh's working paper and the Delhi conference proceedings. Three U.S. law journals gave favorable reviews.[15] *Journal* commentary elaborated varied perspectives on the principles. In visits to seventy-five countries, ICJ legal officers and staff presented the rule of law message to public officials, university groups, and lawyers' organizations.

ICJ promotional activities complemented the United Nations "action plan." The United States discouraged human rights standard setting and encouraged studies and seminars on arbitrary detention and criminal procedure. Between 1955 and 1966 the U.N. Division of Human Rights organized a total of twenty-eight seminars on civil liberties, economic development, women's rights, and minorities.[16] Marsh participated in a U.N. criminal justice seminar in the Philippines. Oscar Schachter represented the United Nations at the ICJ

TABLE 3.1. ICJ Reports Defining the Rule of Law.

Reports of Meetings
- *Report of the 1955 International Congress of Jurists: Athens, Greece.*
- *The Rule of Law in a Free Society: A Report on the International Congress of Jurists, New Delhi.* Geneva: ICJ, 1960.
- *African Conference on the Rule of Law: A Report on the Proceedings.* Geneva: ICJ, 1961.
- *Executive Action and the Rule of Law: A Report on the Proceedings of the International Congress of Jurists, Rio de Janeiro, Brazil.* Geneva: ICJ, 1962.
- *Regional Conference on Legal Education.* Singapore, 1962.
- *Dynamic Aspects of the Rule of Law.* Bangkok, 1965 (Eng./Fr./Sp.).
- *The Rule of Law and Human Rights: Basic principles of the rule of law elaborated at ICJ Congresses and Conferences, 1955–1966.* 83 pp., hardcover (Eng./Fr./Sp.).
- *Congres de Juristes Africain Francophones.* Dakar, 1967.
- *Right to Freedom of Movement.* Bangalore, 1968.

Reports of National Surveys
- ABA Committee to Cooperate with the International Commission of Jurists. *The Rule of Law in the United States.* Geneva, 1958. 108 pp.
- ———. *The Rule of Law in the United States: A Survey.* Geneva, 1962. 184 pp.
- *The Rule of Law in the Federal Republic of Germany: A Statement by the German National Section.* Geneva: ICJ, 1958. 41 pp.
- *The Rule of Law in Italy.* Geneva: ICJ, 1958.

Delhi meeting. Kabes attended a 1957 UNESCO colloquium in Chicago on "The Rule of Law as Understood in the West," but the ICJ did not send a representative to the Warsaw meeting on communist systems. The ICJ reached legal elites with more scholarly publications in noncommunist countries; the United Nations attempted to fashion a more comprehensive communication system.

Conclusions on Standard Setting

Articulation and Aggregation

How effectively did the ICJ articulate the rule of law as a universal value? At four international meetings between 1955 and 1963, the ICJ defined the rule of law to include two groups of substantive rights:

1. Well-established civil liberties of speech, press, religion, assembly, democratic elections, and
2. Undefined rights of economic justice including education.

The ICJ also progressively identified four procedural mechanisms to limit arbitrary state power:

1. An independent judiciary to restrain the executive,
2. A popularly elected legislature,
3. A responsible bar committed to social justice, and
4. International law enforced by regional courts.

Did the jurists independently synthesize universal human rights that incorporated third world concerns, or were they agents of socialization for Western values? The ICJ's liberal democratic, natural law principles reject Western positivism, Marxism, Koranic law, and the informal dispute resolution procedures of traditional societies. The simplest, most powerful ICJ principle is the very first declaration in the Act of Athens: "The State is subject to the law." That NGO clarion call affirms constitutional limits on state sovereignty. The concept clearly has Western natural law roots in the French Declaration on the Rights of Man and the Citizen, the U.S. Declaration of Independence, and Dicey's *Law of the Constitution*. The Fourteenth Amendment of the U.S. Constitution asserts: "No state shall deny to any person life, liberty or property without due process of law." European and American jurists refined their ideals at meetings with third world elites trained to practice in the two dominant Western legal systems who nonetheless demanded independence and economic justice.

Initially, Western jurists envisioned ICJ principles primarily as norms for domestic legal reform. ICJ support for regional courts to enforce human rights was a significant departure from traditional concepts of state sovereignty. The ICJ's European members were most eager to strengthen international checks on state power. The 1950 European Convention for the Protection of Human Rights created regional institutions authorized to protect individuals from state abuse. The ICJ then recommended regional courts in Africa and Latin America.

Members from former colonies, including President Bose, resisted. Lawyers throughout the British Empire had to take appeals to the Privy Council in London for final review. Bose saw ICJ principles solely as a guide for local adaptation and opposed international enforcement through U.N. organs in the West. In 1946 Lord Shawcross, representing Britain, argued that a General Assembly resolution condemning South Africa's racist policies would set a dangerous precedent of intervention in domestic affairs.[17] Conservative U.S. lawyers similarly distrusted international enforcement. A few internationalists led by former ABA President Charles S. Rhyne founded a Special Committee on World Peace Through Law. Rhyne planned a World Conference of Lawyers to strengthen the International Court of Justice and to promote regional courts. His new group did not affiliate with the ICJ. As the United Nations drafted a bill of rights, the

ICJ observed without contributing to the text. Kabes recalled that in the late 1950s he, Charles Raphael, and the General of the Salvation Army stood out at the United Nations: "NGO representation was mainly the domain of elderly ladies in the style of what the French call 'bien-pensant' (something like do-gooders)."[18]

Lawmaking

Did ICJ expertise significantly influence customary international law? Lalive suggested that the ICJ facilitated new "general principles of law" that "contribute to the development of international law."[19] The statutes of both the Permanent Court of International Justice and the International Court of Justice direct the judges to apply not only conventions and customs but also "the general principles of law recognized by civilized nations" and "the teachings of the most highly qualified publicists of the various nations, as subsidiary means for the determination of rules of law."[20] The ICJ surveys of legal practice and *Journal* articles about different countries clarified general principles of law in civilized nations.

How do the ICJ's rule of law norms compare to the international bill of rights? The state-approved U.N. Covenant on Civil and Political Rights allowed more government control of speech, religion, press, and assembly. The ICJ more severely restricted preventive detention in emergencies. The United Nations gave considerably more weight than the ICJ to third world concerns for self-determination and nondiscrimination. The ICJ did not press for U.N. petition procedures but favored enforcement by an independent bench and bar in national courts. The United Nations adopted a detailed Covenant on Economic, Social and Cultural Rights that went far beyond the ICJ's general call for economic justice.

Marsh and most of his colleagues never claimed that the ICJ's proclamations made law. Instead, they were creating a climate for international law to seep into domestic jurisdiction.[21] Whatever their appeal, Western NGO proclamations were far less authoritative than the universal standards proclaimed by the United Nations. The Universal Declaration and two implementing covenants comprised a readily identifiable international Bill of Rights; General Assembly endorsement created legitimacy that no congress of jurists, however eminent, could hope to equal. In the 1960s the ICJ convened two more conferences on the rule of law theme, small regional meetings in Bangkok and Colombo. After the U.N. covenants were completed, the ICJ published a text identifying comparable provisions from its Congress proceedings.[22] Instead of creating law, the ICJ made declarations that resemble NGO policy guidelines and promotional goals. In an era when critics faulted greedy lawyers, the ICJ advocated public responsibility, elevating the community good over personal gain. Their bold campaign against state criminals took the ICJ beyond promotion and lawmaking into well-publicized and innovative protection efforts.

Chapter 4

Protecting Victims

"No, no!" said the Queen.
"Sentence first—verdict afterwards."
"Stuff and Nonsense!" said Alice.
—Lewis Carroll, *Alice's Adventures in Wonderland*

Between 1956 and 1963 the ICJ developed independent authority to investigate violations, judge governments' guilt, and publicly condemn their crimes. Traditionally, states alone enforced international law with diplomatic or military means, and governments recognized few customary rules beyond formal treaty obligations. Over the past century states have gradually allowed intergovernmental organizations more lawmaking and enforcement functions. Inadequate protection by states and the League of Nations failed the millions victimized by genocide and aggression in the 1940s. Idealists envisioned a postwar order in which international NGOs could put wayward governments in the dock. ICJ advocates pressed the United Nations to implement new law and developed outside enforcement strategies to protect victims.

To enforce human rights law, the ICJ brought state criminals to the court of world public opinion. Because the primitive international legal system lacked prosecutors, the jurists performed like private attorneys general indicting state felons.[1] In the absence of international courts with compulsory jurisdiction over recalcitrant states, ICJ experts rendered judgments based on independent investigations. When no intergovernmental organization would compel obedience to the rule of law, the Commission punished offenders with negative publicity. All governments fell short of the ideal, but their failings ranged from negligence, through petty offenses, to heinous crimes against humanity. The ICJ's varied responses ranged from exhortation to denunciation, from quiet diplomacy to negative publicity, from lobbying wayward governments to appealing for U.N. condemnation.

Suasion, unlike coercion, requires moral and professional authority untainted by political bias. The ICJ claimed its authority from eminent membership and staff, national sections in over thirty countries, and as many as forty thousand professional supporters committed to the rule of law. State representatives typically shield allies and skewer adversaries. In selecting targets and methods, the ICJ avoided the double standard of U.N. member governments but still appeared somewhat partisan.[2] The jurists exhorted many governments, including their own; condemned totalitarianism but not colonialism; and waged their most intensive campaigns against the USSR and China. The major tactics included trial observers, country reports, public protests, and inquiry committees.

Trial Observers

At Delhi the ICJ had proclaimed a fundamental right to fair trial. Political trials rather than routine criminal proceedings became the first concern. From its origins, the ICJ condemned trials that were rigged to eliminate political enemies. Under some regimes, emergency laws retroactively criminalized and enhanced penalties for the opposition's prior acts. To assure conviction, governments created special courts with servile judges. Unrepresented traitors convicted in secret proceedings and unable to appeal their sentences were promptly executed. Successful coup leaders prosecuted and executed their ousted rivals. Some regimes welcomed observers to confer legitimacy on show trials.

Rule of law objections to such summary justice threaten tyrants' primary goal—to retain power. As an international NGO, the ICJ would not dispatch lawyers or find local counsel to represent political defendants in different local jurisdictions.[3] Without openly contesting governments' authority to punish criminals, the ICJ sent trial observers to impress on judges and counsel their obligation to proceed fairly. Governments, NGOs, and journalists had all set precedent by sending observers to political trials. Idealists wanted a customary rule of international law that required states to admit observers.[4] The ICJ advanced that emerging norm by overcoming initial state resistance and routinely sending trial observers to many different countries.

To pressure governments for admission, the ICJ publicized each formal request to send observers and protested any denial. The press cooperated by identifying four communist governments that refused visas for ICJ missions.[5] Ceylon's justice minister objected in the press to Munro's public request, but still admitted a Canadian ICJ trial observer. Poland's denial was followed by an invitation to other purportedly impartial observers. Governments that excluded observers did not escape censure, as the *Bulletin* used independent sources to expose unfair proceedings. The ICJ had easiest access in countries where its leaders had visited officials and organized sections. By 1962 seven governments in Europe, the Middle East, Africa, and Asia had admitted ICJ missions. The observers must have disappointed rulers who hoped the ICJ would confer legitimacy on their quasi-legal efforts to eliminate political enemies. Firsthand *Bulletin* reports from Turkey, Ethiopia, and Dahomey criticized grave procedural irregularities.

Instead of sending staff as observers, the ICJ recruited volunteer experts who were able to leave work on short notice.[6] Governments might be more willing to admit attorneys and professors than NGO legal officers not currently employed in practice. For long trials in Ethiopia and South Africa a succession of observers was needed. There were all too few qualified, available experts who could understand both the language and law in another jurisdiction. European jurists in former colonial powers were likely volunteers for trials in the British Commonwealth, Latin America, and Francophone states. The ICJ selected Britain's Gerald Gardiner as its first trial observer after South Africa's 1956 arrest of 156 political activists for treason.[7] Less eminent African, Asian, and Latin American observers had superior nationalist credentials. Even if an ICJ national section could have sent local observers, the goal was to establish an international presence. The British and French sections occasionally sent their own independent observers or undertook joint missions with the ICJ.[8]

A principled commitment to due process causes public interest lawyers to become identified with unpopular extremists. One U.S. attorney general characterized the ACLU as a "criminals' lobby"; many members who survived the Holocaust resigned when the ACLU represented anti-Semitic Nazis. Although the ICJ did not raise legal defense funds, it did advocate fair play for defendants of all political persuasions: anticommunists in Hungary, Poland, Yugoslavia, and Cuba; antifascists in Portugal, South Africa, and Spain; and coup leaders in Ceylon, Dahomey, and Egypt. In principle, even Adolf Eichmann's genocidal crimes did not excuse Israel's improper trial procedures. The ICJ observer from Greece sympathetically approved the Israeli court's "broad-minded spirit" that did not give "too much regard for procedure, as befits consideration of the problems of international penal law."[9] Yet his balanced report also disclosed major flaws: that Israeli penal law was given retroactive effect, that Eichmann's kidnapping in Argentina violated international law, that the defense had been denied a fair opportunity to call witnesses, that prosecution witnesses in absentia had not been cross-examined, and that Israel specially authorized the death penalty only for Nazi criminals.

By intervening in political trials ICJ observers at best modified the rules of play but not the outcome of a high-stakes struggle for power. Following unjust convictions, the ICJ followed up with futile public appeals for clemency, denouncing executions in Turkey and Ethiopia.[10] A few dismissals and acquittals may conceivably have been influenced by ICJ intervention. Ceylon was challenged for adopting retroactive legislation to prosecute alleged coup leaders before specially appointed judges; the charges were dismissed and the emergency procedures rejected as an unconstitutional breach of judicial independence.[11] A Spanish intellectual reportedly believed that an ICJ observer was a decisive factor in his acquittal.[12]

The first ICJ trial observers attempted with little success to enforce a right to fair trial against states conducting political prosecutions. Their greatest success was in establishing a routine NGO presence that helped internationalize criminal court proceedings that had traditionally been within exclusive domestic jurisdiction.

Country Reports and Protests

ICJ public reports about state offenses made governments the defendants in a primitive court of public opinion. Governments themselves submitted self-congratulatory periodic reports to the U.N. Commission on Human Rights. Since no international court had compulsory jurisdiction over lawbreaking states, the ICJ generated negative publicity as a public rebuke. The mildest reprimands appeared as brief articles in the *Bulletin* or as longer country studies in the *Journal.* Press releases announcing each issue highlighted the most egregious offenses. In response to urgent situations, the ICJ released to the news media protest cables demanding action by public officials. Three special book-length reports exposed systemic injustice in South Africa, Spain, and Cuba. Ad hoc inquiry committees investigated Soviet aggression in Hungary, China's occupation of Tibet, and French atrocities in Bizerte, Tunisia.

Periodical Reports

Balanced country reports in the *Bulletin* and *Journal* exhorted the negligent and rebuked the malicious. Each *Bulletin* carried as many as fifteen brief staff reports on legal developments and problems in different countries. Secretariat researchers built an impressive library and had prepared briefing papers for the many countries visited on ICJ missions. The background files described each country's legal system, the position of the bar, the judiciary, the constitution, legal problems, political conditions, and leading personalities. Members, practitioners, and legal scholars prepared longer *Journal* articles reporting on their own national legal systems. Dispassionate academic commentary analyzed preventive detention and wiretapping in both Western and non-Western countries. The authors offered constructive proposals to cure defects in current procedure.

Protests

Police crackdowns on opposition groups, persecution of minorities, and rigged political prosecutions required prompt intervention. Like a foreign minister, the Secretary-General cabled diplomatic protests and appeals to government officials. Unlike some domestic interest groups, the ICJ did not solicit mass mailings from concerned members. Press releases reprinting a cable's text for English, French, and Spanish readers generated extensive negative publicity that increased the pressure. The *New York Times* carried news reports on ICJ press complaints against a dozen different governments. In rare cases, the Secretary-General engaged in quiet diplomacy, making private appeals and personal visits. Public shame rather than personal influence became the primary advocacy tactic to protect victims.

Some members and national sections welcomed public ICJ concern about their own governments; others objected. International NGO criticism and respectful exhortation could advance domestic interest group efforts. Rather than parochially objecting to ICJ complaints about their country, activists occasionally appreciated international endorsement for their domestic goals. The *Journal* published an Indian Commission of Jurists' Inquiry Committee report faulting the communist state government in Kerala.[13] The ICJ cabled Ghana protesting detention of opposition lawyers including J. B. Danquah, section president of "Freedom and Justice."[14] Americans fighting McCarthyism and Southern racism may have welcomed critical commentary and respectful recommendations in the *Bulletin* and *Journal*.[15] An ICJ lament that segregation was "shameful to the good name of the United States"[16] confirmed civil rights leaders' claim that discrimination affected the country's international reputation.

In other cases the independent Secretariat antagonized local supporters. Just prior to completing his term as Secretary-General, Marsh risked offending some Americans: he publicly opposed Alabama's execution of a black man convicted of a $1.95 theft.[17] During Lalive's tenure, the U.K. section "Justice" resented ICJ intervention in British colonies. The French section "Libre Justice" attempted to control inquiries into repressive wartime policies in France and Algeria.[18] When the ICJ faulted French soldiers for atrocities in Bizerte, "Libre Justice" publicly announced it was breaking off all relations with the Secretary-General.

Special Reports on Illegal Systems

The 1952 and 1955 congresses approved strident Cold War exposés of Eastern European communist regimes.[19] Providing improved balance, the next reports on South Africa, Spain, and Cuba exposed the systemic injustices of apartheid, fascism, and communism. By publishing witness statements, protest letters, and affidavits, the ICJ provided an international audience to victims silenced by government censors at home. Documentary appendices included repressive legislation, executive decrees, and court judgments. In a brief preface, the ICJ Secretary-General criticized each government for violating rule of law principles identified in the Declaration of Delhi.

The timely South Africa report appeared after the 1960 Sharpeville massacre. Expressly rejecting positivism, Lalive's introduction asserted that apartheid violated fundamental economic and political rights set out in the Universal Declaration of Human Rights.[20] Ten chapters were introduced by reprinting different articles from the Universal Declaration, but the text never explained their legal significance. South Africa had not voted for the Declaration and defended apartheid as a domestic policy beyond the reach of customary international law. The report's temperate conclusion exhorted white South Africans who opposed apartheid to press for change.

At the Athens Congress, Scandinavian members, among others, had insisted on denouncing Spanish fascism. Some Executive Committee members worried that public condemnation would provoke Francisco Franco to crack down on liberals. The most ardent cold warriors preferred fascism to communism. Others promoted democratic opposition to avoid the communist takeover sought by Spain's IADL activists. Prolonged Executive Committee review and concerns delayed the report's publication until 1962. The final text merely described the legal system without calling it a police state or otherwise passing judgment.[21] In a brief introduction, Munro asserted that state control of the press and military trials of civilian offenders violated the Delhi Declaration, but the main text provided no legal analysis. An appendix reproduced lengthy protest letters from 339 Basque priests and from 350 Spanish intellectuals. Spain's ambassador called Debevoise to Washington to complain. Several ICJ members protested the critical report. No Spanish delegates attended the 1962 Rio Congress, and the Executive Committee denied one Spanish applicant observer status.

Well before the ICJ report condemning Castro, Executive Committee members had pressed for action on other Latin American dictators—the Dominican Republic's Trujillo, Haiti's Duvalier, and Cuba's Batista. Instead, the staff singled out Castro in a partisan report that could find nothing good in Cuba's revolutionary system.[22] The report included 124 pages of witness statements published anonymously to protect informants from retaliation. Readers were assured that typed, signed affidavits were available in Commission files. Such assurances of confidentiality may be the only means to obtain firsthand evidence from vulnerable victims. Inherently unreliable anonymous testimony is particularly suspect, however, when the investigator is politically motivated.

The ICJ report did not identify who conducted the witness interviews or where they took place. Executive Committee minutes indicate that an Argentinian legal officer spent five months gathering evidence in the United States, Mexico, and Venezuela.[23] The interviews were conducted six months after the unsuccessful CIA-sponsored Cuban exile invasion at the Bay of Pigs while the agency was plotting Castro's assassination.[24] Presumably many witnesses were refugees interviewed in Florida, and the United States wanted their message heard widely. The Cuban report can be found in nearly three times as many U.S. libraries as the ICJ studies of Spain and South Africa.[25] The special reports condemning pro-Western South Africa and Spain improved the ICJ's claim to impartiality, but Cold War priorities prevailed in both the Cuba report and a 1962 publication on the Berlin Wall.[26] CIA operative Philip Agee concluded:

> The Agency saw the ICJ as an organization which it hoped would produce prestigious propaganda of the kind wanted on such issues as violations of human rights in the communist bloc. Reports on other areas like South Africa would, so far as the CIA was concerned, merely lend respectability to this object.[27]

Whether or not intended as propaganda, the Cuba study accurately described Castro's egregious mistreatment of political prisoners. *Against All Hope: The Prison Memoirs of Armando Valladares* convincingly documents the summary trials and executions of 1961.[28]

Inquiry Committees

Crimes against humanity inspired ICJ Inquiry Committees patterned on the Nuremberg Tribunal. The proceedings at Nuremberg set a historic precedent for holding individuals responsible under customary international law against aggression and genocide. The four allied governments created a tribunal of eight members and appointed prosecutors who introduced documentary evidence and called witnesses in an eight-month trial. The Nuremberg prosecutor for Britain, Lord Shawcross, had trial responsibility for counts related to German aggression against neutral Norway. Defense counsel cross-examined prosecution witnesses and introduced evidence and legal arguments that won full acquittals for three of the twenty-two Nazis tried. Twelve others were sentenced to death, one in absentia, and six were sentenced to prison.[29]

Nuremberg confirmed for idealists that states could be held accountable under customary international law even if they failed to ratify binding treaties. To codify the principles, states adopted a U.N. convention criminalizing genocide; yet governments refused to create an international court with compulsory jurisdiction over state crimes. The postwar Geneva Conventions granted the ICRC only limited enforcement responsibility subject to state control. State parties to bilateral treaties occasionally agreed to international commissions of inquiry as ad-hoc fact-finding bodies.[30] Could private NGO commissions now render effective judgments about violations by governments that refused to cooperate? Would an ICJ verdict impress the United Nations or have independent impact? The earliest reported precedent by a private group is the 1930s Dewey Commission of Inquiry into the Moscow Trial of Leon Trotsky.[31] An IADL committee found the United States violated Article 6 of the Nuremberg principles by using bacteriological weapons in North Korea.[32] Jurists at the ICJ's inaugural congress in Berlin then reviewed documentary evidence and heard witness testimony before condemning state crimes in the Soviet zone.

The ICJ pursued that quasi-judicial approach with expert bodies that passed judgment on Soviet aggression in Hungary and Chinese genocide in Tibet. The Indian Commission of Jurists appointed a national section Inquiry Committee to investigate the communist state government in Kerala. Under a troublesome double standard, the ICJ disregarded the Anglo-French attack on Egypt, the Algerians' revolt against France, the U.S.-sponsored invasion of Cuba, and India's conquest of Goa. Only in the case of alleged French atrocities in Tunisia did an impartial inquiry challenge a noncommunist power in a major report. Critics have challenged procedural inequities in the Nuremberg prosecution;[33] the ICJ procedures were even more seriously flawed. The two major inquiry bodies included outspoken activists known for their hostility to the governments under investigation. Not surprisingly, the governments charged refused to participate; the ICJ did not provide representation for absent defendants as the Nuremberg tribunal had done for Martin Bormann. Fact-finding interviews with partisan refugees involved friendly questioning with no rigorous cross-examination. Documents accepted in evidence were not authenticated as required by U.S. court rules. The Secretariat released preliminary findings to the press and published major reports without soliciting responses from the governments charged.

Hungary

In 1956 the USSR invaded Hungary, replaced public officials, and brutally suppressed a popular uprising that Americans had long encouraged. The United States offered no military aid to roll back the Iron Curtain; the Soviets installed a puppet regime that prosecuted and then executed noncommunist leaders. The ICJ Secretariat immediately issued press releases and prepared briefing papers challenging Soviet violations of international law. NATO allies denounced the invasion in the United Nations, which appointed a special investigating committee. The same General Assembly responded to Israeli-Anglo-French aggression against Egypt by dispatching a U.N. emergency force to Suez. Only the Soviet intervention in Hungary aroused ICJ concerns for the U.N. Charter's prohibition of force.

Former Nuremburg prosecutor Shawcross acted initially as a representative of "Justice" and then of the ICJ. He had visited Eastern European countries liberated from the Nazis and had also been Britain's postwar U.N. representative. Shawcross chaired an ad hoc Lawyers' Conference to investigate the aggression. Just as anti-Nazi allies had rendered judgment at Nuremberg, twenty-six anticommunist jurists from fourteen Western countries judged the Soviet and Hungarian offenses.[34] The Hungarians refused admission to trial observers, but the ICJ Secretariat obtained extensive information about political defendants and their sentences.

A one-day ICJ Lawyers' Conference at The Hague reviewed and

endorsed the Secretariat's findings.[35] Shawcross then reported to the U.N. Special Committee in Geneva the jurists' conclusion that the USSR had violated the 1947 Hungarian Peace Treaty, the 1948 Geneva Conventions, and the Warsaw Pact.[36] After publishing the initial ICJ conference report, the Secretariat tracked the Hungarian prosecutions through 1958 in two subsequent publications.[37] Hungary denounced as "a baseless fabrication" the finding that from two thousand to five thousand people were executed after the uprising.[38] The government put former premier Imre Nagy to death after the ICJ's 1958 final report.

In its report, the U.N. Special Committee expressly cited the ICJ findings and incorporated the jurists' legal analysis. Marsh issued press releases and sent correspondence to U.N. delegates challenging Hungary's right to attend the General Assembly. In New York, AFFJ executive secretary Raphael circulated the ICJ reports to delegates who used the information to condemn Soviet aggression. New Zealand's ambassador, Sir Leslie Munro, was ultimately designated a powerless U.N. representative on Hungary; unlike the case in Suez, the 1956 aggressor in Hungary prevailed.

Tibet

The ICJ waged an even more vigorous U.N. campaign challenging China's 1959 military occupation of Tibet. Imperial Britain had encouraged Tibetan Buddhists in their defiance of Manchu and Nationalist rule from Peking. In 1951 the Dalai Lama, under duress, accepted Chinese communist sovereignty over the autonomous territory. The exiled Chinese Kuomintang and the CIA recruited, trained, and supplied Tibetans to fight for complete independence.[39] Neighboring India had border disputes with China and sympathized with the Tibetan struggle. The conflict peaked in 1959 when the People's Liberation Army occupied Lhasa in force and installed the Panchen Lama. The Dalai Lama found sanctuary in India with several thousand loyalists.[40] They reported massive atrocities including sixty-five thousand deaths, torture, involuntary sterilization, persecution of monks, and indoctrination of children.

The ICJ represented the Tibetans in the court of world opinion and at the United Nations. Indian Commission of Jurists General-Secretary Purshottam Trikamdas provided on-site research; Lalive and the Geneva Secretariat published the evidence and legal analysis; and Raphael coordinated the U.N. campaign in New York. Trikamdas had served six years in prison during the struggle for India's independence. A staunch anticommunist, he founded its socialist party, which allegedly had links to the CIA-funded Congress for Cultural Freedom.[41]

Within four months of the Chinese crackdown, the ICJ published a 208-page preliminary report comparable to the Nuremberg indictment supporting a *prima facie* case of genocide.[42] Although China had not ratified the Genocide Convention, the ICJ followed the Nuremberg precedent and applied customary international law. At a Geneva press conference, Trikamdas presented evidence of sixty-five thousand deaths.[43] Lalive appointed a nine-member Legal Inquiry Committee to investigate the facts and to evaluate Tibet's claim to independence. At the U.N. General Assembly, five country representatives including Leslie Munro cited the ICJ preliminary report. With nine opposed, forty-five states voted for a resolution that urged respect for Tibetan rights without mentioning China. Britain, France, and India were among twenty-six countries that abstained.[44]

Trikamdas chaired the Inquiry Committee of nine jurists from India, Ceylon, Burma, the Philippines, Malaya, Ghana, and Norway. After initially accepting appointment to the committee, Shawcross objected to the preliminary report and resigned.[45] Trikamdas publicly appealed to China for permission to visit Tibet but received no answer. Administrative Secretary Kozera, accompanied by a legal officer from Geneva, led the field investigation in India. The group gathered documents, accepted written statements, and interviewed the Dalai Lama and Tibetan refugees. The inquiry committee reconvened in Geneva to approve the final staff-prepared report.

The 345-page Legal Inquiry Committee report found (1) genocide in violation of customary international law, (2) sixteen violations of the Universal Declaration of Human Rights, and (3) that Tibet was not within China's domestic jurisdiction. The committee's renewed finding of genocide trumpeted in an ICJ press release made page 1 of the *New York Times*.[46] An accompanying editorial urged those supporting communist China's U.N. admission to consider the findings.[47] Few readers noted a careful distinction made in the final report. China had not sought to exterminate Tibetans as a people.[48] The committee could not verify claims of sixty-five thousand dead and of compulsory sterilization. The ICJ narrowly charged *cultural* genocide: that China attempted to eliminate Buddhism in Tibet by forcibly transferring children and by killing an unknown number of religious leaders. The committee further concluded that Tibet had been legally independent from 1911 to 1950 and that the Dalai Lama was justified in revoking the 1951 surrender to China.

The findings relied heavily on one-sided testimony by uncontested witnesses. An American historian argued that the committee should have interviewed independent journalists to verify refugee claims.[49] The legal analysis appears more like an advocates' brief than a carefully reasoned judgment. A letter in the *Guardian* rejected the committee's legal findings that Tibet had been independent and that China was liable for genocide.[50] The Nuremberg tribunal found that the Nazi program to kill all Jews violated a customary norm against genocide. The Genocide Convention expanded the crime to include forcibly transferring children and other offenses; counsel representing China, if appointed, could have reasonably argued that those additional provisions and the Universal Declaration had not become binding customary international law. The report did acknowledge but then rejected China's contention that Tibet's landless peasants needed support against feudal rulers who violated basic rights.

Courts treat witnesses who testify against their own interest as particularly credible. Committee members' disagreements with their own government can be assessed by examining U.N. votes on a resolution urging respect for Tibetans' cultural and religious life. Six of the nine ICJ Committee members came from four states that abstained in the vote. Perhaps those committee members differed with their respective governments' official position.

Eight of the jurists came from six Asian and African countries that had recently achieved the "self-determination of peoples" promised in the U.N. Charter. Their governments, particularly that of India, had insisted on proclaiming a fundamental right of self-determination in both U.N. human rights covenants. The committee did not base its support for Tibetan independence on a customary law right to self-determination. Instead, the committee defended the principle of nonintervention; the report justified U.N. action on Tibet by finding that the territory was historically not within China's domestic jurisdiction. The committee chairman and two other jurists from India may have been sensitive to their government's distinction between internal and external self-determination. Jawaharlal Nehru demanded that Portugal leave Goa but refused to hold a plebiscite for Kashmiris seeking independence from India. The English legal officer who drafted the final report may have shared his imperial government's objections to affirming a peoples' legal right to self-determination.

In sum, the committee displayed some judicial temperament by not accepting the refugees' most extreme allegations; yet it failed to offer reliable evidence to substantiate major findings. Press releases sensationalized the committee's conclusions and created a false impression that the ICJ had documented proof of mass killing in Tibet. The report may possibly have delayed communist China's U.N. membership, but the Dalai Lama remained a refugee in India. In the 1990s Tibetan advocates continued to cite the ICJ's finding that China had conquered an independent state and committed genocide.

Bizerte

Following a military clash with Tunisia in the disputed North African territory Bizerte, France would not allow a Red Cross visit. Tunisia's government charged French soldiers with atrocities and asked Lalive to appoint an inquiry committee. The ICJ Secretary-General agreed to investigate the allegations despite France's noncooperation. Three European jurists conducted an on-site investigation in Tunisia,[51] but the French would not allow a visit to Bizerte. Based on the available evidence, the jurists unanimously found that French forces had violated the Geneva Conventions by committing summary executions and mutilations.[52] The forty-five-page published report included six grisly photographs of mutilated corpses.

An Executive Committee majority—Kreher, Shawcross, and van Dal—dissociated themselves from the published report. They complained that the committee should have first communicated the report to the French government for its observations and should not have taken sides in an inter-state dispute. In further protest, "Libre Justice" announced that it would break off all relations with the Secretary-General.[53] Lalive demonstrated considerable independence when he disregarded French members' objections. Illegal atrocities merit investigation whether or not the parties involved are governments or private citizens. Yet the committee only contacted partisan sources, so its conclusions remained subject to challenge as unreliable. Ultimately, France and Tunisia negotiated their own settlement of the territorial dispute.

The ICJ's three flawed efforts at quasi-judicial enforcement failed to create either the desired substantive results or an acceptable procedural approach. Ad hoc committees enforcing disputed customary norms against unrepresented defendants ironically resembled the political trials in state courts that ICJ observers condemned. In its haste to challenge crimes against humanity, the ICJ disregarded rule of law principles proclaimed at Delhi. A permanent inquiry committee might have developed more appropriate quasi-judicial procedures. The jurists switched instead to more respectable fact-finding missions that were not limited to communist offenders. British philosopher Bertrand Russell began a radically new NGO quasi-legal tribunal in 1967. His first International War Crimes Tribunal of eminent nonlawyer jurors condemned U.S. atrocities in Vietnam. By 1992 more than fifty tribunals conducted by different NGOs had condemned immoral states with unanimous opinions that read more like manifestos than legal judgments.[54]

Conclusions

Advocacy for Implementation

How did ICJ advocates move the United Nations to demand compliance by state offenders? Unless U.N. members implemented Charter rules, they might just as well have resurrected the failed League of Nations. U.N. consultative status enabled the ICJ to appear only before the Commission on Human Rights, which disclaimed all responsibility for implementation. ICJ advocates pressed the U.N. General Assembly to protect victims of aggression in Hungary and Tibet. Country studies and inquiry committee reports gave some governments ammunition against state rivals—NATO allies to discredit the Soviet invasion of Hungary, the United States to denounce China and Cuba, Tunisia to attack France. The ICJ's negative publicity about uncooperative governments was used to support critical U.N. resolutions. The dominant Western bloc controlled General Assembly decisions to denounce the Soviet invasion of Hungary and to deny communist China admission. The Organization of American States expelled Castro.

Did ICJ lobbying influence U.N. implementation, or did cynical state patrons manipulate the ICJ to advance national interests? Governments had imposed greater limits on the ICRC, which could not intervene over state objections and did not go public with embarrassing reports. Public officials who became ICJ advocates effectively combined insider knowledge with the independence afforded by NGO status. Lord Shawcross and Leslie Munro pursued similar agendas first as ambassadors to the General Assembly and later with the ICJ. An Austrian member of the European and U.N. Commissions on Human Rights had greater opportunity to denounce French atrocities through the ICJ Inquiry Committee on Bizerte. The United Nations did so little that insider lobbying had less impact than outside protest against states that escaped its imperfect procedures.

Protest for Enforcement

The ICJ's first protection efforts were both pretentious and democratic, partisan and principled. An exclusive legal elite demanded that states respect laws guaranteeing due process, popular sovereignty, and civil liberties. Claiming extraordinary authority for a nongovernmental organization, the ICJ sought unprecedented limits on state power.

Did ICJ trial observers contribute to a customary norm that states must allow international visitors to attend open criminal proceedings? Stalin's show trials had been public, but communist governments never allowed ICJ observers. Noncommunist governments that allowed ICJ observers may have assumed that their presence could pose no threat. Trial observers became common at major political trials; the widespread practice established a valuable precedent rather than a legal right to attend.

Did the ICJ select targets for investigation based on legal rather than political criteria? The ICJ skewered communist dictators with partisan fervor, but also made principled judgments condemning fascist, apartheid, and other totalitarian regimes. Within the ICJ most members and staff were idealists who willingly took sides in inter-state disputes but at the same time challenged government allies for their offenses. Circumstantial evidence strongly indicates that Administrative Secretary Kozera acted as a conscious agent of CIA funders. Although the ICJ increasingly faulted noncommunist offenders, lingering imbalance was obvious.

Were ICJ judgments made by impartial experts? Partisan jurists ignored their own procedural scruples to fault communist adversaries but proceeded against others with more professional detachment. ICJ reports on Hungary, Tibet, and Cuba may have been accurate, but the authors were not impartial. As Ermacora noted in a critique of the IADL: "an investigation by an apparently impartial non-governmental organisation may also be used for political purposes by searching for material only supporting a political aim."[55] At a time when Castro's romantic admirers overlooked his failings, NGO criticism was warranted and needed. Covert funding of anonymous investigators did not legitimately meet that need. The ICJ inquiry committees were similarly flawed by one-sided proceedings whose findings could not be accepted as legal authority. The best reports disseminated credible victim statements that fostered international solidarity with local activists. The ICJ's legal expertise and moral authority encouraged local self-help.

Did ICJ interventions and public judgment of state crimes induce government compliance? The press widely publicized ICJ charges, and public officials frequently responded. Communist rulers denounced ICJ propaganda; Spain and South Africa also initiated public relations counteroffensives. Several victims attributed their release to ICJ protest, but public officials would never acknowledge being moved by negative publicity. ICJ intervention weakened some rulers' claim to legitimacy without inducing them to institutionalize the rule of law. After 1963 a new Secretary-General made the ICJ a far more determined advocate for supranational authority.

ICJ Inquiry Reports, 1955–1963

Hungary

The Hungarian Situation and the Rule of Law. The Hague: ICJ, 1957. 144 pp.
The Continuing Challenge of the Hungarian Situation to the Rule of Law. The Hague: ICJ, 1957. 33 pp.
Justice in Hungary Today. Geneva: ICJ, 1958. 72 pp.

Tibet

The Question of Tibet and the Rule of Law. Geneva: ICJ, 1959. 208 pp.
Tibet and the Chinese People's Republic: A Report to the ICJ by its Legal Inquiry Committee on Tibet. Geneva: ICJ, 1960. 341 pp.

South Africa

South Africa and the Rule of Law. Geneva: ICJ, 1960. 239 pp.
South African Incident: The Ganyile Case (June 1962). 20 pp.

Others

Report of the Committee of Enquiry into Events in Bizerte, Tunisia. Geneva: ICJ, 1961.
The Cassell Case: Contempt in Liberia. Geneva: ICJ, 1961.
The Berlin Wall: A Defiance of Human Rights. Geneva: ICJ, 1962. 54 pp.
Cuba and the Rule of Law. Geneva: ICJ, 1962. 240 pp.
Spain and the Rule of Law. Geneva: ICJ, 1962. 153 pp.

Part III
1963–1970: NGO Pioneers for International Human Rights

Chapter 5
Building Coalitions for Global Change

> The Universal Declaration is . . . the Charter of liberty of the oppressed and downtrodden. It defines the limits which the all-mighty state machine should not transgress in its dealings with those whom it rules. . . . Effective implementation machinery should conform to judicial norms, it should be objective and automatic in its operation; it should not be *ad hoc* nor dependent on the political expediency of the moment. . . . It is essential to provide a judicial remedy accessible to those affected. In curbing cruelty and crimes against humanity it is not sufficient to deplore them; it is essential to pass judgment . . . before an International Tribunal to punish crimes against humanity.
>
> —Seán MacBride[1]

Part III Overview, 1963–1970

In an extraordinarily violent decade, millions of innocent victims died in superpower proxy wars, civil conflicts, racial disorders, and independence struggles. The Cold War turned hot in Vietnam; the Congo, Nigeria, and Burundi suffered bloody domestic conflict; black freedom fighters took up arms against white rulers throughout Southern Africa; Warsaw Pact troops occupied Czechoslovakia; Israel seized Arab territories; Chinese and Soviet forces had border clashes; and political assassinations, race riots, and antiwar protests destabilized the United States. A nuclear arms race threatened total holocaust.

Amidst the carnage, the United Nations completed two major human rights covenants and lavishly celebrated the International Year for Human Rights in Teheran. New Afro-Asian members reformed

Human Rights Commission procedures to hear black African and Palestinian demands for self-determination. NGOs pressed the U.N. to hear individual petitioners from Haiti, Greece, or any other country that committed gross human rights violations. Europe's human rights system began effective supranational enforcement, and the American Convention on Human Rights initiated an Organization of American States (OAS) regional court. Human rights activists established new NGOs, and private citizens initiated East–West dialogues on disarmament.[2]

The ICJ soared to proud heights of influence as Secretary-General Seán MacBride organized a global coalition to campaign for a U.N. High Commissioner for Human Rights and for humanitarian law to prevent military atrocities. ICJ mediators facilitated settlements, and inquiry reports shamed recalcitrant governments. The bubble burst in 1967 when press reports of covert CIA funding embarrassed ICJ activists and many other unwitting recipients. Foes at the United Nations sought to revoke the consultative status of several prominent NGOs, including the ICJ.[3] After an official inquiry the CIA ended its support for nonprofit groups. The Executive Committee was assured that the AFFJ would no longer accept secret government grants. The American sponsors obtained Ford Foundation grants for two years to wind up the ICJ's operations. MacBride resigned and notified all staff that their appointments would end on June 30, 1970. European governments then saved the ICJ by funding a considerably reduced staff directed by a new Secretary-General.

This chapter examines how the ICJ shifted from domestic legal reform to international standard setting, and the coalition strategy that was adopted. The first section applies findings about U.S. public interest groups to ICJ leadership and governance. The second section contrasts the strategies and constituency tactics used to advance supranational authority with public interest lobbying in Washington. Two sections in the following chapter analyze the ICJ response to human rights crises and to the 1967 revelations and loss of covert CIA support.

Leadership, Goals, and Strategy

Jeffrey Berry's study of eighty-three U.S. public interest groups explains how such organizations decide on goals, capabilities, strategy, and tactics.[4] Despite considerable variations in size and resources, public interest organizations in Washington display remarkable similarities. Do the same generalizations apply to international human rights NGOs? Barry's research shows that public interest group staffs largely determine policy and program with minimal oversight by governing boards and with literally no control by the membership. U.S. organizations spend more resources relaying information to members than soliciting their ideas. In an unusual exception, Common Cause annually polls its members to determine program priorities. Board decisions are normally a pro forma approval of staff recommendations. Staff expertise and personal interest generate most new initiatives, and established organizations rarely shift priorities or methods. Members unable to remove leaders or to decide policy signal their displeasure by writing complaints, withholding contributions, or quitting the organization. The ACLU lost members when it represented Nazis and picked up support during the Nixon impeachment proceedings.

> In few areas of political life is the discrepancy between the formal juridical guarantees of democratic procedure and the actual practice of oligarchic rule so marked as in private or voluntary organizations such as trade unions, professional and business associations, veterans' groups, and cooperatives. . . . Almost all such organizations are characterized internally by the rule of a one-party oligarchy. That is, one group, which controls the administration, usually retains power indefinitely.[5]

Leadership

ICJ governance closely resembles that of U.S. public interest groups. The high costs of travel and translation services prevent frequent Executive Committee and membership meetings. The Executive Committee met only three times yearly and the full Commission convened only once between 1962 and 1971. At that 1966 session, titular non-European officers were elected; all Executive Committee members retained office without the triennial election required by the Statute. The Statute was amended to delete a requirement that financial accounts be reported at Commission meetings.

Frustrated by the undemocratic proceedings, a newly elected member from Australia sent a nine-page memo to all Commission members calling for major changes. Edward St. John acknowledged the American funders' claim to leadership but insisted that the ICJ must elect Executive Committee members. Speculating correctly that the elected president did not belong to the committee, he proposed giving that officer voting membership. St. John also advocated non-European representation on the committee and proposed that Commission members retire after a fixed term. As one means of improved policy consultation with Commission members, he requested an agenda prior to the next triennial meeting.[6] The Executive Committee, its American chairman, and European members resisted their constituent's reform proposals but relinquished extensive authority to a new Secretary-General. After removing Secretary-General Munro, the Executive Committee appointed a committed internationalist who dominated the organization for seven years.

Seán MacBride was an extraordinary choice to lead the ICJ. Born in Paris to exiled Irish revolutionaries, as a young child MacBride met other freedom fighters such as Nehru and Nkrumah. A journalist and barrister, he was imprisoned three times by the British for revolutionary activities; after independence he became a member of Ireland's Parliament and minister of external affairs. In that capacity he helped found the Council of Europe, served as president of its Council of Foreign Ministers, and jointly sponsored and signed the 1949 Geneva Conventions and the European Convention of Human Rights. After leaving government, MacBride helped found Amnesty International and chaired its International Executive Committee.[7] He organized Ireland's national ICJ section and made impressive contributions to the Congress deliberations in Delhi and Rio. Executive Committee chairman Eli Whitney Debevoise flew to Shannon to make a personal appeal for MacBride to accept the post.

Following his October 1963 appointment, MacBride promptly took decisive control of ICJ administration with strict regard for the Statute. He arranged for the ICJ's first financial audit, which revealed highly irregular bookkeeping. Administrative Secretary Edward Kozera soon resigned. Years after he had left the ICJ, following the public revelations, MacBride asserted that he never knew the CIA had supported the AFFJ; he surmised that Kozera was "undoubtedly a CIA operative."[8] Vladimir Kabes returned to the ICJ from advising the Congo's government to take the retitled post of executive secretary. With seventeen different nationalities, the thirty-six member staff comprised an effective, multilingual, truly international Secretariat. Six legal officers responsible for different regions exerted the a strong non-European influence on ICJ programming. The seven-thousand-volume library and archives had subscriptions to one hundred newspapers, journals, and periodicals.

Policy Goals

MacBride proposed major policy changes that aroused considerable opposition from the Executive Committee.[9] He made the strengthening of international law and institutions a top priority. In order to make the Universal Declaration an enforceable international bill of rights, MacBride wanted the ICJ to campaign for permanent U.N.

Seán MacBride, ICJ Secretary-General from 1963 to 1970, won the Nobel Peace Prize for his extensive international service.

and regional fact-finding machinery and trained mediators. He also proposed support for international peacekeeping machinery and general disarmament.

The Executive Committee initially considered international standard setting beyond the ICJ's scope, but soon endorsed MacBride's ambitious human rights campaign. President Vivian Bose objected to supranational institutions; he argued that the ICJ should continue its focus on third world legal and economic development.[10] In a compromise resolution, the 1966 Commission meeting emphasized that "the maintenance of the Rule of Law is basically a national responsibility," but urged speedy ratification of human rights covenants and pledged support to U.N. endeavors.[11] MacBride believed that new African and Asian governments had violated European legal principles, and he favored international remedies through new Commonwealth institutions.[12] MacBride campaigned without success for an international ombudsman, a U.N. High Commissioner for Human Rights. ICJ activists in Britain and New Zealand worked successfully for parliamentary commissioners at the national level.[13]

MacBride shifted resources from world tours and international congresses to hosting receptions in Geneva for diplomats, U.N. Secretariat officials, Human Rights Commission representatives, and U.N. Sub-Commission experts. Visiting dignitaries paid courtesy calls at the ICJ Secretariat's large new office complex.[14] The Executive Committee effectively blocked MacBride's efforts to associate the ICJ with disarmament negotiations, a U.N. peacekeeping army, and East–West dialogues of legal professionals. In his personal capacity, MacBride participated actively in the International Peace Bureau and related causes. He favored reducing expenditures for publications by merging the *Newsletter* with the *Bulletin* and discontinuing the *Journal*. The Executive Committee insisted on continuing the *Journal* and discouraged joint activities with the IADL, but approved most of the other changes.

Funding

To finance his ambitious program, MacBride proposed professional fund-raising, paid associate memberships for individuals in countries without national sections, and grant applications to U.N. agencies. Debevoise opposed MacBride's recommendation to hire a professional fund-raiser, and the AFFJ continued to provide about 97 percent of the ICJ's annual $400,000 regular budget. Other foundations and contributors supported a separate special-projects budget of about $60,000.[15] Executive Committee members took no responsibility for fund-raising. MacBride sought consultative status with UNESCO to obtain funding for ICJ legal education projects, lawyer recruitment, staff salaries, and conference expenses. A former journalist, MacBride also wanted UNESCO to protect a free press. UNESCO granted consultative status in Category C in 1965 but did not make grants to the ICJ.

TABLE 5.1. ICJ Officers, Members, and Meetings, 1963–1970.

Secretariat (2 Quai de Cheval Blanque, Geneva)
Secretary-General: Seán MacBride, October 10, 1963–December 1, 1970
Executive Secretary, Vladimir R. Kabes, 1964–1969
AFFJ Secretary, New York, Saul Sherman

Executive Committee
Eli Whitney Debevoise, U.S., Chairman
Per T. Federspiel, Denmark
René Meyer, France (beginning 1966)
Lord Hartley Shawcross, United Kingdom (Gerald Gardiner, alternate)
A. J. M. van Dal, Netherlands

Presidents
Vivian Bose, India, 1959–1966
T. S. Fernando, Sri Lanka, 1966–1977

New Members

Year elected		*Final year*
1964	Terje Wold, Norway	1972
	Mohamed A. Abu Rannat, Sudan	1975[a]
1966	Kenzo Takayanagi, Japan, Vice-President, 1966	1968[c]
	René Meyer, France	1972[c]
	Edward St. John, Australia	1977[a]
	Luis Negron Fernandez, Puerto Rico	1976[a]
1970	Chandra Kisan Daphtary, India	1980[a]
	Enrique Garcia-Sayan, Peru	1978[c]
	Bahri Guiga, Tunisia	1980
	Gustaf Petren, Sweden	1985[a]
	Shridath S. Ramphal, Guyana	1985[a]
	Michael A. Triantafyllides, Cyprus	1985[a]
	Masatoshi Yakota, Japan, Vice-President	1981[a]

Meetings
Geneva, 1966

[a] Year elected honorary member. W. J. Ganshof van de Meersch, Belgium, was also named an honorary member.
[b] Resigned.
[c] Deceased.

Networking

Consultative status with international organizations enhanced ICJ leadership of human rights coalitions. NGOs incorporated under national laws lack the "legal personality" international law grants to states, intergovernmental organizations, and the Red Cross. In contrast to the constitutionally protected right of petition in the United States, international organizations can exclude citizen groups.[16] State members decide which NGOs can receive and circulate documents, observe, and occasionally speak in committee meetings. Consultative status could enhance the ICJ's legal status and provide vital access to key officials.

Compared to the United Nations, the Council of Europe had very few consultative organizations and granted NGOs far fewer rights.[17] From his own council experience, MacBride realized how the ICJ might benefit from consultative status in Category I. Recognition in 1965 created important new contacts in the European Secretariat and Consultative Assembly. The International Labor Organization (ILO) added the ICJ to its list of associated groups, and informal contacts were made with OAS, Organization of African Unity (OAU), and Arab League officials. MacBride wanted but never could employ full-time ICJ representatives at the United Nations in New York, UNESCO's Paris headquarters, or the OAU in Ethiopia. Nor did ICJ supporters realize their goal of recognition conferred by the Nobel Peace Prize. Their campaign fell short in 1965 when the Nobel Committee honored UNICEF, and the Commission received an honor both unexpected and unique. At the urging of the national bar, Thailand's king sent a National Assembly member to honor the ICJ with a replica of the Thai "Stone of Justice" at a Geneva Human Rights Day presentation.[18]

To pool resources and enlarge the constituency represented, small domestic groups rely extensively on strategic coalitions.[19] Berry distinguished dependent coalitions dominated by a single group from participatory alliances with shared responsibilities. He also identified both ad hoc and permanent coalitions. Rival egos and each group's need to enhance its own reputation frequently prevent effective long-term resource sharing.[20] Rival national loyalties and fund-raising competition across state boundaries make NGO coalitions difficult. Carefully distinguishing between allies and rivals, MacBride led an ad hoc coalition to establish a U.N. High Commissioner for Human Rights and founded a permanent human rights NGO committee in Geneva.

Coalitions often include not only interest group experts but also key legislators from congressional subcommittees and executive department specialists. Those "subgovernments" or issue networks often make significant policy choices routinely accepted by the U.S. Congress and the president.[21] Within an issue area such as health care, a revolving door may circulate the same individuals between Congress, the Department of Health, and the American Medical Association.

Conflict with the Department of the Interior may lead officials at the Environmental Protection Administration to enlist Sierra Club assistance.

Similarly, NGO human rights coalitions include sympathetic government representatives and U.N. Secretariat officials. ICJ members and staff in an emerging human rights network both came from and went to the European Court of Human Rights, the U.N. Secretariat, and specialized agencies.[22] After leaving the ICJ, MacBride held important posts with UNESCO and as U.N. High Commissioner for Namibia. In the United States, government officials earn higher salaries by switching to private interest groups; low-paid NGO staff find U.N. employment a more lucrative career advance.

The World Campaign for Human Rights

To promote international rather than municipal law reform, the ICJ developed new strategies. How could an international human rights NGO influence international lawmaking?[23] Domestic public interest strategies enlist voters and courts to influence elected legislators. Berry identified four main advocacy strategies: law, embarrassment and confrontation, information, and constituency influence and pressure.[24] Some of the associated tactics—campaign contributions, litigation, publishing legislators' voting records—obviously cannot influence international treaty negotiations conducted by government representatives. Though less effective at the United Nations than in the U.S. Congress, other information and constituency strategies might still make a difference; for example, legal research, personal lobbying, committee testimony, and influential constituent appeals. The Charter preamble attributes power to "We the peoples of the United Nations . . ." and the ICJ insisted that diplomats negotiating treaties regard people as their constituents.

U.N. High Commissioner for Human Rights

Shortly after his appointment, MacBride represented the ICJ at an informal human rights policy planning group convened by the World Veterans' Federation. Along with representatives of Amnesty International, the Red Cross, and the International Committee of Military Doctors, they explored proposals for disarmament, a U.N. peacekeeping force, and methods to resolve disputes.[25] MacBride argued to the ICJ Executive Committee that the ICJ had a responsibility to lead lawyers in a quest for global peace; he worried that lawyers were joining a potential rival organization, Charles Rhyne's Peace Through World Law Center. From his post as its chairman, MacBride viewed

Amnesty International with its nonlawyer members responding to individual victims as a natural ally. While reluctantly willing to endorse international human rights treaties, the Executive Committee considered peacekeeping initiatives beyond the ICJ's scope. There was no objection to continuing informal, private discussions with other organizations.[26]

MacBride chaired the next policy planning session at the offices of "Justice" and Amnesty International in London. The World Jewish Congress representative and John Humphrey, director of the U.N. Division of Human Rights, revived a 1947 proposal. NGOs had collaborated with great success in lobbying for a U.N. Charter provision creating a Commission on Human Rights. They had failed to obtain a global attorney general or ombudsman capable of responding to individual complaints. By the 1960s, the Commission's steadfast refusal to consider individual petitions prompted support for the appointment of a U.N. High Commissioner for Human Rights.[27]

Rather than communicating a demand by constituent members, NGO leaders shaped their proposal in consultation with public officials. During the Kennedy administration, U.S. State Department officers seeking ways to strengthen the U.N. human rights machinery had approached John Humphrey and American NGOs.[28] Jacob Blaustein, former chairman of the American Jewish Committee, then publicly advocated a U.N. High Commissioner with comparatively limited power. Humphrey argued that governments would be more inclined to accept a High Commissioner capable of providing humanitarian good offices at their request rather than to admit fact-finders selected in response to individual complaints. Vietnam had recently invited a fact-finding mission composed of experts whose government associations created an unfortunate appearance of political bias.[29] Humphrey urged the NGOs to give top priority to campaigning for a High Commissioner; he recommended contacting U.S. and British officials to introduce a proposal in the General Assembly's Third Committee.

MacBride accepted responsibility for the initiative and convened a final planning group meeting in Geneva. The New York-based International League for the Rights of Man decided not to participate in the coalition and prepared its own unsuccessful proposal for a special rapporteur or consultant. MacBride drafted a resolution authorizing the appointment of a High Commissioner which seven NGOs endorsed in a joint press release.[30] Election-year politics made the United States an unlikely sponsor, but MacBride speculated that Britain's Labour government might introduce the proposal. Humphrey recommended Costa Rica's ambassador Fernando Volio Jiménez, an expert from the U.N. fact-finding mission to Vietnam.[31]

Without crediting the ICJ authors, Volio introduced the resolution at the Human Rights Commission's 1965 session. The Commission placed the item on the agenda over Soviet objections but never discussed the proposal. The ICJ's senior legal officer strongly endorsed the proposal at the July 1965 ECOSOC session. Ambassador Volio then introduced the resolution directly to the General Assembly. After MacBride wrote to Prime Minister Lester Pearson asking for support, Canada became one of the co-sponsors. Eastern bloc representatives opposed the potential infringement of national sovereignty, and the General Assembly referred the proposal back to the Commission on Human Rights.

To build third world support, the NGOs lobbied African participants at a U.N. seminar on "Human Rights in Developing Countries."[32] Volio chaired the next session of the Human Rights Commission, but could not persuade any Eastern bloc members to join a working group that refined the proposal. The considerably strengthened draft authorized the High Commissioner to review communications and proposed a regionally balanced advisory board. The Human Rights Commission and ECOSOC then approved the draft proposal, two tantalizing victories that heightened NGO expectations for International Human Rights Year, 1968. MacBride obtained increased NGO support at several meetings; their endorsement could never overcome third world government concerns such as India's that the High Commissioner would interfere in internal affairs. The General Assembly indirectly rejected the proposal for a High Commissioner by repeatedly postponing consideration. The bitter disappointment prompted MacBride to criticize "the conservatism of most governments"; he observed "that public opinion is far in advance of the official governmental attitude."[33] While unwilling to accept a High Commissioner, U.N. members did institute a confidential communication procedure which enabled NGOs to present evidence of violations for screening by Sub-Commission experts in closed session.[34]

NGO Human Rights Committee

MacBride the entrepreneur created the first permanent NGO human rights coalition to check spreading atrocities in Vietnam, the Congo, and Southern Africa. The 1907 Hague Convention and the 1949 Geneva Conventions provided insufficient protection for both civilians and combatants brutalized in modern guerrilla war. MacBride launched a World Campaign for Human Rights as part of the U.N.'s 1968 International Human Rights Year. He deliberately involved communist-oriented groups to allay objections by the Soviet bloc and to moderate the more ideologically extreme organizations. Despite reservations by his Executive Committee, MacBride supported renewed U.N. consultative status for the IADL.[35] His revolutionary credentials aided collaboration with third world freedom fighters.

The three-hundred-member Conference of Nongovernmental Organizations in Consultative Status at the U.N. (CONGO) became the coalition vehicle. CONGO coordinated U.N.–NGO procedural relations and had not previously been used to rally a peoples' constituency to make demands. In 1965 MacBride organized and chaired an ad hoc human rights subcommittee of CONGO to prepare for the 1968 U.N. International Conference on Human Rights in Teheran. The committee included mass membership religious organizations with large congregations in many countries as well as dedicated human rights NGOs such as Amnesty International (AI) with its growing multinational base. An ICJ legal officer was also elected in his personal capacity to the CONGO bureau as co-president for Europe.[36] MacBride used the *Bulletin* to proclaim the "World Campaign," and a special issue of the *Journal* was devoted to its major goals.[37]

In 1968 MacBride co-chaired a Geneva meeting of seventy-six U.N. human rights NGOs and of fifty experts sitting as the Montreal Assembly on Human Rights. Both conferences generated recommendations for the Teheran Conference, including MacBride's top priorities: heightened protection for victims of armed conflict and the appointment of a U.N. High Commissioner for Human Rights.[38] NGO representatives could not speak at the Teheran diplomatic conference, but the ICJ and its allies drafted and promoted a resolution committing the government representatives to protect human rights during armed conflicts.

The conference then called on the General Assembly to invite the U.N. Secretary-General to study the need for additional humanitarian international conventions.[39] After Teheran, 127 members of CONGO attended a Paris conference that also supported improved protection for civilians during armed conflict.[40] MacBride then lobbied the Third Committee, helping to obtain twenty sponsors for a resolution unanimously adopted by the General Assembly. He considered the resolution's adoption as "one of the very few worthwhile results emanating from the large and elaborate U.N. Conference" at Teheran.[41] The International Committee of the Red Cross (ICRC) subsequently invited MacBride to serve on a committee of experts that began a process culminating in adoption of Protocols to the Geneva Conventions in 1977.

After 1968 the human rights NGO coalition became a permanent subcommittee of CONGO, with more than sixty member organizations chaired by MacBride and his successor as ICJ Secretary-General. It never again launched a world campaign, nor has the ICJ called on its national sections to do so.[42] Initially the NGO coalition was a useful vehicle for mobilizing a new constituency to influence international organizations. Interdenominational religious NGOs offered a large global membership for influencing governments that the ICJ could never match. Collaboration with communist-oriented and third world NGOs enhanced the movement's legitimacy.

Personal and institutional rivalry reduced the scale of subsequent joint ventures. MacBride's coalition strategies were often viewed as personal initiatives by ICJ members and staff, who rarely participated in his high-level NGO diplomacy. The proliferation of small human rights NGOs made collaboration both more necessary and difficult. NGOs naturally cherish their independence, and they frequently compete for limited resources and recognition. MacBride insisted on a cool and distant relationship with a potential rival for Western lawyers' support—the American-led and generously funded World Peace Through World Law Center. As AI and the major church groups developed more extensive organizational resources, they became less interested in a global NGO coalition. After leaving the ICJ, MacBride initiated an AI world campaign on a single theme, torture. Smaller NGOs continued to rely on the CONGO special committee and its ICJ chairman for information and as a means to aggregate their own limited influence.

Protection of Journalists

The ICJ also provided legal expertise in a lobbying partnership with journalists. The International Federation of Editors-in-Chief asked MacBride, a former journalist, to prepare an instrument that would protect reporters on dangerous missions. Under his direction, ICJ staff prepared the Montecatini Draft convention on war correspondents.[43] The 1949 Geneva Conventions gave journalists inadequate protection, and reporters had been detained and killed covering conflicts in Korea, Southern Africa, Latin America, and Vietnam. ICJ legal officers consulted the International Press Institute before preparing a text intended to protect correspondents from harassment, unjust arrest, and detention.

Journalists attending an international congress approved the proposed convention, but the U.N. Commission on Human Rights considerably weakened three major provisions. The government representatives limited the number of journalists who could qualify for safe conduct cards to individuals from "bona fide" news organizations that provided the correspondent's main source of income. Instead of protection from harassment and arrest, the parties would give foreign journalists the "same protection . . . as [they provide] to their own journalists."[44] Finally, the U.N. committee could withdraw safe conduct cards from journalists who violated a code of ethics requiring high standards of integrity that precluded any "political" activity.

After the General Assembly disregarded the Commission draft, proponents shifted their efforts to UNESCO.[45] The International Association of Democratic Lawyers and the ICJ were asked to consult recognized press organizations in drafting a convention to protect journalists. After several meetings the ICJ decided not to support proposals on journalists' duties that afforded governments a pretext for restricting rather than protecting rights.[46]

Legal Education

MacBride's standard-setting initiatives supplemented rather than replaced the ICJ's ongoing promotional work. At his direction, the ICJ published a legal reference, *The Rule of Law and Human Rights*, compiling the principles and definitions elaborated at Athens, Delhi, Lagos, Rio, and a final regional conference in Bangkok.[47] The *Journal* began publishing a digest of judicial decisions to inform practitioners about case law in other jurisdictions. The ICJ and "Libre Justice" organized a Dakar conference for jurists from French-speaking African countries in 1967.[48] Indian jurists examined freedom of movement.[49] The European sections arranged conferences on the individual and the state and on privacy rights.[50] ICJ staff also regularly attended U.N. human rights seminars and conferences organized by other organizations. Seminars for recent law school graduates and fellowships for work at the ICJ Secretariat were offered to young lawyers, particularly those from developing countries. Britain appointed a parliamentary commissioner or ombudsman in 1967, eight years after a report by "Justice" proposed the reform.

Conclusions

Leadership

The ICJ's strong leaders did not practice the democracy they preached. Seán MacBride wrested more authority from the Executive Committee than did his predecessors, curbing Kozera's influence and elevating international initiatives to top priority. Debevoise complained that MacBride consulted him too often, and the Executive

Committee disapproved of several of the Secretary-General's most idealistic proposals. As in most domestic groups the members had little or no control of policy, program, or budget. The Executive Committee perpetuated its own authority. Publications listed Commissioners and the titular officers, but did not identify the Executive Committee members or its dominant chairman.

Recruitment

Did the ICJ mobilize activists from Western and third world countries? The ICJ recruited staff from Britain, France, Australia, Chile, Argentina, India, and East Africa. Young lawyers received fellowships for up to a year at the Secretariat, and the most promising were hired as ICJ regional officers. Experienced staff moved on to posts at the United Nations, ILO, FAO, WHO, UNESCO, and WIPO (the World Intellectual Property Organization). Just as MacBride had graduated from national to international politics, his recruits became administrators in the growing network of global institutions. The ICJ did not recruit many new members for the Commission or organize local supporters into effective sections or affiliates. MacBride maintained the impressive ICJ communication network of forty thousand subscribers, but did not enlist many new associates.

Articulation

How effectively did the ICJ articulate universal values that balanced Western and third world concerns? Under Seán MacBride the ICJ placed on the legislative agenda liberal European rather than third world initiatives. Western idealists campaigned for a U.N. High Commissioner for Human Rights and protection for journalists. New leaders in Africa and Asia resisted external checks on their authority. Despite major American funding, MacBride reacted to U.S. atrocities in Vietnam by campaigning for new limits on military tactics. His commitment to strengthen the Geneva Conventions served freedom fighters in subject territories, but the world campaign was principally a Western effort.

Aggregation

Did the ICJ create broad-based coalitions of NGO activists and government policy makers? Did ICJ seniority and expertise make it an NGO leader? When did coalition strategies work and when did rivalry prevent collaboration? How did participants compromise their positions, divide responsibility, and share the credit? The ICJ organized and dominated both ad hoc and permanent coalitions. The group advocating a U.N. High Commissioner included several NGOs, the Director of the U.N. Human Rights Division, U.S. State Department officials, and Costa Rica's U.N. representative. Several sponsors wanted credit for the proposal, and MacBride blamed Costa Rica for acting prematurely without consultation. The ad hoc coalition never survived its initial defeat. For the 1968 World Conference, MacBride fashioned and led a permanent NGO coalition, the human rights subcommittee of CONGO. The committee provided a forum primarily for smaller NGOs, and major groups collaborated on only one world campaign. MacBride collaborated effectively with AI and the IADL but viewed the World Peace Through Law Center as a rival for Western lawyers' affections. U.N. Secretariat officials and state representatives joined ICJ activists in an emerging human rights network similar to the issues networks identified by political scientists in the United States.

Lawmaking

How can international laws be made of the people, by the people, and for the people? In the absence of international political parties and contested elections, NGOs serve an even more vital democratic function in world politics than that which interest groups perform at the national level. In contrast to the elected members of a national legislature chosen by a mass constituency, diplomats who negotiate international law only indirectly represent the people. Delegates to international organizations report through foreign ministry superiors to a head of state rather than to the voters. Private citizens seeking protection need some mechanism to influence diplomats who give top priority to maintaining state sovereignty. Human rights NGOs cannot use the economic assets of multinational corporations and the paramilitary attacks of terrorist groups.[51]

Did the ICJ provide democratic representation for world citizens in the international political system? Like U.S. public interest groups, the ICJ provided lawmakers with information and expertise. ICJ experts drafted resolutions and model conventions, enlisted state sponsors, and claimed broad popular support. The ICJ and allied NGOs represented a new global constituency demanding that international organizations protect not only sovereign states but also the world's people. As a coalition leader MacBride had considerable success in placing new proposals on the intergovernmental agenda. None of the proposed reforms became international law during MacBride's ICJ tenure.[52] The U.N. did approve the Covenant on Civil and Political Rights, and the OAS adopted the Inter-American Convention on Human Rights. Those treaties addressed states of emergency and created new international enforcement procedures. The Geneva-based ICJ did not have lobbyists who participated in their drafting, but the *Journal* publicized the new conventions. The next chapter shows how ICJ protest of atrocities also generated pressure for new supranational authority.

Chapter 6
Responding to Crisis

> Justice of any sort, in principle as in execution, emanates from the State.
>
> —Charles De Gaulle

> Real justice must derive its strength equally from the State and from the masses.
>
> —Jean Paul Sartre[1]

Throughout the 1960s states promised justice in new human rights treaties, but they practiced the most extreme barbarism. The ICJ struggled to protect life and liberty in crisis after crisis. In 1963 the ICJ Secretariat received 5,878 letters and sent 6,592.[2] Secretary-General MacBride left to Amnesty International rescue efforts for individual victims and devoted ICJ resources to combat systemic racism, fascism, and communism in states North and South, East and West. African liberation from white minority rule in South Africa, Angola, and Rhodesia became a top priority. Fascist repression in Greece, Spain, Indonesia, Haiti, and the Dominican Republic were investigated and exposed. Communist invaders cut short Czechoslovakia's democratic reforms, and the ICJ publicized injustice throughout the Soviet empire.

The ICJ used both cooperative and confrontational approaches, a range of tactics from quiet diplomacy to public condemnation. After bloody riots, two governments invited the ICJ to conduct inquiry commissions quite unlike its confrontational proceedings on Hungary, Tibet, and Bizerte. In private communications ICJ officials pressed officials to respect law when restoring order. Trial observers could be friendly private advisers to the misguided, or hostile public adversaries to the malicious. The ICJ indicted uncooperative regimes with negative publicity and well-documented complaints to intergovernmental human rights commissions.

Part III of this book concludes by explaining how the ICJ responded to its own nearly fatal crisis. Revelations of covert CIA funding in 1967 threatened the Commission's public standing and triggered a total cutoff of American support in 1970. A new Secretary-General obtained sufficient European government contributions to keep the ICJ barely functioning for another year.

Advocacy, Protest, and Inquiry

African Liberation from White Minority Rule

African winds of change toppled colonial regimes up to a white redoubt south of the Zambezi River. In five territories white minorities of between 2 and 18 percent legalized oppression to retain privilege. Portuguese colonialists used forced African labor, white Rhodesians unilaterally proclaimed independence from Britain, and apartheid created a South African caste system that was also imposed on neighboring South West Africa (Namibia). As liberation movements took up arms for freedom, the ICJ raised international challenges to military repression and racist legality.

In correspondence with South African minister of justice B. J. Vorster, Seán MacBride demonstrated a willingness to use quiet diplomacy even with an unrepentant adversary. MacBride established his bona fides by recalling that his father had fought with the Boers against the British. That credential moved Vorster to write a personal reply that disavowed any official response to the meddlesome ICJ.[3]

The ICJ publicly confronted South Africa for both its internal apartheid and its domination of South West Africa. *The Bulletin* reported on each new piece of repressive legislation—the Sabotage Act, the No Trial Act, the Bantu Laws Amendment Act, and the Terrorism Act. ICJ trial observers praised occasional acts of judicial independence and witnessed political prosecutions of so-called communists. The ICJ protested harassment of defense lawyers and dispatched a British member of Parliament to aid an attorney whose passport was withdrawn.[4] Two special reports exposed South African injustice; the regime countered with its own publication, *South Africa and the Rule of Law*.[5] Two *Journal* articles and a special report criticized the World Court's decision that Ethiopia and Liberia could not bring suit on South West Africa.[6] After the General Assembly officially stripped

South Africa of its right to govern the territory, the ICJ publicly condemned the trials of South West Africa Peoples' Organization (SWAPO) freedom fighters.

In Angola and Rhodesia ICJ members had personal relationships and political sympathies that muted public criticism. The ICJ sent observers to Leopoldville and Angola who prepared a special report on Portugal's brutal response to the Angolan independence movement.[7] MacBride visited Lisbon to discuss the findings with Portuguese officials, and the *Bulletin* announced the forthcoming report. The Executive Committee insisted on seeing the final draft, and it was never published. Instead, the *Bulletin* reported U.N. resolutions opposed by the United States and Britain that condemned Portuguese colonialism and called on NATO allies to cut off military assistance to the Salazar regime.[8] Several press releases and two *Bulletin* articles denounced Rhodesian censorship of the African press, a mandatory death penalty, and separate-development policies.

MacBride effectively coordinated the ICJ campaign on Southern Africa with U.N. pressure. He circulated a U.N. report on apartheid to the ICJ's African readers. The *Bulletin* article on the Bantu Laws was published and circulated as a U.N. Document. MacBride's U.N. seminar paper on how South Africa violated the Universal Declaration appeared both in the *Bulletin* and as a special ICJ report. MacBride chaired an NGO observers' group at a 1967 apartheid seminar and presented thirteen detailed recommendations for U.N. action.[9] The NGOs pressed the United Nations to record the names of South Africans charged with crimes against humanity so that individuals could be held personally liable. MacBride testified before special U.N. committees on apartheid and prison conditions and then received a special invitation to consult with the Security Council subcommittee for Namibia.

Fascism North and South

Anticommunist dictators imprisoned and executed political rivals in Spain, Portugal, Greece, Indonesia, Haiti, the Dominican Republic, and Burundi. Condemning brutal police-state torture and murder, the ICJ challenged several tyrants' right to rule. Spain characterized the ICJ as a communist front and lobbied its members to rein in the staff; Portugal expelled a Secretariat legal officer, and Greece barred trial observers. Dictators protested ICJ support for dissident lawyers as subversive and illegal intervention in their states' internal affairs.

In order to save lives and free political detainees, staff members occasionally avoided publicity and negotiated with the devil. Private correspondence and personal visits produced mixed results. Following MacBride's appeal to Spain's minister of justice, Franco granted a full pardon to lawyer Eduardo Cierco Sanchez.[10] A Brazilian newspaper editor expressed appreciation for an ICJ trial observer whose presence aided his release. Burundi's butchers took advantage of quiet diplomacy to delay negative publicity.

Burundi

A struggle for power between the Bantu-speaking Hutu majority and Burundi's Nilotic Tutsi rulers followed elections in 1965. Hutu candidates won a parliamentary majority, but the minority Tutsi retained power. The traditional king, absent in Geneva, had little control over radical pro-Chinese Tutsi military officers. Conservative, pro-Western Hutu soldiers attempted a coup, which failed. The International Confederation of Trade Unions alerted the ICJ to the mass killing of Hutu leaders. ICJ staff met in Geneva with aides to the king who requested French-speaking judges to try the rebels. Instead, the ICJ sent Swiss professor Philippe Graven to Bujumbura to obtain information and urge respect for law.

MacBride cabled Burundi officials about Graven, who spoke with the minister of justice by phone a day after arriving. The regime had completely silenced the local press, and all foreign correspondents had left the country. Incommunicado at his hotel, Graven heard rumors that more executions were taking place. Pretending ignorance of Graven's presence, the minister cabled MacBride to ask who was coming and when. Graven finally met the minister, who refused to produce documentation of trial procedures for those executed. All the elected leaders in both houses of Parliament had been shot—eighty-six Hutu in all. Reuters broke the story based on travelers' reports in Nairobi. Graven returned to Geneva, and the staff urgently debated what to do next.[11]

Kabes, Graven, the Red Cross representative, and the U.S. State Department encouraged MacBride to send two more observers immediately. Kabes argued that Graven's initial protest had brought concessions from officials who would now be more cooperative. An ICJ presence could assist as many as one thousand detainees awaiting execution, encourage moderate forces, and help defeat the Chinese faction. The minister of justice had offered to cooperate, and a rejection would create ill will at an upcoming ICJ African conference in Dakar. Red Cross representatives in Burundi strongly favored another mission, and the U.S. State Department would help obtain financial support.

Describing himself as a minority of one, MacBride informed Debevoise that he had decided to use adverse publicity rather than muzzled observers. Thus far the killers in Bujumbura had gotten away with murder. "It is extraordinary that in this age a Government can execute all the parliamentary leaders without any publicity."[12] Observers from the United Nations, Red Cross, and the foreign missions could continue quiet diplomacy; the ICJ must publicly denounce the slaughter and the manipulation of its own observer.

In a widely carried press release, the ICJ identified nine parliamentary, union, political party, and cabinet leaders who had been executed. The report estimated that five hundred to twelve hundred detainees remained in jeopardy and urged the United Nations to provide the requested judges and judicial investigating officers. MacBride rejected the minister's offer to grant "all facilities" to "attend trials as these are public," and announced conditions for any future mission. The government must notify accused of the charges, allow defense counsel, provide advance notice of all trials, delay executions to allow time for clemency appeals, and supply all documents used as a basis for past sentences.[13] There were no further executions, but the military completed its takeover in 1966. After the public rebuke, Burundi's ambassador and crown prince visited the ICJ Secretariat and apologized for Graven's treatment.[14] When Greek colonels staged a military coup a year later, MacBride wasted no time on quiet diplomacy.

Greece

In fifty years, the cradle of democracy suffered five military coups. In April 1967, anticommunist colonels preempted scheduled elections, imposing martial law that suspended all constitutional guarantees. An estimated six thousand were detained, torture became routine, the press was entirely controlled, public meetings were banned, political parties and trade unions were dissolved, and independent judges were dismissed. MacBride immediately adopted confrontational tactics—public condemnation and a complaint to the Council of Europe.

As a party to the Statute of the Council of Europe and the European Convention of Human Rights, Greece had pledged to respect civil liberties. Greek citizens could not petition the European Commission of Human Rights because the government had not accepted

Convention Article 25 allowing individual complaints. Unless another state party complained under Article 24, that Commission could not consider any violations. The colonels also invoked Article 15, which authorizes a government to derogate from certain rights during an emergency that threatens the life of the nation.

In a press release denouncing the coup, MacBride detailed the violations of the European Convention as well as the ICJ's Act of Athens. He sent copies to the Council of Europe's secretary-general and to the president of the Consultative Assembly as well as the U.K. secretary of state. In an accompanying letter, MacBride anticipated and challenged the junta's notice of derogation: there had been no public emergency threatening the life of the Greek nation, and the colonels were not a lawfully constituted government. MacBride requested distribution of the ICJ statement to members and committees; he noted that he was personally a signatory of the Council Statute and European Convention and a former member of the Committee of Ministers and of the Assembly. Unless states complained about Greece to the European Commission on Human Rights, the Convention would be rendered completely nugatory.[15]

The Assembly president circulated MacBride's statement. The Legal, Political, and Standing Committees adopted resolutions urging states to complain under Article 24. The Consultative Assembly appointed a rapporteur to contact the Greek regime. The U.N. Sub-Commission unsuccessfully urged the Commission on Human Rights to investigate the Greek situation. MacBride preferred action by the European Commission, which had become a human rights showpiece. In September, Norway, Sweden, Denmark and the Netherlands complained to the European Human Rights Commission on behalf of Greek nationals. Greece's representative urged the Commission to dismiss, because the government was entitled to a "margin of appreciation" in responding to an emergency.[16] The European Human Rights Commission admitted the application in January 1968 and began an investigation that took twenty-three months. The ICJ continued to supply information to the Assembly rapporteur, sent several trial observers to Greece, and publicly denounced each new assault on the rule of law.

The Consultative Assembly recommended that the Council of Ministers expel Greece for violating the Statute, and the Commission found numerous violations of the Human Rights Convention. Greece denounced both, withdrew from the Council of Europe, and refused to participate in the Ministers' review. The Ministers resolved that Greece had violated the Human Rights Convention and remained bound by its terms. Unmoved, the junta implemented a new Constitution without regard for law or international opinion.[17]

Communist Injustice

The ICJ continued to assault the Iron Curtain with *Bulletin* exposés of transgressions by East Germany, Hungary, Rumania, and of course the USSR. Widely distributed special reprints of a *Journal* article, "Economic Crimes in the Soviet Union,"[18] publicized anti-Semitism in state prosecutions. Press releases and periodic reports denounced trials of intellectuals in Moscow, Chinese communism, and Tibet's subjugation. Warsaw Pact aggression against Czechoslovakia provoked sharp protests but no campaign comparable to the 1955 Legal Conference on Hungary.

Selected ICJ members and staff viewed MacBride's priorities and tactics with communist regimes as politically suspect. Dedicated to avoiding nuclear war, MacBride consorted with leftists in the international peace movement. He attempted to engage lawyers from the East in constructive dialogue and to influence officials with quiet diplomacy. The Executive Committee discouraged rapprochement with the IADL, and MacBride's missions to communist capitals were made in his personal capacity. The Austrian national section organized a meeting with Eastern European attorneys and preliminary contacts were established.

Quasi-Judicial Inquiry by Request

MacBride repeatedly noted that ICJ intervention ended when armies started fighting. What influence could the most respected NGO have to arrest the carnage in Kashmir, Nigeria, the Sudan, the Middle East, or Vietnam? Personally outraged at states' barbaric military atrocities, MacBride appealed for international peacekeeping forces and stronger humanitarian law to protect civilians. Rarely did the ICJ condemn specific war crimes or intervene on behalf of individuals. In two unique situations ICJ inquiry commissions attempted to resolve violent disputes peacefully before they escalated into full-scale military conflicts.

The ICJ's first inquiry proceedings had defied uncooperative target governments and passed judgment on the Soviet invasion of Hungary, China's repression in Tibet, and French atrocities in Bizerte. The Netherlands, India, Tunisia, and Switzerland allowed ICJ proceedings on their soil, but it was impossible to visit the territory investigated. After those first confrontational inquiries, the ICJ was assisted by state parties to make quasi-judicial findings on disputes in Panama and British Guiana.

Panama

Four U.S. soldiers and twenty-three Panamanians died during 1964 riots after a confrontation in the canal zone. Panama complained to the Organization of American States, demanding renegotiation of the Canal Treaty. The OAS appointed a five-member mediating committee. Panama's National Bar Association charged the United States with violating Universal Declaration provisions on torture, free assembly, and the right to life. In a letter to ICJ member Fernando Fournier of Costa Rica, the association's president requested an investigation.

Both governments agreed to hearings conducted by an ICJ-appointed Investigating Committee made up of a Swedish judge, a Dutch professor, and an Indian lawyer.[19] During a two-week mission, the committee met informally with government officials and took one hundred hours of public testimony. Responding to the bar representatives, Army general counsel Joseph Califano accused Panama's government and Cuban agents of inciting the riot. Local radio stations had encouraged the attacks. The legal adviser to Panama's Ministry of External Affairs explained why the National Guard was not ordered to stop the rioters. American ballistic experts testified that the bullet that killed one girl could not have been the .30-caliber ammunition used by U.S. forces.[20] As the ICJ hearings concluded, the governments restored diplomatic relations and announced future discussions about the canal under an OAS mediating committee plan.

Two months later, the ICJ committee published a report applying the Universal Declaration rather than treaties ratified by the two governments.[21] Both governments participated in an unprecedented proceeding conducted by private legal authorities who invoked and construed the Universal Declaration as customary law. When the conclusions absolved the United States, a *New York Times* editorial hailed a possible new avenue to practical jurisprudence.[22]

The committee found that Panama's police had failed to restrain the rioters, and that the Americans had not fired until they sustained casualties. U.S. forces were faulted for provoking the Panamanian protest, for not using water jets and more tear gas, and for firing directly into a crowd. The regrettable killings did not violate the Declaration's right to life, because U.S. forces had faced firebombings and hostile fire. The committee invoked Panama's Constitution and unratified provisions on emergency measures in the Inter-American draft Convention on Human Rights to approve U.S. restrictions on freedom of assembly. U.S. news media headlined the "not guilty" verdict.[23] After a new government was elected, a socialist National Assembly deputy castigated the ICJ, charging that it was subsidized by the United States.[24]

British Guiana

The sun has still not set on communal discord in former English colonies. When indigenous Amerindians proved unsuited to plantation labor, Britain first imported African slaves and then indentured East Indians to Guiana. London granted internal self-government in 1961. Indian leader Cheddi Jagan of the People's Progressive Party formed a majority government opposed by Forbes Burnham and the predominantly African People's National Congress. Communal rioting for three successive years disrupted negotiations for full independence. The CIA covertly supported an eighty-day general strike against Jagan's leftist government in 1963.[25] British troops returned to keep order; London proclaimed a state of emergency in April 1964 when 130 people died in communal violence. Over Jagan's objections, Britain instituted proportional representation for new elections. In coalition with another minority party, Burnham formed a bare governing majority. The British governor general used emergency powers to remove Jagan from office. Jagan refused to participate in further independence negotiations and charged discrimination against East Indians in the security forces.

British Guiana's political crisis pitted the ICJ Executive Committee's American chair against the British member and alternate. The British Colonial Office and Burnham invited the ICJ to appoint a three-member commission to investigate racial problems in the public service. Lord Shawcross recommended an ICJ inquiry. After consulting Webster and Bonsal, Debevoise raised the strongest objections to assisting a colonial power deal with a subject territory. Distinguishing British Guiana from Panama, Debevoise argued that investigating racial discrimination exceeded the ICJ's scope, that political rather than legal factors controlled, and that Jagan's party would refuse to participate. He rejected proposed British government funding as improper and recommended referral to the OAS or another body.[26]

Shawcross disavowed any affront to Americans who paid the ICJ's bills in a reply copied to all ICJ members. He noted the ICJ had previously intervened in British colonies, even though "Justice" claimed responsibility for dependencies. Panama's relationship with the United States differed little from the case of Egypt, where Britain had treaty rights to the Suez canal. The ICJ should help those whose fears of a predominantly African police force were delaying final realization of full independence.[27] Marsh, Gardiner, van Dal, and Federspiel all wrote letters supporting Shawcross. The Executive Committee accepted the British Guiana government's invitation and authorized MacBride and Debevoise to appoint suitable commission members. The committee refused financial support from either British Guiana or Britain.

MacBride immediately visited London and Georgetown to finalize the commission's terms of reference and procedures. Burnham insisted that the commission not include any English, American, African, or Indian jurists. The commission's terms of reference were to examine the balance between the races in the security forces and civil services and to make recommendations to eliminate any imbalance caused by racially discriminatory selection procedures.[28] MacBride could not persuade Jagan to participate. His Progressive People's Party (PPP) publicly declared that it would boycott the investigation. Since the Colonial Office had acknowledged that East Indians were underrepresented in the security services, Jagan demanded immediate remedial measures rather than further investigation of discriminatory procedures.

An Irish judge chaired the panel, which included law professors from Austria and Greece.[29] The legislature adopted the Commission of Jurists Ordinance, which granted the commission the powers of the Guiana Supreme Court to subpoena witnesses, receive testimony on oath, and charge individuals with perjury and contempt. The commission decided not to compel testimony or the production of documents. Instead, by public notice the ICJ invited all interested parties to submit memoranda and to make oral statements in public session. Seventy-two witnesses gave testimony and seventeen organizations submitted memoranda. At their request, many Indians and security officers were heard in private session. From August 5 to 20, 1965, the commission held both public and private hearings, received documents from the attorney general, and heard complaints by East Indians not associated with the PPP.

Since racial imbalance per se was not illegal, the commission presented a sociological and political report about appropriate representation for Africans, East Indians, and Europeans in the civil service.[30] Indigenous Amerindians comprising 5 percent of the population were excluded from consideration as a group requiring special protection before ultimate integration into modern society. East Indians made up 50 percent of the population but only 20 percent of the police force. The commission found that historical factors such as

African urbanization, culture, and education rather than intentional discrimination resulted in their overrepresentation in the security forces. So that more Indian applicants would qualify, the Commission recommended eliminating requirements that police be 5 feet, 6 inches tall and unmarried. The *New York Times* selectively reported the commission's opposition to rigid quotas as unconstitutional and a potential cause of racial tension.[31] The commission proposed a constitutional amendment so that for a five-year period 75 percent of new police officers would be Indians. The members also endorsed appointment of an ombudsman, possibly a representative committee, to handle race discrimination complaints.

Constitutional negotiations resumed without Jagan. British Order-in-Council No. 2161 specifically referred to the ICJ report, and the draft constitution incorporated several of its recommendations, including the appointment of an ombudsman. No further race riots delayed independence, and Guyana became a fully sovereign republic in the Commonwealth on May 26, 1966. Burnham assumed the presidency, and minority Afro-Guyanese continued to hold "an overwhelming majority of all senior governmental posts, public service positions, . . . and police."[32] Not until the 1990s did the Indian majority win power in democratic elections.

The British Guiana inquiry was the ICJ's final use of quasi-judicial NGO hearings. Indian members asked the ICJ to inquire into Pakistan's expulsion of non-Muslim minorities, but the inter-state rivalries made formal hearings impossible. In place of further quasi-judicial hearings, the ICJ turned to fact-finding missions based on interviews and field investigation. Reliable fact-finding reports could persuade regional human rights commissions and U.N. bodies to conduct hearings on violations. States party to the European Convention on Human Rights agreed in advance to allow in-country investigations. A European investigating subcommission visited detention centers and took testimony in Greece from March 10 to 19, 1969.[33] MacBride urged the Inter-American Commission to investigate Haiti. The U.N. Commission on Human Rights initiated procedures for reviewing individual communications, and MacBride aided its inquiries on Southern Africa. As the ICJ turned to intergovernmental procedures, other groups sponsored NGO tribunals. British philosopher Bertrand Russell organized the first International War Crimes Tribunal in 1967. Eminent non-lawyer jurors condemned U.S. atrocities in Vietnam. By 1992 other NGOs had convened more than fifty tribunals that condemned immoral states without improving on the flawed procedures employed by the ICJ.[34]

CIA Repudiation, Collapse, and Renewal

CIA Revelations

The CIA exposé reached the ICJ on Sunday, February 19, 1967.[35] A month after *Ramparts* magazine exposed covert funding of the National Student Association, the *New York Times* listed more than forty other recipients, including the AFFJ. A *Washington Post* graphic illustrated how seven CIA conduit funds had paid three legitimate foundations grants for the AFFJ that went to the ICJ.[36] The reports disclosed covert funding of many established groups but did not suggest that the CIA had provided the critical initial funding for any organizations.

MacBride acted promptly to protect the ICJ's reputation. In a press release and interviews he denounced the CIA and asserted that he had no information about covert funding through conduit foundations. MacBride acknowledged support from the AFFJ, but insisted that no contributions to the ICJ from any source had strings attached. He stressed the ICJ's impartial work for human rights in the East and West and its efforts to end colonialism and neo-colonialism in all forms. In letters to ICJ members and national sections, MacBride encouraged a similar local defense; he discouraged publicity unless press articles and inquiries made it necessary.

By telex MacBride called an Executive Committee meeting to take place in the ensuing two weeks. When Debevoise sought a delay, MacBride circulated an angry letter threatening to resign. The disclosure of unscrupulous cloak-and-dagger operations created revulsion. He protested that innocent ICJ supporters would be falsely linked to CIA espionage. "Their integrity and standing in their own country is of importance not only to themselves personally, but to the cause of the free world." Whether or not the allegations could be disproved, MacBride insisted that in future the ICJ only accept funds whose origins were clearly identifiable and published. Open State Department funding of free world democratic organizations would have been preferable. He would resign unless assured that future AFFJ funding had no taint of intelligence service influence.[37]

Peter Benenson exacerbated his dilemma by publicly demanding that MacBride resign as Amnesty International Executive Committee chairman. AI members had been feuding over alleged British secret service penetration, and Benenson had just resigned as chief executive. The CIA revelations confirmed Benenson's fear that government influence had fatally compromised both organizations; he decided to withdraw his resignation and follow through on a plan to move AI to a neutral country. AI's Executive Committee confirmed his resignation, and Benenson became estranged from the organization he had founded.[38] He further lamented that his other initiative, "Justice," might also become tarnished by its regrettable association with the ICJ.[39]

The ICJ Executive Committee met on March 3, 1967. Debevoise did not reveal the extent of past CIA sponsorship but assured that the AFFJ would see that "no such monies shall be included in the grants or contributions which it accepts."[40] The Committee approved for all Commission members confidential information they could use publicly as necessary. The statement disclaimed any prior knowledge of indirect funding from undisclosed government sources.

Members who wrote in response to the limited explanation expressed more support than outrage. Several indicated a willingness to accept public Justice Department contributions, and few sought additional information. Bose wrote: "As I was President at the time, I ought to have known."[41] Nabuco complained that Debevoise had rebuffed his efforts to learn more about ICJ funding and to publicize the source. MacBride's request to keep down publicity led Nabuco to ask whether the CIA contribution had been 100 percent, 50 percent or 10 percent.[42] His question was never answered. The AFFJ never disclosed the extent of CIA support, and ICJ publications never acknowledged unwitting receipt of any covert funds. The Delaware corporation was dissolved, and its board reincorporated in New York as the American Association for the International Commission of Jurists (AAICJ). Debevoise promised a membership drive, and long-dormant ICJ liaison committees with the New York City Bar and the ABA were given new leadership.[43]

President Lyndon Johnson appointed a three-member committee to investigate the massive CIA funding operation.[44] The group recommended ending all covert support for educational institutions and voluntary organizations with some exceptions. The State Department rather than the CIA might begin public funding of certain groups. After Johnson announced a funding cutoff, the CIA arranged for large surge payments that would carry operations such as Radio Free Europe for several years.[45] To keep the ICJ afloat, Debevoise obtained a $250,000 Ford Foundation grant for 1969. Foundation president McGeorge Bundy had been National Security Council director responsible for CIA oversight. As a member of Ford's board, John McCloy had arranged foundation grants for other projects covertly proposed by the CIA.[46] In 1955 McCloy had hired Debevoise as legal counsel for the foundation. Debevoise retained his post as ICJ

Executive Committee chairman and made additional personal contributions. David Rockefeller also responded to appeals for donations.

U.N. Consultative Status Threatened

The CIA exposé created an ideal opportunity to strip selected NGOs of consultative status. Just as the United States managed to exclude the IADL in the 1950s, the USSR now took aim at the ICJ. Third world members obtained greater representation on the Council Committee on Non-Governmental Organizations and objected to NGOs' Western bias. Arab governments attacked pro-Israeli Jewish groups; African nationalists pursued Western NGOs supporting white South Africa. Tanzania's representative, Waldo E. Waldron-Ramsey, strongly protested the exclusion of NGOs from socialist countries. The United States continued blocking the IADL in committee, until ECOSOC restored its consultative status in 1967. ECOSOC approved new rules to govern relations with NGOs and demanded a full accounting from and reclassification of all groups in consultative status.[47]

In thirty-nine meetings between September 1968 and April 1969, the ECOSOC Committee on Non-Governmental Organizations reviewed 166 groups.[48] The U.S. mission gave an advance briefing to help eleven NGOs, including the ICJ.[49] Dissatisfied with the ICJ's reply to its questionnaire, the committee asked for additional information about funding and invited MacBride to testify in person.

At hearings on April 9 and 10, MacBride fended off hostile demands for a full accounting. The USSR representative asked how many thousands of dollars had been received from the CIA; Tanzania's Waldron-Ramsey asked about the ICJ's internal inquiry into the funding of its American affiliate. MacBride's careful answers denied direct funding by the CIA; he noted the Executive Committee's insistence that the American fund assure that no covert government funds would be accepted. He stressed, "I think the test should be whether there has been any influence [on the organization]. I have been quite satisfied that there has been no attempt to influence the policy of the ICJ by the Americans."[50] The Libyan delegate complained that the ICJ had never publicly criticized Israel for violating Palestinian rights. MacBride answered that the ICJ avoided wartime situations. (Within months *The Review* published its first report on the Middle East.)[51] Waldron-Ramsey probed MacBride's personal involvement when AI allegedly provided secret British government support for Rhodesian prisoners.

Friendly delegates from the United States, Britain, France, and

Uruguay raised procedural objections to applying newly adopted penalties for NGO misconduct. MacBride reported that ICJ publications had described problems in ninety-two different countries; he repeatedly mentioned recent joint ventures with the IADL. Press accounts in Spain and Turkey had claimed the ICJ was controlled by Moscow. In a remarkable shift, Waldron-Ramsey expressed satisfaction at MacBride's answers and praised the ICJ's work. He concluded that national sections rather than the international secretariat had been compromised. Nine committee members voted for consultative status in Category II, and only the USSR and Bulgaria opposed. The USSR then urged ECOSOC to deny consultative status but was outvoted twenty-one to four. MacBride's anticolonial credentials and the ICJ's active advocacy for Namibian independence won critical third world support.

The American and British governments that had nurtured and used them effectively protected the Western NGOs; none of those challenged lost consultative status. The U.N. committee exposed little about state funding, because undisclosed aid served the interests of governments as well as NGOs. The USSR did not want communist front groups to reveal Moscow's support. Third world officials realized that NGOs in Africa and Asia would need government aid to compete with wealthier organizations from developed countries. Arab and African states began supporting Palestinian and anti-apartheid freedom fighters whose representatives were given special observer status at the United Nations. NGOs in consultative status were allowed to receive public funds and have government members as long as they did not act as paid state agents or obstruct U.N. goals. For their part, NGOs in the know concealed their government support in order to appear genuinely independent.

Financial and Leadership Crisis

The 1969 Ford grant provided considerably less than indirect CIA support and was insufficient to sustain the ICJ program. As the organization steadily declined, MacBride advocated aggressive fundraising and appealed for a new Secretary-General. Lawyers, national sections, and private foundations failed to increase their minuscule budget share,[52] and the Executive Committee could not find a third world candidate to succeed MacBride. The members rejected MacBride's proposal to expand membership to dues-paying associates.

At last the Committee agreed to discontinue the expensive *Journal* and to eliminate free subscriptions for ICJ publications. The *Bulletin* and *Journal* were combined into a new publication, a small *Review* that began quarterly publication in March 1969. Published in English, French, Spanish, and German, the *Review* included brief country reports, special studies, ICJ news, and book reviews. The Secretariat eliminated 57 percent of the mailing list—twenty-thousand nonpaying subscribers outside the United States who never belonged to a national section.[53] Staff attrition accomplished further savings; Executive Secretary Kabes resigned in late 1968. The Committee rejected a staff petition for wages and benefits comparable to compensation paid by other Geneva NGOs. In preparation for a full Commission meeting in 1970, the Executive Committee recommended amending the ICJ Statute to fix membership at ten years and to provide for honorary members. Seven new members were elected, bringing total membership to thirty-six.[54]

The American sponsors pulled the ICJ's financial plug in 1970. Rejecting an urgent AAICJ appeal, the Ford Foundation concluded that the ICJ should not be so dependent on a single contributor or country. The foundation would not continue to provide general support for the permanent budget. Over Debevoise's objections, an AAICJ board majority resolved to wind up the ICJ's affairs; it would not seek to raise other funds to sustain the organization. Ford approved a final $150,000 grant sufficient to pay off the ICJ staff and to close down the Secretariat but did not make formal dissolution a condition for payment.

MacBride insisted on leaving within six months. To replace him the old-boy network proposed Niall MacDermot, the treasurer of "Justice." The Executive Committee authorized a one-year appointment contingent on available funds. The 1970 Commission meeting was indefinitely postponed. The *Review* ceased publication; a Secretariat report on the occupation of Czechoslovakia was never published; a conference to prepare an African human rights convention, a textbook on the law of human rights, and all other special projects were suspended. MacBride terminated three legal officers as of March 30, and notified all remaining staff that their employment contracts would end on June 30.[55] Swiss law required a substantial reserve fund for severance pay. Empty offices in the Secretariat were sublet.

Seemingly at the final hour, the Executive Committee resolved not to dissolve the ICJ. Per Federspiel recommended an appeal to the ministers of justice from the Council of Europe. At the Justice Ministers' Conference in May, Britain promised $47,000 if other governments made similar contributions. Grants from six European and two Caribbean governments brought the total to $84,000. MacDermot became Assistant Secretary-General in October and continued fundraising to ensure the ICJ's survival. Reduced dependence on a single contributor encouraged grants from private foundations and foreign ministries. Debevoise obtained support from the Aspen Institute for a Commission meeting in Colorado. In November the Executive Committee appointed MacDermot Secretary-General and approved his one-year budget proposal. Staff were continued on a month-to-month basis and all vacant posts abolished. The retrenchment cut the Secretariat to one-fourth of its peak strength, but the ICJ greeted 1971 with a one-year lease on life.

Conclusions

Enforcement

Two ICJ hearings in the 1960s offered an impartial NGO alternative to the imperfect tribunals only sporadically used by states. The 1899 Hague Convention I established an International Commission of Enquiry for states that consented to pacific settlement, but few used the method.[56] States never followed the Nuremberg Tribunal approach to punish homicidal tyrants. The U.N. Commission on Human Rights created inquiry committees on South Africa and the Middle East despite objections by the state targets.[57]

Did ICJ inquiries use fair procedures? The inquiry commissions in Panama and British Guiana enlisted more impartial members and used fairer procedures than the earlier, one-sided, inquiries on East Germany, Hungary, and Tibet. The two studiously balanced reports identified complex realities and avoided simplistic condemnation or exoneration.

On balance the ICJ inquiries, like the U.N. initiatives, were flawed means to a good end. The Panama commission was the only inquiry where all interested state and private parties cooperated. In British Guiana, the complaining opposition party refused to participate; the ICJ accepted a government invitation and advertised for grievants to present evidence. It makes sense for an NGO to investigate an uncooperative state; why assist a government to investigate grievances by a political party that boycotts the inquiry?

Costly hearings may require special funding that arouses suspicion about who paid the piper's tune. The ICJ quite properly refused British support for the Guiana inquiry, but the local government provided board and lodging for the commission. Full disclosure offers the best assurance against improper influence, but none of the ICJ reports acknowledged a funding source. The independent jurists selected to conduct the inquiries had no inside knowledge of ICJ finances. In its public statements the ICJ attributed its income to lawyers and did not identify the American Fund for Free Jurists as the primary contributor. A disgruntled Panamanian deputy still suspected and protested a U.S. subsidy. Public knowledge of American funding, however indirect, would have made the report validating U.S. conduct far less credible.

Each ICJ inquiry was limited to narrow legal questions isolated from larger political disputes. Would Panama or the United States control the canal? Would Africans led by Burnham or Indians organized by Jagan control an independent Guyana? Whoever prevailed, the ICJ could properly insist on respect for human rights and protection for innocent victims. The adversarial inquiry format clarified facts but left insufficient room for the negotiated compromises required to settle ongoing political struggles. An acceptable racial mix for British Guiana's civil service was a nonjusticiable policy question awkwardly reformulated for the inquiry as an issue of illegal race discrimination.

Advocacy for Implementation

By the late 1960s, improved intergovernmental procedures had reduced the need for quasi-judicial NGO inquiries. Standing commissions with permanent budgets are less subject to political manipulation than are ad hoc tribunals. The ICJ helped activate U.N. and regional procedures by preparing widely publicized charges that resembled legal indictments. ICJ fact-finding missions based on interviews and field investigation encouraged European and Latin American officials to investigate violations in Greece and Haiti. The United Nations began monitoring more situations just as the ICJ lost the financial support required for major NGO enforcement efforts. In response, the ICJ increasingly functioned as a victims' advocate before intergovernmental implementation groups.

Funding

What did the United States buy with its investment in the ICJ? Foreign policy realists used ICJ reports to attack communist rivals; more idealistic officials also welcomed criticism of wayward allies and misconduct by their own government.[58] The Kennedy administration disapproved of Spanish fascism and French colonialism in Algeria, but a State Department protest about human rights violations would be challenged as improper intervention or an unfriendly act. Covertly supported NGO criticism would avoid diplomatic friction, as long as there was deniability. Spanish officials unaware of U.S. funding had done their utmost to refute and silence the ICJ. The foreign ministry published a white paper in response to *Spain and the Rule of Law*. Spain's ambassador to Washington rebuked Debevoise, and the ambassador in Paris worked on Executive Committee member Meyer. An attaché in Geneva visited the ICJ Secretariat twice and threatened to contact Commission members.[59] The ICJ's continuing public criticism undermined Franco's effort to improve foreign relations. After the CIA disclosures, Spain publicly charged the United States with unfriendly acts in supporting the ICJ's critical publications. Although the United States had not directed the ICJ publicity, it could have withheld funding from activities that threatened American interests.

Did the ICJ compromise its independence in return for U.S. support? Staff and members who did not know where the AFFJ obtained its funds felt they had full autonomy. The ICJ legitimately earned a reputation for impartially representing individuals abused by oppressive sovereigns. MacBride vigorously attacked U.S. policy in Vietnam. "Justice" criticized British criminal procedure, and the *Review* decried violations in Northern Ireland, but Britain still helped the ICJ survive. Perhaps Debevoise consciously wanted the ICJ to support U.S. foreign policy, but he granted staff broad discretion. The Ford Foundation cut off support in 1970 because the ICJ had found no other revenue, not because of political considerations.

Government funding per se need not impose unacceptable costs for NGOs. The U.S. Supreme Court established as constitutional law that government must fund defense counsel to oppose state prosecutors. Publicly supported legal aid societies sharply challenge government policy. To an extent, U.S. subsidies to the ICJ had offset costs imposed by other governments. Switzerland required the ICJ to maintain a costly reserve fund for staff severance payments and regulated work permits. Some governments imposed export currency restrictions that impeded subscriptions and contributions to the international Secretariat.

Revelations of covert government funding could have destroyed the organization, but MacBride effectively controlled the damage. If he did not know for certain about the CIA role, he must have chosen not to know. His denials effectively blocked full disclosure. After the first public revelations, a *Ramparts* editor specifically asked MacBride about the CIA employee who had set up the ICJ. MacBride gave an interview, correctly noted that the individual named had been employed by the AFFJ in New York, and reported that his search had revealed no indication of a CIA link in the Geneva records.[60] *Ramparts* never publicly identified the individual or the CIA role in creating the ICJ. When supporters in Sweden sought information to rebut charges that the Tibet report was CIA propaganda, MacBride held fast to the careful disclaimers in his initial press release: The Secretariat had never known the actual source of foundation grants, and there were never any conditions attached.

The AFFJ never provided a full accounting, and its leaders remained in good standing. ICJ publications never reported the CIA revelations, the Executive Committee's response, or the reason MacBride was invited to appear before the U.N. committee.[61] Without a forthright acknowledgment and repudiation of the covert CIA support, speculation continued about when or whether CIA ties had begun and ended. Silence must have seemed less costly than confirmation of members' worst suspicions. Disclosure that the CIA had fully sponsored the organization since 1952 might have destroyed forever its credibility as the independent NGO it truly became after 1967. Individuals compromised their personal integrity without irreparable damage to cherished reputations. The ICJ managed to survive the 1960s in desperate financial shape but with its excellent reputation largely undiminished. Highly dedicated legal officers had impartially applied human rights principles with impressive effect. MacBride had added significantly to the organization's credentials and contacts. Despite its government links, other NGOs reelected the ICJ to the CONGO Bureau in 1969 with the highest vote total of any organization.

The 1970 funding crisis weaned the ICJ from dependence on a single major contributor, but governments rather than private lawyers insured its survival. Confronted with possible dissolution of the organization, top leaders rejected proposals for a large paid associate membership and for greater representation of national sections. They preferred highly selective Commission membership to mass support and capitalized on excellent connections with the political establishment. European government grants permitted appointment of a distinguished new ICJ Secretary-General in 1970. New government support enabled Executive Committee leaders and their nonmember alternates to remain highly independent of their nominal private constituents. The Committee resolved to announce the appointment without mentioning the government subsidies,[62] thus perpetuating a governance structure with minimal accounting and accountability.

Leadership

Seán MacBride's strategy for a global NGO movement that enlisted the IADL in challenging both East and West was remarkably bold and partly successful. His fervor for nuclear disarmament exceeded the

ICJ's scope. The Secretary-General's ambitions for a large membership also conflicted with the leaders' determination to preserve the organization as an exclusive elite. After leaving the ICJ, MacBride's personal star continued to rise with award of the Nobel Peace Prize in 1974 and the Lenin Prize in 1976. He became U.N. Commissioner for Namibia, head of a UNESCO study commission on world communications, president of the International Peace Bureau, and a major player in Amnesty International's remarkable growth.[63] He helped launch AI's mass membership development that rejected government funds, while the ICJ remained dependent on state support. Both organizations were nearly destroyed by a leadership crisis and allegations of intelligence service influence. After 1970, AI's membership strategy and leadership change spurred unprecedented growth, while the ICJ attempted to do more with less.[64] During an unparalleled twenty-year tenure as Secretary-General, Niall MacDermot redirected the ICJ into a highly regarded campaign for economic and political justice.

ICJ Reports on Violations, 1963–1970

Report on the Events in Panama. Investigating Committee appointed by the ICJ. Geneva: ICJ, 1964. 46 pp.

Report of the British Guiana Commission of Inquiry: Racial Problems in the Public Service. Geneva: ICJ, 1965. 199 pp.

The Dynamic Aspects of the Rule of Law in the Modern Age: Bangkok Conference Report. Geneva: ICJ, 1965. 192 pp.

The Rule of Law and Human Rights: Principles and Definitions. Geneva: ICJ, 1966. 83 pp.

South West Africa: The Court's Judgment. Geneva: ICJ, 1966. (Engl./Fr./Sp.).

Apartheid in South Africa and South West Africa. Geneva: ICJ, 1967. 29 pp. (Engl./Fr.)

Erosion of the Rule of Law in South Africa. Geneva: ICJ, 1968. 66 pp.

Part IV
1970–1990: Elite Advocates for Economic and Social Justice

Chapter 7
Mobilizing Advocates for Development

> The enjoyment of the totality of human rights calls for the organisation and mobilisation of the poor in developing countries for self-reliant development. . . . Development should be understood as a process designed progressively to create conditions in which every person can enjoy, exercise and utilise under the Rule of Law all his human rights, whether economic, social, cultural, civil or political.
>
> —From Conclusions to 1981 ICJ Conference on Development, Human Rights and the Rule of Law

Part IV Overview, 1970–1990

After extraordinary atrocities in the 1970s, the human rights movement came of age. Cambodia's killing fields, South African apartheid, disappearances in Argentina, and widespread torture pricked the global conscience. Human rights NGOs, sympathetic national officials, and international organizations responded together with apparent effect. First the U.S. Congress and then President Jimmy Carter insisted that aid recipients respect human rights. The United Nations began seriously investigating disappearances, arbitrary killings, and torture. A new American Court of Human Rights followed the European model by rendering judgments against defendant states. African governments ratified a human rights convention that established a regional commission. Economic sanctions punished South Africa. Hundreds of new national and international NGOs organized. Amnesty International attracted an unprecedented global membership.

Democratic change arrived first in Western Europe. Portugal,

Spain, and Greece removed their dictators in the 1970s. A decade later, Latin American juntas, Eastern European Marxists, and Asian despots fell. By 1990 dictators confronted broad human rights laws that limited domestic jurisdiction; international organizations, aroused citizens, and other governments demanded change. The Cold War, apartheid, colonialism, fascism, and communism were all historic relics. Yet unresolved problems remained. Economic justice was still a distant, improbable goal. Old barbarisms continued—war crimes, torture, communal massacres. China, Haiti, Indonesia, Iran, Iraq, and Israel withstood international pressure.

Human rights advocates developed promotion, standard-setting, and protection activities that parallel the public education, lobbying, and litigation of domestic interest groups. Part IV of this book evaluates how the ICJ performed those three functions during Niall MacDermot's twenty-year tenure as Secretary-General. For fourteen of those years, New York attorney William J. Butler chaired the Executive Committee. Chapter 7 examines promotion—in social science parlance, the political mobilization of groups and socialization of individuals for world citizenship and global leadership. Chapter 8 examines standard setting or lawmaking, and Chapter 9 assesses protection or enforcement activities. The final chapter in Part IV illustrates how the ICJ's Centre for the Independence of Judges and Lawyers (CIJL) performed all three functions.

New Direction for a Global Mission

Social Movements and Interest Group Entrepreneurs

Social movement theorists contend that injustice triggers mass protest. Outraged victims will spontaneously organize and demand radical change.[1] A major study on mobilizing American interest groups found to the contrary that social movements rarely begin as insurgencies by exploited victims against their oppressors. "Distress and anger over perceived injustice are a persistent fact of life among disadvantaged elements of any society and are only one of a number of factors that must exist before a social movement begins."[2] U.S. interest groups typically spread through "the intervention of sympathetic patrons who provide fresh resources and crucial assistance for entrepreneurial leaders at a critical time."[3]

Theories about international politics give conflicting perspectives of the human rights movement. Are idealists correct that mass demands for universal rights contribute to a global consciousness that could doom state sovereignty?[4] Realists forecast an enduring clash of civilizations unaffected by a futile campaign to propagate Englightenment values in non-Western societies.[5] Are the major battles of the twenty-first century more likely to feature world citizens' assaults on arbitrary state power or Islamic, Hindu, and Buddhist challenges to Western Christendom? From 1970 to 1990, the ICJ systematically cultivated non-Western offshoots, grass roots with uneven growth that put rival theories to the test.

Unlike a social movement, the ICJ mobilized new groups in the same way it had been founded—from the top down. ICJ leaders were elite entrepreneurs who used government, church, and foundation patrons to start third world organizations. The ICJ's longest serving Secretary-General was another dominant entrepreneur who came to embody the organization. Niall MacDermot was a committed internationalist who ardently championed both civil liberties and economic justice. As a youth in the 1930s MacDermot belonged to the "New Britain Group," which espoused utopian plans for European federation and syndicalist politics.[6] MacDermot completed legal study at Balliol College, Oxford, before enlisting for military duty during World War II. He won the Order of the British Empire for success as a Lieutenant-Colonel in charge of counterintelligence for the Normandy landings. After the war, MacDermot practiced law for eighteen years, joined the ICJ national section, sat as a part-time judge, and became a Labour member of Parliament. In 1964 his political career blossomed with appointment as Secretary to the Treasury and prospects of promotion to solicitor general.

Instead, MacDermot became the second casualty of a British intelligence agency (MI5) campaign against Labour prime minister Harold Wilson and associates on the political left. MI5 officers possibly bore a grudge against MacDermot for revealing in Parliament that Soviet spy Kim Philby had had an important intelligence position during the war. MacDermot's 1966 divorce and subsequent marriage in Geneva to a half-Soviet, half-Italian U.N. translator provided an opportunity for revenge. Notified of MI5 concerns about MacDermot's wife, Wilson removed him from the cabinet defense committee and shifted him from Treasury to become Minister of State for Planning and Land. His British political career crippled, MacDermot announced his resignation from the government for personal reasons. With poetic justice, a victim of British intelligence revived the ICJ after its nearly fatal CIA exposé and financial crisis.

A friendly journalist wrote an admirable personal description of the ICJ Secretary-General.

Niall MacDermot, Q.C., a former U.K. cabinet minister, served as ICJ Secretary-General from 1970 to 1990.

In many ways MacDermot was an anachronism, a throwback to an earlier era. Long after leaving Britain, he continued to look and act like a British cabinet minister with his mane of white hair, craggy features, and rich aristocratic delivery. He loved his British-made Rover car, the BBC World Service, and the London *Times*. His pinstriped suit stood out among the long hair and jeans worn by many other human rights lobbyists. He discouraged intimacy and could be cuttingly rude to people who thought they were his friends. But this only added to the impression of incorruptibility. As a former minister he owed no one any favors. No one talked down to MacDermot, and no one ignored him. Diplomats deferred to him and dreaded his rebukes.[7]

Financial exigency plagued MacDermot for his first five years as Secretary-General. He moved the Secretariat from its spacious offices to a low-rent, five-room residence, where he shared an office in a converted bedroom.[8] An Indian judge once paid a courtesy call at the cramped, suburban office and proposed that on a subsequent visit he would like to see the Secretariat building. First the Spanish and then the French editions of the *Review* were suspended. MacDermot found commercial publishers for major ICJ conference reports. The shrunken budget would not permit a "triennial" business meeting for six years. Full-time staff declined to seven, and law student interns assumed major responsibilities. The World Council of Churches paid the salary of one legal officer.

Few lawyers became patrons, contributors, or even dues-paying associate members. The ICJ's human rights gentry did not approach wealthy individuals for major contributions. Modest annual grants from a dozen European governments barely covered operating expenses. Renewal was never assured, and bankruptcy repeatedly threatened. Funds raised and contributed through the AAICJ declined to less than one-third of total revenues. Pressed to recognize the ICJ's urgent needs, Whitney Debevoise relinquished the Executive Committee chair to a more active New York attorney, William J. Butler.

A practicing lawyer, Butler had been counsel and executor for ACLU founder Roger Baldwin. As counsel for the International League for Human Rights, he had testified before the ECOSOC committee reviewing NGOs' consultative status. Butler had joined a fact-finding mission to Greece, argued an ACLU school prayer case before the U.S. Supreme Court, and was well connected to the U.S. State Department. MacDermot visited Butler's chalet in Zermatt and discussed the possibility of his becoming Executive Committee chairman. When Bonsal's regular Commission membership expired, Debevoise invited Butler to a 1975 Executive Committee meeting. He was formally recommended for election to the Commission and continued to attend Committee meetings. When Debevoise announced his resignation from the committee, he asked the members to co-opt Butler. The informal tradition of New York leadership continued under Butler from 1976 until his term on the Commission expired in 1990. Debevoise was elected vice president after his fourteen years as chairman.

Public and Private Patrons

By the late 1970s changes in Western development assistance and human rights policy generated additional public funding for the ICJ. Foreign aid officials in Western democracies had greater confidence in private NGOs than in multilateral development agencies or recipient governments. Soviet influence at the United Nations and corruption by local officials persuaded Organization for Economic Cooperation and Development (OECD) donors to enlist church groups and charities to disburse relief and development funds directly to grass-roots organizations.[9] Legal aid became part of development aid when donor states insisted that recipients respect human rights.[10]

The U.S. Congress pressed the Agency for International Development (AID) to maximize participation by local organizations in development projects and to use private charities to reach those most in need.[11] Butler secured a $100,000 AID grant for an ICJ study on states of emergency. Congressional liberals also made U.S. military and economic assistance conditional on respect for human rights. The Carter administration began making annual grants to the ICJ which Republican successors continued until 1983. The Reagan administration then sought to involve the ICJ in the National Endowment for Democracy. In Congressional testimony Secretary of State George Schultz mentioned the ICJ as a potential grant recipient. Third world staff denounced the U.S. effort to co-opt ICJ advocates into promoting opposition to pro-Soviet communist governments. MacDermot vigorously protested the unsolicited, unwelcome endorsement, and the ICJ received no politically tainted U.S. grants after 1983.

Grants from European governments were accepted without fear of interference. During the 1980s about twenty-five states made unrestricted grants that ranged between 30 and 37 percent of total annual income. The Ford Foundation's annual $100,000 grant was the next major income source.[12] Those subsidies for the ICJ general budget paid for staff salaries, rent, publications, and administrative expenses. Restricted grants went into a separate special-projects budget for missions, reports, conferences, training seminars, and studies. Special-project costs ranged from 24 to more than 50 percent of total expenses. European governments provided the major grants through development ministries and cofinancing of quasi-private foundations.

Sweden's socialist government allocated 1 percent of its gross national product for development aid. For popular causes such as human rights and democracy, Parliament mandated spending more than the foreign ministry requested.[13] Sweden's International Development Authority (SIDA) initially funded the ICJ's special project Legal Services in Rural Areas. The agency then paid half of the publications expenses and began providing a reliable base for the general budget. By 1990 SIDA provided over one-third of the ICJ's rapidly growing income.

Indirect government funding through quasi-private charities also increased rapidly. Several governments cofinanced foundations administered by Catholic, Protestant, and nondenominational boards—most importantly, NOVIB in the Netherlands and Evangelischen Kirche in Deutschland (EKD) in Germany. Their restricted grants supported relief, development, and human rights projects abroad. ICJ regional legal officers budgeted each project separately, securing multiple sponsors for programs in third world countries where free churches and the professional bar were at risk. Each special project grant included a share for administrative overhead in the general budget.[14] With the exception of Ford, private foundations contributed far less than those cofinanced by European governments. Butler obtained a small Rockefeller Brothers Fund start-up grant for an ICJ Centre for the Independence of Judges and Lawyers (CIJL). Table 7.1 displays ICJ income and expenses in 1990 after development and foundation grants had grown to exceed government subsidies for the general budget.

As funding gradually improved in the 1970s, MacDermot employed Secretariat legal officers from Latin America, Asia, and Africa, resumed publication of the *Review* in French and Spanish, and produced a quarterly ICJ *Newsletter*.[15] Local cosponsors helped organize regional seminars in English-speaking and Francophone Africa, the Caribbean, South America, the Middle East, and Asia. At each meeting the ICJ expanded its third world contacts, recruited members and staff, and organized regional jurists' organizations, new national

TABLE 7.1. Revenue Sources for ICJ Expenses, 1990.

Major donors	*Income (Swiss francs)*		*Expenditure categories*
General Budget			Salaries, rent, administration
15 Governments	447,757	(22%)	
Ford Foundation	326,900	(16%)	
SIDA	140,000	(7%)	Publications
Special Projects overhead	163,256	(8%)	
Other	60,187	(3%)	
Special Projects			Missions, seminars, studies
SIDA, NOVIB, EKD, others	913,179	(45%)	
Total (Swiss francs)	2,051,279	(100%)	

Adapted from tables in *International Human Rights Organizations: The Meaning of Their Work for Local Organizations.* Series of Program Evaluations DGIS/NOVIB #45 (The Hague: March 1992), 80 nn. 88, 89.

sections, and indigenous lawyers' groups. Special-project funding for conferences paid travel expenses for Commission members to hold triennial business meetings at The Hague in 1981, Nairobi in 1985, and Caracas in 1989.

Development and the Rule of Law

ICJ advocacy of development as a human right sought to bridge a major North-South divide. Both MacDermot and Butler viewed economic rights as fundamental. Some third world officials insist that human rights begin after breakfast. Famine, disease, and extreme poverty cause more death and suffering than torture or genocide. Southern leaders challenged Northern states to remove trade barriers and provide economic aid during the 1960s, the U.N. Development Decade. Frustrated by slow growth, third world governments next promoted a right to development. The Senegalese jurist who introduced the development proposal at the United Nations, Kéba Mbaye, was elected ICJ President.

The nonaligned movement also demanded a New International Economic Order (NIEO) that would require major reallocation of Northern wealth. Apologists for one-party states insisted that citizens must sacrifice political and civil liberties in order to realize swift economic growth. Western experts attributed slow growth to corrupt management of market economies and sought reallocation of power within third world oligarchies. Many private relief agencies disbursing government funds favored political restructuring that would threaten governing elites both North and South. As dependency theorists and development experts debated economic rights, the ICJ reexamined its rule of law principles.

Most Western lawyers' organizations and Amnesty International exclusively championed political rights. Since 1959 the ICJ had advocated a dynamic rule of law that included economic justice. In a major 1981 conference at The Hague, the ICJ connected development to the rule of law. The Dutch government, which hosted and partially funded the meeting, had also financed the 1976 RIO study on Reshaping the International Order.[16] MacDermot commissioned a conference working paper from Australian Philip Alston, a U.N. consultant on the right to development.[17] His views strongly shaped the ICJ conclusions, as well as a U.N. Secretariat report submitted by the Dutch director of the Human Rights Division, Theo van Boven.[18]

The ICJ repudiated claims that civil liberties must be sacrificed to permit economic growth. The jurists concluded that political and economic rights are inseparable and deserve equal emphasis. Development requires maximum participation by individuals able to associate freely and to speak out on policies affecting their future. Individuals should be the subject, not the object, of development, a human right inextricably linked with political liberty. Beyond third world self-reliance, "industrialised countries should cooperate with the developing nations to achieve a New International Economic Order with a more just and equitable distribution of the world's resources and wealth."[19] Progressive jurists must dismantle structural obstacles to development, such as militarization and export policies that enrich multinational corporations. Pergamon Press published the conference report, and the conclusions appeared in the U.N. monthly *Development Forum*.

The ICJ's support for a right to development appealed to German and Dutch church foundations and third world elites. Churches used Northern government grants to fund ICJ seminars in the South that promoted the interdependence rather than the incompatibility of political and economic rights. Without formally disavowing its prior critique of socialist legality, the ICJ sympathetically considered how African one-party states could protect human rights. ICJ seminars in Asia and Latin America challenged wealthy landholders and economic exploitation. MacDermot invited Muslim elites to examine how Islam respected human rights. Glasnost led to dialogue with Soviet jurists.

Proselytizing in All Regions

Sub-Saharan Africa

MacDermot's first major regional conference departed significantly from the multiparty Western parliamentary model celebrated in the ICJ's early Congresses. An 1976 East and Central African ICJ conference promoted "Human Rights in a One Party State." After their independence, Tanzanian and Zambian one-party democracies had experimented with contested elections within the party and professed to respect the independent bench and bar. The ICJ conference report included working papers and speeches by party officials endorsing preventive detention during emergencies, political education, and party direction of the executive, legislature, and judiciary. MacDermot's introduction noted the importance of "changing circumstances" and "the new political philosophy and system."[20]

The report's conclusions satisfied neither Zambia's President Kaunda nor the Commission members who attended the 1977 triennial business meeting in Vienna. Commissioners' objections were appended to the final report. Democratic purists complained that the one-party rule endorsed at Dar es Salaam violated ICJ ideals. For pragmatists, single-party constitutions with procedural guarantees for individual rights appeared preferable to the ubiquitous African military dictatorships. A compromise statement warned of the inherent dangers in both one-party systems and ineffective attempts to duplicate the Westminster model. The ICJ adopted eleven principles calling for electoral choice, freedom of association, an ombudsman, independent judges, and free expression. A London publisher issued the report and its non-judgmental recommendations for procedural fairness favorably impressed third world nationalists who resented Western attacks on newly independent governments. In follow-up visits to six countries, ICJ representatives encouraged ministers of justice, attorneys general, judges, and lawyers to implement the recommendations.

For twelve countries in Francophone West Africa, the Senegalese affiliate ASERJ (Association sénégalaise d'études et de recherches juridiques) cosponsored a 1978 regional conference that attracted forty-eight jurists. ICJ President Kéba Mbaye used the session to promote a third generation of solidarity rights, which included the right to development, peace, a satisfactory environment, and a just economic order.[21] Mbaye's personal assistant, Adama Dieng, a Muslim, began his ascent to ICJ Secretary-General at the meeting. After training in law at Dakar University, Dieng worked as an administrative officer and registrar in the Senegalese courts. He also assisted Mbaye in drafting a proposed African Charter on Human and Peoples' Rights. Dieng completed several research projects on racism as a UNESCO consultant and was a legal columnist for a daily newspaper. After earning a diploma at the Research Center of The Hague Academy of International Law, he taught a course on journalism at the Institute of Human Rights in Strasbourg. MacDermot asked the Senegalese expert on the U.N. Sub-Commission to recommend an African legal officer, and Dieng joined the ICJ Secretariat in 1982.

Dieng managed a new ICJ program to introduce in Africa the type of legal services in rural areas pioneered in Asia and Latin America. The ICJ assisted grass-roots development organizations trusted in rural areas to train paralegals. Litigation would be a last resort. Paralegals from villages, development organizations, or universities would work for legal reform and only involve urban lawyers as needed. Between 1983 and 1990 the ICJ sponsored seven training and follow-up sessions for paralegals in both French- and English-speaking Africa.[22] (The following chapters detail the ICJ's 1985 Nairobi conference on the African Charter and CIJL seminars on the Independence of the Judiciary.)

From Africa's legal elite, the ICJ elected eleven members in a

Left to right: William Butler of New York, Executive Committee chairman from 1976 to 1990; Kéba Mbaye, former President, Supreme Court of Senegal, Judge of the International Court of Justice, and ICJ President from 1977 to 1985; and T. O. Elias of Nigeria, an ICJ member and President of the International Court of Justice, spoke at the ICJ's 1986 Nairobi meeting to promote the African Charter on Human and Peoples' Rights.

twenty-year period, including Supreme Court presidents Kéba Mbaye of Senegal and T. O. Elias of Nigeria. Mbaye led the ICJ as its President from 1977 to 1985, campaigning for the right to development and the African Charter. Highly regarded at the United Nations, Mbaye was elected chairman of the Human Rights Commission. He and Elias organized an African Association of International Law for research on decolonization, development, human rights, and humanitarian law. Both won election to the International Court of Justice. ICJ members Rajsoomer Lallah and Amos Wako were elected to the U.N. Human Rights Committee.[23]

Wako came to ICJ notice through his efforts to organize a regional lawyers' organization as the first secretary-general of the Inter-African Union of Lawyers. He served on the Committee of Experts and as Kenya's delegate to the OAU ministerial meeting to draft the African Charter. Following election to the ICJ, he became special rapporteur on summary and arbitrary executions for the U.N. Human Rights Commission, a member of the U.N. Human Rights Committee, and the U.N. Secretary-General's personal envoy to Indonesia after a massacre in East Timor. He was the first African member on the ICJ's Executive Committee.

Human rights advocates have publicly asked whether Wako became a "fallen angel."[24] Opposition lawyers in Kenya learned that he resisted ICJ intervention on behalf of a detained editor who advocated multiparty elections.[25] President Daniel arap Moi continued repressive measures to preserve one-party rule, but Wako became his attorney general in 1991. In order to avoid potential conflicts, Wako suspended his ICJ membership under a Statute amendment applied during his tenure as a government minister. Promising reforms, Wako released political detainees, lifted a ban on the *Nairobi Law Monthly*, and secured ratification of the African Charter on Human and Peoples' Rights. He also supported a constitutional amendment requiring counsel for human rights defendants.[26] Only after Western aid donors cut off assistance did Moi allow multiparty elections, which he won in December 1992. Critics complain that Wako has manipulated law to protect an undemocratic regime and his own power.[27] If so, his career perversely reveals that leadership in the international human rights movement now confers a status coveted by ambitious politicians.

Wako was never active in the ICJ's Kenya national section. That group held sporadic meetings and retained its first staff in 1992, when younger lawyers began to challenge one-party rule. At a 1991 seminar organized by the section, an old-guard Kenya African National Union (KANU) minority approvingly cited the ICJ report on *Human Rights in a One-Party State*.[28] Kenya's notoriously undemocratic single party routinely violated human rights, and the majority pressed for a multiparty system. U.S. AID funded a major election project in 1992 that employed eighteen thousand poll watchers. The other six registered African affiliates did not send representatives to the ICJ's business meetings, notify the Geneva Secretariat of activities, or provide requested information.

Middle East and North Africa

Religious doctrine bedevils human rights advocates in the Middle East. Saudi Arabia did not support the Universal Declaration of Human Rights, and the Organization of Islamic Countries has proposed a regional code more consistent with Koranic law. The IADL organized widely in the region with anticolonial zeal. The ICJ recruited few members from Arab countries, and none ever played prominent roles in the organization. Israeli Supreme Court judge Haim Cohn was an early member.

The Egyptian member was law professor Boutros Boutros-Ghali, a Coptic Christian whose wife is Jewish. At that time the ICJ had no restriction on cabinet ministers serving as members during their period of government service, and several did so. After Boutros-Ghali became Egypt's minister of state for foreign affairs in 1981, the statute was amended. Thereafter, the Executive Committee on its own initiative or at a member's request could hold Commission membership in abeyance until the official position was relinquished.[29] However much the ICJ might be enhanced by gaining a U.N. Secretary-General as a member, there is no prospect that Boutros-Ghali would resume his affiliation.

To bridge the cultural divide, MacDermot organized a regional conference on "Human Rights in Islam." Kuwait University and the Arab Lawyers Union cosponsored a 1980 conference attended by sixty scholars and lawyers from twenty-six predominantly Islamic countries. Instead of challenging current government practice, MacDermot encouraged general debate on how Islamic law promoted justice. Commission member A. K. Brohi, Pakistan's former minister of law and religious affairs, delivered the keynote address. Free of Western commentary or judgment, the Muslim participants discussed human rights principles in the Koran and Shari'a.[30] One participant, Kuwait's Dean of the Faculty of Law and Shari'a, became one of the first female members but was never active.

MacDermot's U.N. interventions condemning Israeli violations of Palestinian rights won more converts. Unlike other Western NGOs, the ICJ had no dominant Jewish leaders and frequently denounced Israel. A Palestinian group in the Occupied West Bank, "Law in the Service of Man," applied to become an ICJ affiliate. A Ramallah barrister approached MacDermot for assistance in publishing a carefully documented study showing how Palestinians in the occupied territories were subject to secret orders enforced by military courts. The British-trained activists demonstrated convincingly that lawyers appearing in court had no prior knowledge of the applicable rules. MacDermot was outraged at the practice and impressed that the highly professional non-Muslim lawyers were not fronting for the PLO. "Law in the Service of Man" registered as a corporation to avoid government regulations for charitable societies. The ICJ accepted an application for affiliate status separate from the inactive Israeli national section nominally headed by Haim Cohn.

A Kuwaiti donor funded ICJ publication of the affiliate study entitled *The West Bank and the Rule of Law*. National sections translated the report into five languages, giving the new affiliate legitimacy and exposure in Europe. The U.N. Human Rights Division purchased five hundred copies for a Special Committee report to the General Assembly; foreign missions in Geneva made bulk purchases. "Law in the Service of Man" took the name Al Haq and received financial support from OXFAM, ICCO, the Ford Foundation, and church groups. Its offices provided the only public law library in the West Bank, its lawyers took victim affidavits, and its publications systematically exposed Israeli human rights violations.[31] The organization refused all contributions from Arabs and Israelis and limited any single source to 20 percent of the budget.[32] The group became the largest ICJ affiliate, with three times the staff of the Geneva Secretariat. In 1988 the Gaza Centre for Peace and Law affiliated. The Israeli national section discontinued its limited operations, and Jewish activists there founded new human rights groups. A Tunisian group was the ICJ's only other affiliate in a region where governments severely restricted both NGOs and Western influence.

Asia

In a diverse region of Hindus, Muslims, and Buddhists, many ICJ activists were Parsis, Christians, and women disadvantaged by dominant religions. Legal officer Daniel Ravindran of India began serving India's poor while still a law student. As a member of the All India Catholic University Federation, he taught school dropouts in the slums. After joining the Bar Council he provided legal aid to rural farmers from 1977 until 1981. To gain international experience, he contacted the University of Minnesota human rights intern program. Based on Ravindran's outstanding resumé, MacDermot hired him for a Southeast Asia regional seminar and Geneva internship, which led to a permanent appointment. Fali Nariman, a Parsi, was elected to the ICJ and its Executive Committee after resigning as India's solicitor general when Indira Gandhi proclaimed a state of emergency.

Most Asian jurists recruited as ICJ members had high status. T. S. Fernando, ICJ President from 1966 to 1977, was president of the Ceylon Court of Appeal and a former attorney general and solicitor general. Sir Guy Powles of New Zealand and Sir Moti Tikaram of Fiji each served as an ombudsman. Cooperation with Fiji's unconstitutional regime upset Tikaram's reelection to the ICJ after an initial five-year term. At first Tikaram protested a military coup, but he then replaced on the bench independent judges removed for defending the constitution. The ICJ rejected Tikaram's explanation that his appointment could ameliorate an unjust situation. Tikaram attended his final Commission meeting in 1989 when the ICJ protested the dismissal of Malaysian judges who had remained faithful to the rule of law.

Several new women members from Asia breached the all-male bastion.[33] Former law professor and Dean Mrs. Tai-Young Lee of South Korea was elected vice president. As founder and director of the Korean Legal Aid Center for Family Relations, she actively campaigned on behalf of "comfort" women enslaved by Japanese troops during World War II. A Muslim woman from Indonesia, Nana Moeljadi, became an administrative mainstay in the Geneva Secretariat.

Australian judge Michael Kirby inherited from his compatriot St. John the gadfly member role, advocated democratizing ICJ governance, and was elected to the Executive Committee. From the bench he promoted domestic application of international human rights norms. The large Australian national section initiated missions to regional trouble spots, occasionally without consulting MacDermot. After one embarrassing incident, MacDermot made clear the Australian section did not speak for the ICJ and pressed the group to apologize for a misstatement.

About ten other national sections and affiliates in Asia were considerably weaker. The predominantly Catholic Philippines offered more fertile ground than Islamic Indonesia, which sought to block Dutch aid for local NGOs. In three countries studied by NOVIB, local activists complained of inadequate feedback and follow-up from the Geneva Secretariat.[34] Sri Lankans appreciated ICJ support when a presidential commission threatened citizen groups.[35] Weak ICJ sections and affiliates in India, Malaysia, and Nepal distributed ICJ publications and arranged occasional conferences.

British and American jurists dominated the ICJ's 1959 New Delhi Congress. The 1980s development seminars were of Asians, by Asians, and for Asians. A 1981 ICJ seminar on "Rural Development and Human Rights in South East Asia" brought forty participants from five Association of Southeast Asian Nations (ASEAN) countries to Malaysia. The ILO, FAO, UNESCO, and the Economic and Social Commission for Asia and the Pacific all sent representatives. The Dutch foreign ministry and foundations with ties to Indonesia and Catholic churches provided funding. The cosponsoring Consumers' Association of Penang rallied opposition to deforestation, powdered milk, tourist exploitation, and high-technology growth strategies based on production for export. Participants advocated the NIEO, a nuclear free zone, and international protection of the environment.[36]

The ICJ encouraged ASEAN civil rights lawyers to create a Regional Council on Human Rights in Asia (RCHRA). ICJ members Roberto Concepción of the Philippines and Thiam-Hien Yap of Indonesia were among the twelve founders from five countries.[37] The first RCHRA General Assembly issued a strongly worded "Declaration of the Basic Duties of ASEAN Peoples and Governments," which was submitted to the ASEAN Secretariat. After attending the second annual RCHRA General Assembly, Ravindran published the declaration in the ICJ *Newsletter*.[38] With Ford Foundation support, RCHRA members and staff in the Philippines lobbied for ratification of the international covenants, promoted law reform, worked to free political prisoners, and obtained U.N. consultative status.

A 1982 seminar in Lucknow, India, launched a second ICJ regional enterprise, the South Asian Association for the Right to Development (SAARD). The cosponsoring Human Rights Institute hosted forty participants from five countries and published seminar papers advocating third world development perspectives.[39] Participation by Fali Nariman, a highly respected New Delhi lawyer and former solicitor general of India, revealed the paradox of ICJ elites promoting rights for the oppressed. Seminar advocates for the Asian masses rebuked lawyers who sold their services to dominant groups. The keynote speaker warned against energy-dependent agricultural systems and heavy petrochemical-based inputs for productivity. Two years later the Bhopal chemical plant disaster took twenty-five hundred lives, and the Indian government sued Union Carbide for damages. Nariman, a member of the ICJ Executive Committee, successfully defended the U.S. corporation; to the dismay of critics, a negotiated settlement provided only $450,000 for compensation.[40]

At a SAARD follow-up conference in Nepal, Ravindran struggled to make the organization an agent of change for India's untouchables and bonded laborers throughout the region. SAARD adopted a plan of action, but the organization failed to take root. The ICJ expanded its own promotion of legal services in rural areas, with Ravindran organizing twelve training seminars for paralegals in six Asian countries.[41] He edited a handbook that local groups translated for use in the Philippines and India. NGO populists mobilized rural activists to challenge agribusiness, corrupt public officials, and postcolonial legal systems that preserved vast wealth disparities.

> [Pathologies] are endemic in the legal systems of most developing countries. Our legal systems are both alien and alienating to our masses. . . . Access to legal process is usually restricted and available often only through the intermediary of lawyers operating in what is undoubtedly a "disabling" profession. . . . Our laws and legal institutions seem to have been developed to be geared to the needs and interests of the rich, the powerful, the transna-

tionals. . . . The cumulative effect of these pathologies has made our legal systems an instrument for the production and reproduction of exclusion, dependency, impoverishment and evasion of accountability. . . . [W]e must strive for an "alternative" conception of law—law for a society whose vision reaffirms self-reliance, participation, endogeny, redistribution of resources and power, and development, above all else, of the human being.[42]

The ICJ promoted a new breed of lawyers to work with social action groups against centralized development projects that oppressed the poor.[43]

Latin America

At times ICJ affiliates in predominantly Catholic Latin American countries outnumbered those in Western Europe, although many were organizational shells without substance. MacDermot recruited Alejandro Artucio as Latin American legal officer. Artucio, a Uruguayan defense lawyer, had been imprisoned and tortured by the junta after representing Tupomaro guerrillas. For eleven months of incommunicado detention he experienced the military's most refined skills—near suffocation in tubs of water, beatings, and days with his head in a hood. Released with head shaved, he was placed on a plane to Paris by a squad of soldiers armed with machine guns. In 1974 MacDermot offered him work, and the World Council of Churches provided his initial salary.

The ICJ's first development seminar in Barbados, though intellectually stimulating, failed to launch the desired Caribbean regional organization.[44] With the Latin American Council for Law and Development, the ICJ arranged a 1979 seminar in Bogotá, Colombia on Human Rights in the Rural Areas of the Andes Region. Sixty-one professors, advocates, academics, unionists, and peasant and Indian leaders from six countries attended. In a rare display of assertiveness, indigenous representatives spoke forcefully of their needs. The participants concluded that repression of civil and political rights is the cause of economic failure. They called for greater popular participation in agricultural and development policies and advocated agrarian reform, labor legislation, Indian rights, and a regional jurists' association.[45]

MacDermot then invited one leading jurist from each country to be a founding member of the Andean Commission of Jurists (ACJ); he arranged for a Colombian who had worked in the ICJ Secretariat to become ACJ secretary-general.[46] The ICJ obtained $180,000 from foundations and $10,000 from Norway to launch the ACJ. Colombia withheld approval of the ACJ Charter for months, and the secretary-general resigned before the organization was legally registered. MacDermot then contacted the Commission members to appoint a Peruvian national, Diego Garcia-Sayan, as executive secretary. Start-up funds deposited in Colombia that could not be remitted abroad were lost as the ACJ became the first international NGO recognized by Peru.

The Lima office quickly became fully independent, with its own foundation and support from Catholic and other European groups. The ACJ published a 323-page seminar report, "International Rules on Human Rights and Internal Law," and lobbied the Peruvian government on behalf of the disappeared in Argentina. The ACJ published a quarterly *Boletín* and a monthly *Andean Newsletter*, and obtained consultative status at the U.N. In 1987 the ACJ cosponsored a Lima seminar on legal services in rural areas of the Andean countries. Peasant and indigenous leaders, lawyers, and social science professionals from five Andean countries attended. After regularly attending ICJ business meetings, Diego Garcia-Sayan was elected to the ICJ and its Executive Committee in 1992. He also joined the U.N. Commission on Human Rights Working Group on Disappearances.

Andrés Aguilar Mawdsley, Venezuela's U.N. ambassador, succeeded Mbaye as ICJ President from 1985 to 1991 and, like his predecessor, was elected to the International Court of Justice. As president of the Inter-American Commission on Human Rights, Aguilar was credited with effectively pressing Argentina's junta to stop the disappearances. With U.N. funding for a conference on an independent judiciary, he hosted the ICJ's 1989 triennial meeting in Caracas. After his election to the ICJ, Guyana's attorney general and minister of state, Shridath S. Ramphal, became secretary-general of the Commonwealth Secretariat.[47]

It was difficult to recruit and hold members from countries under military rule. Alberto Ramón Real of Uruguay resigned to avoid military retribution for the ICJ's attack on his government. Former vice president Osvaldo Illanes Benítez resigned and protested that MacDermot's negative reports on Chile were inaccurate. Chilean professor Alfredo Etcheberry was elected in his place and joined the Executive Committee.

The North

The well-advanced ICJ network in the North produced a growing pool of national section activists and prospective leaders. European Executive Committee members included P. J. G. Kapteyn, councilor of state for the Netherlands; Rudolf Machacek, member of Austria's

Constitutional Court; Louis Joxe, ambassador of France and minister of state; Christian Tomuschat, professor of International Law, Bonn; and Gerald Gardiner, former Lord Chancellor of England. Paul Sieghart of "Justice" frequently attended committee meetings as an alternate but was never elected to the ICJ. Two members of the European Human Rights Commission were elected: Michael A. Triantafyllides, president of the Supreme Court of Cyprus, and Norwegian professor Torkel Opsahl. Former prime minister of France Edgar Faure was unanimously elected in 1971. Former Secretaries-General Marsh and Lalive were named Honorary Members.

In 1987 and 1988 three women succeeded such elder statesmen as John Humphrey, former director of the U.N. Human Rights Division. Claire L'Heureux-Dube was a Canadian Supreme Court judge. Nicole Questiaux was a member of the Council of State of France, former minister of state, and an expert on the U.N. Sub-Commission on Prevention of Discrimination and Protection of Minorities. Ireland's feminist senator Mary Robinson complained at the triennial meeting in Caracas about the underrepresentation of women. She suspended her membership when elected as Ireland's president.

The European sections conducted extensive activities at both the national and regional level without assistance from Geneva.[48] Section representatives regularly attended triennial ICJ meetings and renewed requests for closer collaboration. MacDermot and Butler both resisted staff and membership pressures for closer integration of local affiliates and the Geneva Secretariat. They did not seek their financial support and did not want responsibility for settling local problems. Section leaders elected to the Commission or hired as staff qualified on their individual merits and did not represent national groups. New sections might organize with a minimal start-up grant, but then MacDermot insisted on full autonomy. Independent ICJ sections thus had less difficulty organizing under local law than did new AI groups, which registered as branches of the international secretariat in London.

In the late 1970s ICJ executive secretary Hans Thoolen, of the Netherlands, urged MacDermot to seize a unique opportunity for growth resulting from unprecedented public support for human rights. As new NGOs grew dramatically, Britain's former secretary to the treasurer cautiously kept the ICJ from bankruptcy with a modest staff and budget. In the United States, Bill Butler did not recruit new AAICJ members or encourage new lawyers' groups to affiliate. Former ICJ interns joined the new International Human Rights Law Group in Washington, the New York Lawyers Committee for Human Rights, and the Minnesota Lawyers International Human Rights

Committee. All sought grants from the same U.S. foundations and appealed to the same bar constituency. Amnesty International USA organized a legal support network with urban chapters throughout the country. If the growing human rights bar in the United States had affiliated with the ICJ, Americans would undoubtedly have resumed their domination of the organization.

In Europe, MacDermot helped launch several new organizations. Thoolen served on a planning committee that followed the ICJ model in establishing the International Commission of Health Professionals for Health and Human Rights based in Geneva.[49] Lawyers organized new national sections in the new democracies, first in Spain and Portugal, then in South Africa, Hungary, and Poland. Spain's former ombudsman, Professor Don Joaquin Ruiz-Gimenez was elected as an ICJ member and Vice President. Young activist lawyers in the Netherlands organized a new section, Nederlands Juristen Comité vor den Mensenrechten (NJCM), which took major initiatives on European issues. Thoolen helped initiate the Human Rights International Documentation System (HURIDOCS) to assist NGOs in handling and exchanging information. He also campaigned at the Council of Europe, which awarded the ICJ its first Human Rights Prize in 1981. In the Netherlands the ICJ received the Wateler Peace Prize and the Erasmus Prize.

Thirty years after beginning its war on socialist legality, the ICJ welcomed opportunities for dialogue with Soviet jurists. The Nixon-Brezhnev experiment with détente encouraged people-to-people and professional-to-professional exchanges, including lawyers. In 1972 fifty members of the Washington, D.C. Bar Association visited Moscow, and seven observed a civil trial. The USSR honored former ICJ Secretary-General MacBride with the Lenin Peace Prize, and MacDermot made valuable official contacts during a 1974 holiday in Moscow. The Austrian section arranged for joint meetings with Eastern European counterparts. A conference on children's rights in Poland, cosponsored with the IADL, was the ICJ's first friendly appearance behind the Iron Curtain.

In 1984 the Association of Soviet Lawyers (ASL) initiated formal exchange arrangements with both the ICJ and the American Bar Association (ABA). The ASL hosted twenty ICJ representatives in Moscow for a discussion on nuclear weapons, human rights internal legislation, and judicial procedure. Practicing attorneys constituted about half of the ICJ representatives, while academics dominated the Soviet delegation. ICJ members unsuccessfully sought permission to observe prosecutions involving slander against the state, to visit psychiatric hospitals, and to obtain statistics on trials.

In October 1986 the ICJ reciprocated by hosting a session for the ASL in Madrid that took up free expression, economic rights, and human rights and peace. The participants did not mention specific violations or seek relief for particular individuals. Law as a means for securing international peace remained a paramount concern for the Soviet participants. The Soviets eschewed rhetoric about bourgeois imperialism and requested that the summary report not refer to "socialist" legality or "socialist" justice. By the time the ASL-ICJ representatives met for the last time in 1989, Gorbachev's constitutional revolution had brought about *pravovoye gosudarstvo*—a state based on law.[50] The rule of law had still not arrived, but the communist empire soon crumbled. By 1990, new entrepreneurs and patrons were needed to mobilize advocates for development in Northern Asia and Eastern Europe.

Summary

During the two decades when human rights activism mushroomed, the ICJ switched government patrons, recruited leading Southern jurists, launched new affiliates, and revitalized its membership. Amendments to the Statute enlarged the Executive Committee from five to seven and reduced the length of members' terms. Early members with more than twenty years' service were given honorary status; new members were elected to five-year renewable terms up to fifteen years. Table 7.2 lists ICJ leaders and new members after 1970.

ICJ tactics for spreading human rights values included seminars, conferences, lectures, publications, and local organizing. In regional seminars the ICJ proclaimed development as a basic right, recruited third world lawyers, and launched new groups. In conferences with jurists from Islamic countries, African one-party states, and the Soviet Union, the ICJ proselytized among non-Western elites. ICJ experts preached rule of law gospel in lectures to professional groups, at U.N. human rights seminars and NGO conferences, in publications, and in private meetings with public officials. Sweden's development agency funded technical assistance through ICJ training seminars on legal services in rural areas. A practitioner's manual was developed to help paralegals represent third world peasants. ICJ studies on asylum, privacy, and states of emergency promoted international protection for basic civil liberties.

The ICJ launched new NGOs of local advocates for universal human rights and also recruited elite members who were or who became leaders of international organizations. Individual recruits to the global movement left their home countries with varying degrees of

TABLE 7.2. ICJ Officers, Members, and Meetings, 1970–1990.

Secretariat (109 Route de Chêne, Chêne Bougeries, Geneva 1972–1992)
Secretary-General, Niall MacDermot, Dec. 1, 1970–June 1990
Executive Secretary, Hans Thoolen, 1977–1981
Adama Dieng, 1990

Executive Committee

1977–1981	*1985–1989*
William J. Butler, U.S., Chairman	W. J. Butler, U.S., Chairman
Per T. Federspiel, Denmark	A. Etcheberry, Chile
Heleno Claudio Fragoso, Brazil	P. J. Kapteyn, Netherlands
Gerald Gardiner, U.K.	R. Machacek, Austria
Louis Joxe, France	Fali Nariman, India
Michael A. Triantafyllides, Cyprus	C. Tomuschat, Germany
John Thiam-Hien Yap, Indonesia	Amos Wako, Kenya

Presidents
Kéba Mbaye, Senegal, 1977–1985
Andres Aguilar, Venezuela, 1985–1991

New Members

Year elected		*Final year*
1971	Rt. Hon. Lord Gerald Gardiner, U.K., Executive Committee	1986[a]
	Seán MacBride, Ireland	1986[a]
	John Thiam-Hien Yap, Indonesia, Executive Committee	1986[a]
	Edgar Faure, France, Executive Committee, 1972–1976	1976
	Godfrey L. Binaisa, Uganda (U.S.)	1981
	Joel Carlson, South Africa (U.S.)	1981
1972	Allah-Bakhash K. Brohi, Pakistan	1982
	Haim Cohn, Israel	1987[a]
	John D. Humphrey, Canada, Vice President, 1981–1987	1987[a]
	Kéba Mbaye, Senegal, President, 1977–1985	1987[a]
1973	Boutros Boutros-Ghali, Egypt	1981[d]
	Torkel Opsahl, Norway	1988[a]
	Heleno Claudio Fragoso, Brazil, Vice President, 1981	1984[c]
	Alberto Ramón Real, Uruguay	1974[b]
1974	Alphonse Boni, Ivory Coast	1985
	Mrs. Ngo Ba Thanh, Vietnam	1989
	Kwamena Bentsi-Enchill	1974[c]
1975	Alfredo Etcheberry, Chile, Executive Committee, 1985–1989	1990[a]

TABLE 7.2. (*continued*)

New Members

Year elected		*Final year*
	William Butler, U.S., Executive Committee Chairman, 1976–1990	1990[a]
	Sir Guy Powles, New Zealand	1990[a]
1976	P.J. Kapteyn, Netherlands, Executive Committee, 1978–1991	1991[a]
	Rudolf Machacek, Austria, Executive Committee, 1985–1989	1991[a]
	Roberto Concepción, Philippines, Vice President, 1981	1986
	Louis Joxe, France, Executive Committee, 1976–	1986[a]
	Miguel Lleras Pizarro, Colombia, Vice President	1980
	Taslim O. Elias, Nigeria	1990[a]
1977	P. Telford Georges, Bahamas, Barbados, West Indies	1992
1979	Andres Aguilar Mawdsley, Venezuela, President, 1985–1991	
	François-Xavier Mbouyom, Cameroon	
	Don Joaquin Ruiz-Gimenez, Spain, President, 1992–1994	
1981	Miss Kinuko Kubota, Japan	1986[c]
	Mrs. Tai-Yung Lee, South Korea, Vice President, 1985–1994	
	Amos Wako, Kenya, Executive Committee, 1985–1991	1991[d]
	Badria Al-Awadhi, Kuwait	1991
	Guillermo Figallo, Peru	1991
	Tun Mohamed Suffian, Malaysia	1986[a]
	Rahsoomer Lallah, Mauritius	
	Christian Tomuschat, Germany, Executive Committee, 1985–	
1982	Fali Nariman, India Executive Committee, 1985	
	Juma Reginal Sawaya Mawalla, Tanzania	
1983	Chitti Tingsabadh, Thailand	
1984	Michael Kirby, Australia, Executive Committee Chairman, 1992	
	Augusto Conte-MacDonnell, Argentina	1990
	Sir Moti Tikaram, Fiji	1989
	Raul F. Cardena, Mexico	1989
1987	Henry de Boulay Forde, Barbados	1992
	Adela Reta Sosa Diaz, Uruguay	1992
	Nicole Questiaux, France	1992
	Senator Mary Robinson, Ireland	1990[d]
	Lord Scarman, U.K.	1992
	Dorab Patel, Pakistan	

TABLE 7.2. (*continued*)

New Members

Year elected		*Final year*
1988	Desmond Fernando, Sri Lanka, Executive Committee, 1992	
	Lennart Groll, Sweden, Vice President, 1992	
	Madame Justice Claire L'Heureux-Dube, Quebec, Vice President	1991[b]
	Kofi Kumado, Ghana, Executive Committee, 1992	
	Yuichi Takano, Japan	
1989	Dalmo de Abreu Dallari, Brazil, Executive Committee, 1992	
Meetings		
	Aspen, 1971	
	Vienna, 1977	
	The Hague, 1981	
	Nairobi, 1985	
	Caracas, 1989	

[a] Year elected honorary member.
[b] Resigned.
[c] Deceased.
[d] Membership suspended after taking official post.

TABLE 7.3. ICJ Regional Contacts as of 1970 and 1990.

	ICJ members		*National sections*		*Executive Committee*		*Officers*	
Region	*1970*	*1990*	*1970*	*1990*	*1970*	*1990*	*1970*	*1990*
W. Europe	9	8	14	17	4	2		Vice President
Asia	8	7	13	11		2	President	Vice President
Middle East	1	1	2	2				
Africa	3	7	8	9		1		
S. America	5	7	15	13		1		President
N. America	4	2	2	2	1	1	Chairman	Chairman
Total	30	32	54	54	5	7		

commitment and understanding. Transnational contacts arranged by the ICJ socialized third world activists and elites to global norms and weakened national loyalties. New affiliates replaced ICJ national sections founded in the 1950s which had become dormant. A summary tally of members and national sections in Table 7.3 reveals increased third world representation but little absolute growth.

Conclusions

Funding

Remarkably, the NGO honored for challenging state sovereignty elected public officials as members and depended heavily on government support. Other NGOs may confirm social movement theories about grass-roots protest. The ICJ developed as a political interest group with state patrons, following a corporatist approach. Why did Northern governments fund, and Southern governments allow, ICJ programs that advocated subversive political and economic ideas? Industrialized states with multinational corporations funded development experts who bit the hand providing grants. Community activists in totalitarian states organized national and regional groups to change unjust systems. At a Swedish-funded seminar in Indonesia, for example, the ICJ might inveigh against European arms sales and organize local activists to demand land reform.

A major study of North Atlantic foreign aid found that governments collaborated with seemingly hostile private organizations because the benefits outweighed the costs.[51] Northern donors want cost-effective aid programs that circumvent corrupt public officials. Direct foreign aid to local organizations would violate national sovereignty. NGOs such as the ICJ can reduce bureaucratic overhead, avoid legal obstacles, and directly promote local self-help. For their part, third world governments too poor to provide rural legal aid prefer NGO technical assistance over government grants that have more strings attached. Radical community activists may organize as a result, but such reform groups might harness passions that would otherwise ignite revolutionary movements.

With its reputable cadre of establishment figures, the ICJ enjoyed a special entrée with many governments, churches, and foundations. The secretary for human rights of EKD, a church foundation, was a member of the German national section. To an extent, the ICJ's individualist human rights doctrine offered ideological support for both North and South. The third world had a right to development and the North a duty to assist, as long as modernizing states allowed popular participation and respected human rights. Economic growth must be accompanied by political development.

That ICJ prescription for development enticed Western donors and some third world elites, even though the correlation between democratic institutions and economic growth has been uncertain at best. Totalitarian South Korea developed more wealth per capita and much higher literacy than democratic Portugal. Undemocratic ASEAN countries that violated human rights—Malaysia, Thailand, and Indonesia—had twice the per capita growth rates of countries in other regions; they enjoyed 7 to 9 percent real economic growth in 1991.[52] A growing middle class in Southeast Asia has now demanded the democratic reforms the ICJ proclaimed as prerequisites of development.

Socialization

The time for powerful democratic ideas appeared to arrive around 1990, and the ICJ was a small agent of transnational socialization. The organization took several hundred third world lawyers, judges, scholars, public officials, and community activists outside their own countries for meetings with people from other states. They received working papers, heard speakers, met U.N. and foundation officials, discussed human rights, and were urged to organize for action. ICJ staff conducted follow-up meetings and secured start-up funds for selected groups. Middle-class activists inspired by Western democratic ideals were exposed to radical economic demands by more populist groups in the movement. That cross-fertilization has had little impact on Western views of civil society and the state. MacDermot viewed ICJ promotional activities as "bread upon the waters." The scattered particles spawned minimal commitments to universal values, but could nurture future links across cultural fault lines. Alternately, fundamentalist religious movements in the third world could frustrate global integration by challenging human rights NGOs as alien agents of Westernization.

By educating members and staff, the ICJ socialized human rights advocates for democracy, modernization, and world citizenship. The organization enhanced idealists' commitment to service but also attracted opportunists seeking personal gain. Attendance at ICJ promotional activities and leadership in the organization were no guarantees of principled commitment to human rights. Conflicts of interest were unavoidable given the ICJ preference for established jurists with high government experience. On balance, the celebrated heroes far outnumber the few fallen angels.

Recruitment

After retirement, MacDermot reflected that his ICJ career had been far more rewarding than the limited experience of his bar-association and party colleagues in Britain.[53] His sympathetic understanding of non-Western political and economic conditions attracted to Geneva capable Secretariat staff from Uruguay, Senegal, India, and Indonesia. They left their third world homes to serve a transnational cause that transcended partisan or personal interests. Their enthusiasm influenced young interns from Argentina, Chile, Hong Kong, Bangladesh, and Sri Lanka. Underpaid staff made the greatest economic sacrifices and developed the strongest loyalty to transnational ideals. Few third world lawyers in Africa and Asia could sustain effective local organizations without Northern patrons. Christians educated in Western institutions became active recruits. Affiliates in South America and the Occupied Territories became highly respected independent organizations with staff, publications, and extensive programs.

The ICJ's prestige attracted well-known jurists to accept membership and propelled lesser known recruits into international leadership positions. Three third world members won election to the International Court of Justice, two members served on the European Commission of Human Rights, and one member each served on the Inter-American Commission, the U.N. Commission on Human Rights, its Working Group on Disappearances, and as U.N. Rapporteur on Summary and Arbitrary Executions. Other members and staff took leadership positions in the U.N. and Commonwealth Secretariats, the ILO, and the U.N. High Commissioner for Refugees.

The activists enlisted by the ICJ joined a global human rights network. With limited resources, the ICJ reached comparatively few individuals, and some of its own leaders have not always practiced what they preached. Its profound influence on others reveals why idealists conclude that a new transnational consciousness could result from the cumulative impact of many such groups mobilizing advocates for human rights.

ICJ Reports on Development

Human Rights and Development

Human Rights in a One-Party State. London: Search Press, 1978. 130 pp.

Human Rights and Development: Report of a Seminar on Human Rights and Their Promotion in the Caribbean. Bridgetown, Barbados: Cedar Press, 1978. 208 pp.

Le Développement et les Droits de l'Homme: Rapport d'un colloque africain francophone, a Dakar. Numéro Spécial de la Revue Sénégalaise de Droit, 255 pp.

Derechos Humanos en las Zonas Rurales, Bolivia, Colombia, Chile, Ecuador, Perú, Venezuela: Informe del seminario de la región andina, en Bogotá. Bogotá: Ediciones Internacionales, 1980.

Human Rights in Islam: Report of a Seminar Held in Kuwait, December 1980. Geneva: ICJ, 1982. 95 pp.

Development, Human Rights and the Rule of Law: Report of a Conference Held in The Hague on 27 April–1 May 1981. New York: Pergamon, 1981. 244 pp.

Rural Development and Human Rights in South East Asia: Report of a Seminar in Penang, December 1981. Penang, Malaysia: Consumers Association of Penang, 1982.

Rural Development and Human Rights in South Asia. Report of a Seminar held in Lucknow, India, December 1982. Bombay: Human Rights Institute, 1984.

The Erosion of the Rule of Law in Asia: Report of the Seminar held in Bangkok 18–22 December 1987. Christian Conference of Asia.

Legal Services in Rural Areas

Development and Legal Services in Africa. Report of 1983 Dakar Seminar with CODESRIA.

Legal Services in Rural Africa. Report of a Seminar at Limuru 1–4 October 1984. Geneva: ICJ, 1984. 84 pp.

Report of Seminars on Legal Services for the Rural Poor in South-East Asia (Jakarta) 11–16 January 1987 and South-Asia (Rajpipla) 27–31 December 1987. Geneva: 1988. 98 pp.

Paralegals in Rural Africa. Seminars in the Gambia, Banjul, November 1989, and Harare, Zimbabwe February 1990. Geneva: ICJ, 1991.

Les services juridiques en milieu rural (Libreville Seminar), 1989. 154 pp.

Asian Seminar on Paralegal Trainers. Puncak, Indonesia January 6–10, 1990. ICJ and Women's Communication and Information Centre. Kalyanamitra, Indonesia. 30 pp.

Report of ICJ's National Seminar on Paralegal Training for Women's Organizations, Bombay, September 24–26, 1991.

Chapter 8
Setting Standards and Procedures

> The United Nations Charter was proclaimed in the name of "We the Peoples." The principal decision-makers in the Organization are Governments . . . [which] in many instances cannot be considered as genuine representatives of the people. . . . The international law of human rights is a peoples' oriented law and it is only natural that the shaping of this law should be a process in which representative sectors of society participate. This is a logical requirement of democracy.
>
> —Theo van Boven[1]

Advocacy for international human rights law resembles the U.S. civil rights movement. Just as American civil rights leaders appealed for federal protection against segregationist states, so human rights groups lobbied for international protection against national governments. NAACP litigation forced school desegregation, and mass demonstrations prompted federal laws on employment discrimination, voting rights, and fair housing. International human rights NGOs neither have courts in which to litigate nor elected legislators to influence with votes and campaign contributions. Instead the ICJ used technical expertise and elite contacts to lobby public officials for limits on state power.

Just as civil rights leaders sought both new laws and institutions, human rights advocates campaigned for both standards and procedures. African-Americans demanded voting rights and federal registrars, laws against job discrimination, and an Equal Employment Opportunity Commission. Without a world court to hear individual grievances, the ICJ had even greater need to institute procedures for protecting rights. A U.N. Commissioner for Human Rights could have institutionalized procedures to challenge many different crimes against humanity. Instead the lawmaking U.N. Commission on Human Rights disregarded proper separation of powers and passed judgment on offending governments. Part-time implementation procedures proliferated with new human rights treaties. NGOs promoted many different rapporteurs, working groups, and committees on torture, disappearances, summary executions, arbitrary detention, and women's and children's rights. States consistently resisted meaningful enforcement mechanisms.

The U.N. Human Rights Committee and two regional commissions may have increased rather than satisfied demands for more effective institutions. The worst offenders remained beyond the law's reach, unwilling to ratify or comply with the comprehensive human rights treaties. Perhaps states could be persuaded to accept treaties limited to a single fundamental right. NGOs soon filled the legislative agenda with proposed norms and improved procedures on torture, religious liberty, prisoners of conscience, and the rights of women, children, and minorities. With minimal direction from members, staff largely determined the ICJ's legislative priorities: torture, disappearances, arbitrary detention, states of emergency, and the African Charter on Human and Peoples' Rights. Some third world jurists blocked ICJ support for an optional protocol to abolish the death penalty. Chapter 10, on the Centre for the Independence of Judges and Lawyers (CIJL), deals separately with ICJ drafted standards to assure an independent bench and bar.

Forum shopping in the United States leads civil rights groups to different state and federal courts or legislatures in search of sympathetic judges and friendly lawmakers. At the international level, the ICJ advanced its proposals through different U.N. agencies, European and Latin American regional institutions, and the Japanese Diet. U.N. Sub-Commission experts were so responsive that the Commission on Human Rights became the most frequented path to the U.N. General Assembly. An alternate route through Vienna involved the Congress on the Prevention of Crime and the Treatment of Offenders and its Committee on Crime Prevention and Control.

Governments that kidnap and torture do not ratify treaties that undercut their power. U.S. laws govern Alabama far more than U.N. treaties affect South Africa. Yet even outlaw governments that totally reject treaty restraints may not legally practice slavery and other crimes against humanity. The ICJ promoted new standards to make torture and disappearances universally proscribed crimes. When states would not approve legally binding conventions, the ICJ promoted declarations and principles that could later be invoked as customary international law.

Torture: U.N. and European Conventions

Amnesty International first aroused the international conscience about torture in 1973.[2] To promote action at the national level, the ICJ recommended amendments to the Standard Minimum Rules for the Treatment of Prisoners. MacDermot sought legal protection not merely for torture victims but for all detainees subjected to any type of mistreatment. At the Fifth U.N. Congress on the Prevention of Crime and Treatment of Offenders, the ICJ recommended twenty-seven principles to govern interrogation, administrative detainees, judicial control, legal advice, access by relatives, and remedies.[3] After the congress, MacDermot served on a committee that prepared a Declaration Against Torture, which was adopted by the General Assembly in 1975.[4]

In the following decade, the ICJ helped draft a U.N. torture convention, as well as an optional protocol and two regional treaties providing for outside visits to places of detention. The first goal was a global treaty making torture an international crime. Assisted by six experts at the Institute for International Penal Law (IAPL) in Siracusa, Italy, MacDermot drafted a convention for consideration by the U.N. Commission on Human Rights.[5] Sweden introduced its own draft torture convention. Both proposals were circulated to governments for comment, and the Swedish text became the basic draft for a Commission working group.

During six years of Commission deliberations, MacDermot collaborated with experts from AI, the ICRC, and the World Council of Churches to work for the strongest possible final text. As full participants in meetings of the Commission working group on torture, the highly respected NGO experts provided valued advice to the government negotiators. The ICJ and its NGO partners vigorously supported provisions giving all state parties universal jurisdiction to prosecute individual torturers. AI and the ICJ jointly proposed an amendment extending limited coverage to mistreatment that did not amount to torture.[6] The NGO group also wanted the new Committee Against Torture created by the convention to investigate and make "specific recommendations" to reporting governments. Soviet representatives opposed the threatened encroachment on national sovereignty. The final text only allows "general comments" on government reports[7] and expressly authorizes reservations denying the committee's authority to question governments about allegations.[8] The General Assembly approved the U.N. Convention Against Torture in 1984.[9]

Even before the convention was completed, MacDermot had drafted a supplemental protocol authorizing unannounced visits to detention centers. During the Commission's prolonged negotiation, the president of the Swiss Committee Against Torture (SCAT) asked MacDermot to join in writing an optional protocol modeled after the ICRC's prison visits.[10] The plan was designed to deter abuses so common in closed institutions by authorizing a Torture Committee to organize unannounced visits to places of detention. Unlike the ICRC procedures, experts could visit all places of detention, not just prisons, and would not need to negotiate in advance for government permission.[11] Costa Rica's ambassador to the Commission prematurely presented the protocol before the ICJ had obtained other cosponsors. MacDermot feared that debate on the optional protocol would delay approval of the torture convention, so the proposal for prison visits was deferred at the Commission.

Council of Europe officials then requested that the SCAT and the ICJ draft a regional torture convention providing for prison visits.[12] MacDermot took a calculated risk that the U.N. would still approve the optional protocol following adoption of similar measures in Europe. He drafted a working text for a European Committee for the Prevention of Torture and Inhuman, Degrading Treatment or Punishment. MacDermot made timely and effective use of ICJ consultative status with the Steering Committee on Human Rights of the European Council of Ministers.[13] At a confidential drafting session MacDermot, supported by several members, opposed efforts to limit the committee's authority.[14] The Parliamentary Assembly and Council of Ministers approved a final text in 1987.[15] The newly constituted torture committee makes four visits per year with two weeks' notice and one visit on two days' notice. Experts from Strasbourg make unaccompanied visits for up to two days. Britain, Denmark, and the Netherlands have published committee reports. After the Austrian government released information about a visit, the committee published its own findings.

The ICJ also lobbied, thus far without success, for a Draft American Convention on a System of Visits to Prisons. The ICJ and SCAT organized four preparatory meetings[16] and helped found the Committee of Experts for the Prevention of Torture in the Americas. That committee completed a text providing for a new monitoring mechanism separate from the existing Inter-American Commission on Human Rights. The OAS Secretary-General and legal adviser pointed out the difficulty of winning approval for a new mechanism. The ICJ committee began seeking government support but delayed submitting the draft text until after the OAS General Assembly had received a proposed convention on disappearances.[17] The U.N. Commission has now resumed consideration of an optional protocol for prison visits that would overlap the proposed Latin American regional procedure.

The widespread effort to outlaw torture convinced U.S. judges to recognize a prohibition under customary international law, enforceable without ratification of any convention. In two celebrated cases, torturers from Paraguay and Argentina in U.S. custody were found liable to their victims.[18] Yet one of the same judges dismissed tort claims for "disappearance," because that offense did not violate the law of nations.[19]

Disappearances: U.N. Working Group and Declaration

Initially, the ICJ lobbied for improved procedures to stop disappearances rather than for a new law making the offense a crime against humanity. Provisions of the universal declaration and international covenant guarantee liberty and prohibit arbitrary arrest, so state-instigated disappearances had already been outlawed. The failed campaign for a High Commissioner for Human Rights left the United Nations ill equipped to respond in emergencies. As one alternative, the Commission instituted a confidential communication procedure that enabled NGOs to present evidence of violations for screening by U.N. Sub-Commission experts.[20] In carefully documented written submissions, the ICJ and other NGOs had conclusively shown the Sub-Commission on Prevention of Discrimination and Protection of Minorities how Argentina's junta had caused eight thousand disappearances. The government's canny representative in Geneva used the 1503 confidential procedure to shield Argentina from public scrutiny.[21]

MacDermot repeatedly pressed the Commission to strengthen the 1503 procedure by conducting thorough investigations of offending governments or by publicizing their misconduct. By 1980 Chile was the only case brought out of confidential proceedings. The Commission appointed a five-member working group and then a single rapporteur to investigate disappearances and other offenses of the Pinochet regime. The ICJ drafted a statement signed by twenty-nine NGOs criticizing the inadequate 1503 procedures and prepared, but did not press, a resolution providing for reform.

Since it was politically difficult to target a single offending state for public investigation, the ICJ pressed the U.N. Sub-Commission to look at the problem of disappearances in all countries. At the Commission, MacDermot delegated an Argentinian exile as ICJ representative to present witness testimony of disappearances. Theo van Boven, the Dutch director of the U.N. Centre, met with mothers of the disappeared and strongly supported a more effective response.

Success came in 1980 when President Carter appointed as U.S. ambassador to the Commission the NGO head of the International League for Human Rights. The Western representatives began daily strategy meetings, and France proposed creation of a working group to investigate disappearances. As chairman of the Geneva NGO Special Committee on Human Rights, MacDermot hosted, with Canadian Ambassador Beaulne, an NGO information seminar on disappearances.[22] Government representatives from eighteen delegations to the Commission heard moving testimony from relatives of the disappeared. An Iraqi representative attended and unexpectedly became a key supporter. The ICJ presented detailed written reports on Argentina, the Philippines, El Salvador, and Uruguay. With AI and the International League, the ICJ circulated a statement on disappearances as a U.N. document.

None of the representatives negotiating a proposed resolution were ready to take the floor when the public session opened. NGOs had the unusual opportunity to speak first, and Artucio addressed the Commission in Spanish for the ICJ. Third world governments resisted Argentina's entreaties for solidarity. Senegal's representative, ICJ President Kéba Mbaye, actively promoted the novel thematic approach.

After rejecting last-ditch Latin American objections, the Commission created a five-member working group to receive complaints and to prepare nonaccusatory annual reports identifying the number of disappeared in different countries. The regionally balanced working group on disappearances created a primitive form of international habeas corpus. Creative members initiated an urgent action procedure, sending telegrams of inquiry to governments immediately after receiving a complaint. The U.N. human rights system had its first thematic approach that NGOs could enlist to publicize specific complaints against many different governments. In subsequent years, the Commission appointed theme rapporteurs on summary executions, torture, religious intolerance, and mercenaries. By 1990 many of the functions MacBride had envisioned for a single High Commissioner for Human Rights had been assigned to distinct working groups and theme rapporteurs.[23]

Argentina did not lose gracefully. Its representatives unsuccessfully attempted to revoke the ICJ's consultative status and successfully opposed van Boven's reappointment as director of the Centre for Human Rights. A joint statement by thirty-two NGOs protested the Secretary-General's termination of van Boven.[24] He left Geneva a martyr in 1982 but soon returned as a Dutch expert on the Sub-Commission. Van Boven turned down the opportunity to succeed MacDermot as Secretary-General. In 1991 he was elected to ICJ membership along with his former U.N. deputy, B. G. Ramcharan. After democratically elected leaders replaced the junta, Argentina supported the U.N. working group on disappearances. The executive director of the Andean Commission of Jurists, Diego Garcia-Sayan, became a member.

As the number of disappearances declined, more and more governments copied the crime. In 1989 the working group identified 721 new cases in countries from all regions. The group recommended a new international standard that would expressly outlaw disappearances and establish steps authorities should take to clarify cases and punish those responsible.[25] Their recommendation gave impetus to the Sub-Commission's stalled proposals for a declaration on unlawful detention. In 1988 ICJ legal officer Reed Brody and Sub-Commission expert Louis Joinet prepared the first draft of a U.N. Declaration on the Protection of All Persons from Enforced or Involuntary Disappearances. The co-authors drew heavily on the torture convention and a regional draft convention on forced disappearances by the Inter-American Commission on Human Rights.

Both the OAS General Assembly and the European Parliament had found disappearances a crime against humanity. Brody personally accepted that characterization, but worried that many U.N. members would reject a declaration using that phrase. The original ICJ draft included the elements of a crime against humanity without using the politically charged label. Disappearances could not fall under the political offense exception to extradition requests; statutory limits would not apply.

After two sessions revising the text in the Sub-Commission's annual working group, Brody organized a 1990 interim meeting of experts. The ICJ hosted in Geneva four Sub-Commission experts, two members of the U.N. working group on disappearances, and representatives of five NGOs, the U.N. Centre, and Portugal. The experts revised the ICJ draft to make "systematized" disappearances a crime against humanity. In three days the experts completed a twenty-two-article text that might have taken the Sub-Commission several years. Government representatives at the Commission weakened the reference to crimes against humanity and forwarded the Declaration to the General Assembly for approval.[26]

Arbitrary Detention: U.N. Principles and Working Group

Although "arbitrary" detention has never been considered a crime against humanity, both the Universal Declaration and the Covenant on Civil and Political Rights forbid that offense. The U.S. Supreme Court's tortuous opinions on criminal due process reveal the political obstacles to clear definition. There is little prospect the United Nations will soon agree on a binding convention governing detention procedures. Instead, the ICJ and AI lobbied for a set of principles to be endorsed by the General Assembly as recommendations for national legislation. A supportive Sub-Commission expert provided the necessary entrée. MacDermot convened a subcommittee on detention of the Special NGO Committee on Human Rights to assist rapporteur Erik Nettel of Austria in drafting principles.[27] Twenty-seven NGOs endorsed the "Draft Body of Principles for the Protection of All Persons in Any Form of Detention or Imprisonment." The Western-inspired provisions affirm detainees' rights to be presumed innocent, informed of the charges against them, assisted by counsel, allowed to communicate with family, released prior to trial, and granted a speedy hearing.

Communist experts on the Sub-Commission had surprisingly few reservations about the draft. A Bulgarian expressed surprised that Western laws permitted preventive detention and administrative internment without charge of prior criminal conduct. A cooperative Soviet expert offered only a few amendments.[28] The Sub-Commission recommended the principles with slight modification in 1978. Without review, the Human Rights Commission sent the draft directly to the General Assembly. Normally the Assembly's third or Social, Humanitarian and Cultural Committee completes the drafting of human rights instruments. The detention principles went instead to the sixth or Legal Committee. For ten years that committee's lawyers delayed and weakened the principles in New York without significant follow-up from the European-based AI and ICJ. In 1987 the NGOs prodded the Sub-Commission to question revisions made by the Sixth Committee Working Group.[29] The committee belatedly reported out a text which the General Assembly adopted in 1988.[30]

AI's worldwide campaign to free prisoners of conscience inspired U.N. monitoring that became progressively more systematic. In the 1970s the ICJ and AI annually supplied the U.N. Centre with information about detainees. Each year the ICJ Secretariat prepared for the U.N. Sub-Commission a sanitized synopsis that did not name any governments. In the 1980s conscientious experts demanded more detailed information and additional funding for a pre-sessional investigatory working group. When the Commission refused, the experts convened a sessional detention working group to review NGO complaints. The French expert Louis Joinet prepared a study on administrative detention; the Sub-Commission approved his recommendation for a Human Rights Commission theme mechanism to investigate arbitrary detention.

ICJ legal officer Reed Brody actively promoted the initiative. France's representative followed up Joinet's proposal with a resolution endorsed by the Western group over similar proposals by the United States and Britain.[31] Commission chairman Enrique Bernales Ballesteros of Peru agreed not only to support the proposal but also to introduce the resolution as a chairman's draft. After the Western and Latin American groups approved the concept, the French coordinator invited Brody and the AI representative to two negotiating meetings with government representatives from all five regional groups.

The drafters decided on a regionally balanced working group rather than a single rapporteur. Its broad terms of reference extended to arbitrary detention both pretrial and by judicial order. That vast mandate would include for a start 3,376 possible "prisoners of conscience" identified by AI in 1989.[32] Frustrated with inadequacies of other theme procedures, NGOs wanted the new group to determine responsibility for offenses and provide feedback to complainants.[33] In most instances reports to the Commission on disappearances, torture, and summary killings had merely summarized initial complaints and government replies, which complainants had no opportunity to rebut. The detention group was given unprecedented authorization to "investigate," not merely to examine and report on situations. The U.N. Committee on Crime Prevention and Control had already been directed to "examine" the question of pretrial detention. The Commission unanimously approved the Working Group on Arbitrary Detention.[34] Joinet was appointed and elected as the first chair, assuring further close collaboration with the ICJ. NGOs recognized the French representative who facilitated the successful negotiations by awarding him the Ruth Pearce Award, presented after each Commission session to the diplomat making the greatest contribution. In its first year, the new working groups contacted more than twenty governments inquiring about more than two hundred cases of arbitrary detention.[35]

States of Emergency: Covenant Guidelines and Rapporteur

For more than thirty years, Paraguay's strongman systematically renewed a state of siege every three months. In Uruguay, Argentina, and Chile generals exercised emergency powers against suspected terrorists. Even governments firmly committed to individual liberty retain extraordinary emergency powers to suppress revolutionary violence. The Covenant on Civil and Political Rights expressly authorizes a government, when seriously threatened, to derogate from certain political rights; guarantees against torture and summary execution are non-derogable, even in the gravest emergency. The ICJ has sought limits on pretextual claims of emergency to justify unreasonable detention and press censorship. MacDermot worked for guidelines delimiting emergency powers and for international monitoring of governments claiming extraordinary authority.

The ICJ documented the problem with its most extensive study, detailed reports on states of emergency in twenty countries.[36] The case studies by twenty-two outside experts took years to complete, and the difficult project was plagued by unanticipated expense and delays. MacDermot shared the experts' papers and ICJ recommendations with Sub-Commission rapporteur Nicole Questiaux, of France, for a 1982 U.N. study.[37] She recommended legal criteria mandating that emergencies be officially proclaimed with publicly stated reasons; the threats to be met should be exceptional, emergency measures proportional to the threat, and nonderogable rights should be strictly respected.[38] MacDermot followed up by supporting a Sub-Commission rapporteur to report annually on states exercising emergency powers. Each year rapporteur Leandro Despouy writes to governments that have proclaimed a state of emergency, inquiring about the legal basis. His annual Sub-Commission report lists countries that have proclaimed, extended, or terminated a state of emergency.

In 1984 MacDermot convened a meeting of thirty-one specialists in criminal law to draft principles clarifying when governments could derogate from or limit rights contained in the Covenant on Civil and Political Rights. Bringing experts together for a week-long consultation avoided the delays experienced in the emergency study and offered several advantages to preparation by ICJ legal officers. Drafters must be sensitive not only to the differences between the common and civil law tradition, but also to unavoidable North-South and East-West ideological conflicts. Expert members of a properly constituted committee successfully addressing such divisions can become effective proponents for the text with officials of their respective governments. Increasing the number of contributors also increased the available expertise and the technical sufficiency of the finished product. Recommendations from a broad-based committee have greater legitimacy in politically diverse international organizations than do proposals from one or two small NGOs. MacDermot specifically included Hungarian and Polish experts whose governments had been examined in the emergency study.

Committee preparation also creates several problems. The larger the group, the more difficult to attain consensus and the more likely the paralysis that so often afflicts intergovernmental drafting efforts. The costs of travel, lodging, documentation, and conference facilities may be prohibitive. The high cost of simultaneous translation may limit participation to individuals able to communicate in one working language. Despite the difficulties, the ICJ committee approach worked. ICJ Executive Committee chairman William J. Butler secured partial funding from the Morgan Institute of Human Rights at the Cincinnati College of Law; the IAPL's International Institute of Higher Studies in Criminal Sciences, directed by Professor Cherif Bassiouni in Siracusa, Italy, provided the facility.

The ICJ circulated papers to the invited experts in advance. MacDermot then chaired working groups and led the experts in a thorough review of each recommended principle.[39] After a week of deliberation, the experts adopted the "Siracusa Principles," designed to maximize individual liberty by restricting broad interpretation of limitation clauses in the Covenant's substantive articles. The principles also specified the types of emergency during which states could suspend certain obligations. "Whenever a government applied a limitation it had to pursue a legitimate aim and use measures proportional to that aim. Respect for human rights was itself part of public order, and violation of human rights undermined national security."[40] A Dutch foreign service officer attending the meeting encouraged his government to sponsor the Siracusa Principles in the General Assembly, which approved it by consensus.[41] Some of the principles were followed in redrafting Hungary's Constitution.[42] *The Human Rights Quarterly* published a symposium edition of the working papers, commentary, and principles,[43] and the AAICJ published a pocket-sized edition of the Principles. MacDermot sent the publications to members of the U.N. Commission, Sub-Commission, and Human Rights Committee.

Economic Rights: Limburg Principles and ECOSOC Committee

The Dutch government then supported a 1986 ICJ meeting of experts which drafted implementation principles for the International Covenant on Economic, Social and Cultural Rights. That covenant had been in effect for ten years, and ECOSOC had just constituted an Implementation Committee to examine reports from the states parties. The ICJ set out to clarify gray areas about the government obligations and states parties' reports. Executive Committee chairman William J. Butler and the Dutch Foreign Ministry official who had attended the meeting on the political covenant proposed the meeting on economic rights. Supported by university cosponsors from the Netherlands and the United States, the ICJ convened twenty-nine experts, including four members of the ECOSOC committee. Experts came from twelve countries, including two Eastern bloc nations, the U.N. Centre for Human Rights, the ILO, UNESCO, WHO, the Commonwealth Secretariat, and the sponsoring organizations. The experts prepared the "Limburg Principles" to guide states parties in preparing their reports to the committee and in meeting their obligations to help citizens realize economic and social rights. The Dutch government introduced the principles in the U.N. General Assembly. Philip Alston, who wrote the working papers used at the meeting, became the ECOSOC committee rapporteur.[44]

Mentally Ill Detainees: U.N. Principles and Japanese Law

Soviet abuse of psychiatry triggered ICJ work that unexpectedly contributed to major reform of Japan's Mental Health Act. Britain responded to political detention in Soviet psychiatric hospitals by proposing a U.N. study on due process for mental patients. Sub-Commission expert Erica-Irene A. Daes began the U.N. study and headed a sessional working group.[45] MacDermot convened two meetings of experts at the IAPL in Siracusa, which were attended by Daes as well as a Soviet mental health authority.[46] The understaffed U.N. Secretariat could offer so little support to its rapporteurs that ICJ assistance was needed and welcome. The ICJ in turn obtained easier access to the U.N. system through quasi-independent Sub-Commission experts than was possible through NGO interventions in the government-dominated Commission.

The experts recommended principles that Daes included as an appendix to her report. Involuntary mental patients were to be assured legal representation and a right of appeal to an impartial tribunal. WHO was asked to comment on the proposed principles, and the ICJ was consulted in the agency review and recommendations. The Sub-Commission spent five years reviewing the principles before a new working-group chairman and a more cooperative Soviet expert completed a draft in 1988.[47] In 1991 the U.N. Commission and General Assembly endorsed the Body of Principles for the Protection of Persons with Mental Illness and for the Improvement of Mental Health Care.[48]

Profiteering in Japan's private psychiatric hospitals aroused protests by a small Civil Liberties Union, psychiatrists, bar associations, and journalists. Involuntary commitments accounted for an extraordinary 80 percent of more than three hundred thousand patients held for an average of eight years.[49] "For those subject to detention proceedings . . . the Mental Hygiene Act provided no court procedure, no independent tribunal, no communication, no visiting, no lawyer, no advocate, no hearing, no access to any report or document, no free and independent expert witness and no notification of the reasons for detention." After two patients died as a result of brutal beatings, investigative journalists reported 222 deaths out of one thousand patients at a single privately owned hospital over a three-year period. Critics found "arbitrary detention over long periods of time without proper treatment; suspicious deaths, the alleged abuse of psychosurgery techniques and other therapies such as electroconvulsive and drug therapy; torture and inhuman or degrading treatment; human experiments; forced labour; and appalling conditions and overcrowding in wards."[50]

The opposition Socialist party was more responsive to public complaints than were the ruling Liberal Democrats, whose leaders had financial ties to the hospitals. Frustrated at the government's recalcitrance, attorney Etsuro Totsuka decided to generate international pressure. A paper presented to the International Congress of Psychiatry Law and Ethics charged that Japan's mass detentions violated Article 9 of the International Covenant on Civil and Political Rights. MacDermot relayed a complaint from Totsuka to the United Nations, and Daes reported the information to the U.N. Sub-Commission in 1982. Two years later a *Review* article exposed the inhumane conditions, and MacDermot wrote to Prime Minister Nakasone proposing an independent inquiry.[51] The International League for Human Rights and Disabled Peoples' International also complained publicly to the Sub-Commission about the scandalous abuse of Japan's mentally ill. When the government denied the allegations, the ILHR wrote to Nakasone. The NGO interventions triggered criticism in Parliament but no legal reform.

When Nakasone failed to respond, Totsuka requested a fact-finding mission. MacDermot arranged for the ICJ-inspired International Commission of Health Professionals (ICHP) to cosponsor the mission. Two internationally renowned psychiatrists from the United States and Britain and a Chicago judge experienced in mental health law conducted a two-week inquiry in 1985.[52] Before publicizing any conclusions, the ICJ provided government officials with an advance report. The Ministry of Health initially ignored the recommendations. The final conclusions and recommendations were then published in

English and Japanese, attracting extensive press coverage. MacDermot believes the turning point came after the ICJ complained to the Foreign Ministry that Japan was violating its obligations under the Covenant. In response to continued NGO complaints in the Sub-Commission, Japan's representative announced plans to reform the Mental Health Law.

The ICJ published the full mission report as the Diet began debating an amendment bill.[53] The Private Mental Hospitals Association resisted sweeping reforms, and the new act adopted only some of the ICJ's recommendations. Physicians were to encourage voluntary commitment, hospitals would improve rehabilitation services, and involuntary patients obtained rights before Psychiatric Review Boards. The ICJ/ICHP fact finders conducted a second mission in 1988 to meet with hospital and prefectural authorities on implementing the new law. Their second report noted ongoing legal disabilities, discrimination, and abuse and recommended an inspectorate system.[54] Totsuka wrote an article for the *Review* calling for additional reform. The government invited the ICJ to send experts for follow-up consultations in 1992 to review the act's operation after three years.

The remarkable collaboration of Japanese interest groups and international NGOs brought national legislation into accord with the Covenant. By allowing outside NGOs such influence, Japanese officials displayed extraordinary respect for international human rights. The ICJ success in Japan could be replicated in other democracies that allow interest groups to enlist international allies.

African Charter and Commission on Human and Peoples' Rights

For twenty-five years of labor, the ICJ functioned as a midwife for an African human rights convention, and ICJ elite contacts were instrumental to if not decisive in its creation. Final delivery in 1986 culminated a conception first endorsed by the ICJ at a 1961 conference in Lagos.[55] In the interval an Inter-American Commission began emulating the successful European system, and the United Nations organized seminars encouraging an African instrument. The ICJ participated at the 1969 U.N. seminar in Cairo,[56] and MacBride planned a follow-up ICJ conference to formulate specific proposals. An ICJ budget crisis and severe retrenchment set the effort back until the election of Senegal's Supreme Court president as ICJ president in 1977. With Mbaye as chair, the U.N. Commission on Human Rights adopted a Nigerian-sponsored resolution urging the Organization of African Unity to adopt a human rights convention.

A year later the ICJ convened a seminar in Dakar on development and human rights for forty Africans from twelve Francophone countries. In addition to the familiar call for an African convention, the participants created a follow-up committee.[57] MacDermot met with the African members and raised funds for the committee's correspondence and visits to ten heads of Francophone states.[58] Mbaye approached Senegal's President Senghor, who agreed to introduce a resolution calling for a regional convention at a 1979 meeting of the African heads of state.[59] The resolution drafted by Mbaye and introduced by Senghor directed the OAU Secretary-General to convene African experts to prepare a draft convention.[60] The African heads of state had become increasingly embarrassed by critical reports of the ICJ and others detailing atrocities in Uganda, Equatorial Guinea, and the Central African Empire. The heads of state approved the Senghor resolution at a meeting dominated by debate over Ugandan dictator Idi Amin's overthrow by Tanzanian forces.[61]

Mbaye became rapporteur for the OAU Committee of Experts and prepared a text they approved in Dakar. Two ministerial conferences in Banjul, Gambia revised the draft charter which the 1981 OAU Assembly of Heads of State and Government adopted in Nairobi.[62] While incorporating many key provisions of the international covenants, Mbaye's draft had a distinctively African orientation. The final text recognized first-generation individual civil liberties as well as duties to the community, second-generation economic rights, and third-generation solidarity rights for "peoples" collectively. An eleven-member commission would review inter-state complaints, but its relations with NGOs and individual petitioners was ill defined. The Commission would report in confidence to the OAU heads of state, and the Charter did not establish a regional human rights court.

A Western critic acknowledged the difficulty of reconciling common law, Napoleonic Code, Koranic-Shari'a and Marxist-Leninist legal systems, but decried the "largely cosmetic instrument calculated to be minimally intrusive."[63] Claw-back clauses qualified basic civil-political liberties such as the right to express opinions "within the law."

> [T]he African Charter is woefully deficient with regard to the right to liberty. As that right is subject to national law, the Charter is incapable of supplying even a scintilla of external restraint upon a government's power to create laws contrary to the spirit of the rights granted.[64]

The fair trial guarantees did not expressly require proceedings before civilian courts. The general assurance of free assembly did not expressly mention labor unions. In the absence of any provision on limiting derogation, governments might conceivably suspend all rights in emergency. Despite its substantive defects the ICJ welcomed the Charter as a tool to end the African conspiracy of silence on human rights atrocities.

Twenty-six ratifactions were required to bring the Charter into force. After only fifteen governments deposited ratifications in the first three years, the ICJ organized a conference to complete the task. In addition to ICJ members and staff, sixteen experts from thirteen African countries attended the December 1985 session in Nairobi. The participants adopted a resolution appealing for ratification and offering legal assistance following approval. After the conference, Senegal's President Diouf, in his capacity as OAU President, wrote to heads of state requesting ratification. ICJ legal officer Adama Dieng of Senegal enclosed with Diouf's message copies of the African Charter and the Nairobi conference resolution.[65] The ICJ delegated regional coordinators to follow up with local authorities, bar associations, and others who might influence a decision to ratify. Conference participants from Gabon and Cape Verde reported success in their follow-up efforts; Somalia finally conveyed to the OAU a 1985 ratification that had never been officially deposited. Seven months after the Nairobi conference, the twenty-sixth ratification was deposited; an ICJ press release celebrated the convention's entry into force on October 21, 1986.

Dieng acted promptly to make the new regional commission effective. Not only the individuals chosen to interpret the Charter but also the rules of procedure adopted for its implementation could either cripple or empower the new institution. A month before the OAU elected Commission members, the ICJ invited to a colloquium in Dakar forty distinguished African jurists from twenty countries, including many lawyers eager to serve.[66] The colloquium examined what Mbaye characterized as "grey areas" in the Charter and prepared recommendations for procedures. Representatives of the European and Inter-American Commissions shared their experiences. Some participants favored a procedural rule that would limit NGO interventions to African groups. Dieng pointed out that the first NGO intervention to the Inter-American Commission came from the Geneva-based ICJ, and the colloquium did not recommend any regional limit. Some participants competing for election to the Commission not only welcomed the expert advice but also sought ICJ support for their candidacies.[67] Six colloquium participants were elected to the Commission; its first president had assisted in ratification efforts after the Nairobi conference and paid tribute to the ICJ in his opening speech.[68]

The African Commission President then asked the ICJ to comment on the draft rules of procedure prepared by the OAU Secretariat.

MacDermot and Dieng recommended fifty amendments including some to maximize NGO participation, even in closed meetings.[69] The African Commission accepted all but two, and the OAU Secretary-General expressed appreciation for the contribution.[70] By 1990 the Commission "had received more than 100 petitions which it examined in confidential sessions, but had yet either to make public any steps taken relative to them or to name the states from which they had come."[71] Frustrated by the Commission's political compromises and slow start, Dieng personally lobbied the OAU Secretariat for improved support. The Commission retained Dieng and Wolfgang Benedek of the University of Graz to recommend ways of enhancing its performance. (Chapter 11 reports on Dieng's ongoing campaign to mobilize African NGOs at the Commission after he became ICJ Secretary-General in 1990.)

The ICJ had unmatched NGO influence on the African Charter and Commission because a Senegalese president and executive secretary carried to fruition more than thirty years of sustained ICJ activities. On a continent dominated by little Caesars, access to ruling elites was critical. Animated by a passionate distaste for their excesses, ICJ leaders effectively influenced key heads of state, who grudgingly approved minimalist human rights institutions. Persistent efforts for another thirty years may be required before the fragile regional system affords meaningful protection.

Foreign Policy: AAICJ Colloquia of Human Rights Desk Officers

In addition to campaigning for improved intergovernmental procedures, the ICJ also promoted government foreign policy initiatives to enforce human rights standards. John Salzberg left his AAICJ staff position in New York to assist U.S. Congressman Donald Fraser, chairman of the Subcommittee on International Organizations of the House Foreign Affairs Committee. In 1973 Fraser welcomed the former Parliamentarian MacDermot as the lead-off speaker for "consciousness raising" hearings on international organizations and U.S. foreign policy.[72] After several years of growing concern, Congress established an Assistant Secretary of State for Human Rights and mandated annual country reports. Other legislation directed the executive to apply human rights criteria when granting military assistance and foreign aid or voting for loans in multilateral institutions.

ICJ Executive Committee chairman William Butler then began organizing colloquia for NGO and government specialists. The first series of bilateral meetings introduced U.S. State Department officials and members of Congress to their counterparts in Canada, Britain,

Germany, and the Netherlands. Participants compared the criteria used to ensure respect for human rights in formulating foreign policy and granting foreign aid. In 1983 Butler changed from a bilateral to multilateral format, and his AAICJ brought together human rights desk officers from Western foreign ministries.[73] As many as nineteen attended, coming from as far away as Australia and Japan. Representatives from Switzerland and, more recently, Eastern Europe have joined the annual colloquia.[74] The specialists explain their government machinery to implement human rights and share "day-to-day problems and difficulties encountered in carrying out their governments' human rights decisions in the United Nations . . . ; the international financial institutions; in the various multilateral and regional institutions, as well as in the area of bilateral arrangements between their own and other governments."[75]

Butler and MacDermot presided over sessions where officials spoke off the record about their ideas and policy differences. A Dutch participant concluded that no government could have hosted such effective informal consultations; he praised the ICJ's unique role in facilitating valuable personal contacts and exchange.[76] In setting the agenda for discussion, the ICJ could call attention to proposed initiatives such as establishment of the U.N. High Commissioner. In the most recent meetings, cost-conscious American officials have called for streamlining duplicate international procedures; the Dutch human rights coordinator defended "pluriformity"—multiple procedures on torture and overlapping global and regional procedures.[77] After concluding his term as ICJ chairman, Butler continued the AAICJ colloquia with MacDermot's successor, Adama Dieng.

Conclusions

Governments should not be above the law, but how can the people become sovereign in a nation-state system? Abused citizens seeking protection need some means to influence lawmaking by their state oppressors. Can NGOs democratize an anarchic political world that lacks international political parties and contested elections? The ICJ illustrates how a successful NGO articulates popular demands, aggregates common interests, and shapes intergovernmental lawmaking.[78]

Articulation

ICJ diplomats articulated demands for, rather than by, the people. Victims of torture, disappearances, and arbitrary detention desperately needed representation but did not define ICJ legislative demands. As in most domestic interest groups, staff and key leaders articulated the constituents' goals. Their voice for the oppressed had a Western accent on institutional protection for civil liberties. Progressive American and European leaders advocated economic rights to a greater extent than did other NGOs but made minimal demands for enforceable standards. Kéba Mbaye articulated distinctive African human rights principles of which Western critics disapproved.

Did money talk? Domestic interest groups transfer constituents' money to lawmakers. The ICJ reversed that relationship by accepting grants from government ministries that negotiated international law. Did the ICJ in return articulate the sponsors' message? European sponsors that promoted torture standards did not dictate the ICJ's work for U.N. and regional conventions. AI's global campaign aginst torture moved both governments and NGOs to act. Sweden submitted a draft to the Commission, and the ICJ prepared its own draft as well as an optional protocol. The ICJ actively promoted the rights of all mental patients after an anti-Soviet resolution sponsored by the United Kingdom. MacDermot was clearly not co-opted by the British or any other government sponsor. He deplored mistreatment in noncommunist countries and arranged effective law reform missions to Japan.[79] MacDermot also worked for detainee standards that challenged British internment policies in Northern Ireland. USAID funded the states of emergency study that criticized several American allies. Governments paid the bills but did not call the piper's tune. Principled ICJ leaders independently made demands on their government benefactors and exploited their inside contacts to recruit allies.

Aggregation/Coalition Building

The ICJ aggregated its demands with allies that included other NGOs, Secretariat officials from the U.N. Centre for Human Rights, experts on the Sub-Commmission, and diplomats on the U.N. Human Rights Commission. MacDermot brought organizational representatives together to find common ground before proposing new standards on torture, arbitrary detention, and mental hospitals. Butler effectively used key relationships in arranging foreign policy colloquia. The international human rights network resembles policy communities in the United States. Until the 1980s most political scientists characterized as "subgovernments" the "iron triangles" dominated by interest groups, legislators, and agency administrators. Recent research challenging that model concludes that most policies result from competition between groups in less cohesive "issue networks."[80] Whether national or international, key policy makers circulate through revolving doors that connect legislatures, administrative agencies, and interest groups. ICJ president Mbaye chaired the U.N. Human Rights Commission as a representative from Senegal. The U.N. Human Rights director won election as a Sub-Commission expert and ICJ member.[81]

Network partners typically display unequal strength in reconciling their varied demands. Powerful interest groups can "capture" weak agencies or be "co-opted" by superior political allies. The ICJ and other NGOs dominated U.N. Sub-Commission experts but accepted major compromises when collaborating with diplomats at the U.N. Human Rights Commission. ICJ experts prepared essential materials for Sub-Commission rapporteurs. When the United Nations canceled the Sub-Commission's 1986 meeting, NGOs brought its members together for a three-day meeting.[82] Two working groups drafted recommendations that MacDermot and three fellow NGO leaders circulated to the General Assembly and delivered personally to the U.N. Secretary-General.[83] After his 1990 election as Sub-Commission chairman, Joinet consulted Dieng, Brody, and other NGO representatives to plan priorities and procedures.[84] Western activists dominated the coalitions and agenda setting by the Sub-Commission, NGOs, the U.N. Centre, and the Human Rights Commission. The ICJ aggregated African demands for a regional convention and cultivated nonaligned support at the Commission for the Working Group on Disappearances.

Lawmaking

Did the ICJ significantly influence customary international law as well as human rights conventions? Consistent leadership and institutional memory are critical in prolonged deliberations for international standards. Longevity, perseverance, technical expertise, diplomatic skills, status, and contacts all contributed to ICJ success. MacDermot persevered for twenty years, extending the jurists' cumulative experience to four decades. ICJ elites displayed the requisite manners to secure access with key decision makers. The staff had superior legal expertise, essential language skills, and political savvy.

Carefully nurtured expertise and elite contacts had considerable impact. The African Charter triumphantly climaxed a twenty-five-year quest. The ICJ contributed significantly to U.N. Commission working groups on disappearances and arbitrary detention and to the Convention Against Torture. The European Torture Convention may be a more qualified victory. If the United Nations does not adopt an optional protocol for parties to the global torture convention, regional instruments will be needed in Latin America and Africa.

Fundamental principles approved by the General Assembly as guides to national legislation are "bread upon the waters," with as yet uncertain effects upon customary international law and state practice. Some critics bemoan the disproportionate attention given to drafting additional standards before earlier norms have been ratified or effectively implemented. Yet the principles could foster new values that produce self-help victories which are impossible to document. In some instances the use of effective procedures to enforce weak standards accomplished more than the drafting of improved norms. The Working Group on Disappearances began monitoring government abuses ten years before the Declaration on Disappearances was approved. Successful reform of Japan's Mental Health Act predated completion of U.N. principles on rights of the mentally ill.

Although ICJ lobbying appears quite impressive, U.N. adoption could also mean that governments regard the measures as insignificant. The U.N. Human Rights Commission and General Assembly adopted most human rights declarations and principles by acclamation. Civil rights bills in the United States created higher stakes and intense competition for votes needed to win a bare majority. Has the proliferation of international law and institutions established a human rights "regime?"[85] None of the standards creates supranational institutions that enforce compliance, but regimes are defined as sets of rules that condition states' expectations.[86] The ICJ-influenced standards and procedures created some new legal obligations for states which establish a promotional rather than an enforcement regime. States uniformly call torture a crime against humanity, but the widespread practice reveals that government expectations are largely unaffected.[87] The ICJ protection activities detailed in the following chapter sought to enforce state compliance with human rights law.

ICJ Studies and Standard-Setting Publications, 1970–1990

Asylum in Latin America: The Application in Latin America of International Declarations and Conventions Relating to Asylum. Geneva: ICJ, 1975. 64 pp.

Conference of European National Sections. AIDS and Human Rights European Social Charter. The Hague, September 1989. ICJ and NJCM-Boekerij 14.

"Gross Violations of Human Rights: A Practical Guide for Non-Governmental Organizations Wishing to File Communications with the United Nations." Geneva: ICJ, 1973. 27 pp.

How to Make the Convention Against Torture Effective. Geneva: ICJ, 1979. 44 pp.

Human and Peoples' Rights in Africa and the African Charter. Nairobi Seminar, 1986. 102 pp. (Engl./Fr.).

The Protection of Persons Suffering from Mental Disorder. Proceedings of Two Meetings of Experts held at the International Institute of Higher Studies in Criminal Sciences in Siracusa, May 29–31, 1980, and December 1–4, 1980. Nouvelles Études Pénales, Association Internationale de Droit Pénal. 87 pp.

"The Protection of Privacy: A Comparative Study of the Legal Protection of Privacy in Ten Countries." *UNESCO International Social Science Journal* 24, no. 3 (1972).

States of Emergency: Their Impact on Human Rights. Geneva: ICJ, 1983. 477 pp.

Stromholm, Stig. *Rights of Privacy and Rights of the Personality.* Stockholm: P. A. Norstedt and Sonen, 1967.

Chapter 9
Enforcing Civil Liberties

> The 1989 Erasmus Prize for Human Rights is awarded to the International Commission of Jurists . . .
>
> because the ICJ contributes to promoting and protecting human rights where these are in grave jeopardy through the delegation of research missions and publication of findings;
>
> because the quality and the objectivity of the ICJ is beyond all doubt, . . .
>
> —From November 21, 1989 award presentation

Righteous anger erupts when tyrants murder for power, soldiers gun down protesters, torturers maim children, death squads terrorize peasants, and racists subjugate their equals. Victimized students, workers, lawyers, and religious leaders, their families, friends, churches, and unions appealed in desperation for ICJ help. Speaking truth to power became a defining mission, a moral cause. In rescuing prisoners tortured by sadistic officials of whatever ideology, the ICJ categorically rejected partisan political goals. Inspired by moral outrage, ICJ activists invoked nonpolitical principles of universal justice. Human life and dignity have so much more value than financial gain that ICJ advocates resent comparison with political interest groups.

Yet atrocities result from struggles for power which the ICJ confronted with political skill and legal expertise. South American military juntas secured their power against threats real and imagined with unimaginable torture devices. The ICJ countered with quiet diplomacy, public protest, and lobbying for sanctions. Complaints to the United Nations challenged semiofficial death squads in Central

America and mass murders by African tyrants. Fact-finding missions produced embarrassing reports about Iran's secret police, repression in Sri Lanka, martial law in the Philippines, mass detention in Indonesia, and racial injustice throughout Southern Africa. A Cold War neutral, the ICJ faulted both Eastern repression in the USSR, Romania, and Czechoslovakia and Western abuses in Greece, Portugal, Spain, Turkey, and Northern Ireland. Political dissidents and rival governments used the ICJ's principled efforts for partisan advantage.

To assist individuals arbitrarily detained or unjustly condemned, MacDermot made interventions by letter, cable, telephone, or in person with presidents, ministers, and diplomats. As freedom waned in the 1970s, cries for help greatly exceeded the capacity of four ICJ legal officers to respond effectively. Governments occasionally released a detainee represented by the ICJ, but most complaints arose from systematic abuses beyond a single NGO's influence. MacDermot used the ICJ network to activate other NGOs, regional and U.N. agencies, and national officials responsible for human rights. The three sections below illustrate and evaluate ICJ tactics to (1) aid individual victims, (2) publicize gross violations, and (3) activate international protection procedures.

Casework for Individual Victims

In the United States, public legal aid offices assist the indigent in civil disputes with merchants, landlords, and government agencies. Public defenders represent detainees awaiting criminal trial and the condemned facing execution. ICJ casework for individuals has similar ends but very different means. The "clients" are political prisoners held without trial, torture victims, death row inmates, citizens denied permission to emigrate, or dissidents forced into exile. Their cases reach Geneva from local ICJ members and affiliates, the press, churches, family members, other NGOs, or a concerned government official. Journalists, students, labor leaders, church workers, lawyers, and ICJ members detained by local authorities have required an international public defender.

In twenty years, the ICJ has made nearly six hundred interventions in more than one hundred countries.[1] Over three-fourths involved third world governments, with roughly equal numbers from Africa, Asia, and the Middle East. As other NGOs became active, the average number of ICJ interventions declined from thirty-eight a year in the early 1970s to twenty-two in the late 1980s. Compared with Amnesty

International, the ICJ had a very small caseload and relied more on private interventions than on public pressure.

Quiet Diplomacy

As the first line of defense, MacDermot personally contacted a government official—the president, prime minister, attorney general, foreign minister, or U.N. ambassador. Foreign ministers and ambassadors sensitive to international pressure were generally more cooperative than justice ministers. MacDermot became thoroughly acquainted with diplomats in Geneva. Some who disagreed with their own governments provided information off the record and pressed other departments to respond. When MacDermot personally knew the head of state, he went directly to the top. In diplomatically worded cables, letters, and phone calls, the Secretary-General made humanitarian appeals for clemency or requested information about reported detainees. Responding to summary executions, MacDermot's blunt telephone rebukes berated officials for their "uncivilized" response to political protest.

So many governments and NGOs intervened to help the most celebrated political prisoners that the ICJ's independent impact cannot be determined. A few cases were resolved so soon after MacDermot complained that the ICJ may have made the difference. A day after contacts with the country's ministers of justice, foreign affairs, and interior, Spain released two lawyers in 1976.[2] The Council of the Revolution in Portugal informed the ICJ that an individual had been set free a week after a 1975 intervention. In other cases, letters of gratitude and financial support testified to ICJ influence. The Dutch development organization NOVIB expressed appreciation for a cable to Ecuador's minister of external relations which had helped persuade authorities to release an economist six days after his disappearance.[3] A grateful father thanked MacDermot for assistance in obtaining his son's release in Ghana. Other interventions were credited with commuted death sentences for Czech chess grand master Ludwig Pachman and Professor Ofusu Amaah in Ghana.[4] After a 1973 protest to Japan's U.N. ambassador in Geneva, Jan Zorbas was released and not repatriated to Greece. Numerous NGOs pressed Eastern European governments to allow emigration and family reunification, and the ICJ made seventeen interventions with Romania; in three cases, the government allowed emigration.

In extraordinary cases, the ICJ made personal visits to assist individual victims. An emissary to Mozambique was barred from meeting two detained Spanish priests but did visit other political prisoners.[5] Butler was remarkably more successful in personally negotiating the release of José Esteban González. The Sandinista government arrested the coordinator of the Permanent Commission of Human Rights of Nicaragua for reporting disappearances to the U.N. Working Group. In public statements reported in the press, he complained about Somocista political prisoners while visiting the Vatican, Brussels, and Madrid. Charged with slandering the revolution, González was rushed to trial four days after his arrest in February 1981. The prosecution aroused worldwide protest from those familiar with González's courageous opposition to Somoza. U.N. Secretary-General Kurt Waldheim made an exceptional request for his release.

U.S. ambassador to Nicaragua Lawrence Pezzullo proposed ICJ intervention. Alejandro Artucio and Heleno Fragoso had conducted an ICJ mission to Nicaragua the previous April which had concluded that González's complaints were contradicted by other evidence. Their report, acclaimed by the Sandinistas, enraged González and other critics.[6] The ICJ concluded that despite some abuses, the Sandinistas had eliminated the worst excesses of the discredited Somoza regime. Butler requested permission from Nicaragua's U.N. ambassador to observe the González trial, and the foreign ministry promptly approved. Before leaving New York, Butler asked Tom Farer of the Inter-American Commission on Human Rights (IACHR) to hold up publication of its report on Nicaragua.

After observing the Saturday trial in Managua, Butler began negotiating for González's release with members of the junta, the minister of justice, and ambassadors of the United States, Venezuela, and Mexico. Pezzullo managed delicate diplomatic contacts with government representatives. Nicaragua's interior minister, Commander Tomas Borge, called González a "reactionary" enemy for painting the Sandinistas as torturers during his visit to the Vatican. Butler urged Borge to consider how conviction would affect the pending IAHRC report, the current U.N. Human Rights Commission meeting, and debates in the U.S. Congress over future economic aid. Other junta members and the minister of justice agreed to withdraw the charges if González signed a "Statement of Clarification." Using a translator, Butler hastily negotiated language acceptable to all. González reiterated support for the revolution against Somoza's dictatorship; he stated that ongoing instances of torture, disappearances, and political detention were not systematic or officially condoned. At the final trial hearing set for judgment, González's lawyer filed the statement, and the prosecutor withdrew all charges. At the military prison, the head of state security delivered González to Butler "as president of the

ICJ." A security escort of soldiers with automatic weapons saw them home through hostile crowds.[7] The Nicaraguan press published González's statement in full.

Public Pressure

The few governments that quietly respond to NGO private interventions do so in part to avoid embarrassing publicity. In situations where private correspondence alone was futile, MacDermot issued press releases publicizing an intervention. One weekend in 1983 MacDermot heard BBC reports that Ghana's military government planned to abolish the office of chief justice and dissolve the Judicial Council. First thing Monday morning he sent Dieng to the United Nations for wire service reports and to check the story with a journalist related to Ghana's chief justice. MacDermot pressed Ghana's U.N. ambassador for official clarification of a Worker's Defence Committee statement about a new system of lay justice and people's courts. He considered offering to delay a press release for twenty-four hours but decided that immediate publicity would maximize pressure for prompt action. The ambassador called MacDermot at home, reporting a telex from Accra. The attorney-general and secretary for justice categorically denied that the judiciary had been abolished and assured him that the chief justice remained at his post. A year later a Dutch expert conducted a mission to Ghana that criticized public tribunals created by the military, which duplicated regular courts.[8]

Trial observers also publicized ICJ concern for individual victims. Press releases announced the missions, and *Review* articles reported egregious proceedings. Supported by an annual $10,000 grant from the Rockefeller Foundation, the ICJ sent an average of five observers a year, more than one hundred from 1970 to 1990. South African trials accounted for one-fourth of the total. First world jurists conducted two-thirds of the remaining missions in Africa, Asia, and Latin America, but third world jurists did not observe trials in Europe. In the late 1980s the ICJ recruited more third world jurists for observer missions in their own regions.

In 1977, German churches in dialogue with Buddhists in Thailand asked MacDermot to sponsor an observer for the trial of eighteen students being tried by an illegal military tribunal. When English solicitor David Hallmark attended, he witnessed further military detentions of students protesting the Bangkok political charade. He promptly issued public statements for the ICJ condemning the arbitrary arrests, and the students were released. The military convicted the "Thamassat 18," but within a year the king arranged for an amnesty.[9]

Activating International Procedures

When its own resources were inadequate, the ICJ assisted individual victims through other NGOs, foreign ministries, and intergovernmental human rights agencies. MacDermot provided the Inter-Parliamentary Union Special Committee on Violations with information about detained legislators in eleven countries. The Australian national section persuaded the foreign office to press Chile about detainees. After an ICJ mission to Athens fueled bar association protest over detained lawyers, State Department officials argued that U.S. politics made Greek repression a legitimate concern in bilateral relations. Within weeks of the U.S. protest, the Greek junta released six defense lawyers.[10]

When Malawi's president disregarded NGO appeals to spare the life of Orton Chirwa, ICJ legal officer Tina Dolgopol successfully lobbied the U.N. Human Rights Commission for a cable urging clemency. The 1984 Human Rights Commission chairman from the Netherlands cabled Uruguay's minister of external affairs after the ICJ sought assistance for a presidential candidate brought before a military tribunal.[11] Artucio regularly documented for the IACHR cases of arbitrary detention in Brazil, Chile, Argentina, and Uruguay. National sections filed amicus briefs in two cases before the European Court of Human Rights. The ICJ alerted the U.N. Working Group on Disappearances about individuals missing in Chile, the Philippines, and Sri Lanka.

Individual case work revealed systematic abuse that required a class action approach. Intervention for selected detainees could win political favors for those with special connections but could not ensure due process for all. The ICJ awarded highest priority to redressing gross violations that condemned large groups to summary killing, torture, and racial oppression. To combat those crimes, the ICJ published investigatory reports exposing injustice, solicited condemnation by international organizations, and encouraged bilateral pressure from governments with clout.

Reports on Gross Violations

The ICJ initiated reports on government abuse with regular *Bulletin* articles in the 1950s but never had sufficient resources for systematic monitoring of every country. In the 1970s, AI and the U.S. State Department began annual volumes surveying all states. The *Review* reported on about ten governments each year and reached an attentive audience of fifteen thousand. Articles about third world governments accounted for 84 percent of the total, with Asia and South Africa the most frequently covered. Press releases announcing each edition highlighted the most egregious violations and generated articles in major papers and radio commentary. Costa Rica's government published the *Review* in Spanish for several years in the 1970s. When the regular budget stabilized, the ICJ resumed publication of its French and Spanish editions.

Between 1970 and 1990 the ICJ published separately more than twenty mission reports following on-site investigations and another ten country studies based on desk research. The cumulative output ranks fifth among the major NGOs that conduct fact-finding research. AI, the International Federation of Human Rights, the IADL, and the Watch Committees published two to three times as many special reports.[12] In substance, the ICJ legal experts paid more attention to economic and social conditions than did other NGOs, which focused exclusively on civil and political rights.

Fact-finding missions replaced the inquiry-commissions approach developed by the ICJ on Hungary and Tibet. Commissions of inquiry envisioned by the Hague Conventions were quasi-judicial procedures to resolve disputes between cooperating governments. When Bangladesh and India accused Pakistan of war crimes, the ICJ appointed a commission of inquiry to render an impartial judgment. Pakistan refused to cooperate, and the 1971 war against India restricted the ICJ to a report based on desk research.[13] The ICJ's last report characterized as a "commission of inquiry" was in reality something quite different. Three experts visited Athens in 1973 to investigate the incommunicado detention and possible torture of six defense lawyers. The junta denounced illegal interference in Greece's internal affairs and refused to meet the experts or allow a prison visit. The commission published a report with findings of fact and law based on interviews and documentary evidence.[14] Subsequent on-site investigations were called missions rather than inquiry commissions, employed either a single jurist or an expert panel, and relied on interviews rather than formal hearings or sworn affidavits.

As country visits became routine, human rights advocates grew concerned about reliability and credibility. Politically stacked U.N. working groups sought evidence to confirm prior judgments. NGOs alternately behaved as advocacy watchdogs gathering evidence of abuse and principled investigators engaged in nonpartisan fact-finding. Even impartial jurists found it impossible to follow evidentiary requirements of judicial proceedings. They could not rigorously

TABLE 9.1. ICJ Protection Activities, 1970–1990.

Region	*Inter-vention*	*Trial ob-servers*	*Review articles*	*Report*	*IGO*	*Number of states*
Sub-Saharan Africa	20%	30%	21%	23%		33
Equatorial Guinea		1	3	1	U.N.	
Ethiopia	6		1			
Ghana	12		2	1		
Guinea	5		1			
Kenya	6		1			
Namibia/S.W. Africa	2	1	4		U.N.	
South Africa	33	21	11	3	U.N.	
Tanzania	5	1	4			
Uganda	3	2	1		U.N., U.K.	
Zimbabwe/Rhodesia	3	2	7	1		
23 Others	38	6	11	1		
N. Africa/Middle East	16%	10%	8%	13%		15
Egypt	9	1				
Iran	9		5	1	U.S.	
Israel/West Bank	34	3	3	2	U.N.	
Sudan	9		4	1		
Syria	6		1			
10 Others	23	7	4			
Asia/Far East	20%	17%	29%	32%		18
Bangladesh/E. Pak	8		5	1	U.N.	
India	10		7			
Indonesia	10	3	9	1	U.N.	
South Korea	15	3	3	2		
Malaysia	12	1	7			
Philippines	10	2	5	3		
Sri Lanka	1		5	2	U.N.	
Thailand	7	3	3			
10 Others	37	6	20	1	U.N.	
Latin America	22%	9%	26%	29%		20
Argentina	15	1	6	1	IACHR U.N.	
Bolivia	7		2			
Brazil	10		7		IACHR	
Chile	21	3	5	1	IACHR U.N.	
El Salvador	8	1	5	1		
Guatemala	7		1	1	U.N.	
Nicaragua	5	1	3	1		
Uruguay	10		7	1	IACHR U.N.	
12 Others	57	4	20	3		
E. Europe	12%	4%	6%			8
Romania	17		1			
USSR	18		4			
6 Others	35	4	9			

TABLE 9.1. (*continued*)

Region	*Inter-vention*	*Trial ob-servers*	*Review articles*	*Report*	*IGO*	*Number of states*
W. Europe/U.S./Can./Aus./N.Z.	10%	29%	10%	3%		14
Greece	6	7	2	1	U.N. 1503	
Spain	13	11	5			
Turkey	11	7	5	1	European Commission	
11 Others	29	6	9			
Total	579	106	219	31		108

cross-examine traumatized torture victims, ask detainees to make public complaints against their captors, or subject government officials to discovery of documents or oaths to speak truthfully. Unfamiliar with the local language and law, visiting jurists had less than two weeks in country. The United Nations and NGOs have debated but never adopted standardized procedures for missions, which have varied widely in quality. The following evaluation of ICJ reports applies eight guidelines derived from commonly proposed approaches to human rights fact-finding missions.[15]

1. *Selecting Targets*. Even-handed prosecutors should be scrupulously nonpolitical in choosing defendants.

U.N. representatives in political organs made ad hoc judgments revealing a prosecutorial double standard based on national rivalry. The ICJ functioned more like the ILO Standing Committee of Experts, which took cases on the merits instead of partisan interest. The jurists selected violations to investigate rather than opposition groups to support. Target states objected that the ICJ improperly intervened in domestic politics, but their halting cooperation gradually expanded the scope of legitimate international inquiry. Table 9.1 displays the ICJ's balanced attention to all regions in the third world, and minimal response to Eastern Europe and Soviet client states. Four states were subject to repeated inquiries: South Africa, Israel, Sri Lanka, and the Philippines.

The issue priorities and the nationalities of key members and staff best explain the situations investigated. Genocide in East Pakistan and Burundi, military dictatorships in Europe and South America, and colonial rule and apartheid in southern Africa were consensus choices in the 1970s. After MacDermot pressed a reluctant Executive Committee to recognize Palestinian rights, the ICJ became one of the few noncommunist NGOs to criticize Israel. Following T. S. Fernando's tenure as president, the ICJ conducted two missions to his country, Sri Lanka. British and Dutch jurists initiated missions to former colonial territories—South Africa, Rhodesia, Indonesia, and Suriname. American concern about former territories and current allies brought repeated attention to the Philippines, South Korea, and Guatemala. The ICJ strictly monitored abuse of defense lawyers and judges but declined to send election observers.

Misery often attracted a crowd. By the time of the ICJ's third mission to the Philippines in 1990, three other NGOs were preparing simultaneous reports. Just as the ICJ had developed a special relationship with local lawyers, other NGOs sent missions to support their constituents. Target states complained about multiple investigations, but the ICJ did not await exhaustion of domestic remedies or defer to other procedures.

The ICJ investigated anticommunist dictators far more rigorously than communist totalitarians in Cuba, North Korea, Ethiopia, and Albania. Right-wing targets charged the ICJ with a pro-Marxist bias, illustrated by its sympathetic approach to Nicaragua's Sandinistas. The Israeli government also complained about being unfairly singled out. ICJ activists spanned an ideological range that included left-wing socialists and free-market democrats, equally suspect to rightist dictators stoking fears of a "communist" menace. Persistent rumors that the ICJ had been a CIA pawn led MacDermot to emphasize third world rather than Soviet bloc violations. Few NGOs managed to crack closed communist societies; most investigated more cooperative targets and responsive leaders with ties to the West. The ICJ did sufficient reporting on violations behind the Iron Curtain and in Arab states to disprove politically inspired charges of pro-Marxist or anti-Israeli bias.

Conservatives criticized the ICJ for ignoring human rights violations by antigovernment rebels. A U.S. representative charged that MacDermot's support for Palestinians was pro-terrorist.[16] In response MacDermot insisted that the ICJ opposed terror waged by liberation armies or by superior government forces. At the United Nations Artucio complained about Somocista exiles in Honduras committing war crimes. Before appointment as the CIJL director, Reed Brody took affidavits exposing American-supported contra terror in Nicaragua.[17] Yet the ICJ never investigated systematic atrocities by rebel forces engaged in lawless conflict with repressive juntas. Not until 1991 did AI expand its mandate to consider abuses by "nongovernmental entities."

2. *Selecting Jurists*. Fact-finders should be independent, impartial, expert, and honest.

In most instances, the ICJ chose respected jurists who were not beholden to governments and had no direct stake in the situation. In two exceptional cases, Palestinian lawyers prepared investigatory reports on the Israeli Occupied Territories, and a South African lawyer joined a 1990 mission to his own country. When Israelis objected to Palestinian bias, MacDermot replied that Jews would not be disqualified from investigating anti-Semitism. ICJ missions ranged in size from one to five practicing attorneys, law school professors, and judges. Staff legal officers occasionally assisted or led the delegation. More than seventy individuals participated in missions between 1970 and 1990, including twenty from the United States and eleven from Britain. Western experts dominated most inquiries. Sri Lanka's President expressly invited a trusted British jurist to visit following unwelcome criticism from an American expert.[18] Third world jurists constituted just 29 percent of those who investigated situations in Africa, Asia, and Latin America. New members and staff from the third world have recently conducted more missions in their own respective regions.[19]

3. *Finances*. Fact-finding sponsors should be identified and prevented from influencing the investigation.

Each ICJ mission needed special project funding, but nearly half the reports do not identify a source. Separate grants for travel expenses and publishing reports reduced the risk of undue influence by a dominant sponsor. Butler persuaded U.S. foundations—Ford, Levinson, Richmond, Rockefeller Brothers, Weyerhauser—to fund reports on governments of particular conern to Americans, including Iran, Nicaragua, Uganda, South Korea, Guatemala, and Palau. Church councils and Christian denominations with third world congregations and missionaries supported missions to Indonesia and the Philippines. A Muslim Kuwaiti benefactor funded publication of *The West Bank and the Rule of Law*. Not until the Swedish International Development Authority (SIDA) made large grants for the general budget in the late 1980s could the ICJ undertake a mission without first securing special project sponsors.

ICJ reports occasionally nipped a government hand that fed the general budget. A press release called on Britain to allow an international tribunal on civilian killings in Northern Ireland.[20] After an ICJ inquiry commission expedited its independence, Guyana made small annual grants; they stopped after the *Review* publicized new complaints about racial discrimination in the security forces. Elected Greek officials who replaced the junta began making contributions presumably out of appreciation for prior ICJ support rather than in expectation of buying respect.

4. *Official Contacts.* Target states should have an opportunity to answer complaints but cannot be allowed to thwart a valid inquiry.

Government collaboration was the critical ingredient for successful ICJ on-site investigations. MacDermot knew better than to ask Idi Amin for permission to visit Uganda. Argentina detained and deported three ICJ experts studying refugee problems in South America. Morocco expelled a jurist from Quebec.[21] Western diplomats occasionally promoted an ICJ visit by prodding aid recipients to cooperate. As a condition of exchanging ambassadors, Denmark pressed Uganda to accept an ICJ mission. Formal authorization for a mission created opportunities to interview officials, visit prisoners, and discuss recommendations before publication. Cooperating governments might improve conditions with preinspection housecleaning. Giving governments an opportunity to comment on a draft report enhanced the credibility of vulnerable witnesses who could not be identified or cross-examined. Official follow-up meetings with members of the mission could be used to negotiate recommended reforms. In contrast to U.S. trial court procedure, MacDermot treated a state defendant's refusal to deny or explain as acceptable evidence supporting allegations.

A report on Indonesia illustrates the critical interplay of individual commitment, special project funding, and government collaboration. In conjunction with the Australian section, Netherlands attorneys proposed an Indonesian inquiry to their colleague Hans Thoolen. For years, thousands in the former Dutch colony had been detained without trial. Executive Committee member J. Thiem-Hien Yap had been imprisoned for eleven months and supported the inquiry. Churches in the Netherlands agreed to provide most of the funds. Professor Kooijmans, a former junior minister of Foreign Affairs, would head a delegation including Executive Secretary Thoolen and Rodney Lewis of the Australian section.

MacDermot wrote the Indonesian minister of justice, asking him to receive a mission for two weeks in September 1979. The experts applied separately for visas; staff members asked the ministry to arrange appointments with government officials. The minister replied that a heavy work schedule made it impossible to receive a visit. Thoolen and Lewis kept their bookings to visit Indonesia as planned after attending a Lawasia conference in Sri Lanka. They interviewed private citizens but did not contact government officials. MacDermot then wrote the Indonesian minister of foreign affairs, proposing a June 1980 mission. Officials from the United States, Australia, and the Netherlands applied pressure; the prime minister of the Netherlands was asked to raise the issue during an official visit. Fearing a report would be too critical, the Indonesian government reiterated that the proposed time was inconvenient.

Refusing to be stymied by recalcitrant officials, the ICJ used Thoolen's extensive preparatory research for a commercially published hardcover study, *Indonesia and the Rule of Law: Twenty Years of "New Order" Government*.[22] In the six years required to complete the project, the government released most detainees and revised major criminal laws. Professor J.'t Hart visited Indonesia to consult professors and practicing lawyers for a specially commissioned section on criminal justice. His chapter was translated into Bahasa Indonesia as a guide for local practitioners.

5. *Investigation Procedures.* Terms of reference should make clear whether a mission is engaged in fact-finding or evidence gathering.

While attempting the former, ICJ on-site investigations generally accomplished the latter. Visiting jurists could rarely answer precise questions of fact definitively without subpoena and contempt powers. Advance staff research provided essential background information on the political and legal system. In country, delegations often split up to interview as many sources as possible. Most governments allowed unsupervised travel, a few denied interviews with political prisoners. Interviews rarely involved sworn affidavits, cross-examination, or rebuttal. To test allegations the jurists evaluated witness conduct, weighed direct testimony more heavily than hearsay, sought corroboration, and noted admissions against interest. Newspaper clippings, even in countries with a free press, were not reliable evidence. Despite efforts to shield anonymous sources from reprisals, some individuals who provided information became targets of government harassment.

When Chile and Israel publicly disputed ICJ findings based on undisclosed sources, MacDermot responded vigorously. Palestinian lawyers on the Occupied West Bank collected sworn affidavits from torture victims at Al-Fara'a prison; the ICJ published their statements verbatim without naming the victims. Israeli officials denounced the affidavits as false. MacDermot then cited the Israeli conviction of one Al-Fara'a torturer and a petition by the Israeli League for Civil and Human Rights to enjoin further torture.[23]

The World Council of Churches requested an ICJ mission to Chile in 1974 after the Pinochet junta launched a reign of terror. Chile's foreign minister invited "respected organizations" to come see for themselves. MacDermot led the mission, which included Dr. Kurt Madlener of Germany and Professor Covey Oliver, former U.S. assistant secretary of state for inter-American affairs. Longtime ICJ member Sr Osvaldo Illanes Benítez, former president of the Supreme Court, arranged many local contacts.[24] After a ten-day visit, the mission announced preliminary findings to the press: Chile's "state of war" violated Article 3 of the Geneva Conventions, and interrogators systematically practiced torture. When Pinochet announced an end to the state of war in September, the ICJ publicized new facts disputed by the junta. A press release revealed a decree law that continued "military justice" and reported that military supervisors had been assigned to both public and private schools. In U.S. Congressional testimony, MacDermot disclosed secret junta plans disclosed by reliable sources for reeducation camps to rehabilitate six hundred thousand children.[25]

Chile denounced the widely reported ICJ statements with three half-page ads in the *New York Times* and *Washington Post,* a letter to the *Times* editor from the ambassador, statements at the United Nations, and an article in the embassy's monthly periodical, *Chile Today.*[26] The junta's public relations offensive condemned ICJ lies as part of a propaganda blitz by Marxist and Soviet sympathizers. Two ads signed by Chilean lawyers and students decried as a "grotesque invention" claims that the military controlled schools and planned reeducation camps. Illanes Benítez, who had not objected to the mission report, now accused MacDermot of bad faith; he resigned from the ICJ.

MacDermot responded in two press releases and two letters to the *New York Times.* He disclosed a confidential circular issued by a brigadier general to all schools in greater Santiago confirming that military officers had been assigned. The junta never did establish reeducation camps. MacDermot steadfastly defended his confidential source, and it is possible the public row disrupted the government's plans. Chile's counteroffensive persuaded at least one author that MacDermot had exaggerated.[27] *New York Times* editorial writers found the ICJ version credible in light of other documented abuses.[28] In two supplements to the mission report, MacDermot updated information on detention, torture, and disappearances through 1976.

The factual dispute over disappearances in Nicaragua proved more damaging to the ICJ. González rebuked Artucio and MacDermot for not including his evidence in the published report. In a separate confidential report to the Sandinistas, the ICJ had criticized special tribunals established to try members of the National Guard. MacDermot calculated that the vulnerable new regime would take offense if publicly attacked and be more willing to respond to quiet diplomacy.[29] Cynics suggested that both González and Artucio were politically motivated. González had attacked the Sandinistas only after he was excluded from the revolutionary government. Under threat of imprisonment, he made a statement of clarification at trial qualifying his charges. The U.N. Working Group on Disappearances investigated a few of the cases González had identified.[30] The Sandinistas impressed human rights advocates by ratifying international human rights treaties. Iain Guest suggests that Artucio was sympathetic to the Sandinista revolution and also was impressed by their good faith efforts in a difficult situation. Inability to resolve the disputed claims with greater certainty illustrates that missions engage in more prosecutorial evidence gathering than quasi-judicial fact-finding.

6. *Legal Analysis.* The mission should clearly identify which national and international laws apply.

After finding the facts, ICJ experts offered conclusions of law that distinguished bad policy from illegal conduct. The jurists summarized evidence of lawless action and recommended specific legal reforms. They linked as many obligations as possible first to national law and then to human rights treaties. For countries without effective constitutional guarantees whose governments rejected U.N. and regional conventions, the jurists treated the Universal Declaration's fundamental principles as binding law. New York attorney Donald Fox conducted a 1978 mission that concluded El Salvador's Law of Defense and Guarantee of Public Order violated the constitution and the recently ratified American Convention on Human Rights. The government repealed the law. As death squad activity mounted, the United Nations appointed a special rapporteur on El Salvador.

7. *Findings and Recommendations*. The mission should distinguish conclusions of fact from recommendations and solicit a government response.

Most ICJ missions were likely to find a glass half full rather than half empty. Crediting government good deeds wherever possible made criticism appear constructive, and recommendations more acceptable. ICJ representatives typically shared preliminary findings and proposals with local officials. Prompt reforms would be credited. A timely response could influence the mission to revise conclusions or include the response as a rejoinder. The *Review* published one rebuttal by Uruguay. No dissenting opinion ever appeared in the final conclusions, perhaps to avoid disunity that would encourage a hostile government. Two local ICJ members resigned over reports on Uruguay, including one arrested the day after publication.[31]

8. *Publication and Use*. Reports should be timely, published in their entirety or not at all, identify all fact-finders, and explain the terms of reference, funding, and methodology.

ICJ reports varied from ten ditto pages to hardcover books produced by commercial publishers. The ICJ's published reports are highly regarded for their legal analysis, thorough description of political and economic background, and the clear distinction made between conclusions and recommendations. Many reports still fall short of the recommended ideal. About half the publications do not identify a funding source, primary authors are rarely named, and several do not give a date of publication. Information on the terms of reference, interview evidence, and authentication of documents was often incomplete. The ICJ published only its most favorable conclusions about Nicaragua. Volunteer fact-finders often missed publication deadlines, and their delayed reports were occasionally outdated. Missions supported by permanent staff did more timely work. Overall, the reports won high marks for reliability based on the quality of evidence reported, the experts' status, and the ICJ's solid reputation.

To publish or not to publish was an easy question. Mobilizing shame was the norm, and local human rights victims desperately needed international recognition. Even when using reports to activate the U.N. confidential communication procedure, the ICJ publicized its findings. Extensive press contacts, a large distribution network, and translation into the local language maximized the reports' impact. Over a fifteen-year period, the *New York Times* carried articles and editorials based on ICJ reports involving seventeeen different countries.

Widespread dissemination influenced image-conscious targets dependent on the West. A balanced report of a 1976 mission to Iran embarrassed the Shah. Butler acknowledged Iran's progress on economic and social rights, but criticized the secret police, SAVAK, for torture and suppression of political opposition. Iran initially countered with a newspaper ad claiming the ICJ was CIA funded. That summer the Shah commissioned "[a leading] pollster to survey American attitudes toward him and Iran. . . . The poll results hurt [his] *amour propre*."[32] Butler presented his findings in testimony before a House committee and shared the Shah's comments on the ICJ report. Human rights concerns in the Carter administration and Congress jeopardized the Shah's opportunity to purchase U.S. AWACS and F-16 aircraft. The State Department's country reports on human rights practices expressly noted NGO criticism of aid recipients.

In a dramatic change, Iran allowed ICRC investigators to visit prisons and invited AI and ICJ representatives to separate audiences with the Shah. The Shah's brother had been a classmate of Butler at Harvard College. In his first meeting, Butler presented an ICJ memorandum recommending amendments to the military justice system and penal code. If Iran adopted the proposals, he indicated the ICJ would comment favorably on the situation. Without consulting the Ministry of Justice, the Shah directed Parliament to amend five articles of the Iranian Military Court rules. The promptly approved amendments provided for civilian defense counsel, public trials, and preliminary interrogation within twenty-four hours. Assured that the Shah would not object to public disclosure of their discussion, Butler favorably reported the partial reforms to Congress.[33] He expressed regret that Iran had not yet assured medical exams for arrested detainees or removed SAVAK's power to arraign. The U.S. ambassador to Iran offered to facilitate further discussions.

Butler had a second meeting with the Shah in 1978. His Imperial Majesty agreed to transfer trials of civilians from military to regular courts and to lift the ban on three human rights groups, including the Iranian Association of Jurists. AI and the ICJ had made the same complaints, but U.S. Ambassador William Sullivan concluded that Butler's "constructive" tenor had been more persuasive.[34] When the dynasty fell, conservatives charged that the liberalization had aided fanatics who then rescinded the Shah's progressive economic policies and instituted a far more oppressive reign of terror. Following his exile to Panama, the Shah reportedly told a U.S. State Department officer "I never should have listened to Butler."[35] Human rights advocates concluded the Shah's reforms had been too little, too late. The Carter administration received the ultimate credit, or blame, for pulling the Shah's plug.

The ICJ confronted more recalcitrant offenders in human rights arenas where major powers could be enlisted to impose stiffer penalties. MacDermot offered U.S. congressional testimony on Chile and South Africa and worked effectively to activate intergovernmental procedures.

Confrontation at the United Nations

For all their limitations, U.N. and regional human rights bodies have considerably more clout than small NGOs, however reputable. Professionally produced ICJ reports were more readable and reached a larger public than poorly reproduced and difficult-to-obtain U.N. documents. Yet U.N. reports distributed in five working languages commanded greater attention from sensitive officials. The ICJ pressed ten different U.N. and regional bodies of diplomats and experts to investigate regimes committing gross violations. The jurists documented atrocities, presented victim testimony, pressed for official investigations, and proposed resolutions for adoption. At NGO conferences on Palestinian rights, Namibia, and South America, the ICJ joined the international equivalent of domestic protest rallies.

When target governments effectively manipulated U.N. procedures to their advantage, the ICJ repeated complaints wherever action was possible. African delegates and the nonaligned bloc suppressed ICJ evidence on Uganda at the U.N. Commission on Human Rights. MacDermot published the reports and distributed copies to prime ministers attending a Commonwealth meeting in London. They adopted a resolution condemning Idi Amin.[36] The U.N. Commission and the OAU showed even less interest in Butler's report on genocide in Burundi, which the International Labor Organization took more seriously.[37] The U.N. Sub-Commission disregarded an urgent ICJ appeal on East Pakistan, leaving the U.N. High Commissioner for Refugees to help the Bengalis.[38] A staff study circulated to the European Parliament detailed how martial law in Turkey breached the European Convention on Human Rights.[39] Well briefed by the ICJ and other NGOs, the IACHR conducted major on-site investigations that confirmed gross violations in Chile, Haiti, and Argentina. When the U.N. Human Rights Committee began receiving country reports, ICJ memoranda to sympathetic experts encouraged tough questioning of government representatives.

The worst offenders were not parties to regional conventions or the international covenant. Specialized U.N. agencies with global membership protected only selected rights. The U.N. Commission on Human Rights and its Sub-Commission provided a forum for confronting any government about any violation. In 1973 those bodies moved with the U.N. Secretariat's Human Rights Division to Geneva, creating easy access for ICJ staff. AI had only a local volunteer and sent representatives from London to the annual meetings. MacDermot chaired the Geneva NGO Special Committee on Human Rights until 1988.

New third world members initiated U.N. Commission protection measures in 1967 to support self-determination in Southern Africa and the Israeli Occupied Territories. NGOs and Western governments demanded investigations of other gross violations. A procedural compromise allowed public debate criticizing a few selected pariahs and confidential review of all other communications alleging a consistent pattern of violations. Experts on the Sub-Commission screened private communications for referral to government representatives on the U.N. Commission who were authorized to investigate.

The ICJ zealously took on the pariahs—South Africa, Rhodesia, Israel, Chile—reporting from its own missions to U.N. working groups that were denied permission for on-site visits. A 1971 ICJ Aspen Conference statement on Southern Africa was circulated to Commission members as a U.N. document. MacDermot repeatedly testified on apartheid laws and Rhodesian violations before a Commission working group of experts chaired by ICJ member Kéba Mbaye. In New York, ICJ representatives regularly gave evidence to the U.N. Committees on decolonization, Namibia, and apartheid. At the Sub-Commission, ICJ legal experts challenged South African laws denationalizing citizens assigned to "independent" homelands, recommended World Court review of the white-imposed constitution, and distributed the 1988 mission report, *South Africa and the Rule of Law*. The U.N. Centre Against Apartheid published an ICJ report on children and affidavits on torture in South Africa. The ICJ supplied a working group on Chile with firsthand evidence and contributed to a U.N. Sub-Commission report on the consequences of economic aid to the junta. The ICJ's legal expertise discredited Pinochet's attempt to legalize his rule under a new constitution.

MacDermot began confronting Israel in 1980. He reported to the Commission about his visit to the West Bank and Gaza and his discussions with Prime Minister Begin. In balanced remarks, MacDermot challenged military administration but did not endorse extreme charges of systematic torture. Israel had not allowed the U.N. Special Committee to visit the Occupied Territories. *The West Bank and the*

Rule of Law was distributed with the Special Committee report to the General Assembly, and Jordan requested copies for U.N. Commission members. When the ICJ presented its Palestinian affiliate report on torture at Al Fara'a prison, Israeli representatives made outraged denials. The U.N. Commission devoted nearly one-third of each annual meeting for politically contentious condemnation of South Africa and Israel. While supporting those investigations, the ICJ also lobbied persistently to pierce the veil of silence shielding other offenders from public shame.

Tyrants with allies had considerable advantages over NGOs in a U.N. confrontation. Forty-three government representatives comprised the U.N. Commission on Human Rights, a constituency more devoted to sovereign prerogatives than to human rights. Major states targeted by the ICJ became U.N. Commission members in order to prevent scrutiny. Governments limited NGO access, deciding who could speak, for how long, and on what subject. Outspoken ICJ witnesses provoked counterattacks on its consultative status and right to name its own representative. The U.N. Commission elected twenty-eight experts to the Sub-Commission, supposedly in their personal capacity. Governments targeted for scrutiny voted to replace principled experts with instructed individuals. The nonaligned movement countered Western-initiated complaints by enlarging the Commission to fifty-three, with ten additional third world members. A South African intelligence officer infiltrated a respected Geneva NGO, presumably to provide cover for attacking critics of apartheid.[40]

Confidential Procedures

Initially, NGO speakers at the U.N. Commission could only mention by name those few situations its government members had approved for public discussion. All other private complaints began under resolution 1503 with confidential Sub-Commission screening. The ICJ published a guide for NGOs explaining how to file communications.[41] With three other NGOs, the ICJ submitted the first major complaint against the Greek colonels.

The procedure imposed inordinate delays that prevented timely action. Communications had to arrive for processing six weeks before the Sub-Commission's August meeting. Whenever the ICJ presented supplemental evidence after the deadline, the U.N. Secretariat held it for a year. Before referring a complaint to the U.N. Commission, experts invited the government charged to respond by the following year. The U.N. never informed the ICJ whether its petitions had been rejected or forwarded to the Commission. Governments could learn which Sub-Commission experts had voted for Commission review. The Commission invited governments charged to send representatives but offered no such opportunities to complainants. The Commission kept situations under confidential review for years without ever initiating formal inquiries.

MacDermot confronted and exposed the charade. The ICJ first publicized a 1503 communication against Uganda in a June 1974 press release and in TV and radio broadcasts. Amin threatened to expel all remaining Britons if the BBC broadcasts continued. His exiled brother-in-law and former foreign minister, Wanume Kibedi, responded in an open letter that confirmed Amin's crimes. Two weeks before the Sub-Commission convened, MacDermot supplemented the initial communication with two statements by Kibedi linking Amin to the chief justice's disappearance. The Kibedi supplement arrived too late for distribution as an official document, but MacDermot provided copies to Sub-Commission members. They referred the situation to the Commission for review, but could not incorporate the latest evidence from Kibedi. Another exile wrote to MacDermot reporting on how security forces had killed a foreign official and had left the writer, a former civil servant, for dead. The ICJ forwarded his testimony to the U.N. Secretariat.

As atrocities mounted, the U.N. Commission granted every courtesy to Uganda's representatives for two years. A 1975 resolution adopted in closed session threatened to strip NGOs that violated confidentiality of their consultative status. Uganda's ambassador denounced the ICJ at the General Assembly, provoking a reply by the British delegate. Amin became OAU chairman, and Uganda won election to the Commission in 1977. The nonaligned bloc resisted Western calls for public investigation of the atrocities. Amin publicly claimed that he had been cleared by the Commission.

For the Commission's third Uganda debate, the ICJ prepared another 1503 communication—ninety-two pages of eyewitness accounts describing torture as well as individual and mass killings. Heeding the earlier warning about confidentiality, MacDermot did not publish the evidence. The Sub-Commission forwarded the fresh complaint. By the time the Commission met in 1977, troops had massacred university students on campus, and Amin had had Archbishop Luvum killed. Over the protest of British Foreign Secretary David Owen, the Commission approved a confidential rather than public inquiry. After three missed opportunities, MacDermot called the Commission out. Within two months the ICJ published its five thoroughly documented communications—167 pages in all—which the U.N. Commission had ignored for three years.[42] The Commonwealth prime ministers took the evidence seriously enough to condemn Amin publicly. Realpolitik terminated his reign of terror when Tanzania invaded. Disregarding ICJ calls for a full accounting, the Commission canceled its inquiry. Instead of an embarrassing report on government lawlessness, the Commission offered Uganda advisory services to improve respect for human rights.

On behalf of the Geneva NGOs, MacDermot proposed reforming the 1503 procedure. He recommended treating unanswered complaints as valid and giving petitioners fair opportunity to comment on government replies. Little changed. In 1978 the U.N. Commission chairman began publicly announcing which countries were subject to confidential proceedings. The only information made public involved two governments that had never responded to inquiries. With minimal cooperation, egregious offenders such as Uruguay kept all details confidential for eight years.

Uruguay's Commission representative feigned cooperation for three years before the Commission asked the U.N. Secretary-General to send an envoy to Montevideo. The Peruvian-born Undersecretary-General for political affairs, Javier Pérez de Cuéllar, visited Liberty jail. His leaked report to the Commission read like a brief for the government. Pérez de Cuéllar reported meeting the pianist Miguel Estrella, who appeared healthy. The favorable account supported Uruguay's effort to avoid further scrutiny. Estrella was released before the Commission convened, and Artucio contacted him in Paris. In a visit to Geneva, Estrella gave human rights director van Boven written notes denying any meeting or interview with Pérez de Cuéllar. Van Boven circulated the statement discrediting Pérez de Cuéllar's report.[43] The Commission kept Uruguay under confidential review but obtained only token concessions until democracy was restored. Ironically, a process created to pressure governments became a refuge, shielding offenders from public U.N. criticism.

Public Investigation

The ICJ cultivated alternative approaches to open up U.N. monitoring and condemnation. The Working Group on Disappearances and U.N. Commission rapporteurs on torture and summary killing created expert fact-finding that generated public reports. The Sub-Commission offered a comprehensive public forum for ICJ complaints and possible monitoring. Western governments nominated as experts principled human rights advocates—the Minority Rights Group director from Britain, Canadian and Dutch former directors of the U.N. Human Rights Division, Belgian and Dutch jurists who conducted ICJ missions. The ICJ documented genocide in Kampuchea and exposed forced labor practices in Uganda at the Sub-Commission Working Group on Slavery. Daniel Ravindran urged that group to denounce prostitution in Thailand, sex tourism in the Philippines, and bonded labor in India. The Working Group on Detention heard ICJ complaints about South Korea, Taiwan, Malaysia, and Singapore. Professor Virginia Leary briefed the experts about her ICJ mission to Sri Lanka. Artucio provided documentation on Guatemala, El Salvador, and Bolivia. Target states and their U.N. Commission allies replaced experts responsive to NGO concerns; they defeated activists from Tunisia, Italy, and Norway who were up for reelection and chose experts more responsive to national interests. An independent Sub-Commission expert from Romania and a Commission representative from Iraq were prevented by their governments from attending meetings of U.N. experts.

MacDermot's six-year confrontation with Argentina helped secure NGOs' right to name state offenders publicly and to present victim witnesses at the Commission. Argentina challenged the NGO's consultative status after MacDermot sponsored an exiled lawyer's presentation to the Sub-Commission. In a mission to Argentina, Heleno Fragoso had identified Rodolfo Matarollo as one of sixteen defense lawyers whose lives were threatened. Matarollo got out alive, but his law partner disappeared.

Palestinian and Chilean exiles had previously given firsthand witness testimony at the United Nations, but Argentina had not previously been subjected to public review. For the first time, MacDermot allowed someone other than a staff member to present an ICJ statement. Argentina's ambassador charged the ICJ with violating U.N. rules against "politically motivated" statements. Matarollo had known connections to a guerrilla organization. MacDermot rationalized that law and lawyers were ICJ concerns, "and in Latin America of 1976 both were endangered species. . . . Someone had to speak up for the legion of murdered lawyers, and Matarollo was the right man at the right time."[44] To former British Minister MacDermot, Matarollo was no different than a Sinn Fein dissident who did not become an IRA gunman. Matarollo next spoke at the Commission as a Pax Romana representative.

An Argentine diplomat pretending to be a graduate student examined U.N. files on the ICJ and three other NGOs. None had submitted the quadrennial reports required after the 1960s ECOSOC review of NGOs. At Argentina's insistence, the U.N. Secretariat called on all NGOs to report promptly, and also called on governments to comment. Argentina denounced the ICJ for making slanderous attacks and designating a terrorist as its representative. A blizzard prevented Argentina's top representatives from reaching New York when the ECOSOC Committee on NGOs reviewed their status. The junior representative could not rebut an ICJ report that Matarollo was a distinguished lawyer who had been a minister of education for the provincial government of Buenos Aires from 1965 to 1969.[45] A British representative questioned leftist NGOs about their financing. The ICJ spokesman candidly acknowledged funding by U.S. foundations and twenty-one governments rather than by local human rights groups. ECOSOC routinely approved ongoing consultative status for all.

The ICJ's most celebrated confrontation with Argentina deadlocked a Human Rights Commission meeting in 1982. Several local lawyers whose children had disappeared formed a center for legal and social studies that affiliated with the ICJ. Security forces raided the office and detained its director, Emilio Mignone, for seven days in 1981. MacDermot authorized Mignone to report for the ICJ about his daughter's kidnapping in the Commission's public debate on disappearances. MacDermot asked the Bulgarian chairman in advance to allow him to reply to any objection, and if necessary, to allow Artucio to speak as an alternate. At the meeting, Argentina's ambassador objected to Mignone; the chairman called on Artucio without giving MacDermot a chance to respond. When Artucio mentioned Mignone, the Argentinian objected again. Senegal's delegate came to the ICJ's rescue, insisting that NGOs were entitled to nominate their own representatives. In the ensuing hour of debate, seven governments and van Boven spoke up for that principle.

During a recess for negotiations, MacDermot encountered strange bedfellows. The Eastern bloc and Cuba wanted free representation for their NGOs. The U.K. and U.S. urged compromise; Argentina and its Latin American allies threatened to break a consensus to renew the Working Group on Disappearances and refuse future cooperation. NGOs denounced the blackmail and insisted that Mignone should speak. Debate resumed with delegates from Zambia and the Netherlands forcefully supporting the ICJ. When the chairman called on Artucio to continue, MacDermot took the floor. If he could not answer the allegations against Mignone, the ICJ had nothing more to say.

After another protracted debate, the chairman allowed MacDermot to answer the allegations; then Artucio would resume. MacDermot concluded his response by proposing that if no one objected, he would pass the microphone to Mignone. Argentina's ambassador missed his cue until Mignone had spoken for several moments. Denouncing the politically motivated attack, the ambassador promised to pursue the matter at a higher level if the chairman ruled against him. The chairman allowed Mignone to complete his poignant account of how the entire family watched soldiers take his daughter Mónica from their home. Two other NGOs then called Argentinians without difficulty; a Mother of the Plaza de Mayo represented Pax Christi.[46] MacDermot's bold defense of NGO rights had kept the U.N. Commission open to firsthand witness testimony.[47] Yet Argentina's dirty war had toppled van Boven, whose dismissal the NGOs protested in vain.

Success at the U.N. Commission was rare. The ICJ had only moral approbation to offer state representatives for doing the right thing. A few friendly diplomats might enlist other government cosponsors. The Western bloc, with only a fourth of the membership, had the most ICJ sympathizers, particularly from the Netherlands and Scandinavia. During the Carter administration, an NGO director once represented the United States. Appointees of presidents Reagan and Bush were decidedly less supportive. Within the African and Latin American regional blocs, Senegal and Costa Rica pushed ICJ proposals. Representatives of postcommunist Eastern bloc governments from Poland and Hungary offer new access. Other states not known for taking principled action backed those ICJ complaints which embarrassed political rivals. Most target governments had more U.N. Commission friends than did the ICJ. Tragically, but not surprisingly, the Commission ignored ICJ and AI complaints that Iraq had massacred Kurds. Members saw no evil until Saddam Hussein seized Kuwait's oil.

A confrontation with China after the 1989 Tiananmen Square massacre illustrated ICJ tactics and NGO weakness. The U.N. Sub-Commission was the first to convene after the killings, and its quasi-independent experts were more likely than instructed diplomats to challenge a major power. Twenty-three NGOs coordinated an extraordinary Sub-Commission complaint against China, the first naming a permanent Security Council member. They sponsored an exiled student from Beijing's most-wanted list as the first speaker. China protested allowing an exiled "criminal" to speak. The Sub-Commission chairman, French expert and longtime ICJ supporter Louis Joinet, allowed the witness testimony. Different NGOs reported on students, trade unions, the press, and the legal system. In a closing speech for the NGOs, MacDermot summarized the evidence and urged the Sub-Commission to act. China threatened economic retaliation against governments whose experts supported a critical resolution. Joinet

ICJ Secretary-General Niall MacDermot and CIJL Director Reed Brody attending a 1988 meeting of the U.N. Commission on Human Rights.

arranged to suspend the rules so that the experts could cast a secret ballot. Fifteen voted to pass a resolution requesting the Secretary-General to provide information on China to the Commission.[48]

Responding to the U.N. request for information, China condemned the resolution as a brutal interference in its internal affairs, null and void.[49] The Secretariat's thirty-three-page report to the Human Rights Commission summarized materials from three NGOs. China objected without success to an exiled NGO witness who addressed the Commission. A Western-initiated resolution called on China to release detainees. Nonaligned members narrowly won a vote to take no further action.[50]

In 1990 the United Nations was neither a dangerous place nor an effective forum for protecting civil liberties. The ICJ had helped NGOs dominate the Sub-Commission and publicize embarrassing evidence at the Commission. Ever-increasing protest testimony by victim witnesses sparked new efforts to silence NGOs. A budget crisis created cover for governments opposed to the Sub-Commission's independent monitoring. An unholy alliance of target governments and the frugal proposed to eliminate protection activities that duplicated Commission procedures or to abolish the Sub-Commission altogether.

The Group of 77, or nonaligned states, proposed diverting all individual communications from special rapporteurs to the confidential 1503 procedure, creating a Commission group to monitor complaints against NGOs, and reviewing NGO oral statements twenty-four hours in advance. Western members blocked those crippling reforms but yielded to demands for enlarging the Commission by adding ten third world members.

Conclusions

In national political systems, courts and regulatory agencies implement and enforce the law. In the primitive international system, negative opinion is the most common sanction. The United Nations denounces, diplomats protest, and NGOs condemn. Realists consider public opinion unimportant. "In closed systems or in totalitarian regimes, governments consult neither domestic nor foreign opinions. . . . They manufacture opinion more than they are constrained by it. . . . many governments most of the time see external manifestations of public opinion as only a peripheral consideration in policy making."[51] Did ICJ advocacy check any state misconduct or trigger effective sanctions by others?

Enforcement

ICJ protest is obviously a poor substitute for an international judicial system with compulsory jurisdiction over state criminals. Instead of adjudication by a world court that can enforce judgments, NGOs comprise an opinion tribunal that induces compliance by shaming the guilty. The ICJ's quiet diplomacy directed elite criticism to officials who violated international norms, and its negative publicity generated wider condemnation. ICJ individual casework clearly helped some grateful political prisoners win freedom or clemency. Solidarity with an outside NGO encouraged local self-help groups to demand fundamental human rights. The ousted Shah of Iran reportedly blamed himself for adopting ICJ recommendations.

Implementation

When the ICJ received the first European Human Rights Prize, MacDermot spoke to the European Parliamentary Assembly of the complementary roles played by governments and NGOs.[52] The ICJ had only the ability to expose; governments retained superior power to enforce. Successful international protection against government abuse, ironically, depends on positive state action. ICJ quiet diplomacy, negative publicity, legislative testimony, and U.N. lobbying required both adversarial confrontation and government alliances. ICJ fact-finding reports and U.N. interventions added to the unquantifiable mix of pressures that brought dramatic changes to nine oppressive regimes in Spain, Greece, Chile, Iran, Argentina, Uruguay, South Africa, South Korea, and the Philippines. Argentina's junta took the ICJ as a serious enough threat to attempt revocation of its U.N. consultative status and to silence its representative at the Human Rights Commission.

ICJ protection activities reveal that NGOs contribute significantly to the rudimentary implementation and enforcement of international human rights law. To confront injustice, the ICJ published fact-finding reports, encouraged bilateral sanctions, and activated intergovernmental procedures. A tiny staff maximized its impact by collaborating effectively with other NGOs, committee experts, and democratic governments. In a developed political system, supranational institutions would perform the protection functions that obviously exceed NGO capabilities. Yet human rights advocacy has affected states sufficiently to reveal incremental development of embryonic implementation and enforcement mechanisms. The following chapter provides further evidence of that development in an arena central to the jurists' primary mission.

ICJ/CIJL Reports on Violations, 1970–1990

Argentina

The Situation of Defence Lawyers in Argentina. 1975.

Central African Republic

Brody, Reed. *"Ou est l'honneur"—le proces de Maître Nicolas Tiangaye.* Geneva: ICJ/CIJL, 1990. 38 pp. Report of a 1990 trial in the Central African Republic.

Chile

Report of Mission to Chile, the Legal System and the Protection of Human Rights. Geneva: ICJ, 1974. *Supplement,* Janunary 1975; *Supplement,* September 1976.

Brett, Sebastian. *Chile: A Time of Reckoning—Human Rights and the Judiciary.* Geneva: CIJL, 1992. 259 pp.

Colombia

Violencia en Colombia. Lima, Peru: ICJ/Andean Commission of Jurists, 1990. 130 pp.

El Salvador

Fox, Donald. *Report of Mission to El Salvador.* 1978. 14 pp. (Engl./Fr./Sp.).
Artucio, Alejandro. *El Salvador: Un Brecha a la Impunidad.* Geneva: ICJ, 1991. Trans. as *A Breach of Impunity: The Trial for the Murder of Jesuits in El Salvador.* New York: Fordham University Press, 1992.

Equatorial Guinea

The Trial of Macias in Equatorial Guinea. Geneva: ICJ, 1979. 90 pp. (Engl./Sp.).

Guatemala

Fox, Donald. *Human Rights in Guatemala.* 1979. 58 pp.
Butler, William, and George Edwards. *Guatemala: A New Beginning.* New York: AAICJ, 1987.

Guinea

L'indépendence des magistrats, des avocats et des officiers ministériels en République de Guinée. Geneva: ICJ/CIJL, 1988. 31 pp.

Indonesia

Thoolen, Hans ed. *Indonesia: Twenty Years of "New Order" Government.* London: Frances Pinter, 1987. 208 pp.

Iran

Human Rights and the Legal System in Iran. Two reports by ICJ Observers, William J. Butler and Professor Georges Levasseur. Geneva: ICJ, 1976. 80 pp.

Israel

The West Bank and the Rule of Law. 1980. 128 pp. (Engl./Fr.).
Civilian Administration in the Occupied West Bank. 1982. 44 pp.
Academic Freedom Under Israeli Military Occupation. 1984. 87 pp.
Torture and Intimidation in the West Bank: The case of Al-Fara'a Prison. A staff report of Law in the Service of Man. 1984. 56 pp.

Inquiry into the Israeli Military Court System in the Occupied West Bank and Gaza. Report of a Mission by Jordan J. Paust, Gerhard von Glahn, and Günter Woratsch. Geneva: ICJ, 1989.

Japan

Human Rights and Mental Patients in Japan. Geneva: ICJ, 1986. 84 pp.

Korea

Dewind, Adrian W., and John Woodhouse. *Persecution of Defence Lawyers in South Korea.* Geneva: ICJ, 1979. 68 pp.
South Korea: Human Rights in the Emerging Politics. Geneva: CIJL, 1987. 96 pp.

Morocco

Morocco, Trial in Rabat arising out of Disturbances on 20 and 21 June 1981. Geneva: CIJL, 1981. 25 pp. (Engl./Fr.)

Nicaragua

Human Rights in Nicaragua: Yesterday and Today. Geneva: ICJ, 1980. 85 pp.

Pakistan/Bangladesh

The Events in East Pakistan, 1971. Geneva: ICJ, 1972. 98 pp.
Pakistan: Human Rights after Martial Law. Geneva: ICJ, 1987. 158 pp.

Palau

Palau: A Challenge to the Rule of Law in Micronesia. Report of a Mission. Geneva: ICJ, 1988. 58 pp.

Philippines

Decline of Democracy in the Philippines. A Report on Human Rights under Martial Law by William J. Butler, John P. Humphrey and G. E. Bisson. Geneva: ICJ, 1977. 107 pp.
Human Rights Advocacy in the Philippines. Report of a Mission by the New Zealand and Australian Sections. Sydney, Australia: El Faro, 1985. 72 pp.

Singapore

Report of the International Mission of Jurists to Singapore. 1987. 30 pp.

South Africa

The Trial of Beyers Naudé: Christian Witness and the Rule of Law. London: Search Press, 1974. 188 pp.
Detention of Children in South Africa. Geneva: ICJ, 1978. 8 pp.
Bindman, Geoffrey ed. *South Africa: Human Rights and the Rule of Law.* London: Frances Pinter, 1988. 159 pp.
Will Namibia's Elections be Free and Fair? Geneva: ICJ, 1989. 23 pp.

Southern Rhodesia

Racial Discrimination and Repression in Southern Rhodesia. Geneva: ICJ, 1976. 119 pp.

Sri Lanka

Leary, Virginia. *Ethnic Conflict and Violence in Sri Lanka.* Geneva: ICJ, 1981. 87 pp.
Sieghart, Paul. *Sri Lanka: A Mounting Tragedy of Errors.* Geneva: ICJ, 1984. 95 pp.

Sudan

Halasa, Adib, John D. Cooke, and Ustinia Dolgopol. *The Return to Democracy in Sudan.* Geneva: ICJ/CIJL, 1986. 99 pp.

Suriname

Human Rights in Suriname. Geneva: ICJ, 1983. 14 pp.
Suriname, Recent Developments Relating to Human Rights. Geneva: ICJ, 1981. 34 pp.

Uganda

Uganda and Human Rights: Reports to the UN Commission on Human Rights. Geneva: ICJ, 1977. 167 pp.

Uruguay

Report of Mission to Uruguay. 1974 (Eng./Sp.); *Supplement*, 1975. *Supplement*, 1976.
Amarillo, María del Huerto, and Fernando Urioste. *Uruguay: Independencia del Poder Judicial y de los Jueces.* (*Uruguay: The Independence of the Judiciary and of Judges.*) Uruguay: ICJ, 1990. 220 pp.

Chapter 10
Representing the Bench and Bar

Article 8. Everyone has the right to an effective remedy by the competent national tribunals for acts violating the fundamental rights granted him by the constitution or by law.

Article 10. Everyone is entitled in full equality to a fair and public hearing by an independent and impartial tribunal, in the determination of his rights and obligations and of any criminal charge against him.

Article 11. Everyone charged with a penal offence has the right to be presumed innocent until proved guilty according to law in a public trial at which he has had all the guarantees necessary for his defence.

—Universal Declaration of Human Rights

Lawyers are alternately honored and reviled. In Boston and Bangkok critics detest attorneys' high fees and high living. The bar seems to produce scores of ambulance chasers for each civil liberties hero. Comedians have entire routines of cutting jokes about lawyers' greed, opportunism, bribery, dishonesty, and political connections. "Question: What would you call forty lawyers at the bottom of Lake Geneva? Answer: A good start!" Curmudgeons on the bench defy majority rule, defend privilege, and resist social change. Wags in Chicago claim it is more important to know the judge than to know the law. Yet Chicago attorney Clarence Darrow courageously defended the underdog. U.S. Supreme Court judges appointed by Richard Nixon independently decided a case that doomed his presidency. Brave jurists in Colombia and the Philippines give their lives for human rights.

Politics has threatened judicial independence without respect for ideology. Communist judges functioned as lackeys of the party. Islamic governments favored religious justice in Shari'a courts. Leftist third world leaders painted the bar as a privileged elite beholden to Western interests. Right-wing dictators treated all who challenged their authority as Marxist traitors. Tyrants of varied persuasions abolished the regular courts, prosecuted civilians without counsel before military tribunals, and imprisoned or disbarred outspoken defense lawyers. Drug dealers, large landowners, and terrorists assassinated judges who threatened their interests. Democratically elected executives manipulated judicial appointments, transfers, assignments, promotions, and retirement for political advantage.

Canadian lawyer John Humphrey drafted provisions for the Universal Declaration of Human Rights that endorsed trial before an independent, impartial, competent tribunal with all the necessary guarantees for defense. Those guarantees were not proclaimed to establish a legal elite. Without immunity from political interference, jurists cannot protect fundamental rights. With unchecked power, they become corrupt. When the human rights movement came of age in the 1970s, third world activists became an endangered species. Western lawyers organized to protect defense lawyers tortured as terrorists and judges assassinated for their independence. In 1975 the ABA created a new committee, an inactive New York Bar committee revived, and New York attorneys created the Lawyers Committee for Human Rights (LCHR).

The ICJ acted after a fact-finding mission to Argentina identified twenty-six lawyers subjected to death threats. In 1977 Executive Committee chairman William Butler obtained a Rockefeller Brothers Foundation grant to start an American ICJ Centre for the Independence of Judges and Lawyers (CIJL). The Executive Committee and members attending a Commission meeting endorsed the Centre and a protection strategy. The CIJL would collect information about harassment that could move lawyers' organizations to aid colleagues in distress. ICJ Secretary-General Niall MacDermot persuaded Butler to make the CIJL part of the Geneva Secretariat; its first director joined the staff in 1978.

The start-up grant ended after two years, and attorneys never contributed enough to pay the director's salary. The Centre relied on government and foundation grants rather than membership recruitment and affiliate development. A French judge on the CIJL Advisory Board resigned because his recommendations for government grants to the ICJ might have created a conflict of interest. The Ford Foundation supported publication of a *CIJL Bulletin* in three languages that reached two thousand subscribers in 127 countries. As ICJ Secretary-General, MacDermot ran the CIJL through a young lawyer employed as director. ICJ legal officers assisted with projects in their regions. The first two directors, John Woodhouse of New Zealand and Dan O'Donnell from the United States, each served two years. Americans Ustinia Dolgopol and Reed Brody each directed the Centre for more than four years. Table 10.1 identifies the directors and advisory board members.

TABLE 10.1. CIJL Directors and Advisory Board, 1978–1992.

CIJL Directors	
John Woodhouse (New Zealand)	Feb. 1978–Feb. 1980
Daniel O'Donnell (U.S.)	Feb. 1980–1982
Ustinia Dolgopol (U.S.)	1982–1987
Reed Brody (U.S.)	1987–1991
Mona Rishmawi (West Bank)	1991 Aug.–
CIJL Advisory Board, 1992	
P. N. Bhagwati	Former Chief Justice of India, Chairman
Perfecto Andres Ibañez	Judge, Spain
Lloyd Barnett	President, Organization of Commonwealth Caribbean Bar Associations, Jamaica
Amar Bentoumi	Secretary-General, International Association of Democratic Lawyers, Algeria
Sir Robin Cooke	President, Court of Appeal, New Zealand
Marie-Jose Crespin	Vice President, "Conseil Constitutionnel," Senegal
Param Cumaraswamy	Past President, Malaysia Bar Council; Chairman, Standing Committee on Human Rights, International Bar Association
Jules Deschênes	Former Chief Justice, Superior Court of Quebec, Canada
Enoch Dumbutshena	Former Chief Justice, Zimbabwe
Diego García-Sayan	Executive Director, Andean Commission of Jurists; Peru Member U.N. Working Group on Disappearances
Stephen Klitzman	Chairman, Committee on International Human Rights, American Bar Association
Pablito Sanidad	Chairman, Free Legal Assistance Group, Philippines
Beinusz Szmukler	President, American Association of Jurists, Argentina
Abderahman Yousoffi	Deputy-Secretary General, Arab Lawyers Union, Morocco; Vice President, Arab Organization for Human Rights
Suriya Wickremasinghe	Barrister, Sri Lanka

NGO allies grew considerably larger. Former ICJ intern Michael Posner directed the LCHR with three times the staff available to MacDermot and opened a branch office in Washington, D.C. The Human Rights Watch Committees monitored violations in Eastern Europe and the third world. A former Cold War adversary, the International Association of Democratic Lawyers became another large ally.

As more and more NGOs interconnected in a global protection network, the tiny CIJL also did standard setting and promotion. Its Geneva location and third world affiliates helped the CIJL in drafting United Nations principles for an independent judiciary and in sponsoring seminars for non-Western jurists. The United Nations endorsed a 1989 Caracas Conference on the Independence of Judges and Lawyers, marking the CIJL's tenth anniversary. An ICJ triennial meeting adopted a Caracas plan of action to strengthen the Centre. India's former chief justice, P. N. Bhagwati, chaired a new CIJL Advisory Board with a third world majority. Strengthened by grants from the Swedish International Development Authority (SIDA), the CIJL hired Mona Rishmawi from the Israeli Occupied West Bank to succeed Brody. Third world members, staff, and bar affiliates now passionately advocate the due process model and adversary system developed in Western industrial democracies. This chapter presents a complete account of CIJL protection, standard setting, and promotion activities through 1992; the following chapter in Part V covers other ICJ developments from 1990 to 1992 without further reference to the CIJL.

Protection Casework

From 1978 to 1992 the CIJL dealt with cases from eighty-three countries. Brazilian Supreme Court judge Francisco Rezek clearly differentiated public advocacy case work from special interest pleading for a legal elite:

> The independence of judges and lawyers is not an end in itself; it is a means placed at the service of the community. The judiciary must not stake its claim in the name of the privileges of its members or for the pleasure of an Olympian affirmation of its own power. Its independence and dignity must be defended in the common interest of our peoples, and in particular in the name of the most humble elements of society, of those who most intensely rely upon a free, efficient, altruistic, honest and wise system of justice.[1]

The Centre targeted offenders who, through harassment, obstructed professional activity essential to securing justice for all under the rule of law—"advising and representation of clients, advocacy of law

TABLE 10.2. CIJL Protection Activities, 1978–1992.

Region	*Intervention or circular*	*Trial ob-servers*	*Bulletin articles*	*Visit and report*	*Number of states*
Sub-Saharan Africa	41 (19%)	2	52 (19%)	3	20
Ghana	1		4	1	
Guinea				1	
Kenya	12	1	7		
Namibia	2		4		
South Africa	13		13		
15 Others	13	1	24	1	
N. Africa/Middle East	32 (15%)	1	30 (11%)	2	12
Egypt	6		4	1	
Israel	10				
Sudan	4		4	1	
Syria	2	1	5		
8 Others	10		17		
Asia/Far East	52 (24%)	2	62 (23%)	6	18
Indonesia	3		10	1	
South Korea	1		1	1	
Malaysia	5	1	5	1	
Pakistan	10	1	10	1	
Philippines	15		7	2	
Singapore	2		4		
12 Others	16		25		
Latin America	60 (28%)	1	87 (32%)	6	19
Argentina	5		11		
Brazil	6		6	1	
Chile	10		10		
Colombia	4		6	1	
El Salvador	3	1	8		
Guatemala	10		11		
Haiti	2		5	1	
Honduras	2		4		
Paraguay	3		7	1	
Peru	6		4	1	
Uruguay	1		4	1	
8 Others	8		11		
E. Europe	22 (10%)		18 (7%)		4
Czechoslovakia	7		6		
Yugoslavia	9		8		
2 Others	6		4		
W. Europe, U.S./Can./Aus./N.Z.	11 (5%)	2	25 (9%)		10
Turkey	6	1	8		
9 Others	5	1	17		
Total	218	8	274	16	83

reform for human rights and democracy, the conducting of investigations and the rendering of judicial decisions." Staff responded to victim requests, media reports, and NGO contacts. The CIJL wasted no time on hopeless cases such as North Korea's totalitarian system. In countries where conscientious officials had done their utmost to prevent terrorist attacks, the Centre faulted private death squads. Shakespeare had Dick the Butcher rather than a government official propose: "The first thing we do, let's kill all the lawyers."

The CIJL protection strategy employed five tactics: private intervention, circulars to mobilize lawyers' organizations, published case reports, missions and observers, and complaints to international agencies. When all those failed, some wanted to help lawyers escape with their lives. Attorneys with the courage to remain provided the only support for otherwise helpless victims. Defense lawyer Alfonso Surigao was killed three days after introducing Brody to human rights clients at his home in the Philippines.

Table 10.2 summarizes the best available data on case work by tactic and region. Figures are imprecise estimates because several CIJL missions were jointly sponsored with the ICJ and other NGOs, and some private interventions were not reported. The first column combines circular letters and private interventions. Third world states accounted for all the missions and 85 percent of the published case reports, interventions, and circulars. Latin American and Asian cases comprised the majority.

Private Intervention

Each month saw another quiet diplomatic contact with a U.N. ambassador in Geneva, foreign minister, president, or attorney general. "Can you give the whereabouts of a prominent defense lawyer who suddenly disappeared?" "Urgently request protection for judge receiving anonymous death threats." "Strongly protest incommunicado detention of attorney representing alleged terrorists." "Stop politically motivated disbarment proceedings of civil liberties advocates." "Restore improperly dismissed judge to the bench." Adama Dieng's intervention with Togo's head of state displayed the importance of personal contacts. Ahlonko Dovi, president of Togo's Bar Association and the CIJL affiliate, National Commission for Human Rights, fled when his life was threatened. Dieng telephoned Togo's President, General Gnassingbe Eyadema, and received assurances that Dovi could return without being harmed. Few private interventions had such immediate impact.

Circulars to Mobilize the Bar

The CIJL encouraged professional solidarity—attorneys helping attorneys. Beginning in 1989, the Centre faxed notices about urgent situations to twelve groups most likely to contact a target government. Ten of those were bar associations and international NGOs in Western countries that regularly intervened on behalf of third world jurists. The Arab Lawyers Union and national groups in the Philippines and Brazil were the only third world groups regularly solicited by fax. In another five cases a year the CIJL mailed two hundred circulars to national bar associations, twelve local affiliates, and lawyers worldwide.

In its first year of operation, a CIJL-inspired mission to Uruguay secured the release of four defense lawyers held without trial. The minister of justice had ignored three private ICJ interventions. ICJ legal officer Alejandro Artucio had personally experienced the torture inflicted on attorneys who defended political activists. He gave interviews to Radio Suisse Romande and the Spanish magazine *Cambio 16* and convinced Butler to become personally involved. A 1978 press release detailed fabricated charges against four detained lawyers who had responsibly performed their professional duties. The ICJ sent the information to the Inter-American Commission on Human Rights. A circular urged lawyers organizations to act. Butler arranged a mission to Uruguay sponsored by the New York Bar and the ABA. In five days he held twenty-eight meetings with military commanders, including the president. A carefully negotiated communiqué released to the press reported agreement to reform the system of military tribunals. All four detained lawyers were released. The U.S. ambassador to Uruguay, Lawrence A. Pezzullo, reported that the mission provided a much needed catalyst, a significant human rights advance that influenced the military regime and energized a moribund College of Lawyers.[2]

Other NGOs adapted and surpassed the limited CIJL circulars. In 1987 the LCHR began a "Lawyer to Lawyer Network" that now boasts five thousand lawyers, professors and students as well as bar associations and other groups.[3] The LCHR sends two appeals each month. Many NGOs solicit letters for the same victims. Those pinpricks to officials' consciences have had enough cumulative impact in selected cases to establish letter writing as a basic protection tactic. The CIJL with other NGOs helped involve the International Bar Association and its affiliates to condemn Kenya's systematic assault on judges and lawyers. The ruling party manipulated elections to the Law Society, adopted a law allowing the president to remove judges, banned the

Nairobi Law Monthly, and jailed its courageous editor, Gitobu Imanyara. Kenyan lawyers trained in Britain and the United States had many friends eager to aid their quest for multiparty democracy. President Moi released detainees and relaxed censorship. Perhaps he mistakenly assumed that appointing ICJ Executive Committee member Amos Wako as attorney general would mollify international critics.

Public Protest

Negative publicity also brought positive results. From 1978 to 1989 the biannual *CIJL Bulletin* published 150 case reports exposing government intimidation of jurists. Seven case reports on Kenya reinforced twelve interventions and circulars. In 1989 the CIJL, the LCHR, and the Watch Committees each began publishing separate annual volumes on persecuted human rights defenders. Brody replaced the *CIJL Bulletin* with a far more comprehensive report, *Attacks on Justice*. His press summaries denounced the most flagrant assassinations and tallied the highest body counts. By exchanging information with lawyers' NGOs and Amnesty International, the CIJL reported many additional cases. The third CIJL edition for 1990–91 identified 532 attacks in 51 countries; the 1991 LCHR *In Defense of Rights* publicized for Law Day 497 cases from 49 states. The CIJL also began publishing separate book-length country reports by local lawyers in their own language.[4] Exceptional situations received full dress treatment—an on-site investigation by outside observers, meetings with government officials, and publication of findings/recommendations.

Missions and Observers

Persecuted third world jurists repeatedly pressed the CIJL to send fact-finding missions. Western attorneys and law professors conducted the first on-site investigations in Paraguay, Egypt, Ghana, the Sudan, Pakistan, the Philippines, and South Korea. MacDermot was unable to find a Muslim woman for the Pakistan mission but did assign legal officer Daniel Ravindran of India as rapporteur. Since the late 1980s the CIJL has recruited third world jurists for missions to Brazil, Colombia, Guinea, Kenya, Mali, Malaysia, and Syria. The missions' nationality changed; their legal principles did not. Several of the most recent reports have been published only in Spanish or French, not in English.[5]

In the Philippines and South Korea, Christian activists had close ties with Western churches. South Korea's President Park disbarred and persecuted defense lawyers representing opposition leaders such as Kim Dae Jung. Congressional Democrats objected to coddling an anticommunist dictator. The ABA and New York Bar supported a 1979 mission by CIJL Director John Woodhouse and a New York attorney. The State Department and the National Council of Churches helped the delegates prepare, and the U.S. Embassy in Korea arranged meetings with government officials. Among the lawyers interviewed was the director of the Legal Aid Centre, Ms. Tai Young Lee, suspended from the bar for supporting a Declaration of Democratic National Salvation.

The CIJL delegates personally urged the minister of justice to reinstate several disbarred attorneys and to withdraw criminal proceedings against others.[6] The country's extraordinary economic development cast doubt on the ICJ claim that political and economic rights were interdependent. After Park's 1980 assassination, repression continued for eight years until multiparty elections. Ms. Tai Young Lee continued her legal reform efforts and was elected to the ICJ; she later served as a vice president. In 1987 she assisted an ICJ mission to South Korea that examined the new constitution and forthcoming elections.[7]

In four Islamic countries the ICJ sent missions to assist local bar associations that resisted varied threats to the rule of law. The Arab Lawyers Union and members of the Egyptian Bar Association sought CIJL help when a pro-Western government dissolved the Bar Council. Bar leaders had criticized the Camp David accords with Israel as unconstitutional and imprudent. President Anwar Sadat cracked down on Islamic fundamentalists and other political foes. ICJ member Boutros Boutros-Ghali became Egypt's minister of state for foreign affairs. When the government began harassing opposition lawyers, MacDermot wrote him to protest but received no satisfaction. The ICJ amended its statute so that individuals accepting government posts incompatible with membership could be suspended; Boutros-Ghali asked to step down for the duration of his cabinet appointment and never resumed membership. Prior to his assassination, Sadat obtained a parliamentary act that dissolved the elected Bar Council. In response to a lawsuit challenging that act's constitutionality, Parliament prepared another Bar Council law that was totally unacceptable to the profession.

CIJL director Ustinia Dolgopol went to Egypt for negotiations with bar leaders, Boutros-Ghali, the minister of justice, and members of Parliament. She proposed that the former council leaders accept their removal and that the government allow new elections without interference; the bar leaders accepted but the government rejected the compromise.[8] Parliament enacted another law opposed by the bar. When a court held Parliament's prior act unconstitutional, the legislators repealed the second. Free elections to the Bar Council were resumed.

A Pakistani lawyer visited Malaysia to investigate the removal of the Supreme Court president and to observe the prosecution of a Bar Council vice president. The prime minister had created an ad hoc disciplinary tribunal whose chairman assumed the court presidency after removing the incumbent. Two other Supreme Court justices who resisted the judicial takeover were dismissed.[9] The vice president who protested on behalf of the bar council was convicted of contempt. The unjustly dismissed Malaysian jurist addressed the ICJ triennial meeting at Caracas; the CIJL sent a resolution on his behalf to bar associations worldwide.

The CIJL sent Jordanian experts on missions to the Sudan and Syria, where nationalists and Muslim fundamentalists persecuted human rights advocates. President Nimeiri of Sudan was overthrown before the mission arrived. His notorious "September Law" abridging judicial indpendence and enforcing Shari'a penalties of whipping and amputation remained in force. The Centre's recommendations for legal reform and a follow-up visit to discuss implementation had little impact in a society virtually destroyed by civil war and drought.[10]

Syria prosecuted a human rights lawyer for statements "shaking the confidence of the masses in the aims of the Revolution" and for "receiving money . . . from a foreign country . . . with the aim of committing any verbal . . . act against the goals of the Revolution."[11] The 1992 prosecution took place behind closed doors in a special state security court. ICJ Executive Committee member Asma Khader of Jordan became the first international NGO observer allowed at the security court. After reviewing the *ordre de mission*, the presiding officer allowed her to observe the verdict and sentencing at a final session open to defendants' families. Perhaps officials cooperated because of the CIJL's Palestinian leadership and the observer's Jordanian nationality.

Regional affinity did not mean undue sympathy for the Syrian prosecutors. Khader observed that the defendant lawyer was helped into the courtroom for sentencing, unable to stand or walk on his own. Her report demonstrated how the procedures fell short of international standards. The court ignored allegations that incriminating statements were extracted by torture and did not allow defense witnesses. The court ordered nine years at hard labor even though there were no charges of either practicing or inciting violence. There was no right of appeal to a higher court. The CIJL immediately released

Khader's report with an appeal on behalf of the unjustly convicted attorney and his codefendants.[12]

Complaints to International Agencies

The Centre pressed U.N. and regional agencies to monitor and condemn offending states that resisted private interventions and negative publicity. A 1980 complaint on Guatemala to the Inter-American Commission on Human Rights identified fifteen jurists killed or disappeared. A 1984 CIJL mission to Paraguay documented for the U.N. Sub-Commssion how the executive subordinated the judiciary during a prolonged state of seige.[13] Criticism of one government creates political waves that intergovernmental bodies prefer to avoid. Thematic investigations that in theory subject all states to equal scrutiny are politically more palatable. The Commission on Human Rights had a rapporteur on summary executions, ICJ member Amos Wako. He could include CIJL cases of assassinated judges in his U.N. report but had no mandate to investigate lesser forms of intimidation.

The ICJ successfully lobbied the U.N. Sub-Commission to appoint Louis Joinet as a rapporteur on the independence of the judiciary. The French expert became a founding member of the CIJL advisory board. He began adding to the annual Sub-Commission report specific case information from the CIJL and other NGOs. Brody scheduled publication of *Attacks on Justice* for release at the Sub-Commission's annual review. While not as influential as a Commission rapporteur, Joinet initiated U.N. complaint procedure by an annual theme report on jurists.

Protection casework for individuals at best provided an emergency response to symptoms without reforming unjust institutions that systematically produced new victims. Through standard setting the CIJL attacked underlying structural causes.

Standard Setting for Independent Judges and Lawyers

How empty the Universal Declaration's promise of a fair trial became. Based on security measures employed in the colonies and Northern Ireland, Britain advocated emergency administrative detention not subject to judicial control.[14] The International Covenant on Civil and Political Rights expressly allowed governments to derogate from due process guarantees during emergencies. Without new standards guaranteeing judicial independence, CIJL protection case work rested on a shaky legal foundation. Executives could claim a legal right to suspend habeas corpus and try unrepresented civilians before military courts under martial law. Many different lawyers' groups pressed the United Nations to approve new standards. After ten years of sustained pressure, the General Assembly endorsed principles meeting many NGO goals. CIJL tactics helped significantly to set the agenda, prepare texts, lobby for adoption, and provide follow-up.

Setting the Agenda

Separate U.N. bodies in Geneva and Vienna independently began to draft new standards in 1980. MacDermot chose to approach the General Assembly through Geneva starting at the U.N. Sub-Commission; its parent, the Commission on Human Rights, meets annually. MacDermot influenced Sub-Commission expert L. M. Singvhi of India to propose a study on the independence and impartiality of judges and lawyers.[15] The Commission authorized his research. Both bodies created agenda items on "the independence and impartiality of the judiciary, jurors and assessors and the independence of lawyers." CIJL case reports documenting attacks on judges and lawyers helped Singvhi demonstrate the need for new U.N. standards. To meet that need, the Sub-Commission expert would prepare a draft declaration for adoption by the Commission. Others approached the General Assembly through the Vienna Committee on Crime Prevention and Control; it reported at five-year intervals to the U.N. Congress on the Prevention of Crime and Treatment of Offenders. In 1980 the sixth U.N. Congress on the Prevention of Crime directed the Vienna Crime Committee to elaborate guidelines on the independence of judges. Singvhi had a broader mandate that also included guarantees for lawyers, jurors, and assessors.

Preparing a Text

NGO and U.N. legal experts proposed comprehensive guarantees that few governments granted either in law or in practice. MacDermot arranged for committees of experts to assist Singvhi with separate declarations of principles on judges and lawyers. In 1981 the ICJ and the International Association of Penal Law (IAPL) brought experts to Siracusa, Sicily, for five days to discuss eighteen position papers on an independent judiciary. Americans wrote five of the papers, and all but two of the remainder were by Western Europeans. Papers from the CIJL and the U.N. Crime Prevention Branch in Vienna recommended draft principles. The experts agreed on thirty-two basically Anglo-American common law principles. The judiciary should be an independent branch of government, rather than a service department controlled by the executive and legislature. They proposed nonpolitical appointments, secure tenure, and trial guarantees in ordinary courts. The recommendations did not expressly advocate judicial review that would empower judges to enforce fundamental rights and nullify unconstitutional acts.

In 1982 the same hosts, together with representatives of eleven lawyers' organizations and attorneys from twenty countries, drafted principles for an independent bar. Over half those participating came to Noto, Sicily, from the third world and Eastern Europe. Both the U.N. Human Rights Division in Geneva and the Crime Prevention Branch in Vienna sent representatives. The forty-four principles adopted balance rights and duties. Governments should honor the attorney-client privilege and not punish those who represent political dissidents. Special recruitment of women and minorities may be required to rectify past discrimination and assure equal access for all. The profession should provide legal assistance to the indigent and defend economic as well as civil rights.

In order to protect lawyers from government harassment, the experts proposed that independent bar associations have sole responsibility for discipline in cases of misconduct. As a condition of appearing in court, lawyers should join independent, self-governing bar associations. Those freely elected councils financed by assured dues from all lawyers could reject control by party or government officials. The legal profession should organize to check government attacks on the judiciary, defense counsel, and helpless citizens. The experts did not consider mandatory membership a violation of lawyers' freedom of association. The CIJL principles advocated the judicial institutions of multiparty democracies, a due process model requiring dispute resolution by adversarial confrontation in court. Singvhi appended the Siracusa and Noto recommendations to his progress reports.[16]

By 1982 organizations such as the International Bar Association (IBA) had arranged seven other conferences to prepare similar recommendations. To create a single text, Jules Deschênes, chief justice of Quebec's Superior Court, convened representatives of twenty-four groups at a Montreal World Conference on the Independence of Justice. Invitees from the USSR and China declined, without acknowledging their governments' likely opposition to the NGOs' handiwork. Five commissions at the conference recommended standards on international judges, national judges, lawyers, jurors, and assessors. MacDermot attended the commission on lawyers, whose working paper presented the CIJL draft principles. The group adopted most of those proposals, except for one on affirmative action in recruitment.

Dolgopol attended the commission on national judges. Drawing extensively on IBA recommendations on the judiciary, the group recommended principles that considerably improved on the Siracusa proposals. Judges would review derogations from due process in emergencies; criminal defendants must be tried in ordinary courts, not before ad hoc or military tribunals. Judges should be immune from suit and barred from political activities. In plenary sessions the conference adopted a five-part Universal Declaration on the Independence of Justice.[17] Singvhi's final report to the U.N. Sub-Commission modified the text slightly. He dropped the section on international judges before recommending adoption of the major provisions on judges, lawyers, jurors, and assessors as a U.N. Declaration on the Independence of Justice.[18]

Lobbying for Adoption

The separate drafting stream in Vienna overtook the Geneva proposal with unfortunate results. The Crime Committee asked Deschênes to submit recommendations on an independent judiciary. He obliged with the one section from the Montreal Declaration on national judges. The committee recommended those principles for adoption at the 1985 U.N. Congress on the Prevention of Crime in Milan. Eastern European governments categorically rejected the Western bourgeois concept of independent judges. Faced with the prospect of total loss, Dolgopol worked with a Canadian representative to salvage a consensus on the most acceptable tenets. The congress adopted twenty Basic Principles on the Independence of the Judiciary.

The government representatives accepted in principle constitutional guarantees of judicial independence, secure tenure, limited immunity, judicial authority to decide a court's competence and case assignment, and bars to unwarranted interference or revision of decisions. Dropped were provisions on states of emergency, closing down courts, freedom of thought, speech, and movement for judges, prohibition on transfer of judges, grounds for disqualification, and responsibility for court administration and budget.[19] The congress recommended the diluted text as principles for government consideration in light of local circumstances rather than as a declaration of universal standards. The U.N. General Assembly endorsed the weakened principles, urging governments to take them into account in their national legislation and practice.[20] The Basic Principles, "general though they are, represent the first intergovernmental standards spelling out the minimum standards of judicial independence and are the acknowledged yardstick by which the international community measures that independence."[21]

Implementing Procedures

Apart from a preamble urging states to respect the Basic Principles on the Independence of the Judiciary, the drafters overlooked implementation procedures. The General Assembly had previously endorsed ICJ principles on derogation in times of emergency without any effective U.N. follow-up. Human rights conventions obligate states parties to submit periodic reports on compliance and establish optional complaint procedures. Otherwise, U.N. exhortations fall on deaf ears. The CIJL increased the volume by invoking the principles in published case reports, interventions, and circulars. MacDermot organized seminars for third world judges and lawyers to promote national implementation. He also asked the Human Rights Steering Committee of the Council of Europe to formulate guidelines and principles for the independence of the judiciary and the legal profession.[22] The U.N. Sub-Commission arranged for Joinet to prepare annual reports on judicial independence. The CIJL supplied Joinet with information to facilitate annual U.N. monitoring reports on how governments treated judges and lawyers.

ECOSOC requested states to report at five-year intervals on their implementation measures begining with a 1988 survey by the U.N. Secretary-General. The CIJL helped to develop fifteen implementation procedures that filled a few holes in the principles. MacDermot and Brody attended a 1987 U.N. expert meeting on law enforcement that prepared an initial draft for the Crime Committee.[23] ECOSOC adopted and the General Assembly endorsed procedures by resolving that "all states shall adopt and implement" the principles. States should disseminate the Basic Principles in local languages. The Secretariat should publish the text along with other international human rights standards. Governments are to report to the United Nations at five-year intervals on their dessemination and incorporation in national legislation. The Secretary-General should provide technical cooperation for governments requesting assistance in improving their courts and promote training seminars. The CIJL began receiving U.N. grants for regional jurists' conferences.

Completing Principles for Lawyers

CIJL lobbying for better standards also continued on two fronts. In Vienna, MacDermot and Brody proposed to the Crime Committee principles for an independent legal profession. In Geneva they pushed for Singvhi's comprehensive Declaration on the Independence of Justice, which remained largely intact. If adopted by the

General Assembly, the proposed declaration from the Human Rights Commission would have greater coverage and force than the Crime Committee principles. Deschênes was elected to the Sub-Commission and gave strong support. Review took until 1988 as the Soviet expert resisted and governments were solicited for comments. In response to their objections, Singvhi weakened the provisions on judicial immunity and deleted provisions on states of emergency and the ban on political activities.[24] The result still would have improved on the Basic Principles. In the spirit of *perestroika*, a new Soviet expert accepted the declaration. The Sub-Commission approved it the same month the Crime Committee in Vienna recommended principles on lawyers and the implementation procedures to protect judges.

Vienna once again prevailed over Geneva. In 1989 the Human Rights Commission's government representatives referred the entire declaration prepared by its Sub-Commission to the Crime Committee experts. The Sub-Commission was authorized to monitor implementation of principles drafted in Vienna; the Commission would draft standards to protect all human rights defenders, not just lawyers and judges. A presessional working group continued negotiating a declaration on the right and responsibility of individuals, groups, and organs of society to promote and protect universally recognized human rights.

The Vienna Secretariat hired Brody to help reconcile the Singvhi declaration with the principles on lawyers adopted by preparatory meetings for the next U.N. Crime Congress. Many but not all of the CIJL proposals made it into the final twenty-nine Basic Principles on the Role of Lawyers. Since the Noto conference, the CIJL had insisted that an independent legal profession was essential, as important as an independent judiciary in protecting human rights. The draft principles granted lawyers a "vital" role without using the term *independent* or establishing the bar as a coequal instrument in securing justice. The principles do not require bar association membership but affirm lawyers' right to join self-governing professional groups with elected executives, free of external interference.

Like the Noto draft, the principles call for affirmative action in recruitment and training in ethical duties. Governments should assure competent defense counsel for indigents, allow access to a lawyer within forty-eight hours of arrest, and permit confidential consultations. "Lawyers shall not be identified with their clients or their clients' causes as a result of discharging their functions." Governments must ensure that lawyers can function without intimidation, that they can travel freely at home and abroad, and that they are not prosecuted for performing professional duties. The authorities shall safeguard threatened lawyers and assure immunity for good faith statements made in court. The proposal included modest implementation procedures, including government reports at five-year intervals and publication with other human rights standards.

The U.N. Congress taking up the principles met in Havana, hosted by a Cuban regime not recognized for tolerating independent lawyers. U.S. representatives boycotted the communist isle. Rather than supporting the principles in Havana, the U.S. government set hurdles for NGO representatives traveling to Cuba. Brody managed to attend for the CIJL. His report exposing contra terror in Nicaragua had facilitated a good working relationship with the Cuban expert on the Sub-Commission. The CIJL cosponsored with the Arab Lawyers Union and the Lawyers Committee for Human Rights a special meeting for delegates on an independent judiciary. Judge Bhagwati of the CIJL board chaired a panel of judges and prosecutors from Egypt, Haiti, and Peru.

In contrast to the setback in 1985, the 1990 congress adopted the principles on lawyers by consensus. Altogether the congress adopted forty-six instruments and sets of guidelines, including major initiatives on organized crime, juvenile delinquency, extradition, and information sharing, of greater concern to the delegates.[25] Regional preparatory meetings for the Congress made the experts' revised proposals on lawyers far more acceptable to governments. New representatives from Eastern Europe no longer raised Marxist objections. If MacDermot could have foreseen the communist collapse, the CIJL might have chosen to accept temporary defeat at the 1985 congress. In 1990 NGOs won more detailed principles for lawyers than they had for judges, but none at all for jurors.

In both drafts, governments weakened NGO proposals for extensive independence. Self-regulation in the judiciary and bar may lead to abuse, but externally imposed discipline permits political meddling. The principles encourage peer review but allow disciplinary action by nonlawyers. Servile judges and lawyers co-opted by the state might improperly discipline human rights advocates unless professional colleagues could check their misconduct. State representatives eliminated what may have appeared ludicrous and self-serving proposals for "adequate remuneration." In fact, governments exert financial pressure on underpaid defense counsel and vulnerable judges, the wealthy lawyer's poor cousins. Many principles were couched in general terms such as "reasonable" and "necessary," allowing considerable government discretion in implementation. In any event, the drafts were statements of recommended principles rather than formal declarations or binding conventions.

A General Assembly resolution "welcomed" the Basic Principles on the Role of Lawyers and invited governments to take them into account in national legislation and practice.[26] Brody followed up with demands for meaningful implementation. The final *CIJL Bulletin* published the U.N. principles along with the Singvhi declaration and NGO conference resolutions that proclaimed more extensive guarantees.[27] Brody lobbied the Sub-Commission for an independent rapporteur to monitor the independence of judges and lawyers. With U.N. Commission approval, Joinet began preparing an annual report. Developments in Vienna could once again abort a promising start. The United Nations replaced the expert Crime Committee with an ECOSOC commission of forty government representatives who were to meet annually beginning in 1992. The Commission on Crime Prevention and Criminal Justice could initiate implementation and monitoring that supersedes protection activities in Geneva. NGOs will have greater difficulty gaining access if the new Crime Commission does not elect a committee of experts like the Sub-Commission in Geneva.

The minimal U.N. principles established standards that too many governments failed miserably. Through force of repetition in U.N. resolutions and NGO publications, advocates sought to elevate the principles to binding norms of customary international law. The CIJL also performed a promotional function, educating third world jurists and public officials to adopt the principles in national law.

Promotion for Legal Reform

Promotion empowers local advocates to protect themselves and socializes third world elites to Western due process values. Rapporteur Joinet's first report criticized the U.N. advisory services—seminars, training institutes, and technical assistance. The CIJL began organizing seminars on judicial independence in 1986 and providing legal consultants in 1991. Research publications, legal interns in the Geneva Secretariat, and collaboration with other NGOs also spread the rule of law gospel. CIJL publications now reach more than five thousand individuals in 127 countries. A *Yearbook* has replaced the *Bulletin*.[28]

Seminars

Each year the CIJL convenes two meetings for judges, lawyers, and government officials to promote independence for the bench and bar. Western aid agencies and foundations—USAID, the Ford Foundation,

SIDA, the Commonwealth Foundation—funded seminars as development assistance. In contrast to the confrontational tactics of protection casework, collaboration is the rule. The CIJL seeks a friendly forum in which to educate local elites on the need for legal reform. Typically, top government officials, prime ministers, presidents, and attorneys general opened the proceedings with welcoming remarks. In only one case did a host government disrupt a planned seminar. A dispute between the local bar and government in Bangladesh caused the CIJL to move a seminar to Nepal. Only one country had judges represented, and Indian jurists did not attend.

The program began with seven subregional seminars for Africa, Asia, and the Americas held in Costa Rica, Argentina, Tobago, Nepal, the Philippines, Zambia, and Gambia. MacDermot recruited one or more local cosponsoring organizations; weak groups frustrated planning, strong organizations coordinated follow-up implementation. The cosponsors invited as many as forty jurists from four to twelve states for work sessions lasting two to five days. Six chief justices and six attorneys general attended seminars in the Commonwealth Caribbean. Participants received working papers that laid out basic principles approved by the United Nations or advocated by the CIJL. Keynote speakers from the region detailed local threats to the profession and suggested possible reforms.

Issue working groups debated appointment, compensation, tenure, discipline, removal, and immunity of jurists. New governments' dependence on Western expatriate judges concerned many. In Commonwealth states subject to the Crown, the Privy Council in London heard final appeals. British settlers and foreign nationals continued to staff many African courts. An ICJ member from the West Indies was Tanzania's chief justice. Newly independent Namibia employed judges from South Africa. Popular pressure to Africanize the bench might achieve more independence from the West at the expense of the judiciary's independence from political control. The seminar working groups socialized new judges to the independent roles favored in Western democracies. Final plenary sessions adopted moderate recommendations addressed to governments and a follow-up action plan for the region. Recognizing that life tenure for judges might be unattainable, the seminars advocated secure fixed terms with assured compensation and protection against arbitrary removal.

One jurist from each country served on a follow-up committee to oversee implementation. Attorneys general from two Commonwealth African states announced their intention to bring local practice into harmony with principles learned at the seminar in Lusaka, Zambia.

Law professor Philip Amoah of Ghana, who presented a working paper, later joined the ICJ as a legal officer for Africa. Host universities and law societies expanded the CIJL's local contacts. The cosponsoring African Bar Association was responsible for coordination and communication after two regional meetings. The CIJL published seminar reports to disseminate major working papers and approved recommendations.[29]

In Paraguay, Peru, Pakistan, Nicaragua, and India, the ICJ followed up with national seminars and reports.[30] Two years after an ICJ fact-finding mission on conditions after martial law, Pakistan's Ministry of Law and Justice cosponsored a CIJL seminar.[31] The U.N. Centre for Human Rights supported a seminar that considered methods to innoculate India's legal system against another state of emergency. In Peru, five hundred jurists, including thirty-five judges, attended a seminar on the judiciary and democracy cosponsored by the the Andean Commission of Jurists.[32] In all three countries scarred by bloody civil strife, the CIJL promoted a political/legal order remote from daily reality. Pakistan's president proclaimed an emergency to remove the elected civilian government in 1990 and created special courts; Peru's elected president suspended the constitution to battle Shining Path guerrillas; and India's judges struggled with communal violence and separatist terrorism.

Expert Consultants

NGOs have suspected U.N. advisory services since the United States first proposed the program as an alternative to enforceable human rights covenants. Third world target governments now feign a need for technical assistance in order to avoid rebuke for human rights violations. Politically motivated Human Rights Commission members cooperate by replacing fact-finding rapporteurs with technical advisers. The ICJ joined other NGOs in exposing how U.N. experts disregarded violations in Equatorial Guinea, Haiti, Uganda, and Guatemala. In 1991 the CIJL began making its own expert personnel available for drafting legislation and constitutional provisions. The ICJ cosponsored a colloquium with the Ministry of Justice to prepare recommendations for the Congo's new constitution. About 125 Congolese judges, prosecutors, clerks, bailiffs, and Justice Ministry officials consulted with Western and African experts in preparing draft constitutional provisions and a new law on the judiciary.

An SIDA official on loan to the Centre for Human Rights encouraged U.N. contracting with the CIJL and other NGO consultants to acquire superior expertise. In 1991 the advisory services program hired Brody and Bhaghwati for a two-week consultation with Mongolia's Constitutional Drafting Committee. Following multiparty elections, a new legislature prepared a draft constitution for a parliamentary democracy. The CIJL experts spent thirty-eight hours reviewing the text with the drafting committee. They recommended new or changed articles to guarantee human rights and an independent judiciary.[33] After the experts met with the president, supreme court, political parties, lawyers' association, and NGOs, twenty recommendations were incorporated.[34]

NGO Collaboration

Western human rights activists long for independent third world NGO allies to challenge African and Asian representatives on the Human Rights Commission who oppose U.N. intervention in domestic matters. An unholy alliance of undemocratic governments seeks a Commission majority that can frustrate Western and NGO protection initiatives. The CIJL's allies include national bar associations and international federations such as the International Bar Association, the African Bar Association, and the Union International des Avocats. CIJL staff regularly publish journal articles, present conference papers, and speak to prospective converts. Brody presented a paper entitled "Protecting the Independence of the Legal Profession" at the ninth Commonwealth Law Conference in New Zealand.

At the national level, twelve lawyers' organizations in ten countries have formally affiliated with the CIJL. Three in the West give limited financial support; third world affiliates provide information and casework clients. A fifteen-member CIJL Advisory Board involves leaders of the Commonwealth Caribbean Bar Associations, Algeria's IADL, the American Bar Association Human Rights Committee, the Philippines Free Legal Assistance Group, the Arab Lawyers Union, and the American Association of Jurists. The ICJ boasts over fifty other national sections and affiliates also committed to an independent judiciary. The Kenya section held a series of seminars challenging one-party rule and the President's power to remove judges. Yet none of its members had attended the CIJL Lusaka seminar; few invoked international standards when advocating constitutional reform.[35] The professional bar remains small, but the African continent so vast that the CIJL has not yet established pervasive influence. The next chapter describes how ICJ Secretary-General Adama Dieng focused additional energy on improving Africa's legal infrastructure.

Conclusions

CIJL protection, standard setting, and promotion have nurtured vulnerable advocates and fragile institutions throughout the third world. A tiny staff with limited resources could not work miracles but did make a difference. Unable to undertake as much casework as larger human rights NGOs, the CIJL used third world advocates and high level connections to maximum advantage. Its negative publicity and fact-finding missions replicated by other NGOs were mutually reinforcing rather than wasteful. Multiple reports validated NGO findings and subjected officials to greater pressure than could be accomplished by isolated protest.

In contrast to NGO allies devoted primarily to protection, activist CIJL directors became skilled U.N. lobbyists for new standards. Experience and persistence made them principals in a ten-year drafting process. MacDermot had learned from other ICJ principles endorsed by the General Assembly to follow through with implementation measures. Government delegates rejected international principles granting judges as much job security and independence as conferred by the U.S. Constitution. Yet the CIJL helped set minimal standards in U.N. Basic Principles on the Independence of the Judiciary and on the Role of Lawyers. The reporting and monitoring procedures appear quite ineffective. States parties to binding human rights covenants routinely disregard their reporting obligations. Innumerable U.N. Secretariat questionnaires on varied principles create inordinate paperwork that has had no discernible benefit for jurists at risk. The standards have had greater value as an official imprimatur for CIJL casework and promotion. Just as the Universal Declaration popularized values that subverted totalitarian regimes, the standards on judicial independence may contribute to incremental legal reform. Boys with guns never tire of jailing conscientious judges and lawyers; advocates fighting with ideas, however powerful, need considerably more time to prevail.

A Centre of lawyers helping lawyers appears like a special rather than a public interest group. The ICJ founding conference in Berlin denounced East Germany's perversion of the judiciary and the kidnapping of attorney Walter Linse. Human rights defenders in the press and legislature need independence as much as do judges and lawyers. In fact, the ICJ fulfilled a broad public mission. Before founding the CIJL, the ICJ had assisted the International Parliamentary Union in casework and drafted a convention to protect journalists. Only after the ICJ had helped establish an International

Commission of Health Professionals did it initiate its own Centre for lawyers. Other NGOs such as Article 19 organized to protect an independent press.

On balance the CIJL has impressive public interest credentials. Instead of serving the narrow economic interests of privileged members, the CIJL insisted on lawyers' duty to provide legal aid and pressed bar associations to defend human rights. Volunteer participation involved financial sacrifices for busy practitioners; several supporters were imprisoned for their public service.[36] CIJL reports criticizing a member's government may cause embarrassment and professional liability. Few lawyers with conservative political orientations and lucrative incomes want to join a progressive human rights NGO that challenges official elites. If CIJL-promoted standards prove effective, the prime beneficiaries will not be lawyers and judges but the powerless—detainees, mental patients, torture victims, and political dissidents. The CIJL was not seeking to enrich jurists by protecting judges' tenure and lawyers' independence. Instead, the CIJL enhanced separation of powers for the public interest—government under law.

CIJL Seminars on the Independence of Judges and Lawyers

The Independence of Judges and Lawyers in South Asia. Report of a seminar held in Kathmandu, September 1–5, 1987. CIJL and Nepal Law Society. Geneva: ICJ, 1988. 84 pp.

The Independence of the Judiciary and the Legal Profession in English-Speaking Africa. A report of seminars held in Lusaka, November 10–14, 1986, and in Banjul, April 6–10, 1987. Geneva: CIJL, African Bar Association, ICJ, 1987. 194 pp.

The Independence of Judges and Lawyers in the Commonwealth Caribbean. Reports of a Seminar held in Tobago, September 12–13, 1988. Geneva: CIJL and the UWI/USAID Caribbean Justice Improvement Project, 1989. 66 pp.

La Independencia de Jueces y Abogados en Argentina, Brasil, Paraguay y Uruguay (1988 Buenos Aires Seminar). Geneva: ICJ, 1988. 146 pp.

The Independence of the Judiciary in India. Report of a seminar held in New Delhi, January 20–21, 1990. Geneva: CIJL and U.N. Centre for Human Rights, 1990. 61 pp.

The Independence of Judges and Lawyers in Pakistan. Report of a seminar held in Lahore, November 9–10, 1989. Geneva: ICJ, 1990. 148 pp.

Peru: La Indepedencia del Poder Judicial. Geneva: ICJ, 1989. 97 pp.

Part V
1990–1993: Third World Leadership for a New Order

Chapter 11
Turning Forty

> While the world has changed, the essential mission of the ICJ—to promote the rule of law and the legal protection of human rights—has not changed. As walls which keep people in are replaced by walls that keep people out, as the rivalry between East and West is replaced by conflict between North and South, the role of the ICJ becomes even more vital.
>
> —ICJ Secretary-General Adama Dieng[1]

Public interest groups have a high infant mortality rate and short life expectancy. More than three-thousand international NGOs have dissolved or become inactive.[2] Long after most other nineteenth-century organizations passed away, the government-supported International Red Cross prospered as an exception. Unable to secure permanent funding, many groups die with the entrepreneurs who created and controlled them.

The ICJ belongs to the first generation of human rights NGOs. In 1970 the bankrupt adolescent found new leadership. Approaching forty, a stalled ICJ saw its offspring and new groups flourish. After twenty years as Secretary-General, MacDermot was seventy-three and in failing health. William Butler, Executive Committee chairman since 1976, faced mandatory retirement in 1990 under the ICJ Statute. Both leaders were reluctant to step down. MacDermot proposed a partial retirement that would enable him to continue editing ICJ publications. Butler recommended an amendment to the Statute so he could continue to chair the Executive Committee. Fiscally cautious after lean years when he had cut his own salary, MacDermot resisted staff proposals for expansion. Butler competed with difficulty against other human rights NGOs for U.S. foundation grants. Thoroughly committed, both felt the ICJ needed their considerable experience; new leaders with the requisite skill, commitment, and status would be difficult to find. The ICJ's unique character depended on careful selection from an exclusive elite.

Mobilizing Resources for a New Order

Secretary-General

The search for MacDermot's successor began with Theo van Boven. A hero to NGO activists, van Boven had used his director's post at the U.N. Human Rights Division as a bully pulpit. After publicly criticizing governments that killed their own citizens, he was ousted. Van Boven also knew the Geneva scene well through membership on the U.N. Sub-Commission. He negotiated with Butler for a year before declining the position. The Ford Foundation helped and the ICJ offered 30 percent more than MacDermot's salary. The pay was still not competitive, and shaky finances would mean major fund raising. Van Boven would have lost faculty tenure, a university pension, and health benefits at the age of fifty-four. Unlike MacDermot, whose spouse worked in Geneva, family discouraged van Boven from relocating away from home.

Before van Boven rejected the post, MacDermot announced his retirement for June 1990. Legal officer Adama Dieng served a year as Executive Secretary and then became Acting Secretary-General. After interviewing Swedish ombudsman Peter Nobel and six others, the Executive Committee broke new ground on race, age, language, and status. The ICJ named Adama Dieng Secretary-General in October 1990. The forty-year-old Senegalese jurist preferred French to English and had more experience in international than national institutions. Like the two senior English-speaking cabinet ministers who preceded him, Dieng has a commanding physical presence valued in international diplomacy. During nearly ten years in the ICJ's Geneva Secretariat he had developed both an eloquent passion for the cause and excellent connections, especially in Africa. He had remained at the ICJ after receiving offers from the ICRC and Amnesty International.[3] The elitist jurist's appointment of a young African leader signaled major third world influence in a human rights network dominated by Westerners. Within two years Senegalese nationals had also been appointed as directors of the U.N. Centre on Human Rights and Amnesty International.

Adama Dieng of Senegal was promoted to ICJ Secretary-General in 1990, after service as legal officer for Africa.

Dieng worked to revitalize and redirect the ICJ before its fortieth anniversary. The resulting changes confirm anew the impact of staff in public interest groups. Dieng promoted CIJL director Reed Brody to Executive Secretary; together they prepared a planning document, "Strategies for the Future," and held a brainstorming session with expert consultants. The Executive Committee authorized staff to embark on major expansion before the 1992 ICJ meeting approved a draft plan of action.

Finances

Agencies reassured about the ICJ's prospects gave its new third world leader an immediate vote of confidence. The Swedish International Development Authority (SIDA) doubled its annual grant and funded half the plan's cost in the first two years.[4] An ICJ national section member in Germany arranged a substantial block grant from the church foundation EKD and lobbied development programs for regular support. Annual expenditures increased 20 percent by the end of 1990. Dieng and Brody proposed an additional 41 percent increase by 1992 that would take the annual budget above $2 million. They sought increased project grants from government development programs, state-funded church groups in Europe, the United Nations, the European Community, and private foundations. Twenty European governments, the Ford Foundation, and SIDA provided the unrestricted funds required for salaries, rent, and publications.

Most funding agencies had refused to support the ICJ general budget. Restricted grants for special projects had forced staff to prepare separate applications for each seminar, mission, and report. In order to encourage unrestricted block grants, an annual comprehensive "Request for Funding" was begun to describe all planned special projects. Each special project budget allocated sufficient revenue to cover the Secretariat's real expenses. The ICJ doubled the allocation for administrative overhead from 10 to 20 percent and budgeted additional funds for professional staff time and consultants.

Increased government and foundation support brought opportunities for long-delayed expansion as well as new problems of accountability. The Executive Committee reviewed and approved the general budget, but staff members largely determined the separate special project accounts. In public interest groups funded by individual contributions, members can hold staff accountable by withholding support or quitting the organization. ICJ staff have never been dependent on funding by members. For most of its existence the organization has been a largely government-funded, voluntary organization. Few subscribers even pay for ICJ publications. Local supporters contribute more to national sections than to the Geneva Secretariat. Executive Committee members had paid their own travel expenses to meetings; yet they did not raise funds or share financial reports with the membership. Once appointed by the Executive Committee, the Secretary-General raises income for a highly independent Secretariat. Funding agencies exercise varying degrees of oversight. The Netherlands Foreign Ministry reported to Parliament on NOVIB cofinancing projects with the ICJ but did not indicate the size of its subsidy.[5]

American pluralists champion privately funded interest groups with unqualified freedom to challenge government policy. In European corporatism governments actively support quasi-nongovernmental organizations to represent different social interests. The Swedish Red Cross and Save the Children rely on government for more than 80 percent of their funding.[6] In 1990 twenty Western governments directly and indirectly contributed more than three-fourths of the ICJ budget. Now that SIDA funding exceeds one-third of the total, the ICJ's independence hinges on Sweden's traditional hands-off policy. In only one instance has the Swedish government canceled an NGO grant, after discovering that a South African spy had infiltrated the World University Service. A law professor fond of hypothetical problems could readily suggest conflicts of interest between a human rights NGO and European funding governments. Sweden's non-Socialist government has decided to increase revenues from military exports.[7] Swiss bankers profit from third world dictators who invest embezzled public funds in personal accounts. Independent ICJ staff have repeatedly critized funding governments, but disproportionate reliance on one state still appears suspect. The ICJ's financial collapse in 1970 revealed the peril of dependence on a single major contributor.

Secretariat

Underpaid, overworked activists made the ICJ's reputation. There weren't enough idealists available to staff the desired growth. Effective human rights advocacy now required skilled professionals who were paid competitive wages. Dieng and Brody proposed hiring two legal officers for each region, a librarian, a press officer, CIJL assistants, and an administrative support staff. The ICJ would rent or build more spacious office headquarters properly equipped with the latest technology. More third world interns on short-term appointment to the Secretariat could take home critical skills and contacts. Members and volunteers from local affiliates could assist at international meetings as ICJ representatives. Lawyers conducting lengthy missions that interfered with private practice might require some financial compensation.

SIDA accepted the plan's basic premise to pay improved salaries. Its officials still disapproved of private organizations that resembled government bureaucracies with two hundred professionals. Staff should not exceed thirty,[8] and the ICJ only projected growth from eleven to twenty-two. That increase would not jeopardize informal working relationships, volunteer assistance, and the staff's idealism. The target payroll would still be less than one-tenth of Amnesty International's London Secretariat. Dieng moved the ICJ to spacious offices on the top floor of a modern office building closer to the United Nations;[9] the staff increased to sixteen by 1993.

A new press officer transformed the stodgy *ICJ Newsletter* into a highly readable tabloid with photographs. Alejandro Artucio returned from Uruguay to resume duties as Latin American legal officer. Dieng hired Philip Amoah of Ghana as African legal officer, and Mona Rishmawi from the West Bank to direct the CIJL and Middle East legal affairs. More publications were translated into Arabic. The European Community granted funds for a European legal officer to help promote democratization in the former Soviet empire. Additional third world interns assisted the staff. After many of his pet reforms had been realized, Executive Secretary Reed Brody resigned in 1992 to become director of the International Human Rights Law Group in Washington. His departure left the ICJ without a U.S. attorney on staff at the same time the ICJ had no American member.[10]

Executive Committee

Within eighteen months of Dieng's appointment, a transformed Executive Committee had a new chairman and third world majority. Some members and national section representatives had long resented the ICJ's guided democracy. Since 1952 the Executive Committee had been a self-selected, self-perpetuating group of Western men. A New York lawyer had always chaired the committee, and each chairman had personally selected his own successor. Alternates who were not even ICJ members regularly attended committee meetings. The minutes were not shared with other members until 1986, and MacDermot opposed providing copies to national sections. Poorly attended Commission meetings had rarely convened on the required triennial schedule. Only twelve members, less than a quorum, attended the 1985 meeting in Nairobi. The Executive Committee occasionally used mail ballots, but members had minimal influence on policy decisions. At the 1989 meeting in Caracas, six of the seven Executive Committee members won reelection.

The sole new member, Australian Michael Kirby, had been an outside critic since 1984. Kirby was a Federal Court judge, chairman of the Law Reform Commission, and member of Australian delegations to UNESCO. He joined Butler on a fact-finding mission to Palau before they split over ICJ governance. At the 1985 ICJ meeting in Nairobi, Kirby pressed for democratic reforms—shorter term limits,

ICJ legal officers in 1992. *Left to right*: (seated) Dilbur Parakh of India, Secretary-General Adama Dieng of Senegal, Reed Brody of the United States, and Philip Amoah of Ghana; (standing) Mona Rishmawi from the West Bank and Alejandro Artucio of Uruguay.

financial reports to members, annual Commission meetings, more participation by national sections. Kirby resisted when Butler sought to extend his own term beyond mandatory retirement. The 1989 meeting rejected an amendment that would have allowed Butler an extra term to assist the new Secretary-General.

Following past practice, Butler then sought to select his own replacement from the New York board. All prior Executive Committee chairmen had introduced their successors at meetings where the new leader had been routinely approved. Breaking with that tradition, the committee nominated for ICJ membership an American jurist not associated with the New York affiliate. The AAICJ objection caused a stalemate over which U.S. candidate to elect. For the first time in its history the ICJ had no U.S. member, its Executive Committee no New York chairman.[11] P. J. G. Kapteyn of the Netherlands became chairman for the year before his mandatory retirement, and Kirby was elected chairman in 1992. Butler was elected an honorary ICJ member and remained an active supporter. He continued organizing foreign policy seminars for human rights desk officers, and Dieng became the first non-Western participant.

The change symbolized a decisive reorientation from the ICJ's New York origins. Funding and tradition no longer determined Executive Committee leadership. Since 1970 the Secretary-General had raised far more of the budget than the U.S. chairman. Members from European countries providing the most support had not sought leadership positions. Former ICJ interns and staff active in U.S. human rights groups promoted affiliation. David Weissbrodt was active in the Minnesota Lawyers International Human Rights Committee. When Reed Brody left the Geneva Secretariat in 1992, he insisted on affiliation for the International Human Rights Law Group in Washington, D.C.

The transformed Executive Committee elected in 1992 had five third world members and only one European.[12] The four new members included one woman. Financial security enabled the Commission to pay travel expenses for members from developing countries. Kirby as chairman touted a "new, open ICJ." Following a NOVIB evaluation calling for greater transparency, the Executive Committee approved reports of its meeting and the annual audit for general distribution. A proposed amendment limiting Executive Committee members to two three-year terms was deferred for study. If reelected annually, Kirby could then serve as chairman for seven years through his final term.

Membership

Idealistic staff members encouraged reforms to involve more individuals in ICJ governance but found little support for a mass membership approach or closer relations with national sections. The Statute was amended to increase membership from forty to forty-five so that Eastern Europeans could be added. The members approved an amendment limiting new ICJ members to two five-year terms.[13] Term limits could both promote democratic renewal and enhance staff influence over inexperienced newcomers. Mandatory retirement had forced out the Executive Committee's longtime chairman and produced a new majority, but distant third world members would have difficulty monitoring the Geneva Secretariat.

Prospective nominees were recommended not only by members but also by staff, local affiliates, other NGOs, and activists. Following staff-prepared guidelines, the Executive Committee sought roughly equal regional balance with due regard for Anglophone and Francophone sensitivities. A president and four vice presidents were elected from different regions to largely ceremonial posts.[14] Pressed by funding agencies, the group sporadically attempted to redress the underrepresentation of women. Countries with the most active sections were informally assured representation. As of 1992 the ICJ still had no Eastern European member. Active participation had never been a universal criterion for membership. As many as one-third of the jurists did not cast ballots in electing new members. Only seventeen of the thirty-two members and four honorary members attended the 1992 meeting. Several distinguished absentees gave the ICJ an eminence by association. Table 11.1 identifies members elected through 1993.

In the new order, activist credentials counted more than professional eminence or status, international connections as highly as national position. The ICJ now recruits as members young third world

TABLE 11.1. ICJ Officers, Members, and Meetings, 1990–1993.

Secretariat (28 Chemin de Joinvile [after July 1992])
Secretary-General, Adama Dieng, June 1990–
Executive Secretary, Reed Brody, 1991–1992
Executive Officer (Finance and Administration), Trevor Davies 1993–

Executive Committee, 1992–1995
Michael Kirby, Australia, Chairman
Dalmo de Abreu Dallari, Brazil
Desmond Fernando, Sri Lanka
Asma A. Khader, Jordan
Kofi Kumado, Ghana
Fali Nariman, India
Christian Tomuschat, Germany
Don Joaquín Ruiz-Gimenez, Spain, President

New Members

1990	Antonio Cassese, Italy
	Param Cumaraswamy, Malaysia
	Robert Dossou, Benin
	Enoch Dumbutshena, Zimbabwe, Vice President, 1992
	Niall MacDermot, U.K.
1991	Asma A. Khader, Jordan, Executive Committee
	Diego García Sayan, Peru
	B. G. Ramcharan, Guyana
	Theo van Boven, Netherlands
1993	Mohammed Bedjaoui, Algeria
	Marie José Crespin, Senegal
	Florence Ndepele Mumba, Zambia
	Hipólito Solari Yrigoyen, Argentina
	Robin Cooke, New Zealand
	William Goodhart, U.K.
	Daniel Henri Marchand, France

Meetings
Geneva, 1992

activists as well as senior players in the international human rights network. Judge Enoch Dumbutshena of Zimbabwe, and attorneys Asma Khader of Jordan and Robert Dossou of Benin were elected; ten other positions designated for third world jurists remained vacant. Experienced international activists strengthened links to NGOs and international agencies: van Boven; Peru's Diego García Sayan of the Andean Commission of Jurists; Guyana's B. G. Ramcharan of the United Nations; Italy's Antonio Cassese, chairman of the Council of Europe's Steering Committee for Human Rights; Chile's José Zalaquett, former chairman of AI's International Executive Committee; and MacDermot. Only one of the nine new recruits to the old boys' club was a woman. Canadian member Justice Claire L'Heureux-Dube expressed concerns about equal opportunity. The Secretariat was directed to redraft the statute in nonsexist language.

At the 1992 meeting Butler and others insisted that the Executive Committee must present the AAICJ nominee for election because so many members supported his candidacy. As chair, Kirby refused by ruling that the Statute expressly gave the Executive Committee final say on all nominees. At its prior meeting the committee had reviewed thirty-seven recommended candidates for fifteen vacancies and approved only six nominees. All but one of the committee selections, an Israeli judge, was elected.

The members sustained Kirby's interpretation of the Statute. Indeed, its New York authors had deliberately granted the Executive Committee unchecked power to determine who could stand for election. The undemocratic sins of the fathers were visited on the sons. The founders had established an exclusive inner circle that defeated their successors. Neither the delegates from New York nor anyone else associated with the organization knew that the Statute's Cold War authors had used tight control and financial secrecy to conceal CIA funding. In 1967 the founders had agreed to end covert U.S. support, but they never disclosed even to new AAICJ board members when it had begun or how much had been provided. New leaders have uncritically accepted prior accounts of the ICJ's origins without knowing all the facts.[15] The Statute does not prevent democratically inclined leaders from shared decision making, but does not require open governance.

National Sections and Affiliates

New sections and local affilates developed in countries where ICJ criticism had contributed to democratic reforms—Poland, Hungary,

Namibia, and South Africa. Swiss lawyers also established a section, and the Japanese Civil Liberties Union affiliated. Few new third world groups organized. A new section of "Justice" in Hong Kong requested a fact-finding mission that was funded by other national sections.

Hoping to strengthen the ICJ global network, staff polled local groups about closer ties. Twenty responded. On paper the ICJ had thirty-two national sections and forty-one affiliates in fifty-four countries. Table 11.2 displays the regional distribution. National sections were linked to the ICJ from their founding; they are for lawyers only, and are limited to one per country (except for India). Well over half of the national sections are Western groups. Affiliates may be either ICJ offspring that chose a more independent status or previously established organizations that formally associated with the ICJ. Affiliate members may be either lawyers or non-lawyers. Once established, both sections and affiliates are so autonomous there is little distinction. Few ICJ members actively take part in national groups, and Geneva staff rarely communicate with local counterparts. The ICJ was a conduit for funds to a Tunisian organization that could not otherwise receive grants from abroad. National sections were first invited to send representatives to ICJ meetings in 1977; affiliates began attending in 1985. They paid their own expenses and could not attend business sessions for members only. Twenty-six of the seventy-three national sections and affiliates sent representatives to the 1992 meeting. *Table 11.2* displays the ICJ regional contacts as of 1993.

Some envisioned more effective collaboration similar to the integrated networks of Amnesty International and the International Federation of Human Rights. In return for a voice in ICJ governance, national sections might help implement and coordinate Secretariat

TABLE 11.2. ICJ Regional Contacts as of 1990–1993.

	Actual member	*Target member*	*National section*	*ICJ affiliate*	*CIJL affiliate*	*Professional staff*
Sub-Saharan Africa	8	12	2	7	1	3
N. Africa/Middle East	2			2		1
Asia/Far East	6	12	6	5	6	2
Latin America	6	9	5	6	3	1
E. Europe			1	1		
W. Europe, U.S./ Can./Aus./N.Z.	11	12	18	7	3	2
Total	33	45	32	28	13	9

programs. Local representatives insisted on full autonomy but wanted more information from Geneva, consultation on programs, and regional meetings. They encouraged Western groups to help fund the central office. Revoking the affiliation of dormant groups might undercut local leaders justifiably cautious about government scrutiny. The 1992 meeting approved guidelines calling for an advisory task force to the Executive Committee, regional meetings, a global directory of ICJ experts, local nominees for observers and ICJ representatives to intergovernmental organizations, new sections and affiliates, especially in Eastern Europe, and a hot line for urgent communications.

After forty years, effective collaboration with national sections and affiliates remained a faint hope. A NOVIB evaluation surveyed local ICJ groups in three Asian countries and found little knowledge of or interaction with the Geneva Secretariat.[16] In some countries, ICJ associates were perceived as conservative establishment lawyers reluctant to challenge ruling elites. Outspoken activists elsewhere complained that Geneva failed to give timely notice of regional activities and did not provide needed feedback after requesting information. Uncoordinated decisions of national sections and the Geneva Secretariat led to dual trial observer missions in East Timor. To strengthen the network, Dieng began sharing a summary of Executive Committee meetings and the annual audit statement with local groups. When Tunisia dissolved the League for the Defence of Human Rights, he met with President Zine El-Abidine Ben Ali to protest.[17] Several well-run European sections had valuable personnel and financial assets for export to third world groups with critical needs. The ICJ's sporadic attempts to link sections with each other and Geneva has not created a very effective union. Without close ties, independent local action has produced a decidedly mixed legacy.

Plan of Action

The 1992 triennial meeting approved future priorities on the ICJ's fortieth anniversary. At prior meetings policy planning had been secondary to conferences promoting development, the African Charter, and an independent judiciary.[18] Funding agencies would support conferences as special projects but not underwrite general budget travel costs for a business meeting. Many members also wanted a substantive program. There had been minimal review of organizational issues. Initial plans for a 1992 meeting linked to a conference on Human Rights, Development, and Democracy in New Delhi fell through. SIDA made planning grants to the general budget sufficient to fund a business meeting. Dieng organized the triennial meeting in Geneva primarily for future planning and organizing. Haiti's popularly elected president, Jean-Bertrand Aristide, would keynote an opening anniversary celebration at the United Nations.[19]

In preparatory consultations, staff shared their priorities with the Executive Committee, funding agencies, and third world supporters. Too often Westerners set the human rights agenda without involving third world activists. African critics have accused Western NGOs of perpetuating neocolonial domination in the guise of universal values.[20] ICJ priorities reflect concerns of both European funding agencies and third world victims. Non-western ICJ staff held brainstorming sessions in Argentina and Sri Lanka. Unlike AI's narrow focus, the ICJ's loose rule of law doctrine had always encompassed substantive economic rights and development. An African Secretary-General refashioned that ideal. Opening the triennial meeting in French, Dieng highlighted new priorities for democratic development.

> It is vital . . . to undertake a genuine fight against corruption, the fraudulent acquisition of wealth by high ranking public officials and the shameless transfer of capital from countries of the South to Western banks. These practices lead to the perpetuation of poverty and ever-increasing impoverishment. To this litany of scourges must be added the degradation of the environment, which presents one of the major challenges to confront us as the end of the century approaches. Jurists' contribution will be determinant in the assertion and the genuine fulfillment of the right to the environment as a human right.[21]

Kirby's priorities for a changing human rights agenda stressed the rule of *just* laws to protect minorities and victims of discrimination.[22]

Unlike AI's restrictive policy making, the ICJ's loose governance produced general goals with few clear limits. The meeting approved an action plan that identified three main issue areas: the independence of judges and lawyers; economic, social, and cultural rights; and standard setting. All agreed that the ICJ must continue its technical assistance and training for paralegals, judges, and lawyers. Like an election candidate's litany of concerns, the plan also listed seventeen study themes under six major headings: impunity, land rights, the environment, U.N. peacemaking, self-determination, and oppressed groups including women, children, minorities, and indigenous peoples. While preaching specificity, the 1992 plan provides no clearer a mandate than broad mission statements from the 1950s. Staff retained broad program discretion subject to twice-yearly review by the Executive Committee.

The plan endorsed three proven methods of action—protection, standard setting, and promotion. Future protection casework would concentrate on violations not addressed by other groups and in Francophone countries where ICJ staff had a language advantage. Larger NGOs with permanent research staff dwarfed the ICJ's investigative reports. Little new standard setting was needed. Governments refused to fund existing treaty bodies. The ICJ would stress effective implementation of existing norms through both international and national institutions. The plan envisaged studies as a vital promotional tool. In order to reassert the ICJ's intellectual leadership, major research projects would seek creative approaches to intractable problems and identify emerging issues.

In his second year as Secretary-General, Dieng completed a two-year request for funding, the ICJ "Bible" for 1992–1994.[23] That program for human rights and development advances the new leadership's three major priorities: first, advocating economic and social justice; second, strengthening institutions and legal procedures; and third, confronting criminal rulers.

Renewed Advocacy for Economic and Social Justice

Dieng's first contact with the ICJ had been at a 1978 seminar on development and human rights. His mentor, Senegal Supreme Court chief justice and ICJ President Kéba Mbaye, had pressed for a right to development and the New International Economic Order. The campaign pitted North against South. Former colonial powers resisted third world demands for reparations. Free market devotees defended property rights and decried state economic planning and expropriation. Developing states felt victimized by multinational corporations, crushing debt, and structural adjustment policies mandated by the International Monetary Fund. The ICJ had promoted democratic development and stressed the interdependence of economic and political rights. Economic growth required freedom of speech and association to maximize participation. Dieng took the ICJ a step further, criticizing Western banks and debt relations with the third world. He also challenged corrupt leaders in developing countries and the exploitation of children, women, and indigenous peoples.

Development

Since 1979, ICJ seminars on development and legal services in rural areas have promoted self-help measures. Two female legal officers enhanced the program. Mona Rishmawi expanded paralegal training into North Africa and the Middle East.[24] Dilbur Parak initiated training for workers in Asian women's organizations and arranged a follow-up paralegal seminar in Indonesia.[25] Two paralegal seminars proposed for Africa also centered on helping rural women.

Land rights became a major unifying theme for promoting economic development in all regions. Unjust land laws frustrate rural development. Landless sharecroppers and bonded laborers barely keep afloat in an economic and legal backwater. Large landowners acquire tiny peasant plots, reducing subsistence farmers to rural laborers and vulnerable tenants. South American cattle ranchers and gold prospectors forcibly seize lands from primitive indigenous groups.

The ICJ planned four regional workshops to prepare for a 1994 World Land Rights Conference. The coordinator, Roger Plant, had drafted an ILO Convention on Indigenous Peoples and completed a major study of third world land disputes for the Overseas Development Institute. Redistributive reforms and indigenous land rights topped the Latin American agenda. African participants needed to consider both land restitution for victims of apartheid and land privatization in formerly socialist economies. Participants from the former Soviet bloc would address restitution and compensation to former owners. The Asian workshop agenda featured land markets in China, customary land rights, and forest management. At the world conference, development experts from multilateral agencies and developing countries would draft a preliminary Charter of Rural Rights. The ICJ anticipated a three-year program to set international standards on land reform, land security, rural labor, and tenancy.

Graft by unproductive rulers also impedes development. Dieng estimated that officials on the take had deposited an estimated $200 billion of illicit gains in private European bank accounts. Marcos, Nguema, and the like pocketed development aid for personal gain. Brazenly corrupt elected leaders triggered as much popular unrest as the military rulers they replaced. In addition to business risks, entrepreneurs had to gamble that public officials extorting bribes would stay bought.

Dieng wanted Western cooperation in blocking future transfer of ill-gotten wealth and restitution of money stolen by deposed tyrants. The 1990 U.N. Congress on Crime Prevention had condemned corruption in public administration. Along with other NGOs, the ICJ persuaded the U.N. Sub-Commission to put fraudulent enrichment on the Human Rights Commission agenda. In the Commission debate, Dieng advocated judicial cooperation to restore extorted funds to deprived people in developing countries. The Commission agreed to address the problem along with other obstacles to economic rights. New standards might promote not only steps to prevent fraudulently acquired funds from entering states, but also the extradition of embezzlers and the restitution of stolen funds.

Indigenous Groups

Exploited tribes, women, and children too often become the victims of others' economic advance. Traditionally committed to individual liberty, the ICJ now joined NGOs advocating group rights beyond simple equal protection. With Defence for Children International, the ICJ cosponsored a Siracusa seminar on implementing new standards on child labor and banning the sale of children.[26] When indigenous peoples resisted exploitation of natural resources, the jurists faced conflicting norms on cultural rights, economic development, and new claims for environmental rights.

In Sarawak, Malaysia, natives resisted development that threatened ancestral land and forests. State lands, national parks, reserve forests, large plantation schemes, hydroelectric power dams, and commercial logging displaced native peoples. In 1990 the government prosecuted about two hundred native families for illegally occupying state land. The Netherlands foundation NOVIB encouraged balanced development that prevented environmental degradation and protected native peoples' forest resources. NOVIB's South-North project on sustainable development in Asia funded an ICJ fact-finding mission on forest destruction and native peoples in Sarawak and Indonesia. For the first time, an ICJ on-site investigation gave top priority to economic and social rights. The lead researcher, Roger Plant, examined the customary and statutory law of forest communities threatened with eviction and judicial remedies to protect native peoples' use of the land and its products.[27]

The international human rights network provided indigenous groups a vehicle for self-help. Politically weak at home, native Americans used U.N. norms on self-determination to protest forced assimilation. Leaders in traditional dress made colorful witnesses in Geneva appearances at the Commission and Sub-Commission. In Central America the ICJ cosponsored a legal services seminar in Honduras and a workshop for Indians in Guatemala. Alejandro Artucio and U.N. experts taught forty Guatemala Indians vicitimized in fighting between guerillas and the government about U.N. and OAS human rights mechanisms.[28]

Collaboration for Stronger Institutions and Procedures

United Nations

In 1968 Seán MacBride and the ICJ led a global NGO campaign to lobby the World Conference on Human Rights in Teheran for stronger international law. By the time of the 1993 World Conference in Vienna, U.N. human rights standards had proliferated more rapidly than nuclear weapons and the number of NGOs had grown exponentially. A new ICJ Secretary-General chaired CONGO's Geneva Special Committee on Human Rights, but there was no hope of coordinating activists from two thousand national, regional, and international NGOs. Amnesty International renewed the call for a U.N. High Commissioner for Human Rights. Women's groups and indigenous peoples' representatives advanced their agendas. The ICJ campaigned for an International Penal Court and tried to mediate disputes between competing interests in the movement.[29] The International Service for Human Rights in Geneva assisted small NGOs but could not reconcile many large egos.[30]

Delegates from the South protested domination by Northern NGOs on a Joint Planning Committee. Disagreement over whether to demand full access to drafting committee sessions pitted "inside" groups with consultative status against new national and regional organizations. At the last preparatory conference before the World Conference, Dieng sought to bridge North-South differences and led a contact group separate from the Joint Planning Committee.[31] After dissidents prevented former U.S. President Jimmy Carter from speaking to the NGO forum at the World Conference, the committee was disbanded. A new liaison group of thirty, organized to represent all regions and interests in the movement, included up to six ICJ associates from national and regional affiliates as well as the Geneva office.

The World Conference subjected U.N. decision makers to disruptive pressure from angry victims impatient with diplomatic niceties. Some national NGOs functioned as flags of convenience for opposition groups to attack state rivals. Attendance by representatives of Peru's Shining Path alarmed both governments and human rights activists.[32] At the opposite extreme, China, among others, kept genuine dissidents at home and sent "GONGOs," government agents who claimed to be nongovernmental. In twenty-five years the NGO universe expanded to include combative national and regional groups demanding equal time on the world stage. The most experienced NGO advocates for NGO access to U.N. proceedings found their own voices diluted in the swelling chorus. No longer could one major organization such as the ICJ or Amnesty International provide leadership, although governments recognized their special expertise. The ICJ's African Secretary-General was well positioned to cultivate trust within the fractious global movement. Experience would be needed in Geneva as government representatives began to reexamine and "update" the U.N.'s consultative arrangements with NGOs "in the light of recent experience."[33]

Most NGOs collaborated in Vienna to fend off an Asian government assault on the universality of human rights enforced against states by the United Nations. The 1993 World Conference Final Document and Report reaffirmed rule of law values and urged states to abrogate legislation granting impunity to those responsible for grave violations.[34] The conference also endorsed an optional protocol to the Torture Convention that the ICJ had initiated to authorize unannounced prison visits. Numerous well-organized NGOs representing women reportedly had the greatest lobbying success in Vienna. The NGO presence had greater impact in 1993 than in 1968, but MacBride's harsh appraisal of the Teheran Conference expressed the same disappointment felt by idealists at the meager results in Vienna. Yet MacBride's 1968 campaign for improved humanitarian law did ultimately bear fruit in the 1977 Geneva Protocols, and the High Commissioner became a reality in January 1994. The United States successfully pushed the General Assembly to create the post in December 1993 in a compromise resolution which left the Commissioner's authority unclear. Secretary-General Boutros-Ghali promptly nominated an Ecuadorian diplomat who NGOs feared was unequal to the task.

Other seedlings nurtured by the ICJ in Vienna could sprout in the next decade. The United States favors a criminal court with limited jurisdiction over international terrorists and drug dealers; the ICJ insists on broader penal authority to prosecute human rights offenders.[35] The International Law Commission has completed a draft Code of Crimes against the Peace and Security of Mankind and has now taken up the proposal for a permanent court. Commission member Christian Tomuschat of the ICJ Executive Committee will pursue the campaign for jurisdiction over human rights criminals.

African Commission

Hope must spring eternal for NGO idealists laboring to create effective international institutions. The African Commission on Human and Peoples' Rights (ACHPR) gravely disappointed nearly all. The African Charter itself had so many "claw-back" provisions that states parties incurred no legal obligation to modify national law. The

Organization of African Unity elected government officials of questionable independence to an all-male commission. Sporadic attendance at biennial meetings prevented a quorum at one session. Few states reported as required, and self-serving reports were as brief as three pages stapled to the national constitution. The OAU Secretariat failed to invite representatives to make an oral presentation and answer questions. The commission spent hours rather than days considering state reports and reviewed individual communications in private session.[36]

As part of an international rescue operation, Dieng continued the ICJ's thirty-year quest for regional procedures. Gambia provided office space for a commission headquarters in Banjul, but business meetings were held in hotels. The United Nations and Western governments provided funds for secretariat staff and equipment, but documents were lost and inquiries went unanswered. Dieng served as an expert consultant recommending procedural reforms to give the commission teeth. Western NGOs concurred that the commission urgently needed strong African NGO constituents. Poverty, ethnic loyalty, traditional culture, and government repression left Africa with few of the interest groups so commonly found in the West.[37]

The ICJ has functioned like a midwife, channeling money and expertise to both regional and national groups including the Inter-African Union of Human Rights and the Tunisian League for the Defence of Human Rights. The Secretary-General of the African Committee for Law and Development trained directly with Dieng during an internship in Geneva. For each commission session the ICJ cosponsored workshops for national NGOs.[38] Representatives learned how to obtain consultative status and to comment on country reports. The ICJ prepared and distributed an instruction booklet on how to file communications.[39] African Commission members addressed the workshops and then heard from NGO representatives at their public session. A Canadian Centre, EKD, and SIDA paid all expenses for twenty-five African NGO representatives the ICJ invited to the commission's eleventh session in Tunis. The workshop protested mistreatment of human rights activists in Chad and the Ivory Coast and urged reform in commission procedures. After five disappointing years, observers were grateful that the African Commission convened on time, reviewed two periodic reports, and accepted an invitation to observe elections in Mali.

Still dissatisfied with the inadequate procedures, Dieng obtained European grants to continue NGO workshops and lobbied for amendments to the African Charter. In 1993 the ICJ opened in Geneva its own register of complaints and communications to the African

Commission.[40] The staff could then keep track of documents misplaced by the OAU Secretariat and publicize complaints subject to confidential proceedings under Charter Article 59. On a second track, Dieng convened experts in a brainstorming session attended by six commission members and a representative of the OAU Secretary-General. In a background paper the ICJ identified major weaknesses in the African Charter and proposed amendments to eliminate the claw-back clauses, open up confidential procedures, and create an African regional court. The participants resisted proposals to amend the Charter. Instead they recommended interpretation guidelines to curtail state abuse and improved commission procedures. A larger role for women was urged. The summary report also called for the OAU Summit Conference to approve the human rights budget and for creation of a trust fund financed from extra-budgetary resources. Presumably, European development foundations would provide the needed funds.

Since a regional court was first recommended at the ICJ Lagos conference in 1960, Africans have debated tradition versus alien imports. The background paper for the Dakar brainstorming session forthrightly argues: "Excessive reliance on African tradition may be counter-productive to the progressive development of international human rights law. . . . To reject an African human rights court in the name of tradition may be a retrogressive step."[41] Proponents and opponents of a court at the 1993 meeting ambiguously resolved that "the African concept of the law does not preclude the notion that the evolution of ideas in Africa towards democracy and human rights militates in favour of the proposal to create an African Court."[42] The campaign continues, reinvigorated by an African Secretary-General committed to effective regional institutions.

National Implementation

Forum shopping has made lawyers in the U.S. federal system notorious opportunists searching out the most sympathetic state or federal judge. Civil rights advocates frustrated by a conservative U.S. Supreme Court have turned to more liberal state judges. The ICJ initially favored domestic implementation, then shifted to international enforcement, and now campaigns for both. U.N. lobbying produced superior legal standards without adequate international tribunals for enforcement. Local judges applying U.N. and regional human rights law in national courts would provide far more victims with remedies close to home. In Europe and the United States, human rights advocates have won preliminary victories with a few sympathetic judges who were willing to follow international law. Latin American constitutions allow for direct application of international law, but few lawyers and judges invoke human rights standards. The ICJ attempted to increase their number through training in domestic incorporation of international human rights law. Training courses in Uruguay and Argentina encouraged lawyers to cite, and jurists to apply, international law.[43]

Funding agencies encouraged the ICJ to expand its primary support for legal reform by providing technical assistance for elections. Prior to 1992 the ICJ had not conducted or planned election observer missions. The European Community asked the ICJ for assistance in Madagascar. Dieng welcomed the opportunity to provide experts who could establish democratic procedures and institutions such as a free press, essential in civil society. After endorsing a planned referendum to the European donors, the ICJ provided experts who advised the local media, met with the National Electoral Council, and disseminated information to NGOs and voters. ICJ observers then monitored a constitutional referendum and subsequent voting in three rounds of presidential and legislative elections.[44] The ICJ's use of African experts led to further requests for missions in Burundi, Malawi, the Central African Republic, and Guinea. The United Nations hired ICJ African legal officer Philip Amoah as an election consultant in Lesotho. Dieng also sought technical assistance grants for dispute resolution experts to ameliorate post-apartheid strife in South Africa.

A 1993 U.N. contract to train judges for Cambodia's post-election courts sets impossible expectations. In a three-week training course on Judicial Functions and Independence, the CIJL conducted moot court exercises for prospective appellate court judges who had only paralegal qualifications.[45] Justice Bhaghwati pressed the fundamental evidentiary rule excluding confessions obtained by torture. The institutions of civil society so quickly destroyed during Pol Pot's reign of terror will not be swiftly reconstructed, despite the highest hopes and best intentions.

Confrontation for Protection

Specialization was the watchword of the 1992 action plan. No longer could a small ICJ aspire to protect all the human rights of all the world's people. As an organization of jurists, the ICJ/CIJL had a unique responsibility to protect lawyers and judges. Like clients in pending cases, victims in ICJ local affiliates deserved ongoing support. The ICJ dispatched three missions to Sri Lanka on behalf of local human rights activists harassed and allegedly killed by the government.[46] In three missions to South Africa and Namibia, the ICJ recommended essential prerequisites for free elections.[47] An AICJ-funded mission to Malaysia discouraged the government from adopting legislation that would curtail judicial independence. Other NGOs could attack easy targets at the United Nations, such as Iraq after its invasion of Kuwait; the ICJ's better connected representatives would lobby for U.N. Commission action on difficult cases of governments—such as those of China, India, and Indonesia—with friends in high places.

Executive Secretary Reed Brody coordinated a two-part protection strategy at the United Nations by lobbying the Human Rights Commission to investigate particularly gross situations (in Haiti, Iraq, East Timor, Burma, Tibet) and to create theme mechanisms for widespread problems, including impunity, attacks on judges, and denial of habeas corpus. He drafted resolutions for government sponsors authorizing Commission rapporteurs to investigate Haiti and Iraq. To support Commission action on Indonesia, the ICJ published for the debate a special report on the 1991 massacre in East Timor.[48] Joint lobbying with other NGOs influenced Commission action on Burma, Haiti, and Indonesia; regional voting blocs and political alliances limited meaningful scrutiny to a few pariah states. Few supported ICJ efforts to protect Algerian Islamic fundamentalists, despite the suspension of free elections and disregard for due process.[49]

The ICJ lobbied for thematic approaches on impunity and judicial independence that would apply to any government. Many elected Latin American governments had succumbed to military intimidation by granting amnesty for prior offenses and pardoning convicted torturers. The ICJ influenced Sub-Commission rapporteurs Louis Joinet and Senegalese judge El-Hadji Guissé to initiate a study on impunity. At a meeting on impunity, sixty experts denounced self-amnesty proclamations by several governments and demanded prosecution for war crimes in Bosnia.[50] An ICJ press release decried amnesty provisions in the negotiated settlement to end El Salvador's bloody civil war. Artucio reported on the trial of soldiers who killed four nuns.[51] The ICJ strongly supported exiled Haitian President Jean-Bertrand Aristide's refusal to grant impunity as a condition of returning to office. A major report on Chile welcomed democratic reforms but lamented that the army enjoyed impunity for past violations.[52]

For investigatory missions, Dieng departed from the established fact-finding script. When Burma's government refused entry to a mission, ICJ observers visited as tourists and published a report.[53] China's refusal to allow a 1993 ICJ mission to Tibet poses a greater

Michael Kirby, ICJ Executive Committee chairman since 1991, meeting with the Dalai Lama. China refused to grant permission for an ICJ mission to Tibet in 1993.

obstacle. Dieng himself headed a four-member mission to South Africa.[54] The ICJ gave voice to South American and Arab lawyers, lending its imprimatur by publishing their evidence of violations. The most recent joint publication with Al Haq reported on land rights in the Israeli Occupied Territories. In conjunction with the progressive Arab Lawyers Union, the CIJL planned a regional seminar on independent judicial systems. Lawyers in Argentina, Chile, and Colombia were commissioned to prepare studies documenting attacks on judges in their countries.

ICJ staff from Africa and the Middle East gave those regions high priority. Eight of the ten trial observers assigned in those regions came from other third world countries. In an intervention at the U.N. Commission, Rishmawi criticized Senegal for improperly restructuring the courts. Major missions were planned for Kenya, Sudan, Algeria, Morocco, and Western Sahara. Dieng envisioned predominantly non-Western teams with representatives from different regions delegated to negotiate reforms with government officials before any public denunciation.[55] Collaboration replaces confrontation when the stamp of ICJ approval releases foreign aid suspended by Western donors because of human rights violations. In the 1990s the promise of renewed development assistance may be a more potent weapon than the threat of negative publicity. NGOs that apply a foreign aid stick to third world regimes will appear like Western handmaidens unless they pay due attention to human rights violations in the North.

ICJ representatives have regularly challenged major Western powers. Dieng proposed a U.N. Commission rapporteur for the Israeli Occupied Territories who was appointed despite strenuous U.S. opposition. Rishmawi criticized European trade agreements with Israel and U.S. loan guarantees. The ICJ lobbied the Commission to seek a ruling from the International Court of Justice on whether the Geneva Convention obligated governments to isolate Israel because of its West Bank settlements.[56] Brody accused the United States of scuttling a European-sponsored resolution on Tibet.[57] A lawyer from Ecuador observed a Palestinian deportation trial in Los Angeles.

A fact-finding mission to Hong Kong pressed Britain for democratic reforms before transfer of the territory to China in 1997.[58] A new governor outraged Beijing with a modest proposal to expand the franchise for 1995 legislative elections.[59] The ICJ maintained pressure on Japan to reform its mental health system and sent a mission to investigate restitution for "comfort women" enslaved during World War II.[60] The United States, Japan, and Australia resisted Brody's campaign for decisive action on East Timor. Dieng planned a major mission on xenophobia to Germany, France, and Spain after racist attacks on immigrants.[61] If Western-funded advocates from the third world significantly challenge European abuses, then the idealistic vision of a global human rights regime will appear one step closer. Western funding of third world activists to challenge violations exclusively in the South belies the global ideal.

Conclusions

Recruitment

ICJ recruits from the third world took charge of the Secretariat at the organization's fortieth anniversary. A new Secretary-General from Senegal and the Palestinian director of the CIJL directed a staff that had no leading Western professionals. Non-Western recruits also comprised a new majority on the Executive Committee selected by an informal regional allocation not mandated by the ICJ Statute. Affirmative action also placed a woman from the Middle East on the committee. Recruitment of other Commissioners fell behind as ICJ membership dwindled to thirty-one, well below the authorized level of forty-five. Hiring of additional staff also proceeded slowly. At the national level, European sections remained strong, but very few affiliates in developing countries organized effectively.

Despite its small base, the distinction of its advocates made the ICJ an important source of recruits for transnational human rights service. Brody left to direct the International Human Rights Law Group in Washington. The U.N. Commission on Human Rights named legal officer Alejandro Artucio its rapporteur on Equatorial Guinea. Former U.S. ambassador to the Commission Kenneth Blackwell noted that Western diplomats sought information from the ICJ about new third world recruits being considered for Geneva appointments. He recalled a reception attended by ICJ staff where a French diplomat successfully promoted ICJ member Robert Dossou of Benin as the first U.N. rapporteur on racism.[62]

Articulation

A new Secretary-General gave the "dynamic" rule of law some fresh content at odds with prior ICJ tenets. Dieng urged governments to ban white supremacist organizations.[63] The ICJ's American founders opposed all limits on freedom of association. Dieng advocated the minority protection guarantees of the European Human Rights Convention and the U.N. convention against race discrimination. Conflicting economic and political values also presented the ICJ with difficult choices. Natural law offers no clear mandate for either planned growth or free market economies. Europeans, Americans, and their third world beneficiaries fundamentally disagree over norms for economic development and social democracy. Both indigenous peoples and large plantation owners occupy vast tracts of arable land that could support impoverished peasants. Development depletes natural resources and causes environmental pollution. The rule of law could be misapplied either as a dead hand from the past or as a capricious threat to established rights. Too dynamic a redefinition of fundamental rights implies shifting policy preferences unchecked by legal principle.

The ICJ's substantive rule of law doctrine was expanded to include land rights and more elements of democratic socialism. The strategic plan called for research and future studies that would renew the ICJ's intellectual leadership in the movement. The core values remained procedural and Western—democratic elections, popular participation, and fair laws enforced by an independent judiciary. Elections took priority over land reform. When confronted by challenges to the universality of human rights, Dieng favored global norms over African tradition. Third world leadership and ICJ sensitivity to economic injustice made Western concepts more acceptable as global norms. The ICJ's internal balance between North and South contributes to a global dialogue over Western liberal values in search of a workable synthesis.

Aggregation

At the 1993 World Conference on Human Rights, NGO collaboration was as vital as it was improbable. Rival egos and the vast range of national, regional, and international NGOs produced a loose coalition preoccupied with procedure rather than substance. Amnesty International and the ICJ proposed different institutional reforms, and other groups gave priority to their own agendas. Diversity reflects healthy growth but produces discord that governments can exploit. If NGOs cannot agree on representative leadership, governments may further restrict which groups can speak at U.N. meetings. The Geneva Special Committee on Human Rights chaired by the ICJ Secretary-General wields no coordinating authority, and some hierarchy is needed for more effective aggregation of small group demands. The ICJ and the Lawyers Committee for Human Rights continued to produce similar annual reports describing attacks on the judiciary after years of unproductive discussions about how to avoid future duplication.

Leadership

An organization that had always been governed from the top down experienced a difficult succession. After twenty years in control, a Secretary-General in failing health had to step down. At the same time, members enforced statutory term limits to retire the chairman of the Executive Committee. A new generation of leaders promised democratic reform. The Secretariat consulted extensively with members and national affiliates on a future plan of action. In a struggle for the vacant "U.S." seat, the new Executive Committee retained the undemocratic procedures governing nomination for election to the Commission. The ICJ's future, like its past, would be largely determined by the caliber of its staff rather than by Executive Committee leaders far from Geneva. The Statute forces members to retire after ten years, but sets no term limit for the Secretary-General. Staff and Western development agencies largely determined the ICJ's shifting priorities and methods.

Funding

Western governments and foundations provided increased resources after the ICJ's leadership renewal. Sweden funded the major development initiatives. Staff depend on major donors more than on the Executive Committee. A new chairman promised to make the ICJ more "transparent." The Secretary-General controls how much information is revealed and has begun revealing specific details about government support. An evaluation by the Dutch government's cofinancing program has made public the most complete accounting of current ICJ finances without disclosing the amount of NOVIB project grants. European government patrons allow NGOs, both domestic and international, considerable independence. Third world recipients must manage the funds efficiently and serve the common good. The ICJ's new third world leaders have thus far not been reluctant to fault European sponsors for human rights abuses. Western donors have at the same time retained ICJ expertise for election projects that significantly modified the jurists' program. Without fully democratizing its own governance, the ICJ turned forty with new resources for reform both without and within.

ICJ Reports, 1990–1993

Agenda for Peace: An Independent Survey of the Violence in South Africa. Geneva: ICJ, 1992. 30 pp. Reports on a mission of March 16–29, 1992.

Artucio, Alejandro. *A Breach of Impunity: The Trial for the Murder of Jesuits in El Salvador.* New York: Fordham University Press, 1992. 81 pp.

Blaming the Victims: The 12 November 1991 Massacre in Dili, East Timor, and the Response of the Indonesian Government. Geneva: ICJ, 1992. 26 pp.

The Burmese Way: To Where? Report of a Mission to Myanmar (Burma) by Makhdoom Ali Khan. Geneva: ICJ, 1991. 95 pp.

Countdown to 1997. Report of a Mission to Hong Kong. Geneva: ICJ, 1992. 193 pp.

The Failed Promise: Human Rights in the Philippines since the Revolution of 1986. Geneva: ICJ, 1991. 283 pp.

Guatemala Taller de capacitación par miembros de grupos y comunidades indígenas Ciudad de Guatemala, 31 de marzo–3 de abril 1992. Geneva: ICJ, 1992.

Heaton-Armstrong, Anthony. *Magisterial Inquiry into the Homicide of Richard de Zoysa.* Geneva: ICJ, 1990. 26 pp.

How to Address a Communication to the African Commission on Human and Peoples' Rights. Geneva: ICJ, 1992. 32 pp. (Eng./Fr.)

Human Rights of Psychiatric Patients in Japan: Mission Recommendations. Geneva: ICJ, 1992. 12 pp.
Mbaye, Kéba. *Les droits de l'homme en Afrique.* Paris: Pedone, 1993.
Neff, Stephen C. *Sri Lanka: The Activities of the Presidential Commission of Inquiry in Respect of NGOs.* Report of a Mission, May–June 1991. Geneva: ICJ, 1991. 71 pp.
Refugees from Myanmar. Geneva: ICJ, 1992. 21 pp.
Signposts to Peace: An Independent Survey of the Violence in Natal, South Africa. Geneva: ICJ, 1990. 36 pp.
Towards Universal Justice: International Penal Court. U.N. Human Rights Mechanisms. Geneva: ICJ, 1993. 88 p.
Tragedy in East Timor. Report on the Trials in Dili and Jakarta. Geneva: ICJ, 1992. 69 pp.

Conclusion: **Politics, Law, and Human Rights NGOs**

> Without some working conception of the political role of interest groups, their functions, and the ways in which their powers are exercised, we shall not be able adequately to understand the nature of the political process. Descriptions of that process that treat the nonparty group peripherally and merely anecdotally are not sufficient. The puzzle cannot be solved if some of the pieces are virtually ignored.
>
> —David B. Truman[1]

The puzzle of international politics cannot be solved without understanding NGO functions. Some human rights advocates tout their work as nonpolitical, but the ICJ has participated in a global struggle for power—the individual against the state, international organizations against sovereign governments. Although it may not impress realists, the ICJ is a functional sibling of domestic public interest groups with demonstrable influence on promotion, standard setting, and protection. Although idealists may be impressed, the ICJ has not exercised sufficient influence to herald the imminent arrival of a new world order.

NGO advocacy for human rights since World War II resembles the nineteenth-century campaign that ended the slave trade. Ethan Nadelmann concludes that moral protest mobilized by the British Anti-Slavery Society was the fundamental impetus for change.[2] Paul Lauren also recognizes that group's considerable influence but concludes that structural changes in political, military, and economic power made the critical difference.[3] Nadelmann's work on prohibition regimes suggests that NGOs could contribute to a new moral/legal order that criminalizes torture, summary exections, and disappearances. From Lauren's vantage point, the Cold War's end could have greater impact on human rights than the combined efforts of all NGOs. The first section below contrasts the Anti-Slavery Society impact on nineteenth-century world politics with the findings from this study of the ICJ's influence since 1952. The second section summarizes the key findings about organizational factors that determined the ICJ's effectiveness. A final section offers conclusions about the ICJ's place in a changing world order.

NGO Functions in International Relations

States, intergovernmental organizations, and NGOs all engage in promotion, standard setting, and protection. Their diverse activities have been variously identified as functions, methods, strategies, and tactics. The functional analysis employed throughout this study provides the framework for its main conclusions.

Promotion

Human rights promotion involves socialization, recruitment, and communication. Nadelmann characterizes NGOs as "transnational moral entrepreneurs."

> These groups mobilize popular opinion and political support . . . ; they stimulate and assist in the creation of like-minded organizations in other countries; and they play a significant role in elevating their objective beyond its identification with the national interests of their government. Indeed, their efforts are often directed toward persuading foreign audiences, especially foreign elites, that a particular prohibition regime reflects a widely shared or even universal moral sense, rather than the peculiar moral code of one society.[4]

The Anti-Slavery Society promoted moral outrage through socialization, recruitment, and communication. It sponsored international conventions, translated publications into several languages, "kept in close touch with abolitionists abroad," and sent "propaganda to the press and leading public figures. . . . It played a role in prompting the creation of similar societies in France, the United States, Brazil and elsewhere." The Society "thus represented perhaps the first transnational moral entrepreneur—religious movements aside—to play a significant role in world politics generally and in the evolution of a global prohibition regime specifically."[5]

The ICJ has similarly functioned as a promotional entrepreneur.

Its rule of law congresses, regional conferences, national seminars, and publications have socialized elite recruits in a global communications network. The ICJ has provided legal consultants; cosponsored workshops to train paralegals, community organizers, and police; and provided practitioner handbooks. Development assistance for promoting human rights made educational programming and technical assistance major components of the ICJ's enhanced program.

The message undermined blind patriotism. National loyalty and personal ambition toppled a few fallen angels no longer associated with the ICJ. A considerably larger number of activists appear to have become more committed to the human rights movement than to their national government. African NGO participants at an ICJ workshop adopted a "Profession of Faith" that illustrates their socialization to universal human rights.

> For a century, the African has been denied as an individual: colonial repression was followed, despite the hopes of liberation and the promises of liberty, by the era of the repression of the continent by dictators "with hands stained with blood."
>
> Neither accused nor tried, this is the fate of many thousands of prisoners across the continent, certain of whom run the risk at any time of "disappearing" or being sent to some (sordid) cell in a military camp . . . where he or she will die little by little. . . . Most of these thousands of anonymous prisoners or disappeared persons have committed no other crime than to have dared to criticize the manner in which their governments manage the affairs of their countries.
>
> The world is changing, history is accelerating, the winds of democracy are blowing, democrats are joining ranks, the Rule of Law is (re-)born.[6]

Unlike the Anti-Slavery society's focus on a single evil, the ICJ has promoted a comprehensive human rights code. It took a century to turn world opinion against slavery, and should take even longer to socialize global citizens to the rule of law. After forty years, the organization has had greater success in recruiting individual converts as members, staff, and interns than in mobilizing effective local affiliates. The ICJ recruited third world elites for the international movement, including Kenyan and Peruvian monitors for the United Nations and its own Senegalese Secretary-General. The transfer of power to third world leaders in 1990 and the growing exchange of personnel with intergovernmental organizations shows that the transnational network has expanded considerably since the nineteenth century. The great bulk of humanity in most of Asia and Africa still appears more attuned to Buddhist, Hindu, Islamic, and nationalist creeds than to Western Enlightenment values.[7]

Standard Setting

Standard setting entails the articulation of values, the aggregation of demands from different groups, and the legislation of rules and policies. Nadelmann concludes that Western ideals dictate global standards.

> Virtually all of the norms that are now identified as essential ingredients of international law and global society have their roots in the jurisprudence of European scholars of international law and in the notions and patterns of acceptable behavior established by the more powerful Western European states. This is particularly true of many of the norms reflected in global prohibition regimes. Their emergence within Europe reflected the needs and impositions of the most powerful states as well as the influence of the Enlightenment and contemporaneous religious and moral notions. . . . To an extent virtually unprecedented in world history, a few European states and the United States proved successful in proselytizing to diverse societies, shaping the moral views of substantial sectors of elite opinion outside their borders, and imposing their norms on foreign regimes around the world.[8]

The Anti-Slavery Society demanded the natural rights of man as articulated by Enlightenment principles. It aggregated demands of radical Quakers, legal activists, and African explorers to petition for abolition. In response, Parliament outlawed the slave trade in 1807. When abolitionists lobbied for international action, British representatives negotiated treaties against the trade. Thomas Clarkson prepared a pamphlet illustrating the horrors with a preface addressed to diplomats attending the 1815 Congress of Vienna. William Wilberforce lobbied Parliament and met privately with Czar Alexander I of Russia. Government representatives negotiated the first multinational declaration against the slave trade in 1815, and Britian followed up with bilateral prohibition agreements. Economic sanctions were approved to punish slave-trading states. As slavery actually expanded in the following decades, abolitionists continued the crusade from Brazil to Nepal. In the 1890 Brussels Act, seventeen states adopted a convention that most effectively criminalized the trade.

The ICJ, like its antislavery forefather, articulated demands based on Western Enlightenment principles. Britons Marsh and MacDermot succeeded Clarkson and Wilberforce. Their human rights demands considerably exceeded those of both nineteenth-century abolitionists and contemporary advocates who work for Amnesty International and "Justice" in London. The ICJ aggregated interests with continental and third world activists to expand dramatically Dicey's rule of law doctrine. In addition to procedural guarantees for civil liberties, the ICJ endorsed substantive economic justice and advocated social democracy. With the support of European church foundations, secular advocates preached universal values. In 1976 MacDermot praised the Christian churches for being uniquely equipped to take action and for the will to use available means: "It is often the Churches which play the greatest part. . . . Sometimes they are almost alone in doing so."[9] The ICJ's first non-Western President, Vivian Bose of India, was a Protestant, but non-Christian recruits from the third world subsequently became prominent ICJ leaders. MacDermot reached out to African nationalists by proposing human rights guarantees in one-party states. In turn, Senegalese and Indian activists welcomed the articulation of development rights.

Abolitionists preached morality, which jurists proclaimed as law. Rule of Law congresses and conferences endorsed principles that reinforced emerging norms of customary international law. The ICJ also went beyond the Anti-Slavery Society in demanding supranational enforcement institutions. MacBride moved the ICJ past national implementation with a campaign for a U.N. High Commissioner for Human Rights. Europeans once again took the lead with strong regional institutions that the ICJ promoted as models for Africa, Asia, and Latin America. ICJ member and President Vivian Bose resisted the shift to international institutions, but lobbying for stronger U.N. standards and procedures became a top priority.

ICJ legislative strategies resemble those of U.S. public interest groups. Lobbying is a dirty word for idealists who consider the human rights movement morally superior to political pressure groups. Yet the ICJ pressed the United Nations to adopt international law with expert information, insider contacts, and constituent pressure in the same way the ACLU lobbies Congress. Both MacBride and MacDermot had mastered the process after years of service in their national Parliaments. The Centre for the Independence of Judges and Lawyers did not function like a special interest group for a privileged professional constituency. As a public interest organization, the CIJL protected jurists at risk for defending others' rights.

International lawmaking involves more collaboration than confrontation—elite contacts, expert testimony, workshops to draft proposals, reports documenting a need for action, NGO coalitions, and constituency pressure. A few skilled ICJ lobbyists significantly influenced the adoption of global, regional, and national standards. Without effective implementation, standards amount to empty promises. ICJ follow-up tactics have included setting guidelines for interpretation, lobbying for adequate funding and competent personnel, disseminating handbooks that direct victims in the use of new procedures, and issuing public critiques that goad monitors to act effectively. This study also indicates that national public interest groups have a new strategy to influence their own governments—solidarity with international NGOs. ICJ intervention helped Japanese lawyers obtain major reform of the mental health law.

ICJ participation in NGO coalitions fits with prior findings about ad hoc alliances of domestic groups. Leaders agree to only limited collaboration on occasional joint projects and fiercely protect their distinct identities. Unfortunate rivalry and duplication resulted with the World Peace Through World Law Center and the Lawyers Committee for Human Rights. Each Secretary-General has chaired the Geneva NGO human rights committee since its founding by MacBride. The ICJ could become a victim of its own success in securing access for NGO coalition partners to U.N. bodies. So many small NGOs now intervene with repetitive testimony that victim evidence has less impact, and governments threaten to curtail all NGO speakers. Proudly independent and rapidly growing human rights groups resist direction or control. Without strategic planning, tactical choices by some groups to lobby for national or regional standards could defeat other NGOs' campaigns for global norms. After switching from the United Nations to the European community for improved procedures to deter torture, the ICJ has renewed work on an optional protocol authorizing prison visits under the U.N. convention. After forty years the impact of ICJ standard setting has greater visibility than the fruits of its promotion activities.

Protection

Protection involves rule implementation and enforcement. Nineteenth-century abolitionists effectively mobilized public protest in a global crusade that included fact-finding missions, published reports, and appeals to rulers. Nadelmann concludes that

> among the laggards, the consciousness of being perceived as primitive and deviant surely weighed heavily in the decisions of local rulers to do away with slavery. It is, in short, impossible to explain the abolition of slavery throughout the world during the past two centuries without emphasizing the powerful role of shared moral notions derived primarily from the religious and secular principles of the Enlightenment.[10]

Antislavery opinion also led Britain to use over one-sixth of the Royal Navy as an international criminal police force to suppress the slave traffic.[11]

The ICJ also sought enforcement of international law through both its own interventions and its lobbying of responsible officials to implement sanctions. In the absence of international courts with legal authority over sovereign states, the ICJ used protection tactics different from those of national civil liberties lawyers. Legal representation for client victims occasionally entailed quiet diplomacy but normally required confrontational tactics—fact-finding missions, trial observers, negative publicity, intervention with foreign policy officials and intergovernmental bodies, and witness testimony. Repeated condemnation deligitimized regimes that abused their citizens. Initially, the jurists conducted quasi-judicial inquiry commissions to pronounce judgment on offending governments. Less formal fact-finding missions now produce ICJ reports that resemble prosecutorial indictments for review by newly created international human rights bodies. When state members of the U.N. Human Rights Commission protect their own, the ICJ passes independent judgment condemning both the government charged and the politicized process.

ICJ protection efforts won awards from some governments; target governments paid tribute to its aim by firing back. The ICJ outlived most of the dictatorships and juntas it condemned. Unfortunately, few of the officials charged were ever prosecuted for their crimes. When perceived as representing U.S. or Western policy, the jurists had the greatest influence. The U.S. State Department summarized NGO views in annual country reports. Regular information exchange helped both public and private experts engaged in fact-finding missions. Western ambassadors pressed local officials to admit and receive ICJ representatives investigating violations. Aid donors occasionally suspended assistance until officials made reforms demanded by NGOs. U.S. legislators used ICJ expert witnesses to press a reluctant State Department for more vigorous human rights enforcement. Foreign ministries in some target states quietly support complaints against law enforcement or justice department officials.

The postwar pioneer in human rights protection has now yielded leadership in that field to younger and larger NGOs. Their enforcement functions will continue to be needed until effective judicial institutions acquire jurisdiction over state criminals. When courts adjudicate, interest groups function as lobbyists and advocates rather than as judges.

Interest Group Pluralism and Corporatism

Advocates for popular sovereignty need to understand how NGOs function, organize, and grow in order to enhance their influence. The

ICJ has both unique qualities and more common features that could guide other groups to longevity and success. This study has found great similarity between national and international interest group politics. Research on domestic groups has produced varied accounts of their origins, governance, strategies, and political effectiveness—pluralism, elite theory, democratic corporatism, and social movement research. The ICJ's origins and development most closely fit a corporatist model that may not appeal to proponents of interest group pluralism or populist movements.

Origins and Finances

The first pluralist research found that interest groups originated as grass-roots movements in opposition to the state or rival special interests. Subsequent research revealed the contrary, that U.S. voluntary organizations owed their existence to founding entrepreneurs and major patrons who provided inducements to membership. Democratic corporatist governments in Europe helped organize and support private groups as a means to solicit input from all sectors of the population. The ICJ's American founders portrayed themselves as pluralists, professionals who mobilized to combat communist totalitarianism. In fact, selected members of the New York City Bar were entrepreneurs with a covert patron, the Central Intelligence Agency.

In democratic corporatist fashion, the United States deliberately organized and supported private citizens needing representation in a global political contest with rival Soviet front groups. Unlike fascist corporatism, the CIA allowed the ICJ considerable independence. Autonomous leaders and staff unaware of CIA benefactors took the ICJ beyond narrow anticommunism to attack tyrants of all persuasions. The public disclosure and termination of CIA funding, followed by Seán MacBride's departure, virtually destroyed the original ICJ. Another entrepreneur, Niall MacDermot, and Western European state patrons gave the organization new life in 1970. At its fortieth anniversary, the ICJ again became heavily dependent on one major donor when Sweden made possible significant growth.

The ICJ is not and never was a spontaneous citizens' movement organized to challenge state power. Other human rights NGOs such as Amnesty International may fit the pluralist model, but the ICJ more closely resembles quasi-nongovernmental organizations that use public funds to provide a public service. After years of pretense that the ICJ was member-supported, the organization publicly acknowledges the primacy of governments and foundations. Not until 1993 were members told which governments were supporters and the amounts that were granted by different sources. SIDA openly reports its grants to the Swedish Parliament. In accord with corporatist practice, the ICJ functions like a world legal aid society funded by governments and private foundations. If legal representation for human rights victims serves the U.N. mission, then why not provide multilateral funding? The new order will have truly arrived when governments pay for advocates who challenge their own misconduct in U.N. proceedings. Any multilaterally funded human rights aid must be administered by an autonomous board. A public funding scheme must not force NGO consolidation or curtail fully private advocacy groups. Independently funded NGO watchdogs would still be needed and could ride herd on public groups.

Future research on human rights NGOs should pierce the financial veil to determine who exercises financial control. Until more human rights NGOs disclose their finances, claims for a global citizens' movement remain to be proved. Would greater disclosure be more costly than the aimless complaints about current confidential arrangements? Disclosure would enable target governments to pressure sponsors. Private contributors might find less reason to give. Taxpayers might protest grants for politically controversial activities. Critical fact-finding reports could be discredited as propaganda funded by political rivals.

On balance, disclosure works less mischief than confidential arrangements. The ICJ has shown by example that publicly funded organizations can have considerable independence, but improved financial accounting is required for full trust. Third world skeptics properly complain about the hidden finances of Western NGOs. Greater public disclosure is more than an academic exercise. Funding determines ownership and accountability. The law should require governments to account for taxpayer money appropriated to private voluntary organizations. By rule, NGOs in consultative status should disclose their government funding to the United Nations; they have neither done so nor been required to comply. Many funding governments prefer confidentiality to advance their own policies without political cost through ostensibly private groups.

State-funded NGOs need ethical standards governing their own accountability. All government and foundation grants should be publicly disclosed. Financial reports could reveal the proportion of total income from a specified number of governments in each region without fully identifying which state gave exactly how much. Unrestricted grants should be made for the general budget rather than for special missions that target one country. No government should contribute a disproportionate share of the total budget. The QUANGOs least vulnerable to financial manipulation receive grants from many different governments, foundations, and multilateral institutions. No funds should be accepted from ministries responsible for foreign intelligence; grants from development agencies and legal ministries if disclosed pose less of an ethical problem.

Membership and Governance

The study confirmed that an exclusive inner circle, rather than members, governs the ICJ. Academics have thoroughly debunked the myth of democratically run interest groups, but a participatory image survives. Public-spirited leaders and staff working for progressive reform maintain a façade of collective decision making that rarely acknowledges control by a few key leaders. Disgruntled members have little choice but to vote with their feet or wallets. Niall MacDermot ran a tight ship as Secretary-General for half of the organization's forty years. Chairman Bill Butler dominated the Executive Committee for fourteen years. Excessive dependence on key individuals made for a difficult leadership transition in 1990.

Most ICJ members had too little time for sufficient involvement to offer meaningful policy direction. A few jurists wanted a meaningful voice in governing the organization and periodically sparked internal political division. The New York founders who redirected CIA funds prepared a governing statute establishing procedures like those of the exclusive Council on Foreign Relations. A self-perpetuating Executive Committee controlled ICJ membership and approval of national sections. Local affiliates were excluded from participation in ICJ decision making. In the ICJ's early years, French-speaking members resented Anglo-American control. The Executive Committee corrected the language imbalance but remained predominantly European until 1992. Women have recently pressed for greater representation with moderate success. The Secretariat has provided much better representation for women and third world staff.

The ICJ's fortieth anniversary brought some democratization as a self-proclaimed reformer became the new Executive Committee chair. The ICJ triennial meeting gave members a genuine opportunity to review staff proposals for future directions. Jurists from developing countries achieved a significant Executive Committee majority. A Statute amendment fixed a ten-year term limit for newly elected members. Yet the members did not significantly check the Executive Committee's primacy or integrate national sections and affiliates into decision making. No further member meetings were planned for three years. The new Secretary-General retained budget control through a two-year request to funding agencies, but promised increased disclosure of ICJ finances.

Participatory procedures are far more difficult and expensive for an international NGO than for a domestic interest group. Activists at both levels are economically secure individuals able to commit time and money to the cause. International governing boards meet infrequently and with fewer people, since members must travel from around the world. Members speak different languages, so meetings require costly translation services. International secretariats may have even greater autonomy than their counterparts in largely staff-directed national organizations. Future research on human rights NGOs should recognize the critical importance of secretariat staffing. Elected leaders and prestigious members listed on the organization's letterhead are less important than the executive director and legal officers. An NGO with a third world president may still be dominated by a Western executive and staff. At the time of Adama Dieng's appointment, the ICJ had been shaped by strong European executives. His tenure as Secretary-General could produce policy shifts that reflect more third world priorities.

The ICJ in a Changing World Order

Neorealists acknowledge growing international interdependence but still consider states the only players worth watching. That narrow focus overlooks the promotional functions of both private and public institutions as well as NGO contributions to standard setting and protection. NGOs do not pose a serious threat to state sovereignty, but their activities have affected world politics. Influence, like beauty, may seem greatest in the eye of an idealistic beholder. This study provides considerable evidence of impact that is more substantive than illusory. The ICJ has become as important to world politics and international law as domestic interest groups are to the U.S. legislature, judiciary, and executive. Public opinion has strengthened human rights implementation procedures and influenced state conduct in an unquantifiable but undeniable fashion.

Like its domestic counterparts, the human rights policy community includes both public officials and NGO representatives. Major players are relatively few, and their promotional work has not established an enforcement regime. Key NGO leaders, U.N. Secretariat staffers, and foreign ministry officials have collaborated on the major standard-setting and protection campaigns. The ICJ and large NGO allies appear to have greater influence than do some government officials with selected experts from the U.N. Secretariat, Commission rapporteurs and working groups, the Sub-Commission, and treaty monitoring bodies. The ICJ actively recruited former government and U.N. officials and proudly noted that its distinguished members served on the International Court of Justice, the U.N. Human Rights Committee, the U.N. Commission on Human Rights and its Sub-Commission, the European Commission, the Inter-American Commission, and as special rapporteurs. For several jurists, cabinet-level service was incompatible with ICJ membership. By sponsoring annual seminars for human rights desk officers, Butler created unique contacts for the ICJ with Western foreign policy makers.

NGOs and U.N. Secretariat officials typically claim credit for initiating decisions made at the United Nations while professing an adversary relationship with governments. Reports about U.N. action frequently attribute responsibility to a committee or passively state "It was decided that . . ." The frenetic standard-setting dance has a far more revealing exchange of partners and players that warrants closer scrutiny. Different states' responsibility may go as unreported as their unpublicized funding of NGOs. Idealists cannot create a human rights enforcement regime without using some government collaborators to weaken state sovereignty. To purists, such collaboration means co-optation. Either the public officials are captives of special interests or the private citizens have sold out. Inexperienced activists can easily be co-opted by diplomats manipulating NGOs for the national interest. Savvy ICJ advocates solicited government support without selling services in exchange. States are not monolithic, and the ICJ has both official friends and foes in divided governments.

What's in a name? The ICJ is a "nongovernmental organization" no different from a "public interest group" or "private voluntary organization." Proponents of a supranational legal system label their vision a new world order or international enforcement regime. A promotional regime and epistemic communities resemble domestic policy communities and issue networks. The ICJ belongs to an international human rights policy community that functions like a subsystem in world politics. That community has grown considerably since the nineteenth-century antislavery campaign but has not yet established an effective prohibition regime. The cumulative, incremental impact of human rights NGOs like the ICJ has contributed to an improved world order that is neither radically new nor sufficiently humane. Resurgent loyalty to national identity or fighting faiths could frustrate global integration, or an authoritarian regime could enforce stability without justice. Even if another forty-year campaign produced a just world order, the rule of law would still require an (Independent) Commission of Jurists to promote and protect human rights.

Appendix 1: ICJ/CIJL National Sections and Affiliates, 1993

Africa		
Burkino Faso	Movement Burkinabé des Droits de l'Homme et des Peuples	ICJ Affiliate
Kenya	Kenya Section of the ICJ	
Madagascar	Société Malgache d'Études Juridiques	ICJ Affiliate
Namibia	"Justitia" Namibia	
Senegal	Association Sénégalaise d'Études et de Recheres Juridiques	ICJ Affiliate
South Africa	National Association of Democratic Lawyers	ICJ Affiliate
Togo	Ligue Togoloaise des Droits de l'Homme	ICJ Affiliate
	Ordre des Avocats a la Cour de Lomé	ICJ Affiliate
Zambia	Law Association of Zambia	ICJ Affiliate
Asia		
Bangladesh	Institute of Human Rights and Legal Affairs, Dhaka	ICJ Affiliate
Hong Kong	"Justice Hong Kong"	
India	Indian Commission of Jurists, New Delhi	
	Indian Centre for the Independence of Judges and Lawyers	CIJL Affiliate
	Karnataka State Commission of Jurists, Bangalore	
	Lucknow Branch of the Indian Commission of Jurists	

	Madras Branch of the Indian Commission of Jurists	
Japan	Japan Civil Liberties Union	ICJ Affiliate
Malaysia	The Malaysian Bar Council	CIJL Affiliate
Nepal	Nepal Law Society	ICJ Affiliate
	Nepalese Section of the ICJ	
Pakistan	Human Rights Commission of Pakistan	ICJ Affiliate
Philippines	Integrated Bar of the Philippines	ICJ Affiliate
	Philippine Bar Association	ICJ Affiliate
	Philippines Commission of Jurists	
	Protestant Lawyers League of the Philippines	ICJ Affiliate
Sri Lanka	Sri Lanka Section of the ICJ	
Thailand	Union for Civil Liberty	ICJ Affiliate
North Africa and Middle East		
Egypt	The Egyptian Organization for Human Rights	
Occupied Territories	Al Haq	ICJ Affiliate
	Gaza Centre for Rights and Law	ICJ Affiliate
Tunisia	Ligue Tunisienne pour la Défense des Droits de l'Homme	ICJ Affiliate
South America		
Argentina	Centro Estudios Legales y Sociales (CELS)	ICJ Affiliate
Bolivia	Colegio Nacional de Abogados, La Paz	CIJL Affiliate
Brazil	Secçao Sao Paulo de CIJ	
Chile	Comisión Chilena de Derechos Humanos	ICJ Affiliate
	Comisión de Defensa del Estado de Derecho	
Costa Rica	Costa Rican Section of the ICJ	
Ecuador	Capítulo de Guayaquíl de la CIJ	
	Colegio de Abogados de Quito	ICJ Affiliate
Mexico	Juristas Mexicanos A.C.	
Nicaragua	Sección de Nicaragua de la CIJ	
Peru	Andean Commission of Jurists	ICJ Affiliate
Trinidad and Tobago	Bureau on Human Rights, Dalton House	ICJ Affiliate

Uruguay	Instituto de Estudios Legales y Sociales del Uruguay	ICJ Affiliate

Europe, North America, Australia, and New Zealand

Australia	Australian Section of the ICJ	
	Selborne Chamber, New South Wales Bar Association	CIJL Affiliate
Austria	Osterreichische Juristenkommission	
Belgium	Section Belge de la CIJ	
Canada	Canadian Section of the ICJ	
Cyprus	Legality, Nicosia	
Denmark	Danish Section of the ICJ	
Finland	Finnish Jurists for Human Rights	
France	Libre Justice	
Germany	Deutsche Sektion de IJK	
Hungary	Hungarian Lawyers Association	ICJ Affiliate
Ireland	The Association of Irish Jurists	
Italy	Associazione Italiana Giuristi	
Malta	Chamber of Advocates	ICJ Affiliate
Netherlands	Genootschap voor den Rechtsstaat	ICJ Affiliate
	Nederlands Juristen Comité voor den Mensenrechten	
	Nederlandse Juristen-Verenigung	ICJ Affiliate
	Nederlandse Vereniging voor Rechtspraak	CIJL Affiliate
	Netherlands Order of Advocates	ICJ Affiliate
New Zealand	New Zealand Section of the ICJ	
Norway	Norwegian Association of Judges	CIJL Affiliate
	Norwegian Section of the ICJ	
Poland	Polish Section of the ICJ	
Portugal	Direito e Justiça	
Spain	Asociación Española de Juristas	
	Asociación por los Derechos Humanos	ICJ Affiliate
Sweden	Svenska Avdelningen av IJK	
Switzerland	Schweizeische Sektion der IJK	
U.K.	"Justice"	
U.S.	American Association for the ICJ, Inc.	ICJ Affiliate
	International Human Rights Law Group	ICJ Affiliate
	Minnesota Advocates for Human Rights	ICJ Affiliate

Appendix 2: ICJ/CIJL Periodicals, Yearbooks, and Activity Reports

Periodicals

Bulletin of the International Commission of Jurists. Numbers 1–29 (1954–1967).
Newsletter of the ICJ. Numbers 1–15 (1957–1964).
Journal of the International Commission of Jurists. Volumes 1–9 (1957–1968).
ICJ Review (*ICJ Revista*). Numbers 1–49 (1969–1992).
ICJ Newsletter. Numbers 1–53 (June 1979–April 1993).
CIJL Bulletin. Numbers 1–26 (1978–1990). (Numbers 1–8, Engl./Fr./Sp.).

Yearbooks

Attacks on Justice: The Harassment and Persecution of Judges and Lawyers.
1988–1989. 40 pp.
July 1989–June 1990. 108 pp.
June 1990–May 1991. 143 pp.
June 1991–May 1992. 224 pp.
June 1992–May 1993. 103 pp.

CIJL Yearbook
Vol. 1, 1992. *Constitutional Guarantees for the Independence of the Judiciary.* 125 pp.
Vol. 2, 1993. *Legal Protection of Lawyers.* 103 pp.

Activity reports

The International Commission of Jurists: Basic Facts. 1960, 1966.
The International Commission of Jurists: Objectives, Organization, Activities. 1965, 1972, 1981.

ICJ Report on Activities
1966–1971, 15 pp.
1971–1977, 38 pp.
1977–1980, 109 pp.
1981–1985, 145 pp.
1986–1988, 86 pp.

Notes

Preface

1. An earlier draft of Chapter 1 was presented at the XIV World Congress of the International Political Science Association, September 1, 1988.
2. An earlier version of Chapter 8 appeared as "Popular Sovereignty and International Law: ICJ Strategies for Human Rights Standard Setting," *Human Rights Quarterly* 11, no. 4 (November 1989): 561–85.

Introduction

1. Speech by Niall MacDermot, Secretary-General, on receiving on behalf of the International Commission of Jurists the award of the Wateler Peace Prize at the Peace Palace, The Hague, January 16, 1985. MacDermot carefully noted that he was "expressing personal opinions with which the members of our Comission may or may not agree."
2. P. A. Reynolds and R. D. McKinlay, "The Concept of Interdependence: Its Uses and Misuses," in *Power Capabilities and Interdependence: Problems in the Study of International Influence*, ed. Kjell Goldmann and Gunnar Sjostedt (Beverly Hills, Calif.: Sage, 1979), 154.
3. Hans Morgenthau, *Politics Among Nations*, 6th ed. (New York: Knopf, 1985); Robert Gilpin, *Change and War in World Politics* (Cambridge: Cambridge University Press, 1981).
4. Kenneth Waltz, *Theory of International Politics* (New York: McGraw Hill, 1979).
5. Zbigniew Brzezinski, *Out of Control: Global Turmoil on the Eve of the 21st Century* (New York: Scribners, 1993).
6. Samuel P. Huntington, "The Clash of Civilizations?" *Foreign Affairs* 72, no. 3 (Summer 1993): 22–49.
7. Terry Nardin, *Law, Morality, and the Relations of States* (Princeton, N.J.: Princeton University Press, 1983), 64 n. 29. See also H. L. A. Hart, "Positivism and the Separation of Law and Morals," *Harvard Law Review* 71 (1958): 593–629.
8. J. S. Watson, "The Limited Utility of International Law in the Protection of Human Rights," *American Society of International Law, Proceedings*, 74th Annual Meeting, April, 1980; see also "Legal Theory, Efficacy and Validity in

the Development of Human Rights Norms in International Law," *University of Illinois Law Forum* (1979): 609, at 612, 614.

9. Golunskii and Strogovich, *The Theory of the State and Law*, translated in Hugh Babb, *Soviet Legal Philosophy* (Cambridge, Mass.: Harvard University Press, 1951), 351 at 392–93.

10. Quoted by Seyom Brown, *International Relations in a Changing Global System* (Boulder, Colo.: Westview, 1992), 104–5 from Louis Henkin, "Law and Politics in International Relations: State and Human Values," in *The Evolution of Theory in International Relations: Essays in Honor of William T. R. Fox*, ed. Robert L. Rothstein (Columbia: University of South Carolina Press, 1991), 163–88, at 165.

11. U.N. Charter, Article 71.

12. Yves Beigbeder, *The Role and Status of International Humanitarian Volunteers and Organizations: The Right and Duty to Humanitarian Assistance* (Boston: Martinus Nijhoff, 1991). Paul Ghils, "International civil society: International non-governmental organizations in the international system," *International Social Science Journal* 44 (August 1992, UNESCO): 417–31. Peter H. Rohn, *Relations Between the Council of Europe and International Non-Governmental Associations* (Brussels: Union of International Associations, 1957).

13. Richard Falk and Saul Mendlovitz, eds. *Studies on a Just World Order*, 3 vols. (Boulder, Colo.: Westview, 1982). Richard A. Falk, *The Study of Future Worlds* (New York: Free Press, 1975). Grenville Clark and Louis Sohn, *World Peace Through World Law*, 3d ed. (Cambridge, Mass.: Harvard University Press, 1966).

14. James N. Rosenau, *Turbulence in World Politics* (Princeton, N.J.: Princeton University Press, 1990).

15. Stanley Hoffmann, *Duties Beyond Borders: On the Limits and Possibilities of Ethical International Politics* (Syracuse, N.Y.: Syracuse University Press, 1981), 95.

16. Ian Brownlie, *Principles of Public International Law*, 4th ed. (New York: Oxford University Press, 1990), 33–35.

17. Hersch Lauterpacht, *International Law and Human Rights* (New York: Praeger, 1950).

18. Lauterpacht, *International Law: Being the Collected Papers of Hersch Lauterpacht* 115 (E. Lauterpacht ed. 1970), as quoted by Meron, *Human Rights and Humanitarian Norms in Customary Law* (Oxford: Clarendon, 1989) at 35.

19. Theodore Meron, *Human Rights and Humanitarian Norms in Customary Law* (Oxford: Clarendon, 1989). Paul Sieghart, *The International Law of Human Rights* (London: Oxford University Press, 1983). Peremptory norms or *jus cogens* are so fundamental that they override contrary provisions of treaties or custom.

20. Quincy Wright, *Problems of Stability and Progress in International Relations* (Westport, Conn: Greenwood, 1976 [c1954]).

21. Wright, *Problems in International Relations*, 31–32.

22. Stanley Anderson, "Human Rights and the Structure of International Law," *New York Law School Journal of International and Comparative Law* 12 (1991): 1–28. Covey T. Oliver, "The Future of Idealism in International Law: Structuralism, Humanism and Survival," in *The Structure and Process of International Law: Essays in Legal Philosophy Doctrine and Theory*, ed. R. St. J. Macdonald and Douglas M. Johnston (Boston: Martinus Nijhoff, 1983), 1207–22.

23. Statute of the International Court of Justice, art. 38(1)(b) (c), as an-

nexed to the Charter of the United Nations, 59 Stat. 1055, T. S. No. 993, 3 Bevans 1153 (signed at San Francisco June 26, 1945; entered into force October 24, 1945).

24. Olle Dahlen, "A Governmental Response to Pressure Groups—The Case of Sweden," in *Pressure Groups in the Global System*, ed. Peter Willets (New York: St. Martin's, 1982), 148–70.

25. Lyman C. White, *International Nongovernmental Organizations* (New Brunswick, N.J.: Rutgers University Press, 1951). White at 14 cites the German Zollverein of 1833 and Mazzini's "Young Italy" organization as citizen movements that claimed responsibility for the creation of Germany and Italy. See also Jean Meynaud, *Les Groupes de Pression Internationaux* (Lausanne: Études de Science Politique, 1961); Kjell Skjelsbaek, "The Growth of International Non-Governmental Organizations in the Twentieth Century," *International Organization* 25 (Summer 1971): 420–42.

26. White, *International Nongovernmental Organizations*, 13.

27. J. J. Lador-Lederer, *International Non-Governmental Organizations and Economic Entities* (Leyden, The Netherlands: A.W. Sythoff, 1963), 238–39.

28. Carolyn M. Stephenson of the University of Hawaii puts the number of private groups dealing with international concerns at 13,000. *The New York Times*, April 5, 1992, sec. E at 4. Ghils in "International Civil Society" puts the total at 23,000. See also R. O. Keohane and J. S. Nye, eds., *Transnational Relations and World Politics* (Cambridge, Mass.: Harvard University Press, 1971); Willetts, *Pressure Groups in the International System*; Pei-heng Chiang, *Non-Governmental Organizations at the United Nations: Identity, Role and Function* (New York: Praeger, 1981).

29. "More than 1,200 private environmental organizations accredited themselves as observers" to the 1992 East Summit in Rio de Janeiro. *The New York Times*, April 5, 1992, p. E-4. Maureen R. Berman and Joseph E. Johnson, eds. *Unofficial Diplomats* (New York: Columbia University Press, 1977); Robert C. Angell, *Peace on the March* (New York: Van Nostrand, 1969); Quincy Wright, ed., *Preventing World War III: Some Proposals* (New York: Simon and Schuster, 1962); Ann Thompson Feraru, "Transnational Political Interests and the Global Environment," *International Organization* 28 (Winter 1974): 31–60.

30. Charles R. Beitz, *Political Theory and International Relations* (Princeton, N.J.: Princeton University Press, 1979). Brown, *International Relations in a Changing Global System.*

31. Robert O. Keohane and Joseph Nye, *Power and Interdependence*, 2d ed. (Glenview, Ill.: Scott, Foresman, 1989). Ethan A. Nadelmann, "Global Prohibition Regimes: The Evolution of Norms in International Society," *International Organization* 44, no. 4 (Autumn 1990): 479–526.

32. Douglas Cater, *Power in Washington* (New York: Random House, 1964); Bill Keller, "The Veterans' Lobby as an 'Iron Triangle'," *Congressional Quarterly Weekly Report*, June 10, 1984, p. 1627. See also Eric Redman, *The Dance of Legislation* (New York: Simon and Schuster, 1973).

33. Robert Salisbury, John P. Heinz, Robert L. Nelson, and Edward O. Laumann, "Triangles, Networks, and Hollow Cores: The Complex Geometry of Washington Interest Representation" in *Politics of Interests: Interest Groups Transformed*, ed. Mark Petraca (Boulder, Colo.: Westview, 1992), 130–49. Jeffrey M. Berry, "Subgovernments, Issue Networks, and Political Conflict," in *Remaking American Politics*, ed. Richard A. Harris and Sidney M. Milkis (Boulder, Colo.: Westview, 1989), 239–60.

34. Jack Donnelly, "International Human Rights: A Regime Analysis," *International Organization* 40, no. 3 (Summer 1986): 599–642.
35. David Forsythe, *The Internationalization of Human Rights* (Lexington, Mass.: D.C. Heath, 1991).
36. Howard Tolley, *The U.N. Commission on Human Rights* (Boulder, Colo.: Westview, 1987).
37. Jan Herman Burgers, "The Road to San Francisco: The Revival of the Human Rights Idea in the Twentieth Century," *Human Rights Quarterly* 14, no. 4 (November 1992): 447–78.
38. See *Human Rights Directory: Western Europe* (Washington, D.C., 1982): *North American Directory* (3d ed., 1984), *Latin America* (1990), *Africa* (1989), *Asia* (1981), Human Rights Internet.
39. "Organizational Mayhem Sparks NGO Coup Move," *Terra Viva*, no. 2 (June 12, 1993): 1.
40. Amnesty International, *Facts and Figures about Amnesty International and its Work for Human Rights*, London, June 24, 1992 (AI Index: ORG 10/04/92).
41. Louis Kriesberg, "International Nongovernmental Organizations and Transnational Integration," *International Associations*, no. 11 (1972): 521–25.
42. Laurie Wiseberg, "The Role of Non-Governmental Organizations," in *Put Our World to Rights—Towards a [Canadian] Commonwealth Human Rights Policy* (A Report by a Non-Governmental Advisory Group chaired by the Honorable Flora MacDonald, August 1991), pp. 149–74 (Commonwealth Human Rights Initiative), reprinted in *Human Rights in the World Community, Issues and Action*, 2d ed., ed. Richard Claude and Burns Weston (Philadelphia: University of Pennsylvania Press, 1992), 372–82.
43. Virginia Leary, "A New Role for Non-Governmental Organizations: A Case Study of Non-Governmental Participation in the Development of International Norms on Torture," in *UN Law/Fundamental Rights*, ed. Antonio Cassese, (Netherlands: Sijthoff & Noordhoff, 1979), 197–210. David Weissbrodt, "The Influence of Interest Groups on the Development of United States Human Rights Policies," in *The Dynamics of Human Rights in U.S. Foreign Policy*, ed. Natalie Hevener, (New Brunswick, N.J.: Transaction, 1981), 229–78.
44. Gabriel A. Almond and James S. Coleman, eds., *The Politics of the Developing Areas* (Princeton, N.J.: Princeton University Press, 1960). Gabriel A. Almond, ed., *Comparative Politics Today: A World View* (Boston: Little, Brown, 1974).
45. David Forsythe, *Humanitarian Politics: The International Committee of the Red Cross* (Baltimore: Johns Hopkins University Press, 1977). Georges Willemin and Roger Heacock, *The International Committee of the Red Cross* (Boston: Martinus Nijhoff, 1984). Aaron Levenstein, *Escape to Freedom: The Story of the International Rescue Committee* (Westport, Conn.: Greenwood Press, 1983). Major case studies of Amnesty International include Egon Larsen, *A Flame in Barbed Wire: The Story of Amnesty International* (New York: Norton, 1979), and Jonathan Power, *Amnesty International: The Human Rights Story* (New York: McGraw Hill, 1981). Harry M. Scoble and Laurie S. Wiseberg, "Human Rights and Amnesty International," *The Annals of the American Academy of Political and Social Science* (May 1974): 11–26. Laurie Wiseberg and Harry Scoble, "International League for Human Rights: The Strategy of a Human Rights NGO," *Georgia Journal of International and Comparative Law* 7 (1977): 289–313.
46. Michael Haas followed Almond's eight functions but changed the labels

for three. Haas considered only states and intergovernmental organizations, not NGOs, as agents for articulation, aggregation, socialization, recruitment, transaction, rule making, rule application, and rule supervision. "A Functional Approach to International Organization," *Journal of Politics* 27 (August 1965): 498–517.

47. The humanitarian service identified by Claude and Wiseberg in *Human Rights in the World Community* is treated as one aspect of implementation; other functions they identify, such as information dissemination, advocacy, and solidarity, include different elements of communication, standard-setting, and protection activities.

48. Jan Egelman and Thomas Kerks, eds., *Third World Organizational Development: A Comparison of NGO Strategies* (Geneva: Henry Dunant Institute, 1987). Henry J. Steiner, *Diverse Partners: Non-Governmental Organizations in the Human Rights Movement* (Cambridge, Mass: Harvard Law School and Human Rights Internet, 1991).

49. Wiseberg and Scoble, "International League." Scoble and Wiseberg, "Human Rights and Amnesty International."

50. Haas, "Functional Approach to International Organization," 503.

51. R. J. Vincent, *Human Rights and International Relations* (New York: Cambridge University Press, 1986), 128.

52. Brown, *The Changing Global System*, 101. David Forsythe also concludes that critical NGO reports undermine a government's legitimacy. *Human Rights and World Politics*, 2d ed. (Lincoln: University of Nebraska Press, 1989), 83–101.

53. Theodore H. von Laue, *The World Revolution of Westernization: The Twentieth Century in Global Perspective* (New York: Oxford University Press, 1987). See also Francis Fukuyama, "The End of History?" *The National Interest*, no. 16 (Summer 1989): 3–11. Hedley Bull, "The Emergence of a Universal International Society," in *The Expansion of International Society*, ed. Hedley Bull and Adam Watson (Oxford: Clarendon, 1984), 117–26. Martin Wight, "Western Values in International Relations," in *Diplomatic Investigations: Essays in the Theory of International Politics*, ed. Herbert Butterfield and Martin Wight, (London: Allen & Unwin, 1966): 89–131.

54. Steiner, *Diverse Partners*.

55. Peter R. Baehr, "The General Assembly Negotiating the Convention on Torture," in *Human Rights and Development*, ed. David Forsythe. Theo van Boven, "The Role of NGOs in International Human Rights Standard-Setting; Non-governmental Participation a Prerequisite of Democracy? in *Symposium Organized on the Occasion of the Award of the Praemium Erasmianum to the ICJ* (Leiden: Stichting NJCM-Boekerij, 1989), 53–72. Leary, "New Role for Non-governmental Organizations," 1979. Weissbrodt, "Interest Groups," in *The Dynamics of Human Rights*, 1981. David Forsythe, "Humanizing American Foreign Policy: Nonprofit Lobbying and Human Rights," in *Human Rights and World Politics*, 2d ed. (Lincoln: University of Nebraska, 1989), 127–59.

56. Elizabeth Perkins, "Comparative Pressure Groups Politics and Transnational Relations—The Case of Non-Governmental Organizations at the United Nations" (Ph.D. diss., Texas Tech University, May 1977).

57. Werner J. Feld, *International Organizations, A Comparative Approach*, 2d ed. (New York: Praeger, 1988).

58. Theodore Meron, *Human Rights Law Making in the U.N.: A Critique of Instruments and Process* (Oxford: Clarendon, 1986), 102–3. Theodore Meron,

"Norm Making and Supervision in International Human Rights: Reflections on Institutional Order," *American Journal of International Law* 76 (1982): 754–78.

59. Thomas M. Franck and H. Scott Fairley, "Procedural Due Process in Human Rights Fact-Finding by International Agencies," *American Journal of International Law* 74 (1980): 308–45. Hurst Hannum, "Fact-Finding by Nongovernmental Human Rights Organizations," in *Fact Finding Before International Tribunals*, ed. Richard Lillich (Ardsley-on-Hudson, N.Y.: Transnational Publishers, 1992), 293–304. David Weissbrodt and James McCarthy, "Fact-Finding by International Nongovernmental Human Rights Organizations," *Virginia Journal of International Law* 22, no.1 (1981): 1–89. Nigel Rodley, "Monitoring Human Rights by the U.N. System and Nongovernmental Organizations," in *Human Rights and American Foreign Policy*, ed. Donald Kommers and G. D. Loescher (Notre Dame, Ind.: Notre Dame University Press, 1979), 157–78. Hans Thoolen and Berth Verstappen, *Human Rights Missions: A Study of the Fact-finding Practice of Non-governmental Organizations* (Boston: Martinus Nijhoff, 1986). Randy B. Reiter, M. V. Xunzunegui, and José Quiroga, "Guidelines for Field Reporting of Basic Human Rights Violations," *Human Rights Quarterly* 8, no. 4 (1986): 628–53 (revised and reprinted in *Human Rights and Statistics*, ed. Thomas B. Jabine and Richard Claude [Philadelphia: University of Pennsylvania Press, 1992], 90–126). B. G. Ramcharan, ed., *International Law and Fact-Finding in the Field of Human Rights* (Boston: Martinus Nijhoff, 1982).

60. Political scientists Harry Scoble and Laurie Wiseberg published several journal articles including "Recent Trends in the Expanding Universe of NGOs dedicated to the Protection of Human Rights," *Journal of International Law and Policy* 8 (1979): 627–58. Also in *Global Human Rights: Public Policies, Comparative Measures, and NGO Strategies*, ed. Ved. P. Nanda et al. (Boulder, Colo.: Westview Press, 1981); "Human Rights and Soviet-American Relations: The Role of NGOs," in *Neither Cold War nor Detente*, ed. Richard Melanson, (Charlottesville: University of Virginia. Press, 1982), 151–85. David Weissbrodt, "The Influence of Interest Groups on the Development of United States Human Rights Policies," in Hevener, ed. *The Dynamics of Human Rights*, 229–78; Weissbrodt, "The Role of International NonGovernmental Organizations in the Implementation of Human Rights," *Texas International Law Journal* 12, no. 2/3 (1977): 293–320. Lowell W. Livezey, *Nongovernmental Organizations and the Idea of Human Rights* (Princeton, N.J.: School of Public and International Affairs, 1987).

61. Jeffrey M. Berry, *Lobbying for the People: The Political Behavior of Public Interest Groups* (Princteon, N.J.: Princeton University Press, 1977), 7.

62. Perkins, "Comparative Pressure Group Politics."

63. Berry, *Lobbying for the People*. Andrew McFarland, *Common Cause: Lobbying in the Public Interest* (Chatham, N.J.: Chatham House, 1984). Andrew McFarland, *Public Interest Lobbies* (Washington, D.C.: American Enterprise Institute, 1976). Samuel Walker, *In Defense of American Liberties: A History of the ACLU* (New York: Oxford University Press, 1990).

64. Jeffrey M. Berry, *The Interest Group Society* (Boston: Little Brown, 1984), 113.

65. Philippe C. Schmitter, "Modes of Interest Intermediation and Models of Societal Change in Western Europe," *Comparative Political Studies* 10, no. 1 (April 1977): 7–38, at 9.

66. Harmon Zeigler, *Pluralism, Corporatism and Confucianism. Political Association and Conflict Regulation in the United States, Europe, and Taiwan* (Philadelphia: Temple University Press, 1988). Suzanne Berger, ed., *Organizing Interests in Western Europe: Pluralism, Corporatism and the Transformation of Politics* (Cambridge: Cambridge University Press, 1981). Colin Crouch and Ronald Dore, *Corporatism and Accountability: Organized Interests in British Public Life* (Oxford: Clarendon, 1990). Ilja Scholten, ed., *Political Stability and Neo-Corporatism: Corporatist Integration and Societal Cleavages in Western Europe* (Beverly Hills, Calif.: Sage, 1987). Patrick Birkinshaw, Ian Harden, and Norman Lewis, *Government by Moonlight: The Hybrid Parts of the State* (London: Unwin Hyman, 1990).

67. Wolfgang Streeck and Philippe C. Schmitter, eds., *Private Interest Government: Beyond Market and State* (Beverly Hills, Calif.: Sage, 1985). Schmitter distinguishes "societal corporatism" in democratic countries from "state corporatism" practiced by more authoritarian systems.

68. Berry, *Interest Group Society*, 31.

69. Research by sociologists on new social movements offers an alternative theoretical framework more appropriate for research on grass-roots citizen protest groups than for this study of legal professionals organized to assist victims. Joseph Camilleri and Jim Falk, *The End of Sovereignty? The Politics of a Shrinking and Fragmenting World* (Brookfield, Vt.: Elger, 1992), 199–235. Marta Fuentes and Andre Gunder Frank, "Ten Theses on Social Movements," *World Development* 17, no. 2 (1989): 179–91. Hans Toch, *The Social Psychology of Social Movements* (New York: Bobbs-Merrill, 1965).

70. David B. Truman, *The Governmental Process*, 2d ed. (New York: Knopf, 1971 [c. 1951]). In complex societies when wars and increased government activity upset an equilibrium, adversely affected individuals organize new groups to protect their interest.

71. Robert H. Salisbury, "An Exchange Theory of Interest Groups," *Midwest Journal of Political Science* 13 (February 1969): 1–32. Jack L. Walker, *Mobilizing Interest Groups in America: Patrons, Professions and Social Movements* (Ann Arbor: University of Michigan Press, 1991).

72. Wiseberg and Scoble, "The International League for Human Rights," 296.

73. Berry, *Interest Group Society*, 91.

74. Jack Walker, "The Origins and Maintenance of Interest Groups in America," *The American Political Science Review* 77 (June 1983): 400, cited at 88 in Berry, *Interest Group Society*.

75. "PVO" becomes a U.S. variant of NGO. Brian H. Smith, *More Than Altruism: The Politics of Private Foreign Aid* (Princeton, N.J.: Princeton University Press, 1990). OECD, *Voluntary Aid for Development: The Role of Non-Governmental Organisations* (Paris: 1988).

76. "GONGOs—Are these NGOs or not?" *Terra Viva*, no. 7 (June 18, 1993): 9, complained that the Chinese Human Rights Study Society (CHRSS) was directed by the government through the general secretary of the Chinese Communist Youth League.

77. Smith, *More Than Altruism*, 284.

78. Mancur Olson, Jr. *The Logic of Collective Action* (Cambridge, Mass.: Harvard University Press, 1965).

79. Terry M. Moe, *The Organization of Interests: Incentives and the Internal Dynamics of Political Interest Groups* (Chicago: University of Chicago Press, 1980).

80. Berry, *Interest Group Society*, 93, citing Truman, *The Governmental Process*, 129–39.

81. Berry, *Lobbying for the People*, 186–87. Robert Michels, *Political Parties: A Sociological Study of the Oligarchical Tendencies of Modern Democracy*, trans. Eden and Cedar Paul (1915; reprint, New York: Dover, 1959), 248.

82. E. E. Schattschneider, *The Semisovereign People: A Realist's View of Democracy in America* (New York: Holt, Rinehart and Winston, 1960), 31–34.

83. Wiseberg and Scoble, "International League."

84. Arthur W. Blaser, "Human Rights in the Third World and Development of International Nongovernmental Organizations," in *Human Rights and Third World Development*, ed. George W. Shepherd, Jr., and Ved P. Nanda (London: Greenwood Press, 1985), 273–85. Yash Tandon, "Foreign NGOs, Uses and Abuses: An African Perspective," *IFDA Dossier* 81 (April–June 1991): 67–78.

85. Fred Woodbridge and Richard Rosswurm.

86. Forsythe, *Human Rights and World Politics*, 154–55. For recent improvements in quantifying human rights research, see Thomas B. Jabine and Richard P. Claude, eds., *Human Rights and Statistics: Getting the Record Straight* (Philadelphia: University of Pennsylvania Press, 1991); David L. Cingranelli, ed., *Human Rights: Theory and Measurement* (New York: St. Martin's Press, 1988).

87. John G. Ruggie, "Human Rights and the Future International Community," *Daedalus* 112 (1983): 93–110.

Chapter 1: Recruiting Free World Jurists

1. Christopher Simpson, *Blowback: America's Recruitment of Nazis and Its Effects on the Cold War* (New York: Weidenfeld & Nicolson, 1988), 102.

2. Dudley Bonsal, "Gangsters in the Guise of Jurists," *The Record of the Association of the Bar of the City of New York* 7 (1952): 445, 448.

3. Robert D. Schulzinger, *The Wise Men of Foreign Affairs* (New York: Columbia University Press, 1984). Laurence H. Shoup and William Minter, *Imperial Brain Trust: The Council on Foreign Relations and U.S. Foreign Policy* (New York: Monthly Review, 1977), 62, report that council members filled 42 percent of the top foreign policy posts in the Truman administration and 40 percent under President Eisenhower. In 1947 the council's journal *Foreign Affairs* advocated U.S. containment of the Soviet Union. George F. Kennan, "The Sources of Soviet Conduct," 25 (July 1947): 566–82.

4. The Fighting Group Against Inhumanity and Association of Political Refugees from the East reportedly engaged in propaganda, sabotage, and terrorism "to make the commies look bad." William Blum, *The CIA: A Forgotten History* (London: Zed Books, 1986), 64–65. See also Kai Bird, *The Chairman: John J. McCloy: The Making of the American Establishment* (New York: Simon and Schuster, 1992).

5. Bird, *The Chairman*, 345.

6. General Reinhard Gehlen, Hitler's head of military intelligence for the Eastern front. Bird, *The Chairman*, 353. Simpson, in *Blowback*, describes how the U.S. used other Nazi collaborators and war criminals, both wittingly and unknowingly.

7. "Like Notes from a Flute," *Time* (December 18, 1950): 32–34.

8. Six years after he had helped found the International Commission of Jurists, Friedenau's communist foes published evidence identifying him as nonlawyer Horst Erdmann. The German Association of Democratic Lawyers publicized eighty-seven documents alleging that Friedenau had forged papers to show descent from a Jewish mother and persecution by the Nazis. According to IADL documents, Friedenau's Investigating Committee informants had been espionage agents reporting on troop movements and industrial production. Abbé Jean Boulier, *The Law Above the Rule of Law* (Brussels: International Association of Democratic Lawyers, 1958).

9. John Linehan, "The Soviet Fear of the Law," *American Mercury*, February 1953, pp. 90–94.

10. Joseph Wechsberg, Reporter at Large, "Remember Their Faces, Put Down Their Names," *The New Yorker* (September 8, 1951): 91–106, 99.

11. Wechsberg, "Put Down Their Names," 106. Blum, *The CIA*, 65.

12. Quoted from writings by Georgi Dimitrov by Cord Meyer, *Facing Reality: From World Federalism to the CIA* (New York: Harper and Row, 1980), 98–99.

13. Tom Braden, "I'm Glad the CIA Is 'Immoral,'" *Saturday Evening Post* (May 20, 1967): 10–14, 10.

14. Ibid. See also IADL, Report on U.S. Crimes in Korea of 31 March 1952. Brandweiner, *Facts and Documents Concerning the War in Korea* (Brussels, 1953). Rapport sur l'emploi d'armes bactériologiques sur le territoire chinois par les forces armées des Etats-Unis (April 2, 1952). Cited in F. Ermacora, "International Enquiry Commissions in the Field of Human Rights," *Human Rights Journal* 1 (1968): 180–218, 203, nn. 70, 71.

15. Representative E. E. Cox quoted by Peter D. Bell, "The Ford Foundation as a Transnational Actor," in *Transnational Relations and World Politics*, ed. R. O. Keohane and Joseph Nye (Cambridge, Mass.: Harvard University Press, 1972), 122.

16. In a telephone interview with the author on July 17, 1992, Braden recalled that Dulles periodically had general conversations with Senator Richard Russell, mostly allusions with few details. Meyer reports that Robert Kennedy enthusiastically supported the program when he became Attorney General in 1961. Meyer, *Facing Reality*, 89.

17. Stephen Ambrose, *Ike's Spies* (Garden City, N.Y.: Doubleday, 1981). After leaving the CIA in 1954, Braden became known as a liberal journalist.

18. Meyer's past associations and idealism made him subject to a McCarthy era investigation for leftist leanings; CIA mentors established his loyalty. Meyer, *Facing Reality*.

19. *Annual Report of the Council on Foreign Relations*, 1955–56.

20. By 1967 the organization had built offices in thirty-five countries, employing a staff of 280. Bird, *The Chairman*, 358.

21. Braden, "CIA Is Immoral," p. 14.

22. Ibid., Meyer in *Facing Reality*, 103, also noted that recipients could differ in substantial respects from U.S. policy.

23. John Marks and Victor Marchetti, *The CIA and the Cult of Intelligence* (New York: Knopf, 1974), 172.

24. Philip Agee, *Inside the Company: CIA Diary* (New York: Stonehill, 1975), 66.

25. *New York Times*, February 19, 1967, sec. 1, p. 1, 26. *Washington Post*, February 18, 1967, p. 1.

26. Telephone interview of July 17, 1992, following review of draft text.

27. A *Ramparts* magazine editor, Michael Ansara, identified Robert Bass as the CIA employee assigned to the Commission in a December 24, 1968 letter to Secretary-General Seán MacBride. Tom Braden confirmed the Bass assignment in personal correspondence and a July 17, 1992 telephone interview.

28. Braden reported that the CIA placed one agent in that group. "The CIA Is Immoral," p. 12.

29. Joseph T. Thorson, "The International Commission of Jurists," *Canadian Bar Review* 35 (1957): 898–901. Presumably he was given that cover story by U.S. founders who never revealed the CIA connection. At a 1954 planning session for an ICJ meeting to be held in Athens, the U.S. member indicated the precise budget amount.

30. Seymour also invited New York lawyers General William Donovan and James Grafton Rogers, neither of whom attended. McCloy's counsel, Bethuel Webster, succeeded Seymour as president of the New York Bar Association.

31. Robert G. Storey, President, and George M. Morris, past president, represented the American Bar Association. Paul R. Hays, professor of law at Columbia University, also represented the New York City Bar.

32. Dr. Walter Linse's assailants confessed and received long prison terms in West Germany. *Newsletter of the ICJ*, no. 9, (September 1960): 12, indicates that the Soviet Red Cross first reported that Linse had died in 1953 before informing the West German Red Cross that the prior report was based on mistaken identity. Bonsal, "Gangsters in the Guise of Jurists," 445–46.

33. *International Congress of Jurists, Complete Report: Discourses, Protocols* (West Berlin: ICJ, 1952).

34. Purshottam Trikamdas, head of India's Socialist party.

35. *Right vs. Injustice: The 1952 Berlin Congress* (The Hague: ICJ, 1952), i.

36. The remaining geographically balanced committee members were P. Federspiel of Denmark, J. Nabuco of Brazil, H. B. Tyabji of Pakistan, and Dr. E. Zellweger of Switzerland.

37. After serving as an army officer in World War II, van Dal became a leading advocate at the Supreme Court of the Netherlands.

38. *International Congress of Jurists, Complete Report: Discourses, Protocols* (West Berlin: ICJ, 1952).

39. They also shared memberships not only in the Council on Foreign Relations, but also in the exclusive Century Association and the Harvard Club. Interviews with Bethuel Webster, March 17, 1988, Whitney Debevoise, 1983, and Dudley Bonsal, March 17, 1988.

40. Quoted in the *New York Times* on appointment to the federal bench. Dudley B. Bonsal, "The Judiciary and the Bar—Socialist Legality vs. The Rule of Law," *Texas Law Review* 40 (November 1961): 1–17.

41. *New York Times* obituary, May 22, 1983, sec. 1, pt. 1, p. 37.

42. McCloy, U.S. judge Learned Hand, and former New York judge Joseph Proskauer also addressed the audience of three hundred. Van Dal sought help "in a new crusade for human rights and a free justice, perhaps one of the most bitter crusades in history, the crusade against systematic injustice and the denial of human rights behind the iron curtain." Dudley Bonsal, "Lawyers and the Cold War in Cooperation with the ICJ," Minutes of the Association of the Bar of the City of New York, May 4, 1953, pp. 4, 8–9, 12.

43. Ibid.

44. Samuel Walker, *In Defense of American Liberties: A History of the ACLU*

(New York: Oxford University Press, 1990), 206 citing Charles Silberman, *A Certain People* (New York: Summit Books, 1985), 98–101.

45. J. Grafton Rogers was a former U.S. assistant secretary of state, former dean of law at the University of Colorado, and former dean of Yale University.

46. Prominent New York lawyer Harold R. Medina. Angell was also an AFFJ director.

47. *New York City Bar Association Yearbook*, 1955.

48. "Report of the Special Committee to Cooperate with the International Commission of Jurists," The Record of the Association of the Bar of the City of New York, vol. 8, no. 8, (November 1953): 425.

49. Based on review of the IRS Form 990 Reports made by the Anderson Foundation. *Washington Post*, February 18, 1967, p. 1; *New York Times*, February 19, 1967, p. 26. The Beacon Fund was also mentioned. CIA mail-drop conduits that never filed annual 990-A reports required by the IRS included the Gotham, Price, Tower, Williford-Telford, and San Miguel Funds and the Borden Trust. These dummy foundations then made grants to the M. D. Anderson Foundation of Houston, Texas, the Boston-based Pappas Charitable Trust, and the J. Frederick Brown Foundations.

50. Van Dal and Zellweger, Friedenau, and Henrik Munktell, a conservative M.P. from Sweden, also became members.

51. Osusky and Giuseppe Bettiol of Italy. Standing Committee members not on the Executive Committee were Thorson, Per T. Federspiel of Denmark, José T. Nabuco of Brazil, and H. B. Tyabji of Pakistan.

52. The primary focus was on domestic law reform rather than international legal protection. Some ABA members found objectionable socialism in the U.N. Declaration of Human Rights; after 1952 the U.S. government withdrew support for the draft international covenant on civil and political rights. Bonsal nonetheless wanted the ICJ to rest its claims on the Universal Declaration rather than original standards created independently.

53. Sir Hartley Shawcross, chief prosecutor for the United Kingdom at Nuremberg; Pushottam Trikamdas, senior advocate at the Supreme Court of India; Juan José Cabajal Victorica, lawyer and professor of public law, Uruguay, were added first in 1954. Philippe N. Boulos, former minister of justice and president of the Court of Appeal, Lebanon, joined before the 1955 Athens Congress.

54. *New York Times*, August 25, 1954, p. 10.

55. Marks and Marchetti, *The CIA and the Cult of Intelligence*, 40. *New York Times*, August 2, 1974.

56. In 1962 paid agents helped found the ICJ's national section in Ecuador. Agee, *Inside the Company*.

57. Bonsal, van Dal, and Friedenau drafted the first budget. The AFFJ had an executive secretary with CIA ties at the New York office, which exercised final authority over ICJ expenditures.

58. Replacing several documents are explanatory handwritten notes: "Budget with E. S. Kozera."

59. After a former staff member reported the incident, the new Secretary-General, Seán MacBride, in an internal report entitled "For the Record," noted on pp. 2–3 his objection that Kozera had never requested authorization to copy and remove the mailing list.

60. ICJ Executive Committee Minutes, February 5–8, 1954.

61. *The International Commission of Jurists: Basic Facts*, a periodically published pamphlet on objectives, organization, and activities, stated the ICJ "draws its support from judges, law teachers, practitioners of law and other members of the legal community and their associations."

62. Van Dal had earlier published a report of the Berlin Congress and pamphlets on the Sovietization of Estonia's law courts and criminal penalties given for RIAS propaganda broadcasts.

63. Paul Poom, *Sovietization of Estonia's Law Courts* (The Hague: ICJ, 1953). Father André Bonnichon, *Law in Communist China* (The Hague: ICJ, 1955). Vladimir Gsovski, *The Essence of a Totalitarian State* (The Hague: ICJ, 1955).

64. *Under False Colours: A Report on the Character of the International Association of Democratic Lawyers* (The Hague: ICJ, 1955), 30–31.

65. Abbé Jean Boulier, (Brussels: IADL, 1958): 51 pp.

66. *ICJ Bulletin*, no. 1 (1955): 5.

67. The CIA's Directorate of Plans not only funded groups like the ICJ but also ran covert operations that toppled governments in Guatemala and Iran in 1953 and 1954. Blum, *Forgotten History*.

68. Vyshinsky, *Theory of Evidence in the Soviet Law* (1941)(in Russian), 31, quoted in Gsovski, *The Essence of a Totalitarian State* (The Hague: ICJ, 1955), 52.

69. Alfred M. Bingham, "Law and Justice in the Soviet Union," *Connecticut Bar Journal* 33 (1959): 378, 389 n. 16; Pierre Lochak, "Justice and the Judges in the Soviet Union," *Bulletin of the ICJ*, no. 6 (1956): 41.

70. Harold Berman, "Soviet Law Reform—Dateline Moscow 1957," *Yale Law Journal* (1957): 1191, 1205 n. 600.

71. John Hazard, "The Lawyer Under Socialism," *Wisconsin Law Review* (1946): 90, 92–93.

72. Dudley B. Bonsal, "The Judiciary and the Bar—Socialist Legality vs. The Rule of Law," *Texas Law Review* 40 (1961): 1–17, 6 n. 15.

73. *Report of the International Congress of Jurists: Athens—Greece* (The Hague: ICJ, 1956); Dudley B. Bonsal, "Free Lawyers in Athens," *The Record of the Association of the Bar of the City of New York* 10, no. 7 (October 1955): 352.

74. Ibid.

75. Jan Herman Burgers, "The Road to San Francisco: The Revival of the Human Rights Idea in the Twentieth Century," *Human Rights Quarterly* 14, no. 4 (November 1992): 447–78.

76. Braden, "CIA Is Immoral."

77. *Congressional Record*, 80th Cong., 1st sess., p. 1981 (March 12, 1947), quoted in David L. Cingranelli, *Ethics, American Foreign Policy, and the Third World* (New York: St. Martin's Press, 1993), 126.

78. Patrick Birkinshaw, Ian Harden, and Norman Lewis, *Government by Moonlight: The Hybrid Parts of the State* (London: Unwin Hyman, 1990), argue for sunlight to expose the nature of the bargains struck between public and private leaders to advance the public interest.

79. Bonsal, "Gangsters in the Guise of Jurists," 448.

Chapter 2: Organizing a Global Network

1. Ernest Angell, "Communism or Freedom: The Legal Profession and the Rule of Law," *ABA Journal* 43 (October 1957): 924–927.

2. David Forsythe, *The Internationalization of Human Rights* (Lexington, Mass.: D.C. Heath, 1991). Laurie S. Wiseberg and Harry M. Scoble, "International League for Human Rights: The Strategy of a Human Rights NGO," *Georgia Journal of International and Comparative Law* 7 (1977): 289–313.

3. Bonsal prepared the draft.

4. Webster, Angell, and Debevoise.

5. Bonsal recalled that Sir Hartley Shawcross recommended Marsh, who reported that McDonnell made the initial contact.

6. Personal interview, March 31, 1989.

7. John Ferguson, a U.S. attorney based in Paris, succeeded McDonnell as Bonsal's AFFJ alternate on the Executive Committee. Ferguson was a former deputy director of the policy planning staff of the U.S. Department of State and a member of the Council on Foreign Relations. Ferguson succeeded Bonsal's brother as U.S. ambassador to Morocco in 1961.

8. Lalive had studied law at Harvard and Columbia as well as in his native Geneva.

9. The new office at 6 Rue de Mont de Sion, Geneva, had previously been a personal residence and then a German consulate. Lalive had left his Geneva home and law practice to work at the International Court of Justice in The Hague and was eager to return to Switzerland.

10. As reported by Seán MacBride in a personal interview with Richard Rosswurm and Fred Woodbridge, July 22, 1983.

11. James McDonnell and John Ferguson for Bonsal and Edward Tuck for Debevoise.

12. After election as president of the New York City Bar, Bonsal resigned from the Executive Committee; he arranged for Benjamin Shute's election to both the Commission and the Committee. Bonsal then returned as committee chairman for six months in 1961 until President Kennedy appointed him as a federal judge.

13. Edward Tuck, a U.S. attorney with Shearman and Sterling in Paris.

14. The council could have up to 700 members, the largest number from New York. The Commission's membership, drawn from around the globe, required considerably greater travel expenses for business meetings. A Brazilian member proposed electing a new Commission at each congress; instead, current ICJ members were given indefinite terms.

15. From Australia, Japan, Nigeria, Norway, and Senegal.

16. The U.S. had three members, Bonsal, Shute/Debevoise, and the Czech exile Stephan Osusky; India had two, Trikamdas and Bose.

17. ICJ Statute, Article 35.

18. Form 990-A Report of M. D. Anderson Foundation, 1962, Line 21, B. Funds for an International Congress of Free Jurists. Three other CIA conduit foundations also supported the ICJ through the AFFJ.

19. ICJ Executive Committee Minutes, Explanatory Memo, April 12, 1958, p. 11.

20. *The International Commission of Jurists: Basic Facts* (Geneva: ICJ, 1966), 10. The 1966 mailing list of 47,076 had the following language breakdown: English 22,475; Spanish 11,845; French 8,987; German 3,769.

21. The kings of Norway and Jordan, the emperor of Ethiopia, the president of Liberia, and five Latin American heads of state.

22. Report of the Secretary-General, Meeting, International Commission of Jurists, The Hague, July 7–8, 1958 Appendix I, p. 3.

23. *Newsletter of the ICJ* no. 5, (January 1959): 6.
24. ABA Section on International and Comparative Law, Committee to Cooperate with the International Commission of Jurists.
25. As in the U.S., the national civil liberties organization was not invited to become an ICJ affiliate.
26. Shawcross, a self-described socialist, left the Labour Party in 1958. He was United Kingdom delegate to the United Nations from 1945 to 1949.
27. Egon Larsen, *A Flame in Barbed Wire: The Story of Amnesty International* (New York: W. W. Norton, 1979); Jonathan Power, *Amnesty International: The Human Rights Story* (New York: McGraw Hill, 1981).
28. ICJ Executive Committee Minutes, July 1961 and June 16, 1962.
29. One hundred fifty-eight lawyers from eighteen countries attended from April 24 to April 27.
30. Thirty-eight jurists from the U.K., U.S., and white dominions; thirty-eight from former African and Asian colonies; and thirty-one from India.
31. Schachter later reported that some judges were bothered that their expenses were being paid for by an unknown source. Interview, September 20, 1983, Columbia University School of Law.
32. "Missions and Tours," *Newsletter of the ICJ*, no. 12 (June 1961): 6.
33. Inadequate transportation links between the new countries forced some participants from East Africa to travel via Europe to reach Nigeria.
34. Ford Foundation staff recommendation, 1960.
35. According to Norman Marsh, Ghana's chief justice Sir Arku Korsah was visibly under the instructions of Kwaku Boateng. Letter of April 30, 1992.
36. *Newsletter of the ICJ*, no. 13 (February 1962): 5. The section in Ghana was called "Justice and Freedom."
37. ICJ, *The Cassell Case: Contempt in Liberia* (Geneva, ICJ: 1961).
38. Agee did not identify any others in the section or participants at Rio as CIA agents. Philip Agee, *Inside the Company: CIA Diary* (New York: Stonehill, 1975), 236. After an ICJ protest, Agee reported in a subsequent reprint that he only knew of information about 1961 CIA associations and thought the connection was severed in 1967.
39. In 1960 the ICJ conducted another survey of lawyers' groups leading to a second ABA publication on *The Rule of Law in the United States* by the committee that Ernest Angell chaired.
40. Terry M. Moe, *The Organization of Interests: Incentives and the Internal Dynamics of Political Interest Groups* (Chicago: University of Chicago Press, 1980).
41. Mancur Olson, Jr., *The Logic of Collective Action* (Cambridge, Mass.: Harvard University Press, 1965).

Chapter 3: Defining the Rule of Law

1. Francis Fukuyama characterized the absence of ideological conflict as "The End of History?" *The National Interest*, no. 16 (Summer 1989): 3–11. Robert Gilpin, *War and Change in World Politics* (New York: Cambridge University Press, 1981), disputes the emergence of a global society. See also Theodore H. von Laue, *The World Revolution of Westernization: The Twentieth Century in Global Perspective* (New York: Oxford University Press, 1987).

2. ABA Committee to Cooperate with the International Commission of Jurists, *The Rule of Law in the United States* (Geneva: ICJ, 1958), 108 pp. *The Rule of Law in the Federal Republic of Germany: A Statement by the German National Section* (Geneva: ICJ, 1958), 41 pp. *The Rule of Law in Italy* (Geneva: ICJ, 1958).

3. ABA Committee to Cooperate with the International Commission of Jurists, *The Rule of Law in the United States: A Survey* (Geneva: ICJ, 1962).

4. For years the ACLU resisted proposals by Roger Baldwin and other human rights activists for more human rights work at the United Nations. In 1992 the organization created a human rights task force.

5. A. V. Dicey's classic British text, *The Law of the Constitution*, presented the basic common law formulation stressing individual civil rights protected by an independent judiciary (10th ed., rev. by E. C. S. Wade [London: Macmillan, 1959]).

6. Norman S. Marsh, "The Rule of Law: New Delhi—Lagos—Rio De Janeiro," *Journal of the ICJ* 4 (1963): 257–68.

7. Marsh, "The Rule of Law," 259. Troubled by the overpopulation and low living standards he observed on an ICJ world tour, Marsh concluded, "successful operation of the Rule of Law is only possible where economic and social problems have, to a greater or lesser extent, found a successful solution." "Notes on a World Tour," *Newsletter of the ICJ*, no. 4, (June 1958): 2.

8. Marsh explained that his two-year leave from Oxford was too short and preparations for the Delhi conference too burdensome for effective U.N. action.

9. Norman Marsh, "A Working Paper," *The Rule of Law in a Free Society: Report on the International Congress of Jurists, New Delhi, India, 1959* (Geneva: ICJ, 1959), 197; see also "Editorial: Domestic Jurisdiction and International Concern," *Journal of the ICJ* 1 (Autumn 1957): 2, 6. The 1981 statement of ICJ objectives adds "traditions of lawyers" and changes "essential" to "important."

10. *The Rule of Law in a Free Society*, p. viii.

11. ICJ, *African Conference on the Rule of Law*, p. 173. The chairman of Nigeria's ICJ section "Liberty" deferentially professed: "We shall always be grateful to our former colonial rulers for their tolerance, patience, and understanding." Chief Arthur Prest, p. 88.

12. *African Conference on the Rule of Law: A Report on the Proceedings* (Geneva, ICJ: 1961), 181 pp.

13. *Question*: How can you tell the difference between a lawyer and a leech? *Answer*: A leech will let go and drop off when its victim dies. According to the *New York Times*, John McCloy each year told "the tenderfoots in his law firm 'If a client does not complain about a bill, it isn't high enough.'" David Margolick, "At the Bar" *New York Times*, March 20, 1992, sec. B, p. 16.

14. *Executive Action and the Rule of Law: A Report on the Proceedings of the International Congress of Jurists, Rio de Janeiro, Brazil* (Geneva: ICJ, 1962), 32.

15. William B. Harvey, *Michigan Law Review* 59 (1961): 1286–89. F. H. Newark, *The Law Quarterly Review* 77 (July 1961): 450–51. D. C. M. Yardley, *The Modern Law Review* 24 (September 1961): 673.

16. Howard Tolley, Jr., *The U.N. Commission on Human Rights* (Boulder, Colo.: Westview, 1987), 38.

17. Paul G. Lauren, *Power and Prejudice: The Politics of Diplomacy and Racial Discrimination* (Boulder, Colo.: Westview, 1988), 169.

18. Letter to the author, August 20, 1992.

19. Jean-Flavien Lalive, "Editorial: The Rule of Law in a Changing World," *Journal of the ICJ* 2 (Spring–Summer 1959): 5.

20. Article 38 of the Statute of the International Court of Justice. The other sources are international conventions and custom.

21. Norman S. Marsh, "The Rule of Law as a Supra-National Concept," in *Oxford Essays in Jurisprudence*, ed. A. G. Guest (Oxford: Oxford University Press, 1960), 223–64, 260.

22. *The Rule of Law and Human Rights: Principles and Definitions* (Geneva: ICJ, 1968) compares ICJ principles with provisions of the Universal Declaration and the two international covenants approved by the General Assembly in 1966.

Chapter 4: Protecting Victims

1. Stanley Anderson, "Human Rights and the Structure of International Law," *New York Law School Journal of International and Comparative Law* 12 (1991): 1–28.

2. Thomas M. Franck, "Of Gnats and Camels: Is There a Double Standard at the United Nations?" *American Journal of International Law* 78 (1984): 811–34.

3. The ICJ protested when states denied defendants representation and unsuccessfully pressed Portugal to delay a trial until defense counsel could be sent to appear in Angola. ICJ Press Statement, September 13, 1960. The ICJ did not solicit contributions for a legal defense fund.

4. Governments typically assign diplomatic observers to trials abroad of their own nationals and occasionally monitor politically inspired prosecutions of local citizens. During the 1930s private American and British observers attended trials of socialists and unionists in Nazi Germany; IADL observers monitored Cold War trials of communists in the United States and Spain. David Weissbrodt, "International Trial Observers," *Stanford Journal of International Law* 18 (Spring 1982): 27, 30–31.

5. Hungary, Poland, Yugoslavia, and Castro's Cuba all refused visas to ICJ observers. "Poles Bar Observers: Visas Denied French Jurists to Attend Poznan Trial," *New York Times*, August 21, 1956, p. 5.

6. In an exception to the rule, African legal officer Kabes observed a conspiracy trial in Dahomey in 1962.

7. Even the fairest proceedings to enforce apartheid were an injustice. Gardiner also attended a Portuguese trial and joined a fact-finding mission to Tunisia.

8. The ICJ and "Justice" jointly sponsored missions to South Africa in 1956 and 1962 but sent separate trial observers to other proceedings. On behalf of Commonwealth lawyers, "Justice" claimed special expertise for English-speaking countries.

9. Three hundred and fifty observers attended the trial, including a Zionist sent by the Australian section without notice to the Secretariat. Peter Papdatos, "The Eichmann Trial," *Bulletin of the ICJ* 14 (October 1962): 13–18, at 16. The ICJ did not appeal for clemency or protest Eichmann's execution.

10. Turkey's military regime prosecuted and executed a former prime minister and two cabinet officers despite ICJ appeals for clemency. "The Yas-

siada Trial and Other Recent Developments in Turkey," *Bulletin of the ICJ* 14 (October 1962): 25–29.

11. "The Ceylon Coup d'Etat Trial," *Bulletin of the ICJ* 15 (April 1963): 11–16. The government reinstituted charges before an impartial bench.

12. Silverio Coppa of Italy, along with eight colleagues, observed the Spanish trial of Professor Enrique Tierno. ICJ Executive Committee Minutes, July 2, 1961.

13. Indian Commission of Jurists, "Report of the Kerala Inquiry Committee," *Journal of the ICJ* 2 (Spring–Summer 1960): 139–214.

14. "Press Releases and Telegrams," *Newsletter of the ICJ* no. 13 (February 1962): 5.

15. A French commentator objected to the anticommunist loyalty-security program. André Tunc, "Liberty and Security in the USA," *Bulletin of the ICJ* 6 (December 1956): 50–61. See also Kenneth W. Greenawalt, "Legal Aspects of Civil Liberties in the United States and Recent Developments," *Journal of the ICJ* 2 (Spring–Summer 1959): 81–144.

16. "The Negro Problem in the United States," *Bulletin of the ICJ* 16 (July 1963): 39–48, at 48. A press release condemned racism in Birmingham, Alabama but carefully praised the judiciary's contributions to social change. ICJ Press Statement, "The Negro Situation in Birmingham, Alabama," May 29, 1963.

17. "Fight for Negro Grows: World Jurist Group Urges Clemency in Alabama Case," *New York Times*, September 2, 1958, p. 13. Bose issued a press statement supporting the 1963 civil rights campaign in Birmingham.

18. "The Algerian Conflict and the Rule of Law," *Bulletin of the ICJ* 11 (December 1960): 5–20. Lalive cabled de Gaulle with one protest and obtained a *Bulletin* article written by a "Libre Justice" member when the national section failed to report.

19. *Injustice and the System* and *Justice Enslaved.*

20. ICJ, *South Africa and the Rule of Law* (Geneva, ICJ: 1960), 239 pp. Some members of "Justice" felt a proprietary responsibility for Commonwealth territories and thought the report needed greater British input.

21. ICJ, *Spain and the Rule of Law* (Geneva: ICJ, 1962), 153 pp.

22. ICJ, *Cuba and the Rule of Law* (Geneva: ICJ, 1962) 240+ pp. In another special report, the ICJ declared the Berlin Wall illegal. ICJ, *The Berlin Wall: A Defiance of Human Rights* (Geneva: ICJ, 1962), 54 pp.

23. ICJ Executive Committee Minutes, January 6–7, 1962, Horacio Godoy.

24. Not surprisingly, Cuba refused permission for an ICJ observer to attend the trial of those captured at the Bay of Pigs. The CIA had also targeted Trujillo for assassination.

25. Online Computer Library Center (OCLC) Prism Service, April 8, 1992. Spain—135 libraries in 37 states; South Africa—132 libraries in 34 states; and Cuba—345 libraries in 45 states.

26. ICJ, *The Berlin Wall: A Defiance of Human Rights* (Geneva: ICJ, 1962), 54 pp.

27. Philip Agee, *Inside the Company: CIA Diary* (New York: Stonehill, 1975), 73 n. 8.

28. Translated by Andrew Hurley (New York: Knopf, 1986).

29. Bradley F. Smith, *Reaching Judgment at Nuremberg* (New York: Basic Books, 1977); Ann Tusa and John Tusa, *The Nuremberg Trial* (London: Mac-

millan, 1983). Robert G. Storey, executive trial counsel for the U.S. under Justice Jackson, attended ICJ congresses in the 1950s, when he served as president of the American Bar Association. His work of the trial is *Final Judgment? Pearl Harbor to Nuremberg* (San Antonio: Naylor, 1968). McCloy carried out only five of the death sentences and granted clemency to dozens of Nazi war criminals. Kai Bird, *The Chairman: John J. McCloy* (New York: Simon and Schuster, 1992).

30. Nissim Bar-Yaacov, *The Handling of International Disputes by Means of Inquiry* (New York: Oxford University Press, 1974). Norman L. Hill, "International Commissions of Inquiry and Conciliation," *International Conciliation*, no. 278 (March 1932): 9–94.

31. Arthur W. Blaser, "How to Advance Human Rights Without Really Trying: An Analysis of Nongovernmental Tribunals," *Human Rights Quarterly* 14 (August 1992): 339–70, at 340.

32. IADL, Report on U.S. Crimes in Korea of March 31, 1952. Brandweiner, *Facts and Documents Concerning the War in Korea* (Brussels 1953). Rapport sur l'emploi d'armes bactériologiques sur le territoire chinois par les forces armées des Etats-Unis (April 2, 1952), cited in F. Ermacora, "International Enquiry Commissions in the Field of Human Rights," I *Human Rights Journal* (1968): 180–218, at 203 n. 70, 71. An Austrian professor of constitutional law who chaired the IADL committee repudiated the findings in 1961 after a prosecution that was quashed. Ermacora, "International Enquiry Commissions," 203.

33. Bradley F. Smith, *Reaching Judgment at Nuremberg* (New York: Basic Books, 1977).

34. In addition to Shawcross, other ICJ members included van Dal, Bonsal, Friedenau, Bose, Munktell, and Zellweger. Six of the twenty-six were from Britain, and five from the Netherlands. Two Hungarian exiles participated as experts.

35. ICJ, *The Hungarian Situation and the Rule of Law* (The Hague: ICJ, 1957), 144 pp.

36. "U.N. Hungary Unit Hears Legal View," *New York Times*, March 14, 1957, p. 12. Shawcross also published a summary in the *Times* of London.

37. ICJ, *The Continuing Challenge of the Hungarian Situation to the Rule of Law* (The Hague: ICJ, 1957), 33 pp. ICJ, *Justice in Hungary Today* (Geneva: ICJ, 1958), 72 pp.

38. *New York Times*, September 28, 1957, p. 4.

39. A CIA proprietary air company assisted Kuomintang mercenaries on sabotage raids and trained some Tibetans at Camp Hale in Colorado. Victor Marchetti and John Marks, *The CIA and the Cult of Intelligence* (New York: Knopf, 1974), 115.

40. Tom A. Grunfeld, *The Making of Modern Tibet* (Armonk, N.Y.: M. E. Sharpe, Inc, 1987), Chaps. 7, 8.

41. Ibid., 142.

42. ICJ, *The Question of Tibet and the Rule of Law* (Geneva: ICJ, 1959). 208 pp.

43. "Genocide Is Laid to Reds in Tibet: Jurists Group Says Inquiry Shows Chinese Have Slain 65,000," *New York Times*, June 6, 1959, p. 4.

44. "United Nations Resolution on Tibet," *Bulletin of the ICJ* 10 (January 1960): 37–40.

45. ICJ Executive Committee Minutes, February 6–7, 1960, Doc. 3. "Justice" also decided against giving financial support.

46. "Genocide in Tibet Laid to Red China by World Jurists," *New York Times*, June 20, 1960, p. 1.

47. "Genocide in Tibet," *New York Times*, June 20, 1960.

48. ICJ, *Tibet and the Chinese People's Republic: A Report to the ICJ by its Legal Inquiry Committee on Tibet* (Geneva: ICJ, 1960), 341 pp.

49. "So convinced of Chinese wrongdoing was the LIC that one unsubstantiated charge failed to lead the committee members to question the other charges." Grunfeld, *Modern Tibet*, 144.

50. ICJ Executive Committee Minutes, October 14–16, 1960. Not surprisingly, the Soviet U.N. representative denounced the genocide findings as propaganda, and a pro-communist Swedish-Chinese teach-in faulted the methodology. Executive Committee Minutes, June 15–16, 1968, Document 13.

51. Gerald Gardiner of Britain, Rolf Christopherson of Norway, and Felix Ermacora of Austria, member of the European Commission on Human Rights and U.N. Commission on Human Rights. The mission worked out of the Tunisian Red Crescent offices. Ermacora went on to participate in several U.N. human rights inquiries and wrote the first articles on fact-finding procedures. F. Ermacora, "International Enquiry Commissions in the Field of Human Rights," I *Human Rights Journal* (1968): 180–218. F. Ermacora, "Partiality and Impartiality of Human Rights Enquiry Commissions of International Organizations," I *René Cassin Amicorum discipulorumque liber* (1969): 64–74.

52. ICJ, *Report of the Committee of Enquiry into Events in Bizerte, Tunisia* (Geneva: ICJ, 1961), 45 pp. See also F. Ermacora, "International Enquiry Commissions," 200–203.

53. Press Statement, ICJ Executive Committee Meeting, October 14–15, 1961. *New York Times*, October 21, 1961, p. 7.

54. Arthur Blaser, "How to Advance Human Rights Without Really Trying: An Analysis of Nongovernmental Tribunals," *Human Rights Quarterly* 14 (August 1992). The author's account skips from the 1937 Dewey Commission to the 1966 Russell Tribunal without mentioning the 1952 IADL report on Korea and the 1956 and 1959 ICJ Commissions on Hungary and Tibet. Britain and France both barred Russell's proceedings, and the tribunal held sessions in Stockholm and Copenhagen.

55. Ermacora, "International Enquiry Commissions," 203.

Chapter 5: Building Coalitions for Global Change

1. "The Meaning of Human Rights Year," *Journal of the ICJ* 8 (December 1967): iii–viii.

2. The Pugwash movement founded by Bertrand Russell convened communist and noncommunist scientists, while the Dartmouth Conference series brought together eminent private citizens of the United States and the USSR. Maureen R. Berman and Joseph E. Johnson, eds., *Unofficial Diplomats* (New York: Columbia University Press, 1977), 37, 47.

3. Others included the International Confederation of Free Trade Unions, Pax Romana, and the YWCA.

4. Jeffrey Berry, *Lobbying for the People: The Political Behavior of Public Interest Groups* (Princeton, N.J.: Princeton University Press, 1977), 14.

5. Seymour Martin Lipset, Martin Trow, and James Coleman, *Union Democracy* (Garden City, N.Y.: Anchor Books, 1956), 1.

6. St. John asked the Secretariat to send his nine-page memo to all Commission members. "Memorandum to all members of the Commission from Mr. Edward St. John," ICJ Executive Committee Minutes, February 24–25, 1968. Facing dissolution, the Commission's regularly scheduled 1969 triennial meeting was postponed until 1971. Not until the 1990s did St. John's Australian successor, Michael Kirby, successfully implement reforms that democratized ICJ governance.

7. *Newsletter of the ICJ* 35 (October–December 1987): 1; personal interview, July 22, 1983. *New York Times*, January 16, 1988, p. 10, col. 1.

8. Interviewed by Fred Woodbridge and Richard Rosswurm, July 22, 1983. When he was interviewed, Executive Committee chairman Eli Whitney Debevoise stated that the Secretary-General was informed generally about "government funds." Notes of Fred Woodbridge and Richard Rosswurm, September 19, 1983.

9. Seán MacBride, 1964 Programme and General Policy Memorandum, Executive Committee Minutes, May 9–10, 1964, p. 4. Programme and General Policy Memorandum by Secretary-General for Meeting of Executive Committee, May 9–10, 1964 in Austria; Document XIV.

10. Summary of the President's Memorandum on the Future Work and Policy of the ICJ, Executive Committee Meeting, July 9–10, 1966.

11. "Meeting of the International Commission of Jurists," *Bulletin of the ICJ* 28 (December 1966): 2.

12. "Future Policy and Activities," Secretary-General's Report to the Commission (1966), pp. 31–32. Speech to Commonwealth and Empire Law Conference, Sydney.

13. A. A. de C. Hunter, "Ombudsman for Britain?" *Journal of the ICJ* 4 (Summer 1962): 150–59. A. G. Davis, "The Ombudsman in New Zealand," Part 2, *Journal of the ICJ* 4 (Summer 1963): 316–23.

14. Located at 2, Quai du Cheval-Blanc. The ICJ had two floors of offices.

15. In 1967 the AFFJ provided $400,000 toward a $415,000 general budget; the special projects expenditures were an additional $67,313.

16. The U.N. revoked the IADL's consultative status. Third world governments question the impartiality of NGOs dominated by Western interests and often have no equivalent institution at the national level. The Chinese translation for NGO means "antigovernment" organization. Even some Western democratic cultures find something illegitimate about special interest lobbies. Robert Presthus, "Interest Group Lobbying: Canada and the U.S.," *Annals of the American Academy of Political and Social Science* (May 1974): 44.

17. Peter H. Rohn, *Relations Between the Council of Europe and International Non-Governmental Associations* (Brussels: Union of International Associations, 1957).

18. The stone's thirteenth-century inscriptions represent a Thai Magna Charta "laying down the rules of justice and the rights of the citizen." *Bulletin of the ICJ* 25 (March 1966): 44. The ICJ had conducted a South-East Asian and Pacific Conference of Jurists in Bangkok in February 1965.

19. "[R]arely can any single group achieve its legislative objectives without

assistance from other groups." David Truman, *The Governmental Process* (New York: Knopf, 1967), 362.

20. Lucius J. Barker and Donald Jansiewicz, "Coalitions in the Civil Rights Movement," in *The Study of Coalition Behavior*, ed. Sven Groennings, E. W. Kelley, and Michael Leiserson (New York: Holt, Rinehart and Winston, 1970), 192–208, describes organizational "egos" impeding natural alliance.

21. Douglas Cater, *Power in Washington* (New York: Vintage Books, 1964); Bill Keller, "The Veterans' Lobby as an 'Iron Triangle'," *Congressional Quarterly Weekly Report*, June 10, 1984, p. 1627. See also Eric Redman, *The Dance of Legislation* (New York: Simon and Schuster, 1973).

22. Member Terje Wold, President of Norway's Supreme Court, was a judge on the European Court of Human Rights. Legal officer Karal Vasak was hired by the Council of Europe's Human Rights Division. Hilary Kellerson, Anna Pouyat, Lee Swepston, and Dominick Devlin all took positions at the ILO. Manno Porzio of Chile became an assistant-director-general of WIPO (World Intellectual Property Organization). Annar Cassam took charge of African affairs at UNESCO. Lucian Weeramantry of India worked for the United Nations in the United States.

23. See Virginia Leary, "A New Role for Nongovernmental Organizations in Human Rights: A Case Study of Nongovernmental Participation in the Development of International Norms on Torture," in *UN Law Fundamental Rights*, ed. Antonio Cassese (Netherlands: Sijthoff & Noordhoff, 1979), 197; David Weissbrodt, "The Influence of Interest Groups on the Development of United States Human Rights Policies," *The Dynamics of Human Rights in U.S. Foreign Policy*, ed. Natalie Hevener (New Brunswick: Transaction, 1984), 229–78.

24. Berry, *Lobbying for the People*, fig. IX-1, "Strategies and Tactics: A Decision-Making Framework," 263.

25. The meeting at UNESCO in Paris coincided with a Special Section the veterans organized, chaired by René Cassin, on January 28, 1964. MacBride also discussed with the World Association of World Federalists the need for new international law to govern U.N. peacekeeping forces and the administration of territories under U.N. supervision.

26. ICJ Executive Committee Minutes, May 9–10, 1964, p. 5.

27. Roger Clark, *A United Nations High Commissioner for Human Rights* (The Hague: Martinus Nijhoff, 1972), 58–59; R. St. J. MacDonald, "The United Nations Commissioner for Human Rights," *Canadian Yearbook of International Law* (1967): 84.

28. Clark, *High Commissioner*, 45.

29. John Humphrey, *Human Rights and the United Nations: A Great Adventure* (Dobbs Ferry, N.Y.: Transnational Publishers, 1984), 296–301.

30. Humphrey, *Human Rights and the United Nations*, 298; Clark, *High Commissioner*, 47.

31. Humphrey, *Great Adventure*, 298.

32. Clark, *High Commissioner*, 50.

33. Seán MacBride, "The Promise of Human Rights Year," *Journal of the ICJ* 9 (1968): ii. The Sub-Commission revived the proposal without success in 1983. Sub-Comm. Res. 1983/36 U.N. Doc. E/CN.4/1983/4 (adopted 16-3-3).

34. *Procedures for dealing with communications relating to violations of human rights and fundamental freedoms*, E.S.C. Res. 1503, 48 U.N. ESCOR Supp. (No. 1A) (1970).

35. Interview given by Seán MacBride to Fred Woodbridge and Richard Rosswurm, May 22, 1983. The U.S. had objected to the IADL's consultative status after the organization's anti-U.S. propaganda campaign during the Korean War.

36. V. M. Kabes, ICJ Executive Secretary, who in the 1950s assisted the New York office as an observer at U.N. meetings. Personal interview, August 30, 1988.

37. ICJ, "A World Campaign for Human Rights," *ICJ Bulletin* 24 (December 1965): 1.

38. ICJ, "Geneva Conference on Human Rights," *ICJ Bulletin* 33 (March 1968): 1; "Montreal Statement of the Assembly for Human Rights," *Journal of the ICJ* 9 (June 1968): 94–112.

39. *Human Rights in Armed Conflicts*, G.A. Res. 2442 (XXIII), 23 U.N. GAOR, U.N. Doc. A/Conf. 32/41 (1968).

40. "International NGO Conference on Human Rights," *ICJ Bulletin* 36 (December 1968): 35.

41. Letter to Eli Whitney Debevoise, chairman of the ICJ Executive Committee, January 9, 1969.

42. Ustinia Dolgopol, "The Centre for the Independence of Judges and Lawyers, Its Work and Its Aspirations," *CIJL Bulletin* 19 and 20 (April–October 1987): 43. Interview with Hans Thoolen, December 20, 1987.

43. Melissa Young, "Journalists Precariously Covering the Globe: International Attempts to Provide for Their Protection," *Virginia Journal of International Law* 23 (1982): 135.

44. Young, "Journalists," 146. After leaving the ICJ, MacBride headed a UNESCO commission which alarmed Western foes of a proposed "new information order" by incorporating the convention's provisions on identity cards for journalists.

45. Young, "Journalists," 142–45.

46. "UNESCO: Protection of Journalists," *Newsletter of the ICJ* 1 (1 April–30 June 1979): 8.

47. *The Rule of Law and Human Rights, Principles and Definitions* (Geneva: ICJ, 1966). *The Dynamic Aspects of the Rule of Law in the Modern Age*, Report on the Proceedings of the South-East Asian and Pacific Conference of Jurists, Bangkok, Thailand, February 15–19, 1965 (Geneva: ICJ 1965). One hundred participants from seventeen countries attended.

48. *Congres de Juristes africain francophones*, Dakar, 1967. (Fr.)

49. During the 1968 Human Rights Year, the Mysore State Commission of Jurists held a Bangalore Conference on Freedom of Movement: *Right to Freedom of Movement*, 1968 Conference of Jurists, Bangalore, India, 134 pp.

50. The European sections met in Vienna in 1968 to consider the theme "The Individual and the State" and in Stockholm for the Nordic Conference on the Right to Privacy, May 22–23, 1967, hosted by the Swedish Section. Stig Strömholm, *Right of Privacy and Rights of the Personality: A Comparative Survey* (Stockholm: P. A. Norstedt and Söners Forlag, 1967).

51. Richard Mansbach, Yale H. Ferguson, and Donald E. Lampert, *The Web of World Politics* (Englewood Cliffs, N.J.: Prentice Hall, 1976), Part II.

52. See Harry M. Scoble and Laurie S. Wiseberg, "Human Rights and Amnesty International," *Annals of the American Academy of Political and Social Science* (May 1974): 11–26, for a comparable analytical approach.

Chapter 6: Responding to Crisis

1. April 19, 1967 letter from French president Charles de Gaulle to Jean-Paul Sartre denying a request for the Russell International War Crimes Tribunal to meet in France, and Sartre's reply. *Against the Crime of Silence: Proceedings of the International War Crimes Tribunal* (New York: Simon and Schuster, 1970), 28, 32.

2. Explanatory Notes for the Proposed Agenda, ICJ Executive Committee Meeting January 18–19, 1964, p. 3.

3. Letters of Seán MacBride to The Hon. B. J. Vorster December 17, 1963 and February 27, 1964, and replies from B. J. Vorster of January 14, 1964 and March 19, 1964.

4. "Lindsay's Brother and Briton in South Africa to Aid Lawyer," *New York Times*, July 25, 1969, p. 8, col. 1. Edward Lyons, joined by George Lindsey of the Lawyers Committee for Human Rights, approached the minister of justice on behalf of Joel Carlson, who had represented South African prisoners for thirteen years.

5. *Apartheid in South Africa and South West Africa* (Geneva: ICJ, 1967). *Erosion of the Rule of Law in South Africa* (Geneva: ICJ, 1968). Department of Foreign Affairs, Republic of South Africa, *South Africa and the Rule of Law* (Pretoria: 1968), 68 p.

6. *South West Africa: The Court's Judgment* (Geneva: ICJ, 1967). Staff Study, "Judgment of the International Court of Justice on South West Africa (1966)"; *Journal of the ICJ* 7 (Winter 1966): 163–213; Rosalyn Higgins "The International Court and South West Africa: The Implications of the Judgment," *Journal of the ICJ* 8 (Summer 1967): 3–35.

7. Dr. Hans Rau of Germany visited Angola and Pierre Papdatos of Athens went to Leopoldville in 1965.

8. "Portuguese African Colonies and the United Nations," *ICJ Bulletin* 34 (June 1968): 19–27.

9. Per Westberg of AI co-chaired the NGO group, which included the Africa Bureau, African-American Institute, American Committee on Africa, Commission of Churches on International Affairs, International Confederation of Free Trade Unions, International Defence and Aid Fund, and the Student Non-Violent Co-ordinating Committee. "Recommendations by the Observers of the NGOs at the International Seminar on Apartheid, Racial Discrimination and Colonialism in Southern Africa," Kitwe, Zambia, July 25–August 4, 1967.

10. October 10, 1968 letter from Antonio Ma. de Oriol y Urquijo, Ministry of Justice, to H.E. Seán MacBride. A joint ICJ–Amnesty International mission also met with the minister in 1970 to discuss several concerns.

11. The debate appears in correspondence MacBride sent to Eli Whitney Debevoise, accompanied by Kabes's five-page memorandum summarizing Graven's, the State Department's, and his own views. "Burundi Mission," Documents for ICJ Executive Committee Meeting, March 5–6, 1966.

12. December 30, 1965 letter from Seán MacBride to Eli Whitney Debevoise.

13. "Events in Burundi: Statement of the International Commission of Jurists," January 8, 1966. The BBC and Swiss radio carried the ICJ account.

14. Minutes of staff meeting, June 20, 1966. They also promised to share documents provided to the ILO.

15. May 13, 1967 letter from Seán MacBride to the Right Hon. Sir Geoffrey de Freitas.

16. The "margin of appreciation refers to the latitude allowed to the member states in their observance of the Convention" by the European Commission and Court, which may give "an initial presumption in favor of the defendant state" because of unique local laws or conditions. Thomas A. O'Donnell, "The Margin of Appreciation Doctrine: Standards in the Jurisprudence of the European Court of Human Rights," *Human Rights Quarterly* 4 (Fall 1982): 474–507, at 475.

17. A. H. Robertson and J. G. Merrills, *Human Rights in Europe*, 2d ed. (Manchester, U.K.: Manchester University Press, 1977). A special volume of the *Yearbook* of the Convention on Human Rights—Vol. XII, 1969, Part II, or XII *bis*—contains the report of the Commission on the Greek case.

18. *Journal of the ICJ* 5 (Summer 1964): 3–47.

19. Professor A. D. Belinfante of Amsterdam University, Judge Gustaf Petrén, and Mr. Navroz Vakil of Bombay.

20. "Jurists Leave After Inquiry," *New York Times*, March 15, 1964, p. 31, col. 1.

21. Investigating Committee appointed by the ICJ, *Report on the Events in Panama* (Geneva: ICJ, 1964).

22. "New Avenue to Accord," *New York Times*, June 23, 1964, p. 32, col. 1.

23. "Jurists Absolve U.S. over Panama," *New York Times*, June 10, 1964, p. 11, col. 1. "Panama Verdict: The U.S. Was Not Guilty," *Time* (June 19, 1964): 30.

24. "Panama's Assembly Rejects Hearing on January Riots," *New York Times*, October 8, 1964, p. 9, col. 1. The Assembly adopted a resolution honoring the victims and recommended government compensation for their families. A new government was elected in May, and the opposition unsuccessfully sought to call officials from the prior administration for a hearing.

25. The CIA, which denied the charge, reportedly acted through an affiliate union of the Public Service International, which acknowledged the assistance. *Colliers Encyclopedia*, 1974 ed., *s.v.* "Guyana" (vol. 11, 546).

26. Letter of Whitney Debevoise to the Right Honorable Lord Shawcross, April 12, 1965.

27. Letter of the Right Hon. Lord Shawcross to all members of the ICJ Executive Committee, April 21, 1965.

28. ICJ, *Report of the British Guiana Commission of Inquiry: Racial Problems in the Public Service* (Geneva: ICJ, 1965).

29. Justice Seamus Henchy, Professor Felix Ermacora, and Professor Peter A. Papadatos. Legal officer David Sagar of Australia was registrar for the proceedings and wrote the final report in Geneva. F. Ermacora, "International enquiry commissions in the field of human rights," *Human Rights Journal* 1 (1968): 180–218.

30. *Report of the British Guiana Commission of Inquiry.*

31. "Adverse Effect of Quotas," *New York Times*, October 21, 1965, p. 11, col. 1.

32. U.S. State Department, *1981 Country Reports on Human Rights Practices*, 455. See also *Interim Report of the Joint Mission to Investigate Political Freedom in Guyana*, British Parliamentary Human Rights Group and the Americas Watch Committee, May 1985.

33. Although the regime barred certain witnesses and visits, the Human Rights Commission found ample evidence of torture and other violations.

34. Arthur Blaser, "How to Advance Human Rights Without Really Trying: An Analysis of Nongovernmental Tribunals," *Human Rights Quarterly* 14 (August 1992): 339–70. Britain and France both barred Russell's proceedings, and the tribunal held sessions in Stockholm and Copenhagen.

35. "Units Linked with C.I.A.," *New York Times*, February 19, 1967, p. 27. Based on tax returns from the J. Frederick Brown Foundation and the Granary Fund.

36. "This Is How the Money Goes Around," *Washington Post*, February 26, 1967: a diagram identifying three foundations that made grants to the AFFJ (M.D. Anderson Foundation, Pappas Charitable Trust, and J. Frederick Brown Foundation) and seven conduit funds that channeled CIA money to those three (Price Fund, Borden Trust, Tower Fund, Beacon Fund, Gotham Fund, San Miguel Fund, Wiliford-Telford Fund).

37. Letter from Seán MacBride to Eli Whitney Debevoise, February 24, 1967, with copies to members of the Executive Committee.

38. Benenson alleged that an AI report on Aden that criticized the British government had been suppressed by staff with foreign office connections. He in turn was accused of channeling secret service funds to opposition groups in Rhodesia. Following their early collaboration in founding AI, MacBride and Benenson developed major differences. Egon Larsen, *A Flame in Barbed Wire: The Story of Amnesty International* (New York: Norton, 1979), 31–35. Jonathan Power, *Against Oblivion: Amnesty International's Fight for Human Rights* (London: Fontana, 1981), 14–18.

39. Letter of Peter Benenson to Seán MacBride, February 23, 1967.

40. ICJ Executive Committee Minutes, March 3–4, 1967.

41. Letter from Vivian Bose to Seán MacBride, March 20, 1967.

42. Letter of José T. Nabuco to Seán MacBride, March 9, 1967.

43. Bill Butler of the New York Bar Association, and former AFFJ executive secretary Robert Bass on the ABA committee.

44. Undersecretary of State Nicholas Katzenbach headed the committee, which included HEW secretary John Gardner and CIA director Richard Helms. Church Committee Report, p. 186.

45. U.S. Senate, Report of the Church Committee (1976), p. 187.

46. Kai Bird, *The Chairman: John J. McCloy, The Making of the American Establishment* (New York: Simon and Schuster, 1992), 426–29.

47. ECOSOC Resolution 1296 redesignated categories A and B as I and II; NGOs were required to report every four years and to disclose funding sources.

48. Pei-heng Chiang, *Non-Governmental Organizations at the United Nations: Identity, Role and Function* (New York: Praeger, 1981): 173–87.

49. Others that had received CIA funds included the International Confederation of Free Trade Unions, Pax Romana, and the YWCA.

50. Council Committee on NGOs, Hearing of the International Commission of Jurists, April 10, 1969, p. 7.

51. "The Middle East," *The Review* 3 (September 1969): 10–14.

52. National sections, eighty-five on paper, contributed no more than $15,000 toward the annual budget.

53. ICJ Executive Committee, Secretary-General's Report, October 11–12, 1969, p. 2.

54. Chandra Daphtary, India; Enrique Garcia-Sayan, Peru; Bahri Guiga, Tunisia; Gustaf Petren, Sweden; S. S. Rampahl, Guyana; Michael A. Triantafyllides, Cyprus; Masatoshi Yakota, Japan.

55. ICJ Executive Committee Minutes, April 10–11, 1970.

56. Nissim Bar-Yaacov, *The Handling of International Disputes by Means of Inquiry* (New York: Oxford Press, 1974).

57. F. Ermacora, "International enquiry commissions in the field of human rights," *Human Rights Journal* 1 (1968): 180–218. F. Ermacora, "Partiality and impartiality of human rights enquiry commissions of international organisations," *René Cassin Amicorum discipulorumque liber* 1 (1969): 64–74.

58. Debevoise had pressed for ICJ criticism of racial discrimination in the United States.

59. "Spanish Diplomatic Moves Concerning the International Commission of Jurists," March 4, 1966 memo by V. M. Kabes, Document 11, ICJ Executive Committee Minutes, March 5–6, 1966.

60. Letter from Seán MacBride to Michael Ansara, February 4, 1969.

61. "ICJ News," *The Review* 2 (June 1969): 62–63.

62. ICJ Executive Committee Minutes, November 14–15, 1970, p. 7. Niall MacDermot did publicly thank Austria, Cyprus, Great Britain, France, the Netherlands, Switzerland, West Germany, Canada, Guyana, and Jamaica in *The Review* 6 (April–June 1971): 1.

63. *New York Times*, Obituaries, January 16, 1988, p. 32. MacBride continued to antagonize the United States by supporting military assistance for SWAPO freedom fighters in the struggle for Namibia's independence.

64. AI was confronting financial collapse in 1968 when Martin Ennals became Secretary-General, a post he held for twelve years.

Chapter 7: Mobilizing Advocates for Development

1. "The social movement is the organized collective behaviour of a class actor struggling against his class adversary for the social control of historicity in a concrete community." Alan Touraine, *The Voice and the Eye: An Analysis of Social Movements*, trans. Alan Duff (New York: Cambridge University Press, 1981). *Social Research* 52, no. 4 (Winter 1985) is an issue devoted to writings by sociologists on new social movements. Marta Fuentes and Andre Gunder Frank, "Ten Theses on Social Movements," *World Development* 17, no. 2 (1989): 179–91.

2. Jack L. Walker, *Mobilizing Interest Groups in America: Patrons, Professions, and Social Movements* (Ann Arbor: University of Michigan Press, 1990), 52.

3. Ibid.

4. Two recent works that put social movement theory in the international context are Joseph A. Camilleri and Jim Falk, "The New Social Movements," in *The End of Sovereignty? The Politics of a Shrinking and Fragmenting World* (Brookfield, Vt.: Elger, 1992), 199–235, and Richard A. Falk, "The Global Promise of Social Movements," in *Explorations at the Edge of Time: The Prospects for World Order* (Philadelphia: Temple University Press, 1992), 125–59.

5. Samuel P. Huntington, "The Clash of Civilizations?" *Foreign Affairs* 72, no. 3 (Summer 1993): 22–49. Zbigniew Brzezinski, *Out of Control: Global Turmoil on the Eve of the 21st Century* (New York: Scribners, 1993).

6. In a tragic quarrel, he struck a friend who had an undiagnosed heart

condition, which proved fatal. "MacDermot was forced to go through the formality of a prosecution for manslaughter, at the end of which he was acquitted, without the jury even needing to retire to consider their verdict." David Leigh, *The Wilson Plot: The Intelligence Services and the Discrediting of a Prime Minister* (London: Heinemann, 1988): 143.

7. Iain Guest, *Behind the Disappearances* (Philadelphia: University of Pennsylvania Press, 1990), 112.

8. 109 Route de Chêne, Chêne Bougeries. Remnants of the ICJ archives were stored in the garage and a scaled-down library shelved in the basement.

9. Organisation for Economic Cooperation and Development, *Voluntary Aid for Development: The Role of Non-Governmental Organisations* (Paris: OECD, 1988). Brian H. Smith, *More Than Altruism: The Politics of Private Foreign Aid* (Princeton, N.J.: Princeton University Press, 1990). Thom Kerstiëns, *Are NGOs In? The role of the development non-governmental organizations in the Netherlands*, KDK-brochure 1 (1981).

10. Interview with Werner Lottje, Secretary for Human Rights, Diakonisches Werk der Evangelischen Kirche in Deutschland (EKD) Ecumenical Service, February 25, 1992 in Geneva. *World Development* 15, Supplement (1987) deals exclusively with NGOs providing economic assistance and their relations with government donors.

11. *Foreign Assistance Act of 1967*, Public Law 90–137 (81 stat. 445), part 1, chap. 2, sec. 207(a) and 208(c).

12. Ford significantly increased its support for human rights activities and subsidized many NGOs. Two former ICJ interns became major voices in the emerging movement—Michael Posner, the executive director of the New York Lawyer's Committee for Human Rights, and David Weissbrodt, legal counsel of Minnesota Lawyers International Human Rights Committee, AI Board member, textbook author, and trial observer.

13. Interview with Hakan Falk, SIDA legal officer, February 28, 1992. Other popular themes included environmental protection, population planning, and women's issues. Conservatives who won power as the Soviet empire collapsed sustained the human rights and democracy focus.

14. Interview with Theo van Benning, human rights coordinator, Netherlands Ministry of Foreign Affairs, February 28, 1992. Special project grants allocated 13 percent for vitally needed Secretariat overhead.

15. In 1989 the ICJ published 6,500 copies of the *Review* in English, 1,430 in French, and 1,800 in Spanish. For the *Newsletter* 1,650 copies were published in English.

16. Dutch economist Jan Tinbergen authored the report, *Reshaping the International Order (RIO): A Report to the Club of Rome* (New York: E. P. Dutton, 1976). The governments of Denmark, Norway, and Sweden and the European Economic Community also provided grants.

17. "Development and the Rule of Law: Prevention versus Cure as a Human Rights Strategy."

18. *The International Dimensions of the Right to Development as a Human Right in Relation with other Human Rights based on International Cooperation, including the Right to Peace, Taking into account the Requirements of the New International Economic Order and the fundamental human Needs.* U.N. Doc. E/CN.4/1334 (1979). See also *Popular Participation in Decision Making for Development* (UN Sales No. E.75.IV.10 1975).

19. ICJ, *Development, Human Rights and the Rule of Law: Report of a Confer-*

ence held in The Hague on April 27–May 1, 1981 (New York: Pergamon, 1981): 226.

20. ICJ, *Human Rights in a One-Party State* (London: Search Press, 1978), 129 pp. at 10.

21. ICJ, *Le Développement et les Droits de l'Homme: Rapport d'un colloque africain francophone, a Dakar, Numéro Spécial de la Revue Sénégalaise de Droit*, (1979) 255 pp. A mainstay of the secretarial and administrative staff, Bineta Diop of Senegal joined the Secretariat and assisted at the 1978 seminar.

22. ICJ, *Development and Legal Services in Africa: Report of 1983 Dakar Seminar with CODESRIA* (Geneva: ICJ). *Legal Services in Rural Africa: Report of a Seminar at Limuru*, October 1–4, 1984 (Geneva: ICJ, 1984), 84 pp. *Paralegals in Rural Africa: Seminars in the Gambia, Banjul, November 1989 and Harare, Zimbabwe, February 1990* (Geneva: 1991). As a result of his growing expertise, Dieng assisted the Ford Foundation as a development consultant.

23. Uganda's exiled former attorney-general, Godfrey Binaisa, and South African refugee Joel Carlson in the United States were awarded ICJ membership for past distinction.

24. Pauline Comeau, "Fallen Angels? They were once human rights activists. Now, no one is really sure," *Human Rights Tribune* 1 (Winter 1992): 4–5.

25. Interview with Gitobu Imanyara, Editor, *Nairobi Law Monthly*, April 14, 1992.

26. Interview with Githu Muigai, University of Nairobi Faculty of Law and secretary-general of the Kenya ICJ national section, November 26, 1992.

27. Gitobu Imanyara, Wachira Maina, and Chris Mburu, "Wako: Unravelling Muli's Tangled Web, Will He Make a Difference?" *Nairobi Law Monthly* 33 (June 1991): 19–22. In an October 1991 *Nairobi Law Monthly* editorial, Imanyara challenged Wako's attempt to amend the constitution as an attack on the electoral commission's independence. "The Electoral Commission and the Need to Respect the Constitution," *Nairobi Law Monthly* 37 (October 1991): 2.

28. Christopher Mulei, "Taking Human Rights Seriously: A Review of the Recent Naivasha ICJ Seminar," *Nairobi Law Monthly* 38 (November 1991): 31–42. Telephone interview with Charles Nyachae, President of the Kenyan ICJ national section, February 22, 1992. An earlier Kenyan section seminar is reported in "The ICJ Seminar at Nyeri: KANU as an Instrument for Promoting Democratic Process," *Nairobi Law Monthly* 12/13 (December 1988–January 1989): 26–53.

29. Article 10A. In addition to Boutros-Ghali, the provision resulted in suspended memberships for Ireland's president, Mary Robinson, and Kenya's attorney general, Amos Wako.

30. ICJ, *Human Rights in Islam: Report of a Seminar Held in Kuwait, December 1980* (Geneva: ICJ, 1982). 95 pp.

31. *ICJ Newsletter* no. 21 (April–June 1984): Appendix C, 43–55.

32. Interview with CIJL director Mona Rishmawi, February 26, 1992.

33. Ngo Ba Thanh, secretary of the Institute of Comparative Law, Saigon, was imprisoned twice, won election in 1974, and never became active. Former law professor Kinuko Kubota, elected in 1981, was one of two elderly jurists from Japan who died within years of joining the ICJ. The Dean of Kuwait's law school, Badria Al-Awadhi, also joined the Commission in 1981.

34. *International Human Rights Organizations: The Meaning of Their Work for Local Organizations*, Series of Program Evaluations DGIS/NOVIB #45 (The Hague: March 1992). Indonesians were unfamiliar with a book-length ICJ

study criticizing their government, perhaps because after refusing visas for a mission, officials successfully censored local reporting.

35. Stephen C. Neff, *Sri Lanka: The Activities of the Presidential Commission of Inquiry in Respect of NGOs. Report of a Mission, May–June 1991* (Geneva: ICJ, 1991), 71 pp.

36. ICJ, *Rural Development and Human Rights in South East Asia: Report of a Seminar in Penang, December 1981* (Penang, Malaysia: Consumers Association of Penang, 1982), 254 pp.

37. Indonesia, Thailand, Malaysia, Singapore, and the Philippines.

38. No. 25 (April–June 1985), Appendix A: 41–61.

39. *Rural Development and Human Rights in South Asia. Report of a Seminar in Lucknow, India, December 1982* (Lucknow: Human Rights Institute, 1984), 280 pp.

40. In a lengthy written response to criticism in the *Human Rights Tribune*, Nariman argued that all accused parties are entitled to representation and defended his conduct of the settlement proceedings.

41. ICJ, *Report of Seminars on Legal Services for the Rural Poor South-East Asia (Jakarta) 11–16 January 1987 and South-Asia (Rajpipla) 27–31 December 1987* (Geneva: ICJ, 1988), 98 pp. At another regional conference cosponsored with the Christian Conference of Asia, the ICJ called attention to the deteriorating human rights situation. ICJ, *The Erosion of the Rule of Law in Asia: Report of the Seminar held in Bangkok 18–22 December 1987* (Christian Conference of Asia).

42. Clarence J. Dias, "Rural Development and Human Rights in South Asia," in ICJ, *Rural Development and Human Rights in South Asia: Report of a Seminar in Lucknow, India, December 1982* (Lucknow: Human Rights Institute, 1984), 64.

43. *Asian Seminar on Paralegal Trainers*, Puncak, Indonesia, January 6–10, 1990 (Kalyanamitra: ICJ and Women's Communication and Information Centre, 1990), 30 pp.

44. ICJ, *Human Rights and Development: Report of a Seminar on Human Rights and Their Promotion in the Caribbean* (Bridgetown, Barbados: Cedar Press 1978), 190 pp. U.N. Division of Human Rights official B. G. Ramcharan recalls a particularly refreshing exchange of views in a pool with Grenada's Maurice Bishop.

45. ICJ, *Derechos Humanos en las Zonas Rurales, Bolivia, Colombia, Chile, Ecuador, Perú, Venezuela* (Bogotá: Ediciones Internacionales, 1979), 306 pp.

46. Bolivia, Chile, Colombia, Ecuador, Peru, and Venezuela. Alberto Donadio was secretary-general until August 1981. ICJ members Andrés Aguilar of Venezuela and Alfredo Etcheberry of Chile were among the founders. Colombia had been one of three Latin American governments to make small grants for the ICJ general budget.

47. Guyana and Jamaica made small annual grants to support the ICJ general budget.

48. *Conference of European National Sections. AIDS and Human Rights European Social Charter*, The Hague, Peace Palace September 20–22, 1989 (ICJ and NJCM-Boekerij), 14.

49. *ICJ Report on Activities, 1977–1980*, 31.

50. *Toward the Rule of Law: Soviet Legal Reform and Human Rights Under Perestroika* (New York: Helsinki Watch, 1989), 180 pp. *Glasnost in Jeopardy: Human Rights in the USSR* (New York: Helsinki Watch, 1991), 180 pp.

51. Brian H. Smith, *More Than Altruism* (Princeton: Princeton University Press, 1990).
52. "A Changing Asia: Economic Growth, Especially, Fosters Demands for Political Liberalization," *New York Times*, May 22, 1992, p. 2.
53. Personal interview in Geneva, February 27, 1992.

Chapter 8: Setting Standards and Procedures

1. "The Role of NGOs in International Human Rights Standard-Setting: Non-governmental Participation a Prerequisite of Democracy?" *Symposium Organized on the occasion of the award of the Praemium Erasmianum to the ICJ* (Leiden: Stichting NJCM-Boekerij, 1991), 53–69, at 66, 68.
2. A U.N. committee first studied abusive detention practices in the 1960s. *Study of the Right of Everyone to be Free from Arbitrary Arrest, Detention and Exile*, 17 U.N. ESCOR, U.N. Doc. E/CN.4/813 Corr. 1 (1961). U.N. publication, Sales No. 65.XIV.2.
3. Niall MacDermot, "Proposals by the International Commission of Jurists on the Protection of All Persons Subjected to Any Form of Detention or Imprisonment Against Torture and Other Cruel, Inhuman or Degrading Treatment or Punishment" (Geneva: April 1975, mimeographed).
4. Declaration on Protection from Torture, G.A. Res. 3452 (XXX), 1975.
5. *Draft Convention for the Prevention and Suppression of Torture*, 33 U.N. ESCOR U.N. Doc. E/CN.4/NGO/ 213 (1978); "U.N. Commission on Human Rights," *ICJ Review*, no. 20 (June 1978): 32–33.
6. Article 16. *ICJ Report on Activities 1977–1980* (Geneva), 58–59.
7. Article 19. "U.N. Commission on Human Rights," *ICJ Review*, no. 32 (June 1984): 33–34.
8. Articles 28 and 20. Convention Against Torture and Other Cruel, Inhuman or Degrading Treatment (1984).
9. The Torture Committee soon began reviewing conduct of states parties, but by 1991 only fifty-one governments were parties. To monitor all governments charged with torture, the ICJ supported a new commission rapporteur who made annual reports about states charged with abuse.
10. ICJ and the Swiss Committee Against Torture, *Torture: How to Make the International Convention Effective—A Draft Optional Protocol* (Geneva: ICJ, 1979). Jean-Jacques Gautier was SCAT President.
11. "European Draft Convention Against Torture," *ICJ Review*, no. 31 (December 1983): 50–55.
12. M. Berrier, rapporteur of the Legal Affairs Sub-Committee of the Council of Europe, "Protection against Torture and Other Ill Treatment," *ICJ Report on Activities*, 1981–1985 (Geneva: ICJ, 1985): 16.
13. The Swiss Committee Against Torture did not have consultative status.
14. "The Draft European Convention Against Torture," *ICJ Newsletter*, no. 31 (October–December 1986): 14; personal interview, December 17, 1987.
15. "European Convention against Torture," *ICJ Newsletter*, no. 33 (April–June 1987): 17.
16. A Montevideo seminar in April 1987 attended by forty-three experts, an October 1987 committee meeting of seven in São Paulo, a May 1988 session in Barbados, and a São Paulo committee meeting in October 1988. *ICJ Newsletter*, no. 33 (April–June 1987): 3; *ICJ Newsletter*, no. 35 (October–

December 1987): 13; *ICJ Newsletter*, no. 37 (April–June 1988): 6. Samuel Blixen, "Latin America: Human rights experts propose pact to eradicate torture," *Latin America Press*, May 14, 1987, pp. 6–7.

17. Secretary-General's Report to the ICJ Executive Committee (April 16–October 29, 1988): 2.

18. *Filartiga v. Pena-Irala*, 630 F. 2d 876 2d Cir. (1980); *Forti v. Suarez-Mason*, N.C-87-2058 DJL D.N. Cal. (1987).

19. *Forti v. Suarez-Mason*, 694 F. Supp. 707 N.D. Cal. (1988).

20. *Procedures for dealing with communications relating to violations of human rights and fundamental freedoms*, E.S.C. Res. 1503, 48 U.N. ESCOR Supp. (No. 1A) (1970).

21. Iain Guest, *Behind the Disappearances: Argentina's Dirty War Against Human Rights and the United Nations* (Philadelphia: University of Pennsylvania Press, 1990).

22. David Kramer and David Weissbrodt, "The 1980 U.N. Commission on Human Rights and the Disappeared," *Human Rights Quarterly* 3 (February 1981): 18–33.

23. Howard Tolley, *The U.N. Commission on Human Rights* (Boulder, Colo.: Westview Press, 1987), 104–111.

24. "NGO's Statement on Mr. van Boven's Departure," *ICJ Newsletter*, no. 12 (January 1–March 31, 1982): 25.

25. U.N. Doc. E/CN.4/1985/15, para. 302(c), E/CN.4/1988/19, para. 251(b). Reed Brody, "Commentary on the Draft U.N. 'Declaration on the Protection of All Persons from Enforced or Involuntary Disappearances'," *Netherlands Quarterly of Human Rights* 8, no. 4 (1990): 381–94, 381.

26. U.N. Doc E/CN.4/1992/19/Rev. 1, report of the Working Group on the Declaration on the protection of all persons from enforced disappearance. A preambular paragraph states "the systematic practice of such acts is of the nature of a crime against humanity, . . ."

27. Sub-Commission Intervention by Niall MacDermot, August 23, 1977, "Draft Body of Principles for the Protection of All Persons in Any Form of Detention or Imprisonment," statement submitted by twenty-seven NGOs, May 20, 1977, mimeographed.

28. Personal interview with Niall MacDermot, December 17, 1987.

29. Sub-Commission Decision 1987/108, U.N. Doc. E/1987/18 (1987): 138.

30. *The Review*, no. 42 (June 1989): 82–89.

31. Reed Brody, "The United Nations Creates a Working Group on Arbitrary Detention," *American Journal of International Law* 85 (October 1991): 709–15. "Commentaries: The UN Commission on Human Rights and the New Working Group on Arbitrary Detention," *The Review*, no. 46 (June 1991): 23–41.

32. Amnesty International, *1990 Report*, 298.

33. T. Kamminga, "The Thematic Procedures of the UN Commission on Human Rights," *Netherlands International Law Review* 34 (1987): 299.

34. CHR Res. 1991/42, UN Doc. E/CN.4/1991/22, 105.

35. Joe W. Pitts III and David Weissbrodt, "Major Developments at the UN Commission on Human Rights in 1992," *Human Rights Quarterly* 15 (February 1993): 122–196.

36. *States of Emergency* (Geneva: ICJ, 1983), 477 pp. CIJL Director Daniel O'Donnell edited the report, which included a survey of 158 governments.

37. UN Doc. E/CN.4/Sub.2/NGO/93 (August 26, 1981).

38. Nicole Questiaux, *Question of the Human Rights of Persons Subjected to any Form of Detention or Imprisonment*, study of the implications for human rights of recent developments concerning situations known as states of siege or emergency, 35 U.N. ESCOR, U.N. Doc. E/CN.4/Sub.2/1982/15 (1982). Questiaux was elected an ICJ member in 1987.

39. Personal interview with Professor Bert Lockwood, September 16, 1988.

40. Principle 10.

41. Toine van Dongen. The Netherlands representative to the Commission had the principles circulated as U.N. Doc. E/CN.4/1985/4 (1985).

42. Personal interview with Niall MacDermot, December 17, 1988.

43. "Symposium: Limitation and Derogation Provisions in the International Covenant on Civil and Political Rights," *Human Rights Quarterly* 7 (February 1985): 1–157.

44. "Symposium: The Implementation of the International Covenant on Economic, Social and Cultural Rights," *Human Rights Quarterly* (May 1987): 121–287.

45. "The Rights of Mental Patients," *ICJ Report on Activities, 1981–1985*, (Geneva: ICJ, 1985): 30–33.

46. Aleksander Yakovlev, director, Department of the Theory and Sociology of Criminal Law, Institute of State and Law, Academy of Sciences. *The Protection of Persons Suffering from Mental Disorder* (Siracusa, Italy: Association Internationale de Droit Pénal, 1981).

47. "Guidelines, Principles and Guarantees for the Protection of Persons Detained on Grounds of Mental Ill-health or Suffering from Mental Disorder."

48. CHR Res. 1991/46. U.N. Doc. E/CN.4/1991/39.

49. Niall MacDermot, "The Role of NGO's in the Promotion and Protection of Human Rights," *Symposium Organized on the occasion of the award of the Praemium Erasmianum to the ICJ* (Leiden: Stichting NJCM-Boekerij, 1989), 45–52, at 49.

50. Etsuro Totsuka, "The Changing Face of Mental Health Legislation in Japan," *The Review*, no. 42 (June 1989): 67–81, at 69 and 94.

51. "The Mentally Ill in Japan," *The Review*, no. 32 (June 1984): 15–18.

52. T. W. Harding, head of the Division of Legal Psychiatry at the University Institute of Legal Medecine, Geneva, a former WHO official. The Honourable J. Schnedier, presiding judge, County Division Circuit Court of Cook County; Dr. Harold M. Visotsky, professor and chairman, Department of Psychiatry and Behavioral Sciences, Northwestern University Medical School. Dr. Charles L. Graves, executive secretary of the ICHP, was secretary of the mission.

53. ICJ, *Human Rights and Mental Patients in Japan* (Geneva: ICJ, 1984), 94 pp.

54. "International Commission of Jurists' Mission to Japan, April 1988; Preliminary Report and Recommendations," *ICJ Newsletter*, no. 37 (April–June 1988): 28–44.

55. *Report on the African Conference on the Rule of Law* (Geneva: ICJ, 1961).

56. *Seminar on the Establishment of Regional Commissions on Human Rights with Special Reference to Africa*, Cairo, UAR U.N. Doc. ST/TAO/HR/38 (1969).

57. *ICJ Report on Activities, 1977–1980* (Geneva: ICJ, 1981), 5.

58. *ICJ News*, no. 1 (April 1–June 30 1979): 1. The Secretary-General's Quarterly Report, no. 30 (January 1–March 31, 1979): 8.

59. Kéba Mbaye, "Introduction to the African Charter on Human and

Peoples' Rights," *Human and Peoples' Rights in Africa and the African Charter* (Geneva: ICJ, 1986), 19.

60. Warren Weinstein, "Human Rights in Africa: A Long-Awaited Voice," *Current History* 78 (March 1980): 97.

61. Edward Kannyo, "The Banjul Charter on Human and People's Rights: Genesis and Political Background," in *Human Rights and Development in Africa*, ed. Claude E. Welch, Jr., and Ronald I. Meltzer (Albany, N.Y.: State University Press of New York, 1984), 128–51. A U.N. seminar then met in Monrovia and made specific recommendations for the African regional convention. The ICJ arranged for three African jurists to attend, and all three served on the working group that drafted proposals endorsed at the seminar. ICJ Executive Committee Minutes, October 6, 1979.

62. "African Charter on Human and Peoples' Rights," adopted June 27, 1981, OAU Doc. CAB/LEG/67/3/Rev.5, *Int'l Legal Materials* 21 (1982), 58.

63. Harry M. Scoble, "Human Rights Non-Governmental Organizations in Black Africa: Their Problems and Prospects in the Wake of the Banjul Charter," in *Human Rights and Development in Africa*, ed. Welch and Meltzer, 177–203, at 195.

64. Richard Gittleman, "The Banjul Charter on Human and Peoples' Rights: A Legal Analysis," in *Human Rights and Development in Africa*, ed. Welch and Meltzer, 152–76, at 159.

65. Adama Dieng, "Nairobi Follow-Up: Note for the Executive Committee" (1986, mimeographed).

66. "ICJ Colloquium," *ICJ Newsletter*, no. 33 (April–June 1987): 1; app. A, 25.

67. Personal interview with Adama Dieng, Geneva, December 21, 1987.

68. "Rules of Procedure of the African Commission for Human and Peoples Rights," *ICJ Review*, no. 40 (June 1988): 26.

69. Interview with Adama Dieng, Geneva, December 21, 1987.

70. Letter from Niall MacDermot, September 27, 1988, p. 5. ICJ Executive Committee Minutes, 18 April 1988.

71. Claude E. Welch, Jr., "The African Commission on Human and Peoples' Rights: A Five-Year Report and Assessment," *Human Rights Quarterly* 14 (February 1992): 43–61, at 56.

72. U.S. Congress, House of Representatives, Committee on Foreign Affairs, Subcommittee on International Organizations and Movements, "International Protection of Human Rights: The Work of International Organizations and the Role of U.S. Foreign Policy," *Hearings*, 93rd Cong., 1st sess., August 1, 1973, 29 pp. MacDermot testified and answered questions for more than two hours. When asked about ICJ funding, he reported the severe cutback in U.S. foundation support without mentioning the CIA exposé.

73. AAICJ, *Human Rights and Foreign Policy: The Role of Government*, A Report of Two Colloquia Convened by the AAICJ (New York: AAICJ, 1985), 39 pp. *Human Rights and Foreign Policy: The Role of Government 1985 & 1986* (New York: AAICJ, 1987), 55 pp.

74. Representatives from Czechoslovakia, Hungary, and Poland attended the October 1992 meeting in Stockholm.

75. AAICJ, JUSTICE, British Institute of Human Rights, and Parliamentary Human Rights Group, *Human Rights in United States and United Kingdom Foreign Policy*, Palace of Westminster, November 27–28, 1978 (New York: AAICJ, 1979), 66 pp., ix.

76. Personal interview with Toine van Dongen, former human rights coordinator at the Dutch Ministry of Foreign Affairs, December 15, 1987.

77. Interview with Theo van Benning, human rights coordinator at the Dutch Ministry of Foreign Affairs, February 28, 1992.

78. For works describing other organizations, see Harry M. Scoble and Laurie S. Wiseberg, "Human Rights and Amnesty International," *The Annals of the American Academy of Political and Social Science* (May 1974): 11–26. Virginia Leary, "A New Role for Nongovernmental Organizations in Human Rights," in *UN Law/Fundamental Rights*, ed. Antonio Cassese (Netherlands: Sijthoff & Noordhoff 1979), 197; David Weissbrodt, "The Influence of Interest Groups on the Development of United States Human Rights Policies," in *The Dynamics of Human Rights in U.S. Foreign Policy*, ed. Natalie Hevener (New Brunswick: Transaction, 1981), 229.

79. ICJ, *Human Rights and Mental Patients in Japan, Report of a Mission on behalf of the International Commission of Jurists and the International Commission of Health Professionals* (Geneva: ICJ, 1986).

80. Jeffrey M. Berry, "Subgovernments, Issue Networks, and Political Conflict," in *Remaking American Politics*, ed. Richard A. Harris and Sidney M. Milkis (Boulder, Colo.: Westview, 1989), 239–60. See also Hugh Heclo, "The Emerging Regime," 289–320. Robert Salisbury et al., "Triangles, Networks, and Hollow Cores: The Complex Geometry of Washington Interest Representation," in *The Politics of Interests: Interest Groups Transformed*, ed. Mark P. Petraca (Boulder: Westview, 1992), 130–49.

81. Theo van Boven. His deputy, B. G. Ramcharan, was also elected to the ICJ, as was Sub-Commission expert Nicole Questiaux.

82. The U.N. Secretary-General disregarded MacDermot's appeal that the experts meet on schedule. *ICJ Newsletter*, no. 30 (July–September 1986): 1. The Geneva meeting was attended by fifteen of the twenty-six Sub-Commission members, three former U.N. Commission presidents, the past and present directors of the U.N. Secretariat's human rights office, and fifty-two NGOs.

83. "Recommendations and Conclusions of the NGO Seminar on Human Rights in the United Nations," *ICJ Newsletter*, no. 30 (July–September 1986): 25–31. "Human Rights and the United Nations," *ICJ Review*, no. 37 (December 1986): 31. The Sub-Commission survived the budget crisis and resumed regularly scheduled meetings in 1987.

84. "Consultation on the Enhancement of the UN Sub-Commission on Human Rights," *ICJ Newsletter*, no. 47 (October–December 1990): 25.

85. Jack Donnelly, "International Human Rights: A Regime Analysis," *International Organization* 40, no. 3 (Summer 1986): 599–642.

86. Stephen D. Krasner, "Structural Causes and Regime Consequences: Regimes as Intervening Variables," in *International Regimes*, ed. Stephen Krasner (Ithaca, N.Y.: Cornell University Press, 1983): 2.

87. AI's 1992 report found torture in one hundred countries.

Chapter 9: Enforcing Civil Liberties

1. *Report on the Activities of the International Commission of Jurists 1971–1977*, Appendix III, 25. *ICJ Report on Activities, 1977–1980*, 50.

2. Intervention of October 20, 1976 urging that Juan María Bandrés and Miguel de Castells either be brought to trial or released at an early date. Secretary-General's Report, October 1–December 31, 1976.

3. Letter of September 20, 1976 to Niall MacDermot concerning Rodrigo Egana. In the 1980s NOVIB began regular funding for ICJ special projects.

4. "Current Activities of the ICJ" (Speech by Niall MacDermot to the International Law Section of the ABA, August 5, 1973).

5. Barend van Niekerk, "Report on a Visit to Mozambique" (Geneva: ICJ, 1973), 5 pp.

6. Heleno Claudio Fragoso and Alejandro Artucio, *Human Rights in Nicaragua Yesterday and Today*, Report of a Mission (Geneva: ICJ, 1981), 85 pp.

7. Memorandum, William J. Butler, Esq., to Niall MacDermot on ICJ Mission to Nicaragua February 28–March 4, 1981, The Release of José Esteban González, March 15, 1981. See also *ICJ Newsletter*, no. 8 (January–March 1981).

8. Cees Flinterman, *Human Rights in Ghana*, Report of a Mission for the International Commission of Jurists and Netherlands Committee for Human Rights (Utrecht, Netherlands: SIM, 1984), 47 pp. The account of MacDermot's preliminary intervention in Geneva comes from notes by Fred Woodbridge of his observations and interviews, July 27–28, 1983.

9. Interview with Werner Lottje, EKG "Bread for the World," February 25, 1992, Geneva. In the 1990s the German church foundation began to provide regular funding for ICJ special projects.

10. *Report on the Activities of the International Commission of Jurists, 1971–1977*, 9.

11. *ICJ Newsletter*, no. 22 (July 1984): 9.

12. Hans Thoolen and Berth Verstappen, *Human Rights Missions: A Study of the Fact-finding Practice of Non-governmental Organizations* (Boston: Martinus Nijhoff, 1986), 127.

13. *The Events in East Pakistan, 1971, A Legal Study by the Secretariat of the ICJ* (Geneva: ICJ, 1972), 98 pp. In addition, MacDermot published "Crimes Against Humanity in Bangladesh," *The International Lawyer* 7 (April 1973): 476–84.

14. Morris B. Abram, William J. Butler, John P. Humphrey, "Report of an International Commission of Inquiry into the Detention of: Constantine Alavanos, Antonios Vgonzas, Panayiotis Kanelakis, Nikos Karamanlis, Dimitrios Pappas, Dionysios Bouloukos," *IDOC-North America* 54 (Summer 1973): 21–29. The ICJ cosponsored the commission with the International League for the Rights of Man, the International Law Section of the ABA, and the New York City Bar Association.

15. Thomas M. Franck and H. Scott Fairley, "Procedural Due Process in Human Rights Fact Finding by International Agencies," *American Journal of International Law* 74 (1980): 308–45. David Weissbrodt and James McCarthy, "Fact-Finding by Nongovernmental Organizations," in *International Law and Fact-finding in the Field of Human Rights*, ed. B. Ramcharan (London: Martinus Nijhoff, 1982): 186–230. Hurst Hannum, "Fact-Finding by Nongovernmental Human Rights Organizations," in *Fact Finding Before International Tribunals*, ed. Richard Lillich (Ardsley-on-Hudson, N.Y.: Transnational Publishers, 1991), 293–304. Alex P. Schmid and Albert Jongman, eds., *Monitoring Human Rights Violations* (Netherlands: PIOOM and Center for the Study of Social

Conflicts COMT, 1992). Haim H. Cohn, "International Fact-finding Processes and the Rule of Law," *The Review*, no. 18 (June 1977): 40–48, recommends methods so that states charged are assured due process.

16. At the 1979 International Day of Solidarity with the Palestine People, MacDermot said he was unmoved by the description of those who fought for their liberation as terrorists. The U.S. delegate to the Human Rights Commission objected. *ICJ Newsletter*, no. 4 (January–March, 1980): 30.

17. Reed Brody, *Contra Terror in Nicaragua: Report of a Fact-finding Mission* (Boston: South End Press, 1985).

18. President Jayewardene invited Paul Sieghart, chairman of the Executive Committee of "Justice" and alternate to the ICJ Executive Committee. *Sri Lanka: A Mounting Tragedy of Errors* (London: Justice, 1984). Law professor Virginia Leary of the State University of New York at Buffalo conducted the first mission, as reported in *Ethnic Conflict and Violence in Sri Lanka* with a supplement by the ICJ staff for 1981–1983 (Geneva: ICJ, 1983).

19. Excluding missions to South Africa and Israel, where government officials are of European descent. The most frequently used legal officers were Artucio (Uruguay) in Nicaragua and Equatorial Guinea, Ravindran (India) in the Philippines, and Dieng (Senegal) in Mauritania. ICJ members Yap and Diego Garcia Sayan also participated in missions.

20. February 2, 1972. *The Review*, no. 9 (December 1972): 11–13 also carried an article on preventive detention.

21. André Tremblay, *Morocco: Trial in Rabat arising out of disturbances on 20 and 21 June 1981* (Geneva: ICJ, 1981), 25 pp.

22. (London: Francis Pinter, 1987).

23. *Torture and Intimidation in the West Bank*, a report by the staff of Law in the Service of Man (Geneva: ICJ, 1984), 56 pp.

24. *Final Report of Mission to Chile, April 1974, to Study the Legal System and the Protection of Human Rights* (Geneva: ICJ, 1974), 39 pp., mimeographed.

25. Seymour M. Hersh, "Chile Said to Plan Camps for Children of Allende Backers," *New York Times*, November 20, 1974, p. 7, col. 1. MacDermot appeared before a joint hearing of the House Foreign Affairs Subcommittee on Inter-American Affairs and the Subcommittee on International Organizations and Movements.

26. "Statement: General Council of the Chilean Bar Association," *New York Times*, November 17, 1974, p. IV-9, col. 1. "Letter Sent by the Federation of Students of the Catholic University of Chile to Mr. Niall MacDermot," *New York Times*, December 8, 1974, p. IV-7, col. 1. "The Truth About the International Commission of Jurists and Its Attack on Chile," *Washington Post*, November 8, 1974.

27. Robert Alexander, *Tragedy of Chile* (Westport, Conn.: Greenwood Press, 1978), 373–74. Alexander mistakenly reports MacDermot as alleging that 600,000 had been sent away; he found no camps in personal visits.

28. "More on Chilean Terror," *New York Times*, May 31, 1975, p. 26, col. 1.

29. Iain Guest, *Behind the Disappearances: Argentina's Dirty War Against Human Rights and the United Nations* (Philadelphia: University of Pennsylvania Press, 1990), 221.

30. Ibid., 220–23.

31. Sebastian Soler of Argentina was outraged by a press agency report of an article in *The Review*, no. 8 (June 1972). A day after publication of Mac-

Dermot's 1974 mission to Uruguay, the military arrested Dr. Ramon Real, who was in custody for a month.

32. Charles Naas, "Further Comments on Iran," in *The Diplomacy of Human Rights*, ed. David D. Newsom (New York: University Press of America, 1986), 82–83.

33. "Human Rights in Iran," hearing before the Subcommittee on International Organizations of the Committee on International Relations, House of Representatives, 95th Cong. 1st sess. October 26, 1977.

34. Personal copy of Sullivan letter of December 11, 1977 to William J. Butler quoted in James A. Bill, *The Eagle and the Lion: The Tragedy of American-Iranian Relations* (New Haven: Yale University Press, 1988), 248.

35. Stephen Oxman, as reported in a telephone interview with William J. Butler, July 27, 1992. On a mission to investigate martial law in the Philippines, Butler met President Ferdinand Marcos; he also testified before Congress on South Korea.

36. *Uganda and Human Rights: Reports of the International Commission of Jurists to the United Nations* (Geneva: ICJ, 1977), 167 pp.

37. William J. Butler and George Obiozor, "The Burundi Affair 1972," *IDOC-North America*, no. 52 (April 1973): 23–27.

38. John Salzberg, "UN Prevention of Human Rights Violations: The Bangladesh Case," *International Organization* 27 (1973): 115–27.

39. "The Rule of Law in Turkey and the European Convention on Human Rights," *The Review*, no. 10 (June 1973): 37–56. The study was translated and published in Turkey with a section on the Kurdish minority deleted out of concern for prosecution of "separatist propaganda." German Professor Ernst Hirsch published a critique of the ICJ study, which occasioned a reply in *The Review*, no. 12 (June 1974): 27–29.

40. Craig Williamson, International University Exchange Fund, funded by Swedish Social Democrats. Guest, *Disappearances*, 114, 481–82 n. 7. The IUEF attacked Argentina and funded an ICJ mission to Equatorial Guinea.

41. *Gross Violations of Human Rights, A Practical Guide for Non-Governmental Organizations Wishing to File Communications with the United Nations* (Geneva: ICJ, 1973). 27 pp.

42. ICJ, *Uganda and Human Rights*.

43. Guest, *Disappearances*, 140–44.

44. Ibid., 113.

45. Chiang Pei-heng, *Non-Governmental Oranizations at the United Nations* (New York: Praeger, 1981), 195, reports that he was a "minister of the Argentine government." Guest, *Disappearances*, 114.

46. In a four-page letter to William Butler on March 8, 1982, Niall MacDermot summarized the confrontation.

47. In 1984 small NGOs based outside Geneva founded International Service for Human Rights to facilitate U.N. contacts. There has been little coordination as more and more NGOs sponsor emotional witnesses at the U.N. Human Rights Commission. An appreciative press plays up the contrast between colorfully dressed indigenous peoples and suited diplomats.

48. Sub-Commission Resolution 1989/5. "Commentary: UN Sub-Commission on Discrimination and Minorities," *The Review*, no. 43 (December 1989): 19–20.

49. "Commentary: UN Commission on Human Rights," *The Review*, no. 44 (June 1990): 20.

50. Reed Brody, Penny Parker, and David Weissbrodt, "Major Developments in 1990 at the UN Commission on Human Rights," *Human Rights Quarterly* 12 (November 1990): 559–88.

51. K. J. Holsti, *International Politics: A Framework for Analysis*, 6th ed. (Englewood Cliffs, N.J.: Prentice Hall, 1992): 327.

52. *ICJ Newsletter*, no. 8 (January–March 1981): 39–42, at 40.

Chapter 10: Representing the Bench and Bar

1. Reed Brody, ed., *Attacks on Justice: The Harassment and Persecution of Judges and Lawyers, July 1989–June 1990* (Geneva: ICJ, 1990), 5.

2. Rodolfo Schurmann Pacheco, José Fraga, Hugo Fabbri, Emilio Biasco, *ICJ Report on Activities, 1977–1980* (Geneva: ICJ, 1980), 44. Letter of April 13, 1978 to Adrian W. DeWind, president, Association of the Bar of the City of New York. Pezzullo's cable to the U.S. State Department also praised the mission highly.

3. *1991 Annual Report, Lawyers Committee for Human Rights*. Most contacts are in the United States, but mailings are sent to members in more than ninety countries.

4. María del Huerto Amarillo and Fernando Urioste, *Uruguay: Independencia del Poder Judicial y de los Jueces* (*Uruguay: The Independence of the Judiciary and of Judges*) (Uruguay: ICJ, 1990), 220 pp.

5. *Violencia en Colombia* (Lima Peru: ICJ/Andean Commission of Jurists, 1990), 130 pp. Reed Brody, *"Ou est l'honneur"—le proces de Maître Nicolas Tiangaye* (report of a 1990 trial in the Central African Republic) (Geneva: ICJ, 1990), 38 pp. *L'indépendence des magistrats, des avocats et des officiers ministériels en République de Guinée* (Geneva: ICJ, 1988), 31 pp. Alejandro Artucio, *El Salvador: Un Brecha a la Impunidad* (Geneva: ICJ, 1991), trans. as *A Breach of Impunity: The Trial for the Murder of Jesuits in El Salvador* (New York: Fordham University Press, 1992).

6. Adrian W. Dewind and John Woodhouse, *Persecution of Defence Lawyers in South Korea* (Geneva: ICJ, 1979), 68 pp.

7. Stephen Oxman, Otto Triffterer, and Francisco B. Cruz, *South Korea: Human Rights in the Emerging Politics* (Geneva: ICJ, 1987), 95 pp.

8. "Report of a Mission to Egypt," *CIJL Bulletin* 11 (April 1983): 37–48.

9. Justice Michael Kirby, "Malaysia—The Judiciary and the Rule of Law," *ICJ Review*, no. 41 (December 1988): 40–43.

10. Judge Adib Halasa, John D. Cooke, and Ustinia Dolgopol, *The Return to Democracy in Sudan* (Geneva: ICJ, 1986), 99 pp.

11. "The Exceptional Tribunals in Syria: A Threat to Judicial Independence," *CIJL Yearbook: Constitutional Guarantees for the Independence of the Judiciary* (Geneva: CIJL, 1992), 115–25, at 121.

12. Ibid.

13. Daniel O'Donnell, "Mission Report—Judicial Independence in Paraguay," *CIJL Bulletin*, no. 14 (October 1984): 14–40.

14. Jaime Oraá, *Human Rights in States of Emergency in International Law* (New York: Oxford University Press, 1992).

15. Letter from Niall MacDermot, September 27, 1988.

16. Ustinia Dolgopol, "The Centre for the Independence of Judges and

Lawyers, Its Work and Its Aspirations," *CIJL Bulletin* 19 and 20 (April–October 1987): 33, 36–38. The 1981 Siracusa Draft Principles on the Independence of the Judiciary and the 1982 Noto Draft Principles on the Independence of the Legal Profession are reprinted in *CIJL Bulletin*, nos. 25–26 (April–October 1990): 59–83.

17. *CIJL Bulletin*, no. 12 (October 1983): 13, 27–56.

18. *Final Report of the Special Rapporteur on the Independence and Impartiality of the Judiciary, Jurors and Assessors and the Independence of Lawyers*, U.N. Doc. E/CN.4/Sub.2/1985/18 and Add. 1–6, (1985).

19. Jules Deschênes identifies twenty-five provisions in the declaration that are not found in the Basic Principles. "The International Protection of the Independence of the Judiciary," *CIJL Bulletin*, no. 23 (April 1989): 28–38, 37.

20. Dolgopol, p. 36. "The Milan Principles," *ICJ Review*, no. 37 (Dec. 1986): 62–64. U.N. Doc. A/Res/40/32, November 29, 1985 and A/Res/40/146, December 13, 1985.

21. Sub-Commission rapporteur Louis Joinet, U.N. Doc. E/CN.4/Sub.2/1990/35, para. 15.

22. "Council of Europe—Human Rights Steering Committee," *ICJ Newsletter*, no. 33 (January–March 1987): 18.

23. "Guidelines for the Implementation of the Basic Principles on the Independence of the Judiciary," *ICJ Newsletter*, no. 35 (October–December 1987): 22.

24. Jules Deschênes, "Judicial Independence: An International Perspective," in *The Independence of Judges and Lawyers in Pakistan* (Geneva: ICJ, 1990), 9–24.

25. John Tessitore and Susan Woolfson, eds., *A Global Agenda: Issues Before the 46th General Assembly of the United Nations* (New York: University Press of America, 1991), 213–17, do not even mention the Basic Principles on the Role of Lawyers in their account of the congress.

26. A/Res/45/121.

27. Special Issue, The Independence of Judges and Lawyers: A Compilation of International Standards, *CIJL Bulletin*, nos. 25–26 (April–October 1990).

28. *CIJL Yearbook: Constitutional Guarantees for the Independence of the Judiciary* (Geneva: CIJL, 1992).

29. CIJL and Nepal Law Society, *The Independence of Judges and Lawyers in South Asia, Report of a Seminar held in Kathmandu from September 1–5, 1987* (Geneva: ICJ, 1987), 84 pp. *The Independence of the Judiciary and the Legal Profession in English-Speaking Africa, Report of Seminars held in Lusaka from November 10 to 14, 1986 and in Banjul from April 6 to 10, 1987* (Geneva: CIJL and African Bar Association, 1987), 194 pp. *The Independence of Judges and Lawyers in the Commonwealth Caribbean, Report of a Seminar held in Tobago from September 12 to 13, 1988* (Geneva: CIJL and the UWI/USAID Caribbean Justice Improvement Project, 1989), 66 pp.

30. *The Independence of the Judiciary in India, Report of a Seminar held in New Delhi on January 20–21, 1990*, ed. Reed Brody (Geneva: CIJL and U.N. Centre for Human Rights, 1990), 61 pp. Reports of seminars in Paraguay, Nicaragua, and Peru were published in Spanish.

31. *The Independence of Judges and Lawyers in Pakistan, Report of a Seminar*

held in Lahore, November 9–10, 1989 (Geneva: ICJ, 1990), 148 pp. *Pakistan: Human Rights After Martial Law, Report of an ICJ Mission to Pakistan in December 1986 by Judge G. Petrén, Mrs. Helen Cull, Jeremy McBride and D. Ravindran.* (Geneva: ICJ, 1987), 156 pp.

32. *Peru: La Indepedencia del Poder Judicial* (Geneva: ICJ, 1989), 97 pp.

33. "Brody New Law Group Director," *The Law Group Docket* 7 (Spring 1992): 18.

34. "Mongolia Drafts New Constitution," *ICJ Newsletter*, no. 48 (January 1992): 5. The constitution is called a State *Yassa* in remembrance of the first collection of Mongolian laws promulgated by Genghis Khan.

35. Christopehr Mulei, "Taking Human Rights Seriously—A Review of the Recent Naivasha ICJ Seminar," *Nairobi Law Monthly* 38 (November 1991): 31–42.

36. J. Thiem-Hien Yap of Indonesia, Mrs. Tai Young Lee of South Korea. Dr. J. B. Danquah, chairman of Ghana's national section, was detained without trial for thirteen months before his death in prison. Commission member U Chan Htoon of Burma's Supreme Court was also detained.

Chapter 11: Turning Forty

1. Report of the Secretary-General to the ICJ Triennial Meeting, January 1992, *ICJ Newsletter*, no. 49 (April 1992): 1.

2. *Yearbook of International Organizations*, 16th ed., vol. 1, 1989/90.

3. Interview with Adama Dieng, June 29, 1993, in Geneva.

4. For 1992 SIDA grants were calculated at 36 percent of the proposed general budget, $126,000 for half the publications budget and $364,000 toward strategies for the future. Exchange rates were calculated at $1.45 per Swiss franc.

5. *International Human Rights Organizations: The Meaning of Their Work for Local Organizations*, Series of Program Evaluations DGIS/NOVIB #45 (The Hague, March 1992), 148 pp. Pietje Vervest, Program Evaluation for NOVIB. Interview with Theo van Benning, deputy human rights coordinator, Netherlands Ministry of Foreign Affairs, February 28, 1992.

6. Interview with SIDA legal officer Hakan Falk, February 28, 1992, in Geneva.

7. *New York Times*, February 17, 1992, p. C-1. "The first models of the JAS-39 Gripen . . . a lightweight single-engine economy fighter aircraft that Sweden hopes will become one of its hot new exports. . . . [T]he Swedish government and some of the nation's biggest industries . . . are aggressively looking for markets for other high-technology projects, from radar and torpedoes to submarines."

8. Interview with SIDA officer Hakan Falk, February 28, 1992, in Geneva.

9. 26 Chemin de Joinville, Cointrin.

10. At the time this manuscript was completed in August 1993, Briton Trevor Davies had joined the staff as executive officer for finance and administration and American Peter Wilborn joined as CIJL assistant. The Secretariat had also added a librarian and a press officer.

11. The search for a new member from the United States was still underway in February, 1994.

12. Dalmo de Abreu Dallari, Brazil; Desmond Fernando, Sri Lanka; Asma Khader, Jordan (the only woman); Kofi Kumado, Ghana; Fali S. Nariman, India; Christian Tomuschat, Germany.

13. Amendment to Article 9. Kirby had earlier favored revoking membership for members who missed meetings or otherwise failed expectations. Shortening the initial term from ten to five years enabled the committee to remove with less affront by blocking nomination for reelection.

14. President Joaquín Ruiz-Giménez concluded his remarks in Spanish and offered to host the next meeting. Enoch Dumbutshena, Zimbabwe; Lennart Groll, Sweden; Tai-Young Lee, Korea; Claire L'Heureux-Dube, Canada.

15. German member Christian Tomuschat requested that the 1952 kidnapping case of Walter Linse be reopened. *ICJ Newsletter*, no. 49 (April 1992): 6. Communists siezed attorney Linse in West Berlin. His disappearance in the Eastern Zone enraged jurists attending the Congress that founded the ICJ. They did not appreciate that Linse worked for ICJ founder Theo Friedenau, whose Nazi background and alleged sabotage campaign in East Berlin was never investigated or disclosed by the first Executive Committee.

16. *International Human Rights Organizations: The Meaning of Their Work for Local Organizations*, Series of Program Evaluations DGIS/NOVIB #45 (The Hague, March 1992), 148 pp. The evaluation team visited the Philippines, Indonesia, and Sri Lanka.

17. *ICJ Newsletter*, no. 51 (October 1992): 3.

18. The Hague, 1981; Nairobi, 1985; Caracas, 1989.

19. After losing power to the military, Aristide was unable to attend.

20. Yash Tandon, "Foreign NGOs, Uses and Abuses: An African Perspective," *IFDA Dossier* 81 (April–June 1991): 67–78.

21. Triennial meeting of the Members, National Sections, and Affiliates, Geneva, Switzerland, January 21, 1992. Opening Speech by Secretary-General Adama Dieng, p. 4.

22. Michael Kirby, "Human Rights: Agenda for the Future," *ICJ Review*, no. 49 (December 1992).

23. Request for Funding and Description of Programmes for Human Rights and Development of the International Commission of Jurists, July 1, 1992–June 30, 1994 (Geneva: ICJ, June 1992).

24. A regional seminar in Egypt and national seminars in Morocco and Yemen. Philip Amoah directed a Nairobi paralegal training seminar for Eastern Africa in May 1992 and a July 1993 seminar for rural women from Francophone Africa in Burkina Faso.

25. Report of ICJ's National Seminar on Paralegal Training for Women's Organizations, Bombay, September, 24–26, 1991.

26. "ICJ Seminar on the Rights of the Child, Sicily," *ICJ Newsletter*, no. 46 (July–September 1990): 21–22. In 1992 the same group cosponsored an African seminar on juveniles in conflict with the law.

27. ICJ Request for Funding and Description of Programs, 1 July 1991–30 June 1992, p. 24. NOVIB funded the January 14–February 2, 1992 mission done in cooperation with its Malaysian partner organization, SAM. As with other long-delayed reports, the ICJ had not produced an account of the mission more than a year after its completion.

28. *Guatemala taller de capacitación par miembros de grupos y comunidades indígenas*, Ciudad de Guatemala, 31 de marzo–3 de abril 1992 (Geneva: ICJ, 1992).

29. *Towards Universal Justice: International Penal Court. U.N. Human Rights Mechanisms* (Geneva: ICJ, June 1993), 88 pp.

30. Established in the mid-1980s, the International Service took on some of the responsibility MacDermot had assumed to inform groups outside Geneva about U.N. activities and procedures. Its *Human Rights Monitor*, no. 21 (May 1993), is a special issue on the World Conference that reprints articles from prior issues on preparatory meetings.

31. *Human Rights Tribune* 2, no. 1 (June 1993): 9, 10.

32. Inter Press Service (IPS), with technical cooperation from Der Standard, Vienna, produced the independent daily of the World Conference on Human Rights. *Terra Viva*, no. 10 (22 June 1993): 10.

33. U.N. Doc. E/1993/100, p. 18.

34. U.N. Doc. A/CONF.157/DC1 25 June 1993.

35. An ABA blue ribbon panel lobbying for the proposal has had far more influence on the U.S. Department of State than the ICJ campaign. Interview with Kenneth Blackwell, former U.S. ambassador to the U.N. Commission on Human Rights, July 8, 1993 in Cincinnati.

36. Claude E. Welch, Jr., "The African Commission on Human and Peoples' Rights: A Five-Year Report and Assessment," *Human Rights Quarterly* 14, no. 1 (February 1992): 43–61.

37. Harry M. Scoble, "Human Rights Non-Governmental Organizations in Black Africa: Their Problems and Prospects in the Wake of the Banjul Charter," in *Human Rights and Development in Africa*, ed. Claude E. Welch, Jr., and Ronald I. Meltzer (Albany: State University of New York Press, 1984), 177–203.

38. ICJ Workshop on NGO Participation in the Work of the African Commission on Human and Peoples' Rights, Banjul, the Gambia, October 5–7, 1991; Tunis, Tunisia, February 29–March 1, 1992; Banjul, the Gambia, October 9–11, 1992; Banjul, the Gambia, March 26–28, 1993.

39. *How to Address a Communication to the African Commission on Human and Peoples' Rights* (Geneva: ICJ, 1992), 32 pp. Engl., Fr.

40. "Conclusions and Recommendations of the 4th NGO Workshop," Banjul, March 26–28, 1993. ICJ Press Release, June 11, 1993.

41. Brainstorming Session on the African Charter of Human and Peoples' Rights, Dakar, Senegal, January 13–15, 1993, Background Paper by the ICJ, p. 24. In Europe, the ICJ supported proposals to consolidate the regional Commission and Court of Human Rights in a single tribunal.

42. Brainstorming Session on the African Charter of Human and Peoples' Rights, Dakar, Senegal, January 13–15, 1993, Summary Report, p. 3.

43. Training Course for Judges, Prosecutors and Lawyers on the Domestic Application of International Law in Montevideo, March 22–26, 1993, jointly organized with the Uruguayan Bar Association, and March 29–April 2 in Buenos Aires, Argentina, with CELS.

44. The ICJ retained more than sixty observers paid with a $1.2-million grant from the EEC for voting in August 1992, November 1992, and February 1993. "Madagascar turns out for historic referendum," *ICJ Newsletter*, no. 51 (October 1992): 1.

45. Interview with CIJL Director Mona Rishmawi, June 29, 1993.

46. Stephen C. Neff, *Sri Lanka: The Activities of the Presidential Commission of Inquiry in Respect of NGOs, Report of a Mission May–June 1991* (Geneva: ICJ, 1991), 71 pp. The government objected to ICJ intervention in a matter under

investigation and refused a request to discuss Neff's findings before publication. Anthony Heaton-Armstrong, *Magisterial Inquiry into the Homicide of Richard de Zoysa* (Geneva: ICJ, 1990), 26 pp. Two British lawyers made a follow-up mission in May 1993.

47. *Agenda for Peace: An Independent Survey of the Violence in South Africa* (Geneva: ICJ, 1992), 30 pp., reports on a mission of March 16–29, 1992. *Signposts to Peace: An Independent Survey of the Violence in Natal, South Africa* (Geneva: ICJ, 1990), 36 pp. Geoffrey Bindman, *Will Namibia's Election be Free and Fair?* (Geneva: ICJ, 1989), 23 pp.

48. *Blaming the Victims: The 12 November 1991 Massacre in Dili, East Timor, and the Response of the Indonesian Government* (Geneva: ICJ, 1992), 26 pp.

49. The IADL Secretary-General, an Algerian national and CIJL Advisory Board member, frequently sought ICJ assistance. Interview with CIJL director Mona Rishmawi, June 29, 1993. Algeria used special military tribunals rather than civilian courts to prosecute Islamic Salvation Front leaders and would not admit ICJ trial observers from Sudan and Egypt to the proceedings. *ICJ Newsletter*, no. 50 (July 1992): 7.

50. *ICJ Newsletter*, no. 52–53 (April 1993): 2. In conjunction with the French National Consultative Commission on Human Rights, the ICJ sponsored the meeting in Geneva on November 2–5, 1992.

51. Alejandro Artucio, *A Breach of Impunity: The Trial for the Murder of Jesuits in El Salvador* (New York: Fordham University Press, 1992), 81 pp. (Also available in Spanish.)

52. *Chile: A Time of Reckoning—Human Rights and the Judiciary* (Geneva: ICJ/CIJL, 1992), 259 pp.

53. *The Burmese Way: To Where? Report of a Mission to Myanmar (Burma) by Makhdoom Ali Khan* (Geneva: ICJ, 1991), 95 pp. A year later the ICJ reported on the plight of *Refugees from Myanmar* (Geneva: ICJ, 1992), 21 pp.

54. *Agenda for Peace: An Independent Survey of the Violence in South Africa* (Geneva: ICJ, 1992), 30 pp.

55. Interview of June 29, 1993, in Geneva.

56. "Israeli Settlements and the International Court of Justice," Oral Intervention of the ICJ, 48th session, U.N. Commission on Human Rights, Agenda Item 4. The Commission deferred action in 1992.

57. Reed Brody, "Focus on the United Nations, Prosecution Is a Selective Business," *The Law Group Docket* 7 (Spring 1992): 6.

58. *Countdown to 1997: Report of a Mission to Hong Kong* (Geneva: ICJ, 1992), 193 pp.

59. Governor Christopher Patten also outraged the Chinese with plans to build an airport. *New York Times*, October 29, 1992. Nicholas Kristof, "Fatty Patten's Last Stand," *New York Times Magazine*, February 21, 1993, 36–42.

60. *Human Rights of Psychiatric Patients in Japan, Mission Recommendations* (Geneva: ICJ, 1992), 12 pp. Tina Dolgopol and Snehal Paranjape conducted the Comfort Women Mission, April 15–May 8, 1993.

61. Interview with Adama Dieng, June 29, 1993.

62. Interview of July 8, 1993, in Geneva.

63. Statement made by Adama Dieng on behalf of NGOs at the Commission on Human Rights, 48th Session, February 1992, Item 14 of the Agenda: "Governments should equally ban the creation of any political movement or association which proclaims these doctrines negating human rights."

Conclusion

1. David B. Truman, *The Governmental Process*, 2d ed. (New York: Alfred A. Knopf, 1971), viii.

2. Ethan A. Nadelmann, "Global Prohibition Regimes: The Evolution of Norms in International Society," *International Organization* 44, no. 4 (Autumn 1990): 479–525, at 493, citing Sir Reginal Coupland, *The British Anti-Slavery Movement*, 2d ed. (London: Frank Cass, 1964), among others. Nadelmann concludes that the first global prohibition regime began in 1690 with the enforcement of international law against piracy.

3. Paul Lauren, *Power and Prejudice: The Politics of Diplomacy and Racial Discrimination* (Boulder, Colo.: Westview, 1988), 30, citing David Brion Davis, *The Problem of Slavery in Western Culture* (Ithaca, N.Y.: Cornell University Press, 1975), and others.

4. Nadelmann, "Global Prohibition Regimes," 482.

5. Ibid., 495.

6. General Report: Second NGO Workshop on the African Commission on Human and Peoples Rights, February 29–March 1, 1992, Tunis, Tunisia (Geneva: ICJ, 1992), 3.

7. Samuel P. Huntington, "The Clash of Civilizations?" *Foreign Affairs* 72, no. 3 (Summer 1993): 22–49.

8. Nadelmann, "Global Prohibition Regimes," 484.

9. Niall MacDermot, "The Churches and Human Rights," Address to the Annual General Meeting of the Catholic Institute for International Relations, London, June 18, 1976, p. 1.

10. Nadelmann, "Global Prohibition Regimes," 497.

11. Ibid., 492.

Bibliography

A. World Politics and International Law
B. International Nongovernmental Organizations
C. Human Rights NGOs
D. Interest Groups, Pluralism, and Corporatism

A. World Politics and International Law

Agee, Philip. *Inside the Company.* New York: Stonehill, 1975; Bantam, 1976.

Allott, Philip. *Eunomia: New Order for a New World.* New York: Oxford University Press, 1990.

Alston, Philip. *The United Nations and Human Rights.* Oxford: Clarendon, 1992.

Ambrose, Stephen. *Ike's Spies.* New York: Doubleday, 1981.

Anderson, Stanley. "Human Rights and the Structure of International Law." *New York Law School Journal of International and Comparative Law* 12 (1991): 1–28.

Bar-Yaacov, Nissim. *The Handling of International Disputes by Means of Inquiry.* New York: Oxford University Press, 1974.

Beitz, Charles R. *Political Theory and International Relations.* Princeton, N.J.: Princeton University Press, 1979.

Bird, Kai. *The Chairman: John J. McCloy. The Making of the American Establishment.* New York: Simon and Schuster, 1992.

Blum, William. *The CIA: A Forgotten History.* London: Zed Books, 1986.

Brown, Seyom. *International Relations in a Changing Global System.* Boulder, Colo.: Westview, 1992.

Brownlie, Ian. *Principles of Public International Law.* 4th ed. New York: Oxford University Press, 1990.

Brzezinski, Zbigniew. *Out of Control: Global Turmoil on the Eve of the 21st Century.* New York: Scribners, 1993.

Bull, Hedley. "The Emergence of a Universal International Society." In *The Expansion of International Society*, edited by Hedley Bull and Adam Watson, 117–26. Oxford: Clarendon, 1984.

Camilleri, Joseph A., and Jim Falk. *The End of Sovereignty? The Politics of a Shrinking and Fragmenting World.* Brookfield, Vt.: Elger, 1992.

Clark, Grenville, and Louis Sohn. *World Peace Through World Law*. Cambridge, Mass.: Harvard University Press, 1966.

Cohen, Bernard. *The Public's Impact on Foreign Policy*. Boston: Little, Brown, 1973.

Czempiel, Ernst-Otto, and James N. Rosenau, eds. *Global Changes and Theoretical Challenges: Approaches to World Politics for the 1990s*. Lexington, Mass.: Lexington Books, 1989.

Deutsch, Karl W., and Stanley Hoffmann, eds. *The Relevance of International Law: Essays in Honor of Leo Gross*. Cambridge, Mass.: Schenkman, 1968.

Dicey, A. V. *The Law of the Constitution*. 10th ed., revised by E. C. S. Wade. London: Macmillan, 1959.

Donnelly, Jack. "International Human Rights: A Regime Analysis." *International Organization* 40, no. 3 (Summer 1986): 599–642.

———. *Universal Human Rights in Theory and Practice*. Ithaca, N.Y.: Cornell University Press, 1989.

Ermacora, F. "International enquiry commissions in the field of human rights." *Human Rights Journal* I (1968): 180–218.

———. "Partiality and impartiality of human rights enquiry commissions of international organizations." *René Cassin Amicorum discipulorumque liber* I (1969): 64–74.

Falk, Richard A. *Explorations at the Edge of Time: The Prospects for World Order*. Philadelphia: Temple University Press, 1992.

———. *The Study of Future Worlds*. New York: Free Press, 1958.

Falk, Richard, and Saul Mendlovitz, eds. *Studies on a Just World Order*, 3 vols. Boulder, Colo.: Westview, 1982.

Feld, Werner. *International Organizations: A Comparative Approach*. 2d ed. New York: Praeger, 1988.

Forsythe, David. *Human Rights and World Politics*. 2d ed. Lincoln, Neb.: University of Nebraska Press, 1988.

———. *The Internationalization of Human Rights*. Lexington, Mass.: D.C. Heath, 1991.

———. *The Politics of International Law: U.S. Foreign Policy Reconsidered*. Boulder, Colo.: Lynne Rienner, 1990.

———, ed. *Human Rights and Development*. New York: St. Martin's, 1989.

Franck, Thomas M. "Of Gnats and Camels: Is There a Double Standard at the United Nations?" *American Journal of International Law* 78 (1984): 811–34.

Fukuyama, Francis. "The End of History?" *The National Interest*, no. 16 (Summer 1989): 3–18.

Gilpin, Robert. *Change and War in World Politics*. Cambridge: Cambridge University Press, 1983.

Gross, Leo. *Essays on International Law and Organization*. 2 vols. Dobbs Ferry, N.Y.: Transnational, 1984.

Grunfeld, Tom A. *The Making of Modern Tibet*. Armonk, N.Y.: M. E. Sharpe, 1987.

Guest, Iain. *Behind the Disappearances: Argentina's Dirty War Against Human Rights and the United Nations*. Philadelphia: University of Pennsylvania Press, 1990.

Hart, H. L. A. "Positivism and the Separation of Law and Morals." *Harvard Law Review* 71 (1958): 593–629.

Henkin, Louis. *The Age of Rights*. New York: Columbia University Press, 1990.
Hoffmann, Stanley. *Duties Beyond Borders: On the Limits and Possibilities of Ethical International Politics*. Syracuse, N.Y.: Syracuse University Press, 1981.
Holsti, K. J. *International Politics*. 6th ed. Englewood Cliffs, N.J.: Prentice Hall, 1992.
Humphrey, John. *Human Rights and the United Nations*. Dobbs Ferry, N.Y.: Transnational, 1984.
Huntington, Samuel P. "The Clash of Civilizations?" *Foreign Affairs* 72, no. 3 (Summer 1993): 22–49.
Jacobson, Harold K. *Networks of Interdependence: International Organizations and the Global Political System*. New York: Alfred A. Knopf, 1979.
Kaufmann, Johan. *Conference Diplomacy*. 2d ed. Norwell, Mass.: Martinus Nijhoff, Kluwer, 1988.
Kennedy, Paul. *The Rise and Fall of the Great Powers: Economic Change and Military Conflict from 1500 to 2000*. New York: Random House, 1987.
Keohane, Robert O., ed. *Neorealism and Its Critics*. New York: Columbia University Press, 1986.
Keohane, Robert O., and Joseph S. Nye. *Power and Interdependence: World Politics in Transition*. Boston: Little Brown, 1977.
———. *Power and Interdependence*. 2d ed. Glenview, Ill.: Scott, Foresman, 1989.
———. *Transnational Relations and World Politics*. Cambridge, Mass.: Harvard University Press, 1971.
Kriesberg, Louis. *Social Processes in International Relations*. New York: Wiley, 1968.
Lauren, Paul. *Power and Prejudice: The Politics of Diplomacy and Racial Discrimination*. Boulder, Colo.: Westview, 1988.
Lauterpacht, Hersch. *International Law and Human Rights*. New York: Praeger, 1950.
Linklater, Andrew. *Men and Citizens in the Theory of International Relations*. London: Macmillan, 1982.
Maghoori, Ray, and Bennett Ramberg. *Globalism Versus Realism: International Relations Third Debate*. Boulder, Colo.: Westview, 1982.
Mansbach, Richard, Yale H. Ferguson, and Donald E. Lampert. *The Web of World Politics*. Englewood Cliffs, N.J.: Prentice Hall, 1976.
Marks, John, and Victor Marchetti. *The CIA and the Cult of Intelligence*. New York: Knopf, 1974.
McDougal, Myres S., Harold D. Lasswell, and Lung-chu Chen. *Human Rights and World Public Order: The Basic Policies of an International Law of Human Dignity*. New Haven, Conn.: Yale University Press, 1980.
Meron, Theodore. *Human Rights and Humanitarian Norms in Customary Law*. Oxford: Clarendon, 1989.
———. *Human Rights Law Making in the U.N.: A Critique of Instruments and Process*. Oxford: Clarendon, 1986.
———. "Norm Making and Supervision in International Human Rights: Reflections on Institutional Order." *American Journal of International Law* 76 (1982): 754–78.
Meyer, Cord. *Facing Reality: From World Federalism to the CIA*. New York: Harper and Row, 1980.
Morgenthau, Hans. *Politics Among Nations*. 6th ed. New York: Knopf, 1985.

Nadelmann, Ethan A. "Global Prohibition Regimes: The Evolution of Norms in International Society." *International Organization* 44, no. 4 (Autumn 1990): 479–526.

Nardin, Terry. *Law, Morality, and the Relations of States.* Princeton, N.J.: Princeton University Press, 1983.

Oliver, Covey T. "The Future of Idealism in International Law: Structuralism, Humanism and Survival." In *The Structure and Process of International Law: Essays in Legal Philosophy Doctrine and Theory,* edited by R. St. J. Macdonald and Douglas M. Johnston, 1207–22. Boston: Martinus Nijhoff, 1983.

Oraá, Jaime. *Human Rights in States of Emergency in International Law.* New York: Oxford University Press, 1992.

Ranelagh, John. *The Agency: The Rise and Decline of the CIA.* New York: Simon and Schuster, 1986.

Reynolds, P. A., and R. D. McKinlay, "The Concept of Interdependence: Its Uses and Misuses." In *Power Capabilities and Interdependence Problems in the Study of International Influence*, edited by K. Goldmann and G. Sjostedt. Beverly Hills, Calif.: Sage, 1979.

Rosenau, James N. *Turbulence in World Politics.* Princeton, N.J.: Princeton University Press, 1990.

Ruggie, John G. "Human Rights and the Future International Community." *Daedalus* 112, no. 4 (1983): 93–110.

Sieghart, Paul. *The International Law of Human Rights.* London: Oxford University Press, 1983.

Simpson, Christopher. *Blowback.* New York: Weidenfeld & Nicolson, 1988.

Smith, Bradley F. *Reaching Judgment at Nuremberg.* New York: Basic Books, 1977.

Soroor, Marvin S. *Beyond Sovereignty: The Challenge of Global Policy.* Columbia, S.C.: University of South Carolina Press, 1986.

Storey, Robert G. *Final Judgment? Pearl Harbor to Nuremberg.* San Antonio, Tex.: Naylor, 1968.

Tinbergen, Jan. *Reshaping the International Order (RIO): A Report to the Club of Rome.* New York: E. P. Dutton, 1976.

Tolley, Howard. *The U.N. Commission on Human Rights.* Boulder, Colo.: Westview, 1987.

Tusa, Ann, and John Tusa. *The Nuremberg Trial.* New York: Macmillan, 1983.

Vincent, R. J. *Human Rights and International Relations.* New York: Cambridge University Press, 1986.

von Laue, Theodore H. *The World Revolution of Westernization: The Twentieth Century in Global Perspective.* New York: Oxford University Press, 1987.

Waltz, Kenneth. *Theory of International Politics.* New York: McGraw-Hill, 1979.

Watson, J. S. "Legal Theory, Efficacy and Validity in the Development of Human Rights Norms in International Law." *University of Illinois Law Forum.* 1979, 609.

———. "The Limited Utility of International Law in the Protection of Human Rights." *American Society of International Law, Proceedings*, 74th Annual Meeting (April, 1980).

Welch, Claude E., Jr., and Ronald I. Meltzer. *Human Rights and Development in Africa.* Albany: State University of New York Press, 1984.

Wight, Martin. "Western Values in International Relations." In *Diplomatic In-*

vestigations: Essays in the Theory of International Politics, edited by Herbert Butterfield and Martin Wight, 89–131. London: Allen & Unwin, 1966.
Wright, Quincy. *Problems of Stability and Progress in International Relations.* Westport, Conn. Greenwood, 1976.
———. *The Role of International Law in the Elimination of War.* London: Manchester University Press, 1961.

B. International Nongovernmental Organizations

Angell, Robert. *Peace on the March: Transnational Participation.* New York: Van Nostrand Reinhold, 1969.
Berman, Maureen R., and Joseph E. Johnson, eds. *Unofficial Diplomats.* New York: Columbia University Press, 1977.
Blaisdell, Donald. "Pressure Groups, Foreign Politics, and International Politics." *Annals of the Academy of Political and Social Science* 319 (September 1958): 149–57.
Chiang, Pei-heng. *Non-Governmental Organizations at the United Nations: Identity, Role and Function.* New York: Praeger, 1981.
Claude, Inis. "Collective Legitimization as a Political Function of the United Nations." *International Organization* 20 (Summer 1966): 367–79.
Cohen, Bernard C. *The Influence of Non-governmental Groups on Foreign Policy-Making.* Boston: World Peace Foundation, 1959.
Cosgrove, Carol Ann, and Kenneth Twitchett. *The New International Actors.* New York: St. Martin's Press, 1970.
Dahlen, Olle. "A Governmental Response to Pressure Groups—The Case of Sweden." In *Pressure Groups in the Global System*, edited by Peter Willets, 148–70. Boulder, Colo.: Westview, 1987.
Egelman, Jan, and Thomas Kerks, eds. *Third World Organizational Development: A Comparison of NGO Strategies.* Geneva: Henry Dunant Institute, 1987.
Ehrmann, Henry W., ed. *Interest Groups on Four Continents.* Pittsburgh: University of Pittsburgh, 1958.
Elvander, Nils. "Interest Groups in Sweden." *Annals of the Academy of Political and Social Sciences* 413 (May 1974): 27–43.
Feld, Werner, J. *Non-Governmental Forces and World Politics: A Study of Business, Labor, and Political Groups.* New York: Praeger, 1972.
———. "Nongovernmental Entities and the International System: A Preliminary Quantitative Overview." *Orbis* 15 (Fall 1971): 879–922.
Feraru, Anne Thompson. "Transnational Political Interests and the Global Environment." *International Organization* 28 (Winter 1974): 31–55.
Ghils, Paul. "International Civil Society: International Non-governmental Organizations in the International System." *UNESCO International Social Science Journal* 44 (1992): 417–31.
Gorman, Robert F., ed. *Private Voluntary Organizations as Agents of Development.* Boulder, Colo.: Westview, 1984.
Hercik, Vladimir. "The Worldwide Dimension of the NGOs." *Transnational Associations*, no. 11 (1980): 458–59.
Hudson, Darril. "Case Study of an International Pressure Group," *International Associations*, no. 6 (1968): 405–9.

Huntington, Samuel. "Transnational Organizations in World Politics." *World Politics* 25 (April 1973): 333–68.

Hurwitz, Leon. *The State as Defendant: Governmental Accountability and the Redress of Individual Grievances*. London: Aldwych Press, 1981.

Kerr, Henry J., Jr. "Changing Attitudes through International Participation: European Parliamentarians and Integration." *International Organization* 27 (Winter 1973): 45–84.

Kerstiëns, Thom. *Are NGOs In? The Role of the Development Non-Governmental Organisations in the Netherlands*. KDK-brochures 1. 1981

Kriesberg, Louis. "International Nongovernmental Organizations and Transnational Integration." *International Associations* 24 (1972): 521–25.

———. "U.S. and U.S.S.R. Participation in International Non-Governmental Organizations." In *Social Processes in International Relations*, edited by Louis Kreisberg, 466–85. New York: John Wiley and Sons, 1968.

Lador-Lederer, J. Josef. *International Group Protection, Aims and Methods in Human Rights*. Leyden, Netherlands: A. W. Sythoff-Leyden, 1968.

———. *International Non-Governmental Organizations*. Brussels: Union of International Associations, 1957.

Meynaud, Jean. *La Pression des Groupes Internationaux*. Paris: Centre d'Étude des Relations Internationales Fondation Nationale des Sciences Politiques, 1966.

OECD. *Voluntary Aid for Development: The Role of Non-Governmental Organisations*. Paris, 1988.

Perkins, E. V. "Comparative Pressure Group Politics and Transnational Relations: The Case of NGOs." Ph.D. diss., Texas Tech University, 1977.

Pickard, Bertram. *The Greater United Nations, An Essay Concerning the Place and Significance of International Non-governmental Organizations*. New York: Carnegie Endowment for International Peace, 1956.

Presthus, Robert, ed. "Interest Groups in International Perspective." *Annals of the Academy of Political and Social Sciences* 413 (May 1974).

Rohn, Peter. *Relations Between the Council of Europe and INGOs*. Brussels, 1957.

Skjelsbaek, Kjell. "The Growth of International Nongovernmental Organizations in the 20th Century." *International Organizations* 25 (Summer 1971): 420–42.

Smith, Brian H. *More Than Altruism: The Politics of Private Foreign Aid*. Princeton, N.J.: Princeton University Press, 1990.

Smith, J. Eric. "The Role of Special Purpose and Non-governmental Organizations in the Environmental Crisis." *International Organization* 26 (Spring 1972): 302–26.

Tandon, Y. "Foreign NGOs, Uses and Abuses: An African Perspective." *IFDA Dossier* 81 (April–June 1991): 67–78.

"Transnational Political Interests and the Global Environment." *International Organization* 28 (Winter 1974): 31–60

Union of International Associations (UIA). *Yearbook of International Organizations*. Brussels: UIA, 1990.

White, Lyman C. "The Role of International Non-governmental Organizations (INGOs) in World Affairs." *International Non-governmental Organizations: Their Purposes, Methods and Accomplishments*. New Brunswick, N.J.: Rutgers University Press, 1951.

Willets, Peter. *Pressure Groups in the Global System*. London: Frances Pinter, 1982.

Wright, Quincy, ed. *Preventing World War III: Some Proposals*. New York: Simon and Schuster, 1962.

C. Human Rights NGOs

Archer, Peter. "Action by Unofficial Organizations on Human Rights." In *The International Protection of Human Rights*, edited by Evan Luard. London: Thames Hudson, 1967.

Armstrong, J. D. "Non-governmental Organizations." In *Foreign Policy and Human Rights: Issues and Responses*, edited by R. J. Vincent. Cambridge: Cambridge University Press, 1986.

Beigbeder, Yves. *The Role and Status of International Humanitarian Volunteers and Organizations: The Right and Duty to Humanitarian Assistance*. Boston: Martinus Nijhoff, 1991.

Blaser, Arthur. "How to Advance Human Rights Without Really Trying: An Analysis of Nongovernmental Tribunals." *Human Rights Quarterly* 14 (August 1992): 339–70.

———. "Human Rights in the Third World and Development of International Nongovernmental Organizations. In *Human Rights and Third World Development*, edited by George W. Shepherd, Jr., and Ved P. Nanda, 273–86. Westport, Conn.: Greenwood, 1985.

Cassese, Antonio. "How Could Nongovernmental Organizations Use U.N. Bodies More Effectively." *Universal Human Rights* I, no. 4 (October–December 1979): 73–80.

———. "Progressive Transnational Promotion of Human Rights." In *International Law and Fact Finding in the Field of Human Rights*, edited by B. G. Ramcharan. The Hague: Martinus Nijhoff, 1982: 249–62.

Claude, Richard, and Burns Weston. "Human Rights NGOs." In *Human Rights in the World Community: Issues and Action*. 2d ed., 361–72. Philadelphia: University of Pennsylvania Press, 1992.

Council on Foreign Relations, 1980's Project. *Enhancing Global Human Rights*. New York: McGraw-Hill, 1979.

"Draft Minimal Rules of Procedure for International Human Rights Fact-Finding Missions." *Report of the Subcommittee on Equal Application of Human Rights Laws and Principles of the International Committee on Human Rights*. London: International Law Association, 1982.

Ennals, Martin. "Amnesty International and Human Rights." In *Pressure Groups in the Global System*, edited by Peter Willets, 78–80. London: Frances Pinter, 1982.

Ermacora, F. "Non-Governmental Organizations as Promoters of Human Rights." In *Protecting Human Rights: The European Dimension*, edited by Franz Matscher and Herbert Petzold, 171–80. Köln: Carl Heymanns Verlag KG, 1988.

Forsythe, David. *Humanitarian Politics: The International Committee of the Red Cross*. Baltimore, Md.: Johns Hopkins University Press, 1977.

Franck, Thomas M., and H. Scott Fairley, "Procedural Due Process in Human Rights Fact Finding by International Agencies." *American Journal of International Law* 74 (1980): 308–45.

Green, J. F. "NGOs," In *Human Rights and World Order*, edited by Abdul Aziz Said. New Brunswick: Transaction Books, 1978.

Hannum, Hurst, ed. *Guide to International Human Rights Practice*. Philadelphia: University of Pennsylvania Press, 1984.

International Human Rights Organizations: The Meaning of Their Work for Local Organizations. Series of Program Evaluations DGIS/NOVIB #45. The Hague, March 1992.

International Law Association, Australian Branch. *The International Status of Human Rights NGO's*. Sydney, Australia: Butterworths, 1978.

Jabine, Thomas, and Richard Claude. *Human Rights and Statistics: Getting the Record Straight*. Philadelphia: University of Pennsylvania Press, 1991.

Larsen, Egon. *A Flame in Barbed Wire: The Story of Amnesty International*. New York: Norton, 1979.

Leary, Virginia. "A New Role for Non-Governmental Organizations. A Case Study of Non-Governmental Participation in the Development of International Norms on Torture." In *UN Law/Fundamental Rights*, edited by Antonio Cassese, 197–210. Netherlands: Sitjhoff & Noordhoff, 1979.

Levenstein, Aaron. *Escape to Freedom: The Story of the International Rescue Committee*. Westport, Conn.: Greenwood, 1983.

Lillich, Richard, ed. *Fact Finding Before International Tribunals*. Ardsley-on-Hudson, N.Y.: Transnational Publishers, 1992.

———. *International Human Rights: Problems of Law, Policy, and Practice*. 2d ed. Boston: Little, Brown, 1991.

Livezey, Lowell W. *Nongovernmental Organizations and the Idea of Human Rights*. Princeton, N.J.: School of Public and International Affairs, 1987.

Nanda, Ved P., James R. Scarrit, and George W. Shepherd, Jr. *Global Human Rights: Public Policies, Comparative Measures, and NGO Strategies*. Boulder, Colo.: Westview, 1981.

Newman, Frank, and David Weissbrodt. *International Human Rights*. Cincinnati, Ohio: Anderson, 1990.

Power, Jonathan. *Amnesty International: The Human Rights Story*. New York: McGraw-Hill, 1981.

Ramcharan, B. G., ed. *International Law and Fact-Finding in the Field of Human Rights*. The Hague: Martinus Nijhoff, 1982.

———, ed. *Human Rights Thirty Years after the Universal Declaration*. Boston: Martinus Nijhoff, 1979.

Reiter, Randy B., M .V. Xunzunegui, and José Quiroga. "Guidelines for Field Reporting of Basic Human Rights Violations." *Human Rights Quarterly* 8, no. 4 (1986): 628–53.

Rodley, Nigel. "Monitoring Human Rights Violations in the 1980s." In *Enhancing Global Human Rights*. Council on Foreign Relations, 1980's Project, 117–54. New York: McGraw-Hill, 1979.

———. "Monitoring Human Rights by the U.N. System and Nongovernmental Organizations." In *Human Rights and American Foreign Policy*, edited by Donald Kommers and G. D. Loescher, 157–78. Notre Dame, Ind.: Notre Dame University Press, 1979.

Salzberg, John. "UN Prevention of Human Rights Violations: The Bangladesh Case." *International Organization* 27 (Winter 1973): 115–27.

Schoultz, Lars. *Human Rights and U.S. Policy toward Latin America*. Princeton, N.J.: Princeton University Press, 1981.

Scoble, Harry M. "Human Rights Non-Governmental Organizations in Black Africa: Their Problems and Prospects in the Wake of the Banjul Charter." In *Human Rights and Development in Africa*, edited by Claude E. Welch, Jr., and Ronald I. Meltzer. Albany: State University of New York Press, 1984.

Scoble, Harry M., and Laurie S. Wiseberg. "Amnesty International." *Intellect Magazine* (September–October 1976): 79–82.

———. "Human Rights and Amnesty International." *Annals of the American Academy of Political and Social Science* (May 1974): 11–26.

———. "Human Rights NGOs: Notes Towards Comparative Analysis." *Human Rights* 9, no. 4 (Winter 1976): 611–44.

Shestack, Jerome J. "Sisyphus Endures: The International Human Rights NGO." *New York Law School Review* 24 (1978): 89–123.

Steiner, Henry J. *Diverse Partners: Non-Governmental Organizations in the Human Rights Movement*. Cambridge, Mass.: Harvard Law School and Human Rights Internet, 1991.

Thoolen, Hans, and Berth Verstappen. *Human Rights Missions: A Study of the Fact-finding Practice of Non-governmental Organizations*. Boston: Martinus Nijhoff, 1986.

van Boven, Theo. "The Role of NGOs in International Human Rights Standard-Setting: Non-governmental Participation, a Prerequisite of Democracy?" In *The Role of Non-Governmental Organizations in the Promotion and Protection of Human Rights: Symposium Organized on the occasion of the award of the Praemium Erasmianum to the ICJ*, 53–72. Leiden: Stichting NJCM-Boekerij, 1989.

VerMeulen, Michael. "Forty Lawyers vs. Tyranny." *Quest* 80: 55–58, 101–3.

Verstappen, Berth. ed. *Human Rights Reports: An Annotated Bibliography of Fact-Finding Missions*. New York: Hans Zell, 1987.

Weissbrodt, David. "Human Rights Implementation and Fact Finding by International Organizations." *American Society of International Law, Proceedings*, 1980.

———. "The Influence of Interest Groups on the Development of United States Human Rights Policies." In *The Dynamics of Human Rights in U.S. Foreign Policy*, edited by Natalie Hevener, 229–78. New Brunswick, N.J.: Transaction, 1981.

———. "International Factfinding in Regard to Torture." *Nordic Journal of International Law* 57 (1988): 151.

———. "International Trial Observers." *Stanford Journal of International Law* 18 (1982): 27–121.

———. "The Role of International Non-Governmental Organizations in the Implementation of Human Rights." *Texas International Law Journal* 12 (1977): 293–320.

———. "The Role of International Organizations in the Implementation of Human Rights and Humanitarian Law in Situations of Armed Conflict." *Vanderbilt Journal of Transnational Law* 21 (1988).

———. "Strategies for the Selection and Pursuit of International Human Rights Objectives." *Yale Journal of World Public Order* 8 (1981): 62–86.

Weissbrodt, David, and James McCarthy. "Fact-Finding by International Non-Governmental Human Rights Organizations." *Virginia Journal of International Law* 22, no. 1 (1981): 1–89.

Willemin, Georges, and Roger Heacock. *The International Committee of the Red Cross*. The Hague: Martinus Nijhoff, 1984.

Wiseberg, Laurie S. "Human Rights and Soviet-American Relations: The Role of NGOs." In *Neither Cold War nor Detente*, edited by Richard Melanson, 151–85. Charlottesville: University of Virginia Press, 1982.

———. "Human Rights NGOs." In *The Role of Non-Governmental Organizations in the Promotion and Protection of Human Rights: Symposium organized on the occasion of the award of the Praemium Erasmianum to the ICJ*, 23–44. The Hague: Stichting NCJM-Boekerij, 1989.

———. "Monitoring Human Rights Violations: The Role of NGOs." In *Human Rights and American Foreign Policy*, edited by Donald Kommers and G. D Loescher, 179–210. Notre Dame, Ind.: Notre Dame University Press, 1979.

———. "The Role of Non-Governmental Organizations." In *Put Our World to Rights: Towards a [Canadian] Commonwealth Human Rights Policy*. A Report by a Non-Governmental Advisory Group chaired by the Honorable Flora MacDonald (August 1991): 149–74. Commonwealth Human Rights Initiative. Reprinted in *Human Rights in the World Community: Issues and Action*. 2d ed., edited by Richard Claude and Burns Weston, 372–82. Philadelphia: University of Pennsylvania Press, 1992.

Wiseberg, Laurie S., and Harry M. Scoble. "The International League for Human Rights: Strategy of a Human Rights NGO." *Georgia Journal of International and Comparative Law* 7 (1977): 289–313.

———. "Recent Trends in the Expanding Universe of NGOs Dedicated to the Protection of Human Rights." *Journal of International Law and Policy* 8 (1979): 627–58. Also in *Global Human Rights: Public Policies, Comparative Measures, and NGO Strategies*, edited by Ved. P. Nanda et al., 229–60. Boulder, Colo.: Westview, 1981.

D. Interest Groups, Pluralism, and Corporatism

Almond, Gabriel, ed. *Comparative Politics Today: A World View*. Boston: Little, Brown , 1974.

Almond, Gabriel A., and Sidney Verba. *The Civic Culture: Political Attitudes and Democracy in Five Nations*. Boston: Little, Brown, 1965.

Almond, Gabriel A., and James S. Coleman, eds. *The Politics of the Developing Areas*. Princeton, N.J.: Princeton University Press, 1960.

Barker, Lucius J., and Donald Jansiewicz, "Coalitions in the Civil Rights Movement." In *The Study of Coalition Behavior*, edited by Sven Groennings, E. W. Kelley, and Michael Leiserson, 192–208. New York: Holt, Rinehart and Winston, 1970.

Benewick, Robert. "British Pressure Goups Politics: The National Council for Civil Liberties." *Annals of the Academy of Political and Social Science* 319 (September 1958): 149–157.

Berger, Suzanne, ed. *Organizing Interests in Western Europe: Pluralism, Corporatism and the Transformation of Politics*. Cambridge: Cambridge University Press, 1981.

Berry, Jeffrey. *The Interest Group Society*. Boston: Little, Brown, 1984.

———. *Lobbying for the People*. Princeton, N.J.: Princeton University Press, 1977.

Birkinshaw, Patrick, Ian Harden, and Norman Lewis. *Government by Moonlight: The Hybrid Parts of the State*. London: Unwin Hyman, 1990.

Cater, Douglas. *Power in Washington*. New York: Vintage Books, 1964.

Cohen, Bernard C. *The Influence of Non-Governmental Groups on Foreign Policy Making*. Boston: World Peace Foundation, 1959.

Crouch, Colin, and Ronald Dore. *Corporatism and Accountability: Organized Interests in British Public Life*. Oxford: Clarendon, 1990.
Dahl, Robert. *Dilemmas of Pluralist Democracy*. New Haven: Yale University Press, 1982.
———. *Who Governs?* New Haven: Yale University Press, 1961.
Elder, Klaus. "The 'New Social Movements': Moral Crusades, Political Pressure Groups or Social Movements." *Social Research* 52, no. 4. (Winter 1985): 885.
Etzioni, Amitai. *A Comparative Analysis of Organizations: On Power, Involvement, and Their Correlates*. New York: Free Press, 1961.
Frohlich, Norman, Joe A. Oppenheimer, and Oran R. Young. *Political Leadership and Collective Goods*. Princeton, N.J.: Princeton University Press, 1971.
Fuentes, Marta, and Andre Gunder Frank. "Ten Theses on Social Movements." *World Development* 17, no. 2 (1989): 179–91.
Greenwald, Carol S. *Group Power: Lobbying and Public Policy*. New York: Praeger, 1978.
Hayes, Michael. "The Semi-Sovereign Pressure Groups." *Journal of Politics* 40, no. 1 (February 1978): 134–61.
Kerstiëns, Thom. *Are NGOs In? The role of the development non-governmental organizations in the Netherlands*. KDK-brochure 1 (1981).
Marsh, David. "On Joining Interest Groups." *British Journal of Political Science* 6 (July 1976): 265.
McFarland, Andrew. *Common Cause: Lobbying in the Public Interest*. Chatham, N.J.: Chatham House, 1984.
———. *Public Interest Lobbies*. Washington, D.C.: American Enterprise Institute, 1976.
Michels, Roberto. *Political Parties: A Sociological Study of the Oligarchical Tendencies of Modern Democracy*. 1915. Reprint. New York: Dover, 1959.
Mills, C. Wright. *The Power Elite*. New York: Oxford University Press, 1956.
Moe, Terry. *The Organization of Interests: Incentives and Internal Dynamics of Political Interest Groups*. Chicago: University of Chicago Press, 1980.
Novak, Michael, ed. *Democracy and Mediating Structures*. Washington, D.C.: American Enterprise Institute, 1980.
Olson, Mancur. *The Logic of Collective Action*. Cambridge, Mass.: Harvard University Press, 1971.
———. *The Rise and Decline of Nations*. New Haven, Conn.: Yale University Press, 1982.
Ornstein, Norman J., and Shirley Elder. *Interest Groups, Lobbying and Policy Making*. Washington, D.C.: Congressional Quarterly Press, 1978.
Petraca, Mark. *Politics of Interests: Interest Groups Transformed*. Boulder, Colo.: Westview, 1992.
Presthus, Robert. *Elites in the Policy Process*. New York: Cambridge University Press, 1974.
Redman, Eric. *The Dance of Legislation*. New York: Simon and Schuster, 1973.
Riker, William H. *The Theory of Political Coalitions*. New Haven: Yale University Press, 1962.
Rosenau, James, ed. *Domestic Sources of Foreign Policy*. New York: Free Press, 1967.
Salisbury, Robert, et al. "Triangles, Networks, and Hollow Cores: The Complex Geometry of Washington Interest Representation." In *Politics of Interests*, edited by Mark Petraca, 130–49. Boulder, Colo.: Westview, 1992.

Salisbury, Robert H. "An Exchange Theory of Interest Groups." *Midwest Journal of Political Science* 13 (February 1969): 1–32.

———, ed. *Interest Groups in America.* New York: Harper & Row, 1970.

Schattschneider, E. E. *The Semisovereign People: A Realist's View of Democracy in America.* New York: Holt, Rinehart and Winston, 1960.

Schmitter, Philippe C. "Modes of Interest Intermediation and Models of Societal Change in Western Europe." *Comparative Political Studies* 10, no. 1 (April 1977): 7–38.

Scholten, Ilja, ed. *Political Stability and Neo-Corporatism: Corporatist Integration and Societal Cleavages in Western Europe.* Beverly Hills, Calif.: Sage, 1987.

Schuck, Peter. "Public Interest Groups and Policy Process." *Public Administration Review* (March–April 1977): 133.

Schulzinger, Robert D. *The Wise Men of Foreign Affairs.* New York: Columbia University Press, 1984.

Shoup, Laurence H., and William Minter. *Imperial Brain Trust: The Council on Foreign Relations and U.S. Foreign Policy.* New York: Monthly Review, 1977.

Sinclair, John E. *Interest Groups in America.* Morristown, N.J.: General Learning Press, 1976.

Streeck, Wolfgang, and Philippe C. Schmitter, eds. *Private Interest Government: Beyond Market and State.* Beverly Hills, Calif.: Sage, 1985.

Truman, David. *The Governmental Process.* 2d ed. New York, Knopf, 1971.

Walker, Jack L. *Mobilizing Interest Groups in America: Patrons, Professions and Social Movements.* Ann Arbor: University of Michigan Press, 1991.

———. "The Origins and Maintenance of Interest Groups in America." *American Political Science Review* 77 (June 1983): 396.

Walker, Samuel. *In Defense of American Liberties: A History of the ACLU.* New York: Oxford University Press, 1990.

Wilson, James Q. *Political Organizations.* New York: Basic Books, 1973.

Zeigler, Harmon. *Pluralism, Corporatism and Confucianism: Political Association and Conflict Regulation in the United States, Europe, and Taiwan.* Philadelphia: Temple University Press, 1988.

Zeigler, L. Harmon, and G. Wayne Peak. *Interest Groups in American Society.* 2d ed. Englewood Cliffs, N.J.: Prentice Hall, 1972.

Index

Abolitionist societies, 7
Act of Athens, 41, 68, 71, 76
Ademola, Adetokunbo A., 56, 64
African Association of International Law, 147
African Bar Association, 237, 238
African Charter on Human and Peoples' Rights, 166, 178, 185, 254, 260
African Commission on Human and Peoples' Rights, xv, 73, 260, 262, 269
Agee, Philip, 65, 85, 302 n.38, 333
Aggregation, 12, 75, 111, 183, 268
AIDS, 185
Al Haq, 150, 265
Alafriz, Arturo, 56, 57, 62
Algeria, 49, 131
All-India Association of Democratic Lawyers, 28
Allied High Commission for Occupied Germany, 26, 55
Almond, Gabriel, 8, 342
Alston, Philip, 144, 176, 333
Amaah, Ofusu, 189
American Association for the International Commission of Jurists (AAICJ), 129, 141, 155, 175, 181, 182, 249, 252, 264
American Bar Association (ABA), 31, 33, 34, 38, 61, 69, 76, 126, 156, 219, 224, 238
American Civil Liberties Union (ACLU), 16, 34, 51, 55, 81, 99, 275
American Committee for a Free Europe, 29
American Convention on Human Rights, 98, 201
American Court of Human Rights, 137
American Fund for Free Jurists (AFFJ), 33, 34, 36, 38, 51–55, 57, 58, 60, 61, 65, 88, 98, 100, 102, 125, 126, 131–33, 308 n.15
American Institute of International Law, 6
Amin, Idi, 179, 198, 204, 207
Amnesty International (AI), xiv, 4, 7, 8, 10, 12, 17, 62, 66, 100, 105, 106, 109, 112, 114, 125, 134, 137, 144, 167, 170, 172, 173, 183, 188, 192, 193, 197, 203, 205, 211, 225, 244, 248, 253, 255, 259, 260, 268, 274, 278
Amnesty International USA, 156
Amoah, Philip, 237, 248, 249, 263
Andean Commission of Jurists, 153, 171, 237, 252
Angell, Ernest, 34, 40, 44, 51, 58, 61, 69
Angola, 114, 116
Anti-Slavery Society, 21, 271, 272, 274, 275
Apartheid, 5, 27, 51, 54, 84, 93, 115, 116, 138
Arab Lawyers Union, 149, 224, 226, 234, 238
Arab League, 104
Arbitrary detention, 172
Argentina, xv, 38, 67, 82, 169, 170, 198, 209, 214, 219
Aristide, Jean-Bertrand, 255, 264
Article 19, 240
Articulation, 11, 75, 182, 267
Artucio, Alejandro 153, 170, 190, 192, 196, 201, 209, 210, 224, 248, 249, 258, 267, 269, 331 n.51
Asia Foundation, 30, 58, 62
Aspen Institute, 130

Association of Southeast Asian Nations (ASEAN), 151, 161
Association of Soviet Lawyers, xv, 156, 157
Association sénégalaise d'études et de recherches juridiques (ASERJ), 146
Asylum, 185
Athens Congress, 44, 84
Australia, 199
Australian National Section, 151, 192
Azikiwe, Nnamdi, 64

Baldwin, Roger, 16, 17, 31, 61, 141
Ballesteros, Enrique Bernales, 173
Bandung, 49
Bangkok, 77
Bangkok Conference, 134
Bangladesh, 193, 216
Barbados, 153, 163
Barbie, Klaus, 26
Basic Principles on the Independence of the Judiciary, xv, 231, 239
Basic Principles on the Role of Lawyers, 235
Bass, Robert, 31, 34, 37, 298 n.27, 313 n.43
Bassiouni, Cherif, 175
Batista y Zaldivar, Fulgencio, 85
Beaulne, Yvon, 170
Begin, Menachem, 205
Ben Ali, Zine El-Abidine, 254
Benedek, Wolfgang, 181
Benenson, Peter, 61, 125, 313 nn.38–39
Benítez, Osvaldo Illanes, 56, 57, 65, 154, 200, 342
Berlin, 26
Berlin Congress, 44
Berlin Wall, 85, 94
Berry, Jeffrey, 15, 17, 98, 104, 105
Bettiol, Giuseppe, 37, 57
Bhagwati, P. N., 220, 221, 234, 238, 263
Bissell, Richard, 29, 43
Bizerte, 82, 91, 94, 114, 120
Blackwell, J. Kenneth, 267, 330 n.35
Blaustein, Jacob, 106
Bonsal, Dudley, 31, 34–38, 40, 41, 44, 51, 52, 55, 56, 122, 141, 301 n.12
Borge, Tomas, 190
Bormann, Martin, 87
Bose, Vivian, 53, 55, 56, 62, 66, 72, 76, 101, 126, 275
Bosnia, 264
Boulos, Philippe, 37, 55
Boutros-Ghali, Boutros, 149, 226, 316 n.29
Bowie, Robert, 63
Braden, Tom, 29, 30, 42, 43, 297 nn. 13, 16, 298 nn. 26, 27
Brazil, 65
British Broadcasting Corporation (BBC), 36
British Guiana, 122, 130, 134
Brody, Reed, 171, 173, 184, 196, 220, 232–35, 238, 245, 247–50, 264, 266, 267
Brohi, A. K., 149
Brown, Seyom, 11, 290 n.10, 333
Brownell, Herbert, 63
Brzezinski, Zbigniew, 2, 333
Budget, ICJ annual, 58
Bulgaria, 36
Bundy, McGeorge, 126
Burma, 66, 264, 269
Burmese national section, 63
Burnham, Forbes, 122, 124, 131
Burundi, 97, 204, 117
Butler, William, 138, 141, 144, 155, 175, 176, 181–83, 190, 197, 203, 204, 219, 224, 243, 244, 248, 249, 252, 280, 282

Califano, Joseph, 121
Cambodia, 263
Canadian Bar Association, 61, 71
Carter, Jimmy, 137, 142, 170, 203, 204, 211, 259
Cassell, Christian A., 64
Cassese, Antonio, 252
Cassin, René, 28
Castro, Fidel, 50, 85, 92, 93
Central African Republic, 214
Centre for the Independence of Judges and Lawyers (CIJL), xv, 138, 143, 146, 218–43, 275
Ceylon, 62, 63, 81, 82
Chile, xv, 170, 200, 204, 205, 214, 264
China, xiv, 17, 25, 30, 39, 44, 51, 80, 82, 88, 89, 90, 211
Chirwa, Orton, 192
Civil law, 69, 70
Clarkson, Thomas, 274
Claude, Richard, xii, 8, 293 n.47
Cohn, Haim, 149

Cold War, xvii, 4, 26, 34, 44, 52, 62, 84, 85, 97, 138
Colombia, 215, 218
Colombo, 77
Colonialism, 27, 62, 138
Cominform, 39
Comintern, 6, 28
Common Cause, 16, 99
Common law, 69, 70
Commonwealth, 61, 66, 81, 102, 154, 163, 176, 204, 236, 238
Communication, 11
Concepción, Roberto, 152
Conference of Nongovernmental Organizations in Consultative Status at the U.N. (CONGO), 108
Confidential procedures, 206
Congo, 50, 97, 107, 108, 109, 133, 237
Congress of Cultural Freedom, 31, 89
Congress on Crime Prevention, 257
Congress on the Prevention of Crime and Treatment of Offenders, 166, 167
Consultative status, xiv, 3, 6, 19, 28, 42, 43, 102, 104, 127, 128, 168, 170, 206, 207, 209, 210, 214, 259, 279
Consumers' Association of Penang, 151
Containment, 25, 44
Convention Against Torture, 168, 184
Coordinating Organization of National Unions of Students, 30
Corporatism, xvi, 1, 15, 16, 17, 21, 42, 43, 278, 279, 295 n.67
Costa Rica, 193
Council of Europe, 36, 51, 62, 100, 104, 118, 119, 129, 168, 232
Council on Foreign Relations, 26, 29, 31, 34, 42, 43, 51, 55, 57, 61, 65, 280
Country reports, 82
Cuba, xiv, 50, 81, 82, 84, 85, 87, 93, 94
Cyprus, 41
Czechoslovakia, 25, 33, 36, 97, 114, 120, 129

Daes, Erica-Irene A., 176
Dahomey, 81
Dalai Lama, 88, 89, 90, 265
Danquah, J. B., 64, 83
Dar es Salaam, 146
Darrow, Clarence, 218
Davies, Trevor, 328 n.10
De Gaulle, Charles, 114
Debevoise, Eli Whitney, 26, 34, 35, 37, 40, 43, 55, 56, 85, 100, 102, 103, 111, 118, 122, 123, 125, 126, 129, 130, 132, 141, 308 n.8
Declaration Against Torture, 167
Declaration of Delhi, 68, 71, 72, 84, 85
Declaration of Independence, 69, 76
Declaration on Disappearances, 185
Declaration on the Protection of All Persons from Enforced or Involuntary Disappearances, 171
Defence for Children International, 258
Deschênes, Jules, 220, 230, 231, 327 nn. 19, 24
Despouy, Leandro, 174
Development, xv, 144, 145, 153, 157, 161, 163, 179, 256
Dewey Commission of Inquiry, 86
Dieng, Adama, xv, 146, 180, 181, 182, 184, 191, 223, 238, 244, 281
Diop, Bineta, 316 n.21
Diouf, Abdou, 180
Disturbance theory, 16, 42
Dixon, Owen, 56
Dolgopol, Ustinia, 192, 220, 226, 230, 310 n.42, 326 n.16, 327 n.20, 331 n.60
Dominican Republic, 85, 114
Donnelly, Jack, 7
Dossou, Robert, 252, 267
Dovi, Ahlonko, 223
Draft Body of Principles for the Protection of All Persons in Any Form of Detention or Imprisonment, 172
Dreyfus case, 16
Dualism, xvi, xvii, 2, 5, 21, 70
Dulles, John Foster, 29, 31, 43
Dumbutshena, Enoch, 220, 252
Duvalier, François ("Papa Doc"), 85

East Germany, 25, 26, 27, 31, 130
East Pakistan, 195, 204
East Timor, 148, 264, 266, 269, 270
Ecuador, 65, 66, 189
Egypt, 50, 81, 87, 122
Egyptian Bar Association, 226
Eichmann, Adolf, 81, 304 n.9
Eisenhower, Dwight D., 29
EKD (Evangelischen Kirche in Deutschland), 143, 161, 246, 261
El Salvador, 201, 215
Elias, T. O., 72, 147

Encounter, 30
Enforcement, 14, 92, 130, 214
Enlightenment, 139, 274
Epistemic community, 6
Equatorial Guinea, 179, 215
Erasmus Prize, xiv, 156
Erdmann, Horst, 26
Ermacora, Felix, 93
Escobedo, Manuel, 56
Estonia, 39, 44
Estrella, Miguel, 208
Etcheberry, Alfredo, 154
Ethiopia, 81, 82
European Commission of Human Rights, 118, 163
European Committee for the Prevention of Torture, 168
European Community, 4, 54, 246, 248, 263
European Convention of Human Rights, 72, 76, 100, 118, 267
European Court of Human Rights, 105, 192
European Human Rights Commission, 155
European Human Rights Prize, xiv, 213
Exchange theory, 16, 42
Eyadema, Gnassingbe, 223

Fact-finding, 124, 277
Farer, Tom, 190
Faure, Edgar, 155
Federspiel, Per T., 37, 55, 103, 123, 129
Feld, Werner, 13
Ferguson, John, 55, 301 n.7
Fernandez, Luis Negron, 103
Fernando, T. S., 56, 103, 150, 196
Ford Foundation, xiv, 29, 58, 64, 98, 126, 128, 129, 132, 142, 150, 152, 219, 246
Forster, Isaac, 64
Forsythe, David, 7, 20
Fournier, Fernando, 56, 121
Fox, Donald, 201
Fragoso, Heleno, 190, 209
France, 6, 91
Franco, Francisco, 84
Fraser, Donald, 181
Free Legal Assistance Group, 238
French Declaration on the Rights of Man and the Citizen, 76
Friedenau, Theo, 26, 27, 31–33, 36–40, 44, 57, 297 n.8, 329 n.15
Funding, 16, 17, 21, 57, 102, 131, 161, 197, 269

Gandhi, Indira, 150
García Sayan, Diego, 154, 171, 220, 252
Gardiner, Gerald, 81, 103, 123, 155, 304 n.7
Gardner, John, 16
Gaza Centre for Peace and Law, 150
Geneva Conventions, xiv, 5, 86, 88, 100, 109, 111, 200, 266; Protocols, 108
Genocide, 5, 86, 195
Genocide Convention, 90
Ghana, 66, 83, 189, 191
Goa, 87, 90
GONGOs, 17, 259, 295 n.76
González, José Estaban, 190, 201
Goodhart, William, 52
Graven, Philippe, 117, 118
Greece, 25, 38, 98, 114, 116, 118, 124, 131, 189, 193
Gross, Leo, 5
Group of 77, 213
Guatemala, 196, 215, 269
Guest, Iain, 201
Guinea, 215
Guissé, El-Hadji, 264
Guyana, 198

Habeas corpus, 228
Hague Convention, 130
Hague Peace Conference, 6
Haiti, 85, 98, 114, 124, 131, 264
Hallmark, David, 191
Hammarskjold, Dag, 62
Henkin, Louis, 3, 290 n.10
Henri Texier Prize, 59
Hitler, Adolf, 25, 42
Hoffman, Stanley, 4
Holocaust, 5
Honduras, 196
Hong Kong, 266, 269
Htoon, U Chan, 56, 63
Human Rights Prize, 156
Human Rights Watch Committees, 193, 221, 225
Human Rights Year, 107
Humphrey, John, 106, 155, 219

Hungary, 50, 51, 81, 82, 86, 87, 88, 93, 94, 114, 130
Huntington, Samuel, 2
HURIDOCS (Human Rights International Documentation System), 156
Hussein, Saddam, 211
Hutu, 117

ICCO, 150
Idealism, xvi, 1, 3, 4, 6, 11, 21, 49, 69, 79, 80, 93, 111, 138
Imanyara, Gitobu, 225, 316 nn. 25, 27
Implementation, 13, 92, 131, 214
Impunity, 255, 260, 264
India, 90, 193
Indian Commission of Jurists, 83, 86, 88
Indigenous peoples, 255, 256, 259, 267
Indonesia, 114, 196, 198, 199, 215, 264
Inquiry committees, xiv, 86
Inquisitorial system, 70
Institut de Droit, 6
Institute for International Penal Law, 167
Institute of Human Rights, 146
Inter-African Union of Human Rights, 261
Inter-African Union of Lawyers, 147
Inter-American Commission on Human Rights (IACHR), 124, 154, 171, 190, 224, 228
Interest groups, 18, 20, 21
International Association of Democratic Lawyers (IADL), xiii, xiv, 17, 28, 29, 31, 32, 36, 39, 44, 57, 64, 84, 86, 93, 102, 108, 110, 112, 120, 127, 128, 133, 156, 193, 238, 221, 308 n.16, 310 n.35
International Association of Penal Law (IAPL), 175, 176, 229
International Bar Association, 51, 224, 230, 238
International Chamber of Commerce, 6
International Commission of Health Professionals for Health and Human Rights, 156, 177, 240
International Committee of the Red Cross (ICRC), 3, 4, 8, 51, 55, 57, 60, 65, 91, 92, 103, 105, 108, 117, 118, 167, 168, 203, 243, 244
International Confederation of Free Trade Unions, 30
International Confederation of Trade Unions, 117
International Conference on Human Rights in Teheran, 108
International Congress of Jurists, 40, 41
International Congress of Psychiatry Law and Ethics, 177
International Court of Justice, 5, 52, 76, 77, 147, 154, 163, 282, 290 n.23
International Covenant on Civil and Political Rights, 77, 113, 174, 177, 228
International Covenant on Economic, Social and Cultural Rights, 77, 175
International Federation of Editors-in-Chief, 109
International Federation of Human Rights, 7, 31, 59, 193, 253
International Federation of Trade Unions, 6
International Human Rights Law Group, 155, 248, 250, 267
International Labor Organization (ILO), 104, 111, 151, 163, 176, 195, 204
International Law Commission, 260
International League for Human Rights, 10, 17, 19, 66, 141, 170, 177
International League for the Rights of Man, 31, 51, 106, 323 n.14
International Monetary Fund, 256
International Organization of Journalists, 28
International Parliamentary Union, 6, 192
International Peace Bureau, 102, 134
International Penal Court, 259, 270
International Press Institute, 109
International Rescue Committee, 8
International Service for Human Rights, 259, 325 n.47, 330 n.30
International Union of Students, 28
International War Crimes Tribunal, 91, 124
International Year for Human Rights, 97
Investigating Committee of Free Jurists, 26, 31
Iran, 203, 215
Iranian Association of Jurists, 203
Iraq, 209, 211
Iron Curtain, 33, 36, 39, 42, 44, 51, 87, 120, 196

Iron triangles, 6, 43, 183
Islam, 145, 149, 163
Israel, 81, 97, 149, 195, 196, 197, 200, 205, 215, 226
Issue networks, 6, 104, 183

Jagan, Cheddi, 122, 123, 131
Japan, 176, 178, 189, 216, 270
Japanese Civil Liberties Union, 253
Jefferson, Thomas, 69
Jescheck, Hans-Heinrich, 56
Johnson, Lyndon, 126
Joinet, Louis, 171, 173, 184, 211, 228, 232, 235, 264
Journal of the International Commission of Jurists, 50, 58, 62, 74, 77, 82
Joxe, Louis, 155
"Justice," 110, 122, 126, 129, 132, 274, 305 n.20, 325 n.18

Kabes, Vladimir, 39, 54, 64, 77, 100, 103, 117, 129, 309 n.36
Kampuchea, 209
Kapteyn, P. J. G., 154, 249
Katz, Rudolf, 56
Kashmir, 90, 120
Kaunda, Kenneth, 145
Kenya, 148
Kerala, 83, 87
KGB, 50
Khader, Asma, 227, 252
Kibedi, Wanume, 207
Kirby, Michael, 151, 248, 249, 250, 252, 255, 265, 308 n.6
Kooijmans, Peter, 198
Korea, 25, 28, 30, 109, 161, 216
Kozera, Edward, 37–40, 44, 52, 53, 56, 62, 64, 89, 93, 100, 111
Kréher, Jean, 56, 62, 91
Kuomintang, 88

L'Heureux-Dube, Claire, 155, 252
Laissez-faire, 71
Lalive, Jean-Flavien, 52, 56, 66, 77, 84, 89, 91, 155
Lallah, Rajsoomer, 147
Land rights, 255, 267
Lauren, Paul, 271
Lauterpacht, Hersch, 5
Law of Lagos, 71, 72, 73
Lawmaking, 13, 77, 112, 184
Lawyers Committee for Human Rights (LCHR), 155, 219, 221, 224, 225, 234, 268, 276
Leadership, 16, 19, 65, 98, 99, 110, 133, 268
League for the Defence of Human Rights, 254
League for the Rights of Man and the Citizen, 16
League of Nations, 6, 79
Leary, Virginia, 8, 209, 324 n.18
Lee, Tai-Young, 151, 226
Legal Education, 110
Legal Services in Rural Areas, xv, 142, 146, 164
Lenin Peace Prize, 134, 156
Lewis, Rodney, 199
Liberia, 66, 94
Libre Justice, 62, 91, 110
Limburg Principles, 175, 176
Linse, Walter, 239, 298 n.32, 329 n.15
Lumumba, Patrice, 50
Luvum, Archbishop, 207

M. D. Anderson Foundation, 34, 58, 301 n.18
MacBride, Seán, xiv, 62, 71, 97, 98, 100, 101, 106, 107, 110, 111, 114, 115, 123, 129, 132, 133, 156, 178, 259, 275, 278
McCarthy, Joseph, 28, 29, 83
McCloy, John J., 26, 31, 34, 43, 126
MacDermot, Niall, xiv, 1, 129, 134, 138, 139, 140, 243, 244, 248, 252, 274, 275, 278, 280
McDonnell, James L., 36, 38, 40, 52, 55, 61
Machacek, Rudolf, 154
Madagascar, 263
Madlener, Kurt, 200
Malawi, 192
Malaysia, 227
Marsh, Norman, 52, 56, 61, 62, 71, 74, 88, 123, 155, 274
Marshall Plan, 25
Matarollo, Rodolfo, 209
Mawdsley, Andrés Aguilar, 154
Mbaye, Kéba, 144, 146, 147, 154, 170, 178, 179, 183, 184, 205, 256, 270
Medina, Earnest, 37

Membership, of ICJ, 16, 18, 55, 65, 99, 280
Mentally ill detainees, 176, 186
Meyer, Cord, 29, 43
Meyer, René, 103, 132
MI5, 139
Mignone, Emilio, 210
Minnesota Lawyers International Human Rights Committee, 155
Minority Rights Group, 208
Moeljadi, Nana, 151
Moi, Daniel arap, 148, 225
Monism, xvi, 4, 21, 70
Montecatini Draft Convention on War Correspondents, 109
Montreal Assembly on Human Rights, 108
Montreal World Conference on the Independence of Justice, 230
Mookerjee, Judge, 64
Morgan Institute of Human Rights, 19, 175
Morocco, 198, 216
Mothers of the Plaza de Mayo, 211
Mozambique, 189
Munktell, Henrik, 37, 38, 55, 56, 62
Munro, Leslie, 53, 56, 63, 65, 66, 81, 85, 88, 89, 92, 100

NAACP, 165
Nabuco, Jose T., 37, 126
Nadelmann, Ethan, 271, 272, 274, 276
Nagy, Imre, 88
Nairobi, 180
Nairobi Conference, 180
Nairobi Law Monthly, 148, 225
Nakasone, Etsuro, 177
Namibia, 115, 204, 205, 236, 264
Nariman, Fali, 150, 152
National Endowment for Democracy, 142
National Lawyers Guild, 28
National sections, 38, 59, 133, 248, 253, 254, 283–85
National Student Association, 30, 125
Natural law, xvi, xvii, 3, 4, 21, 69, 76
Nehru, Jawaharlal, 62, 100
Nepal, 151, 236
Netherlands, 199
Nettel, Erik, 172
New Britain Group, 139
New Delhi Congress, 62, 151
New International Economic Order, 144, 145, 256
New York City Bar Association, 33, 34, 38, 43, 126, 219, 224, 323 n.14
NGO Special Committee on Human Rights, 104, 107, 170, 205, 259
Nicaragua, 190, 196, 201, 216
Nigeria, 97, 120
Nimeiri, Gaafar Mohamed, 227
Nixon, Richard, 99, 218
NJCM (Nederlands Juristen Comité voor den Mensenrechten), 156
Nkrumah, Kwame, 64, 100
Nobel, Peter, 244
Nobel Peace Prize, 104, 134
North Atlantic Treaty Organization (NATO), 25
North Korea, 86
Northern Ireland, 198, 228
Norway, 6, 86
Noto, 230, 233
NOVIB, 143, 151, 189, 246, 250, 254, 258, 269, 323 n.3
Nuremberg, 14, 27, 55, 86, 87, 89, 90, 130

O'Donnell, Dan, 220
Occupied Territories, 200, 265
Oliver, Covey, 200
Olson, Mancur, 18
Ombudsman, 73, 102, 110, 124, 146, 156
Operation Crossroads Africa, 30
Opsahl, Torkel, 155
Orban, Paul-Maurice, 56
Organization for Economic Cooperation and Development (OECD), 142
Organization of African Unity (OAU), xv, 104, 178–81, 204, 207, 261, 262
Organization of American States (OAS), 92, 98, 104, 113, 121, 122, 168, 171, 258
Organization of Islamic Countries, 148
Osusky, Stefan, 33, 37
Overseas Development Institute, 257
Owen, David, 207

Pachman, Ludwig, 189
Pakistan, 124, 193, 216

Palau, 216
Palestinian rights, 98, 149
Panama, 121, 130, 131, 134
Panchen Lama, 88
Papadopoulos, George, 38
Paralegals, 10, 146, 152, 164
Park, Chung Hee, 225
Pax Christi, 211
Pax Romana, 209
Pearson, Lester, 107
Pérez de Cuéllar, Javier, 208
Periodical reports, 83, 287
Permanent Court of International Justice, 77
Petren, Gustaf, 103, 312 n.9
Pezzullo, Lawrence, 190, 224
Philby, Kim, 139
Philippines, 62, 195, 196, 216, 218, 269
Pinochet, Augusto, 170, 200, 205
Plant, Roger, 257, 258
Pluralism, xvi, 1, 15, 16, 17, 21, 42, 43, 65, 278
Pol Pot, 263
Poland, 81
Portugal, 49, 61, 81, 90, 116, 161, 189
Positivism, 2, 3, 5, 21, 69, 70
Posner, Michael, 221, 315 n.12
Powles, Sir Guy, 150
Principles for the Protection of Persons with Mental Illness, 176
Privacy, 186
Procuracy, 41
Promotion, xiv, 8, 9, 10, 20, 74, 138, 272
Protection, xiv, 8, 9, 13, 20, 138, 276
Public interest groups, 15, 98, 112
Publications, 58
Pugwash Group, 307 n.2

QUANGOs, 17, 279
Questiaux, Nicole, 155, 174
Quiet diplomacy, xiv, 189

Radio Free Europe, 26, 36, 38, 55, 126
Radio in the American Sector, 27
Radio Liberty, 26
Ramcharan, B. G., 171, 252, 317 n.44
Ramparts, 125, 132
Ramphal, Shridath S., 103, 154
Rannat, Mohamed A. Abu, 103
Raphael, Charles, 40, 53, 56, 61, 88
Rational interest model, 18, 66
Ravindran, Daniel, 150, 152, 209, 225
Regional Council on Human Rights in Asia (RCHRA), 152
Reagan, Ronald, 7
Real, Alberto Ramón, 154, 325 n.31
Realism, xvi, 1, 2, 4, 21, 70
Recruitment, 10, 66, 111, 162, 266
Regimes, 4, 6, 9, 185, 271
Resolution of Rio, 71, 73
Review of the ICJ, 129, 141, 143, 315 n.15
Rezek, Francisco, 221
Rhodesia, 114, 116, 196, 217
Rhyne, Charles S., 76, 105. *See also* World Peace Through World Law Center
Rio Congress, 73, 85
Rishmawi, Mona, 221, 248, 249, 257, 265, 266
Robinson, Mary 155, 316 n.29
Rockefeller, David, 127
Rockefeller Brothers Foundation, 143, 191, 219
Rogers, J. Grafton, 34, 37, 40, 298 n.30, 299 n.45
Romania, 36, 189, 209
Rosenau, James, 4, 290 n.14
Rosenberg, Julius, 28
Ruiz-Gimenez, Don Joaquin, 156
Russell, Bertrand, 91, 124
Ruth Pearce Award, 173

Sadat, Anwar, 226
Salazar, A., 116
Salisbury, Robert, 16
Salzberg, John, 181, 325 n.38
Sandinistas, 190, 196, 201
Sartre, Jean-Paul, 114
SAVAK, 203
Save the Children, 247
Schachter, Oscar, 62, 74, 302 n.31
Schmitter, Philippe, 15
Schultz, George, 142
Senghor, Leopold, 179
Seymour, Whitney North, 31, 34, 37, 51, 61
Shah of Iran, 203, 213
Shari'a, 69, 149, 179, 219, 227
Sharpeville massacre, 84

Shawcross, Hartley, 37, 55, 56, 61, 76, 86, 87, 89, 91, 92, 103, 122, 123, 299 n.53, 301 n.5, 302 n.26, 309 n.27
Shining Path, 237, 259
Shute, Benjamin, 26, 34, 37, 43, 55, 56
Sieghart, Paul, 155, 324 n.18
Singapore, 216
Singvhi, L. M., 229, 231, 232, 233, 235
Sinn Fein, 209
Siracusa Principles, 175, 229, 230, 231
Slavery, 5, 7
Social movements, 138, 139, 296 n.69
Socialist legality, xiii, 33, 39, 40, 68, 157
Socialization, xvi, 9, 10, 138, 162
Soler, Sebastian, 56, 324 n.31
Somoza, Anastasio, 190
South Africa, xiv, 27, 33, 38, 41, 49, 61, 76, 81–85, 93, 94, 114, 130, 134, 195, 205, 217, 263, 264, 265, 269
South Asian Association for the Right to Development, 152
South Korea, 25, 196, 226
South West Africa, 115, 134. *See also* Namibia
Spain, xiv, 27, 38, 41, 49, 51, 81–85, 93, 94, 114, 116, 128, 132, 189
Special Committee on Human Rights. *See* NGO Special Committee on Human Rights
Sri Lanka, 151, 195, 196, 197, 217, 263, 270
St. John, Edward, 99, 151
Stalin, Joseph, 25, 41, 42, 43
Standard Minimum Rules for the Treatment of Prisoners, 167
Standard setting, xiv, 8, 9, 11, 20, 74, 75, 138, 228, 274
Standing Committee of the International Congress of Jurists, 33, 36
States of emergency, 173, 186
Statute of the ICJ, 51, 54, 58, 149
Subgovernments, 6, 43, 104, 183
Sudan, 120, 217
Suez, 49, 88
Sullivan, William, 203
Surigao, Alfonso, 223
Suriname, 196, 217
Sweden, 6, 38, 142
Swedish International Development Authority (SIDA), 142, 197, 221, 236, 237, 246, 247, 254, 261, 279
Swiss Committee Against Torture (SCAT), 168
Switzerland, 132, 182
Syria, 227

Tanaka, Katoro, 56
Tanzania, 208
Teheran, 97
Thailand, 104
Thamassat, 18, 191
Thomas, Norman, 30
Thoolen, Hans, 155, 156, 198, 199
Thorson, Joseph T., 33, 36, 37, 45
Tibet, 50, 51, 82, 86, 88, 89, 93, 94, 114, 130, 133, 264, 266
Tikaram, Moti, 150
Tomuschat, Christian, 155, 260
Torture, 5, 109, 185
Torture Convention, 260
Totsuka, Etsuro, 177
Trial observers, xiv, 80, 119
Triantafyllides, Michael A., 103, 155
Trikamdas, Purshottam, 37, 62, 88, 89
Trujillo, Raphael, 50, 85
Truman, Harry S., 16, 29, 42, 271
Tunisia, 91, 254
Tunisian League for the Defence of Human Rights, 261
Tupomaros, 153
Turkey, 38, 81, 82, 128, 204
Tutsi, 117
Tyabji, Hatim Badrudin, 37

U.N. Centre Against Apartheid, 205
U.N. Centre for Human Rights, 171, 176, 183, 237, 244
U.N. Charter, 5, 290 n.11
U.N. Commission on Crime Prevention and Criminal Justice, 235
U.N. Commission on Human Rights, 5, 7, 8, 27, 50, 68, 82, 92, 98, 107, 109, 119, 124, 130, 154, 163, 166, 167, 172, 178, 183, 204, 205–6, 210, 212, 228, 229, 257, 277, 267, 282; Working Group on Arbitrary Detention, 173; Working Group on Disappearances, 154, 163, 171, 185, 192, 201, 208, 210
U.N. Committee Against Torture, 167
U.N. Committee on Crime Prevention and Control, 166, 173, 229, 231, 232, 233, 235

U.N. Congress on the Prevention of Crime and Treatment of Offenders, 229, 231
U.N. Division of Human Rights, 106
U.N. Economic and Social Council (ECOSOC), 29, 107, 127, 128, 141, 176, 209, 232; Committee on Non-Governmental Organizations, 127, 210
U.N. General Assembly, 50, 53, 76, 77, 89, 92, 106, 108, 150, 166, 172, 184, 206, 229, 231, 232, 235
U.N. High Commissioner for Human Rights, xiv, 98, 102, 104, 105, 106, 108, 111, 166, 169, 170, 259, 260, 275
U.N. High Commissioner for Namibia, 105
U.N. High Commissioner for Refugees, 163, 204
U.N. Human Rights Committee, 148, 166, 204
U.N. Sub-Commission on Prevention of Discrimination and Protection of Minorities, 119, 166, 169, 170, 204–6, 229, 233, 322 nn. 82, 83; Working Group on Detention, 209; Working Group on Slavery, 209
U.S. Agency for International Development (AID), 142, 148, 183, 235
U.S. Central Intelligence Agency (CIA), xiii, xiv, 18, 25, 29, 30, 31, 34, 38, 40, 42, 43, 50, 52, 53, 55, 58, 60, 65, 66, 85, 88, 89, 93, 98, 100, 115, 122, 125, 126, 128, 132, 133, 196, 203, 252, 278, 280
U.S. High Commissioner for Germany, 26
U.S. National Security Council, 25
Uganda, 179, 198, 204, 207, 208, 217
UNESCO, 68, 75, 102, 104, 105, 111, 146, 151, 176, 248
UNICEF, 104
Union International des Avocats, 238
United Kingdom, 61
Universal Declaration of Human Rights, 5, 7, 27, 32, 50, 68, 71, 73, 77, 84, 89, 90, 97, 100, 121, 148, 201, 218, 219, 228, 239
Universal Declaration on the Independence of Justice, 231
Untouchables, 152
Uruguay, 192, 202, 208, 217, 224
USSR, 26, 27, 28, 51, 62, 68, 80, 88, 156

van Boven, Theo, 144, 165, 170, 171, 208, 210, 211, 244, 252
van Dal, A. J. M., 33, 34, 36–39, 52, 56, 65, 91, 103, 123
van Dongen, Toine, 320 n.41, 322 n.76
Vasak, Karel, 39, 40, 54
Victorica, Juan José Cabajal, 37
Vietnam, 30, 49, 91, 97, 106, 107, 109, 111, 120, 124, 132
Vincent, R. J., 11
Voice of America, 36
Volio, Fernando Jiménez, 106, 107
Von Laue, Theodore H., 11, 336
Vorster, B. J., 115
Vyshinsky, Audrey, 41

Wako, Amos, 147, 148, 225, 228, 316 n.29
Waldheim, Kurt, 190
Waldron-Ramsey, Waldo E., 127, 128
Warsaw Pact, 88
Wateler Peace Prize, xiv, 156, 289 n.1
Webster, Bethuel, 26, 34, 37, 40, 43, 52, 122
Webster Commission, 52
Weissbrodt, David, xii, 8, 250, 315 n.12
Westernization, 68
Wilberforce, William, 274
Wilson, Harold, 139
Wiseberg, Laurie, xii, 8, 293 n.47
Wisner, Frank, 29, 43
Wold, Terje, 103, 309 n.22
Women's International Democratic Federation, 29
Woodhouse, John, 220, 226
World Assembly of Youth, 30
World Campaign for Human Rights, 105, 107
World Conference on Human Rights in Teheran, 259
World Conference on Human Rights in Vienna, 3, 7, 17, 19, 259
World Council of Churches, 141, 153, 167, 200
World Federalists, 29
World Federation of Trade Unions, 28
World Jewish Congress, 106

World Peace Council, 28
World Peace Through World Law Center, 76, 105, 109, 112, 276
World University Service, 247
World Veterans' Federation, 105
World War I, 16
Wright, Quincy, 5

Yakota, Masatoshi, 103
Yap, J. Thiam Hien, 152, 198
Yepez del Pozo, Juan, 65
YMCA, 6
Yugoslavia, 38, 81

Zalaquett, José, 252
Zellweger, Edouard, 37, 51, 56
Zorbas, Jan, 189

University of Pennsylvania Press
Pennsylvania Studies in Human Rights
Bert B. Lockwood, Jr., Series Editor
Professor and Director, Urban Morgan Institute for Human Rights, University of Cincinnati College of Law

George J. Andreopoulos, editor. *Genocide: Conceptual and Historical Dimensions*. 1994

Abdullahi Ahmed An-Naʿim, editor. *Human Rights in Cross-Cultural Perspectives: A Quest for Consensus*. 1991

Iain Guest. *Behind the Disappearances: Argentina's Dirty War Against Human Rights and the United Nations*. 1990

Thomas B. Jabine and Richard P. Claude, editors. *Human Rights and Statistics: Getting the Record Straight*. 1991

Menno T. Kamminga. *Inter-State Accountability for Violations of Human Rights*. 1992

Richard L. Siegel. *Employment and Human Rights*. 1993

Howard B. Tolley, Jr. *The International Commission of Jurists: Global Advocates for Human Rights*. 1994

This book was set in Baskerville and Eras typefaces. Baskerville was designed by John Baskerville at his private press in Birmingham, England, in the eighteenth century. The first typeface to depart from oldstyle typeface design, Baskerville has more variation between thick and thin strokes. In an effort to insure that the thick and thin strokes of his typeface reproduced well on paper, John Baskerville developed the first wove paper, the surface of which was much smoother than the laid paper of the time. The development of wove paper was partly responsible for the introduction of typefaces classified as modern, which have even more contrast between thick and thin strokes.

Eras was designed in 1969 by Studio Hollenstein in Paris for the Wagner Typefoundry. A contemporary script-like version of a sans-serif typeface, the letters of Eras have a monotone stroke and are slightly inclined.

Printed on acid-free paper.